Charles Child Walcutt

MAN'S
CHANGING MASK

Modes and Methods of
CHARACTERIZATION IN FICTION

University of Minnesota Press
MINNEAPOLIS

PN
218
.W3

Library of Congress Catalog Card Number: 66-24088

PUBLISHED IN GREAT BRITAIN, INDIA, AND PAKISTAN BY THE OXFORD
UNIVERSITY PRESS, LONDON, BOMBAY, AND KARACHI, AND IN CANADA BY
THE COPP CLARK PUBLISHING CO. LIMITED, TORONTO

An earlier version of the chapter on Hardy appeared in *Twelve Original Essays
on Great English Novels*, edited by Charles Shapiro and published in 1960
by Wayne State University Press, which granted permission to reprint.
The chapter on *Hamlet* appeared in the winter 1965–66 issue of the *Michigan
Quarterly Review* and is reprinted here with the editor's permission. Excerpts
from the poetry of W. H. Auden, T. S. Eliot, Thomas Hardy, Allen Tate,
Elinor Wylie, and William Butler Yeats are taken from the following volumes
and used with permission as noted: *Collected Shorter Poems 1930–44* by W. H.
Auden. Reprinted by permission of Random House, Inc., and Faber and
Faber, Ltd. *Collected Poems 1909–1962* by T. S. Eliot. Copyright 1936 by Harcourt, Brace & World, Inc.; copyright © 1963, 1964 by T. S. Eliot. Reprinted by
permission of Harcourt, Brace & World, Inc., and Faber and Faber, Ltd.
Collected Poems by Thomas Hardy. Copyright 1925 by The Macmillan Company. Reprinted by permission of The Macmillan Company. *Poems 1922–47*
by Allen Tate. Copyright 1932, 1948 by Charles Scribner's Sons. Reprinted by
permission of Charles Scribner's Sons. *Collected Poems* by Elinor Wylie. Copyright 1932 by Alfred A. Knopf, Inc. Reprinted by permission of Alfred A.
Knopf, Inc. *The Tower* by William Butler Yeats. Copyright 1928 by The
Macmillan Company. Copyright renewed 1956 by Georgie Yeats. Reprinted
by permission of The Macmillan Company. The excerpts from *Eternal Fire*
by Calder Willingham are reprinted by permission of the publishers, The
Vanguard Press. Copyright 1963, 1964 by Calder Willingham.

For Janou

PREFACE

THE introductory paragraphs to Part I describe my undertaking in this study — to show how characterization depends upon plot (for which I usually employ the richer term "action"), how the significance of the plot reflects the social and moral values of a society and in turn determines the significance of the characters, and how the patterns of characterization established in fiction influence and affect the image of man that people "recognize" in themselves.

I have tried to confine myself to these matters even at the cost of ignoring many closely related aspects of the art of fiction. So much good criticism has already been devoted to symbol, structure, point of view, theme, tone, and a wide range of ideas that there can be no harm in overstressing — if I have — this central and yet neglected aspect.

Criticism of fiction has also to make sacrifices of another sort in order to cope with the mere size of the novel. If it assumes that the reader has read every novel discussed, it must greatly limit its audience, whereas elaborate summaries perforce limit the number of works that can be treated. In the attempt to show *how* characterization depends on the action, I have elected to work with a relatively small number of fictional exhibits. If I sacrifice range, I hope to gain something not only in depth but also in intelligibility — many readers may find it easier to take hold of my thesis when it is applied in some detail. I hope also that I contribute something to the understanding of the works discussed.

In providing references I have been guided by what I hope is the reader's convenience. Citations by page or chapter number are given parenthetically in the text immediately following quotations from the novels. Page numbers seemed most useful in citing recent novels for which the first American edition is readily available; but where books have been reprinted many times I have used chapter numbers instead. Where I did not believe that anyone would want to check a quotation, I have omitted the reference, but very seldom. I hope this paraphernalia does not distract too many more readers than it helps.

I am indebted to my colleague Robert P. Miller for suggestions that gave me the idea for what I call the psychological symbolism in Conrad's *Victory*. John Gassner and Sears Jayne made helpful suggestions on *Hamlet*. Many students in my seminars at Queens College have helped me work over my first thoughts on problems of characterization. My indebtedness to the legion of colleagues who have written about the techniques of fiction is too great to be specified, and my notes indicate sources only on particular details or issues. Special thanks go to Jeanne Sinnen of the University of Minnesota Press for the best possible editorial guidance and encouragement. I am grateful to the Queens College Faculty Committee on Research for reducing my teaching schedule at the beginning of this undertaking; to the Graduate Office at Queens College for making it possible for Mrs. Waldhetter to type my manuscript; and to her for doing it faster and better than I had any right to expect. Most of all, my wife, Janou, has made the writing of this book a continual pleasure.

C. C. W.

Neuilly-sur-Seine
February 1966

CONTENTS

Man's Changing Mask

PART I

Definitions

A NOVEL is made of action, character, and idea in a great many different proportions. Melodrama may at an extreme be almost entirely action. Character alone presides over the pure stream-of-consciousness, but it does so generally without taking shape. Allegory features the idea, with contrived action and two-dimensional characters. Moving in from these extremes, we find the richest (and perhaps the best) novels where the three elements of action, character, and theme are fused and balanced. My purpose in this study is to explore the what and the how of characterization, in what has turned out to be three aspects: First, I try to show that characterization is a function or product of the action (I use this term always in the Aristotelian sense of plot plus everything that goes with it). Second, in twelve chapters going from *Hamlet* to *Herzog*, I investigate a roughly historical sequence of ways in which characterization depends upon the action. And third — and at the same time — I try to trace the evolution of certain leading ideas of man (let us call them his masks) which are created by and embodied in the kinds of actions that we see from *Hamlet* to Beckett and Bellow. Part III and Chapter 13 of Part V announce in their titles that they are somewhat specially concerned with the dominance of the idea over both character and action; but in fact their central concern is still with the shifting modes of characterization. In a sense, all modern fiction is searching for significant actions while being drawn by symbolism and the idea.

An interest that has grown irresistibly with the subject is the way life copies art in this matter of character. Man is perhaps not "naturally" anything; his sense of self is what he thinks about the world and his place in it, and this is not a product of nature but of society and culture. Thus the more I look at it the more it appears to me that the "nature" of man is something man copies from the masks that he finds in literature; these take their shapes as the actors move through and respond to the problems which are the social substance of their stories. These problems and the human responses to them, which make the self, are surely most convincingly set forth in literary works. The eagerness with which psychiatrists write about Oedipus and Hamlet and Raskolnikov, whom they find more real than real people, underlines the point.

Finally, there comes the ironical consequence that the sparkling canon of objectivity, most generally attributed to Joyce, has produced not crystal clearness but rather ambiguity, which has in turn led to a fashion of irresponsibility. The contemporary aimless hero in the formless novel, not taking form because his author will not define any clear, firm issues to which he can respond with significant choices, is a product of a literary evolution rather than something that art has copied originally from life. Of course life follows hard upon with models for writers to copy in their turn.

I should not presume to exhort writers to return to hearty narratives like *Beowulf* so that characters will have hearty problems; but it has become noticeable during the past two or three years that writers have seemed to sense the emptiness of the forms that are fashionable. One can explore negation only so long. But this is to anticipate, and I must first try to explain in some detail how character depends upon the action and how characterization in a fiction differs from (and yet greatly influences!) the notions and impressions that we get of actual people.

1   *What Is Character?*

MARK TWAIN (or was it Charles Dudley Warner?) said that everybody talks about the weather but nobody does anything about it.
Something of the sort could be said about characterization in fiction.
Every critic talks about it because it must be the axle upon which all
fiction turns; clearly we read fiction because it is about people and
because we expect to learn something about them, which is another
way of saying that character is the central substance of fiction. Why,
then, has it always been so difficult to write about? Why is the criticism of fiction forever dealing with structure, values, point of view,
social and psychological implications — all of which relate to character
— without coming firmly to grips with the question of what *is* character exactly and *how* exactly is it formulated, depicted, developed in a
novel?

I believe that character is like the quantum of the physicists. This
ultimate particle cannot be located except when it jumps, and it
jumps so quick that it cannot be arrested in flight. They know it exists
because it jumps, but they can see only the movement rather than the
particle itself, if particle is indeed what it is. Character manifests itself
in action, obviously; but can we say that it manifests itself only in
action? I think most of us would accept this too, provided that speech
were considered as real an action as any other physical movement. But
if it manifests itself only in action, can we say that it exists apart from
action? This seems to be what we do say and believe with all our
hearts — that character *is* absolutely, quite apart from what it does at
any time. This conviction is, I take it, an expression of the Western

5

drive toward absolutes; we hate even to look at the possibility that only process is real and that with people as with quanta only what happens is actual. We reject the suggestion that people are only what they do, for we must believe that they absolutely and essentially *are* something whether they do anything or not. (I do not wish here to introduce the logical thought that not doing anything is a form of action; as I shall show later, not doing anything in the sense of failing to act when action is called for requires a situation and implies action.)

The belief that character exists absolutely and apart from its acts turns up when almost anybody is asked whether character or plot is more basic in a novel. The general response is that the writer be-gins with his characters and proceeds to display them in one of sev-eral plots that would all serve perhaps equally well. The contrary notion that an author might begin with a good plot and see what characters it turns out would generally be dismissed as leading to in-ferior and melodramatic fiction, for melodrama is defined as that dra-matic (or novelistic) form in which action dominates character. This general belief has expressed itself, during roughly the past hundred years, in a thousand fictional enterprises that deny the validity of the well-made plot and attempt in one way or another to eliminate the classical notion of an action. The slice-of-life, the stream-of-conscious-ness, the mythic pattern, the many experimental forms of naturalism, and the distortions of conventional time-sequence which make what happens a mystery — all these are serious attempts to diminish the significance of plot in favor of what are generally ideas (that is, theses) or the exploration of psychic states that have their being far down below the shallow waters where conventional plots are thought to live.

When Emerson wrote, "The event is the print of your form," he was putting the Romantic image of the human spirit into an aphorism that makes the individual dominant over the inferior world in which he finds himself. Emerson said that nature was a symbol of spirit, and in theory he always urged that the laws of nature and the images of mind were dependent on the unity of Being. But the stress on spirit was always greater with him, and his most memorable sentences expressed its dominance. "Idealism," he wrote, "acquaints us with the total disparity between the evidence of our own being, and the evi-dence of the world's being . . . the mind is a part of the nature of things; the world is a divine dream, from which we may presently awake to the glories and certainties of day." The Romantic notions of spirit, mind, and self are closely connected in pointing to the certainty that mere matter and mere physical event are reflections of prior absolute realities. Essence precedes existence. The absolute self finds and makes its world. That world, as Emerson showed in essay after essay, could be stubborn and unyielding. "Nature's dice are always loaded," he wrote. Yet ultimately the self had access to sources of power that were not natural but spiritual, and from these came its absolute being. What it *did* in the world was inferior in the same way that nature is inferior to spirit: "The world proceeds from the same spirit as the body of man. It is a remoter and inferior incarnation of God, a projection of God in the unconscious [i.e., in brute matter uninformed by spirit, though reflecting its laws]."

Other considerations influence our thinking about the nature of characterization in fiction. The first is that fiction is different from life. In the latter we do empirically sense a character with little evidence beyond the way the person smiles or the intonations in the first sentences he speaks. This sensing of character I take to be an act of our whole emotional selves, drawing upon all the insights, the intuitions, and the emotional habits and patterns that we have accumulated during our lives. It is, fundamentally, an interaction between our selves and the person we are identifying; in such an interaction we are bound to be involved, which is another way of saying that we are as concerned with our own conduct and feelings as we are with those of the other person. What we do in his presence may have consequences: it may enrich our self-image or damage it; it may affect our relations with others; it may have serious practical consequences depending upon whether this new person makes use of us or we of him. These elements of personal involvement make our direct reaction to a new acquaintance a different *kind* of experience from our judgment or understanding of a character in a novel. The latter is detached, aesthetic, and intellectual. The former is fraught with direct emotional and practical consequences; it is immediate, even visceral, and no one can question its practical reality.

But a characterization in a novel is formulated in words, and the fact that one's reaction to the character is entirely a verbal experience makes it a special and different sort of thing. If we are exceptionally sensitive to language, and if the writer is as gifted as a first-class poet, then we may achieve the complex sort of knowledge-experience that comes in reading the best lyric poetry. An ironical consequence of such literary art is that we are tempted to think of the character as a real person and wonder about what he did before he appeared in the action and what he may do after. It is no accident that one unwary critic was impelled to write a book entitled *The Girlhood of Shakespeare's Heroines*; the magic of Shakespeare's language has elicited bodies of speculation about Hamlet, "the man," which have made it impossible for many to see him as a character in a play. I shall return to this problem in some detail. At this point I should like to consider the contemporary drift toward reportage, for we report about real people rather than put them in a work of fiction.

During the twentieth century the line between fiction and reportage has become increasingly unclear. The stories in the *New Yorker* magazine have contributed enormously to this trend, for one of their particular distinctions is that the reader frequently cannot tell whether he is reading a short story or a report. Sometimes the problem is not resolved at the end of the story. And the reverse has been true: what one takes for reports are acknowledged later to be fictions (for example, Joseph Mitchell's famous account of *Old Mr. Flood*, who first appeared as "The Mayor of the Fishmarket"). This blurring of the line suggests that readers today are interested in facts which they can know practically rather than in fictions which they must understand and interpret. Magazines have increasingly large proportions of nonfiction, and several story magazines have ceased publication.* These trends would seem to indicate that people today are identified with their trades, crafts, businesses, and professions. We are curious about what they do, about how they get along in the world, about what is involved in being a "success." Whether because of mass communications, the prevalence of psychological frames of reference, or the massive drift toward the organization man and the organization mind, all of which submerge the freedom of the individual, we seem to grow less concerned with the sort of crucial ethical choices by which fictional characters have in the past defined themselves.

Each of these elements is worth a moment's consideration.

Mass communication makes us know so much that the items of our

*The *Saturday Evening Post* has less fiction; *Collier's* has disappeared, and so have many of the old pulps — *Argosy, Western Stories*, and many more.

knowledge lose significance; there are so many people that people drift into anonymity. The typical adolescent has seen so many faces, brushed elbows with so many patterned contemporaries, and watched the rise and fall of so many public figures that he loses the sense of their personal freedom. The public figure moves through such a vast complex of political and economic forces that the young observer is overwhelmed by the sheer number of factors at work on his life. How can anybody judge what makes the President act as he does? Concerned with a thousand forces and a hundred thousand facts, he makes policy for situations all over the world, and it is almost impossible to know even where the President ends and his advisers begin. The man is unknowable; his public charm is felt, but his ethical center cannot be known because it is impossible for the outsider to know what goes into the choices he makes. This individual is merely a million lesser individuals writ large: people today are wrapped in complexities that make for moral anonymity; they merge with the environment, and the self cannot be separated from the office and the public appearance. To know a character well enough to make a serious evaluation of him we have to know all the elements that are present in the important decisions he makes.

The categories of popular psychology, which enable us to classify people and predict how they will typically act in certain situations, tend to reduce them to mere motives and statistics. This may seem inhuman, but it serves some understandable purposes. One is that there are too many people today who have to be dealt with in one way or another but who cannot be known intimately; the psychological category enables one to make a quick if simple estimate. A second, dubious purpose is the desire to control people without using such tiresome instruments as force or persuasion, and the psychologists suggest that with the right buttons to press we can make most people act as we want them to. A third use is that they enable one to take more convenient attitudes toward himself by in effect eliminating difficult and unmanageable aspects of the self. Let us consider this point by looking at the status of eccentricity today. In general, eccentricities make us uncomfortable, and we do not like to regard them as genuine aspects of the self. Instead, we push them away in two directions – in one we regard them as merely blemishes; in the other we make them aspects of the environment rather than parts of the self.

A tic or a rash can be dismissed as a merely physical defect, like the loss of a leg, which neither affects the character nor is to be regarded as a part of it. It is ignored for reasons interestingly comparable to those operating when a newspaper story fails to tell that a person is a Negro: the assumption surely is that this fact is irrelevant to the person's conduct and status. It is, in short, uncomfortable to notice the fact. This is going further than a Victorian novelist would have gone in concealing physical details, and yet with us the practice may extend much further — to obesity, alcoholism, homosexuality, filthiness. These too are not exactly aspects of the self, and, again, it is not merely tolerance that says so, but rather a notion that such characteristics complicate the problem of knowing and dealing with people: they interfere with communication if they have to be taken into account; they prevent people from being comfortably regarded as normal elements in the statistical bulk of society. They make individuals intractable, embarrassing, and confusing if they have to be taken as intimate and inescapable aspects of the person. Such defects or eccentricities are treated as more or less irrelevant blemishes when they are either permanent defects or qualities that for one reason or another we will not undertake to change. That is, if we do not choose to relate to an individual's obesity or homosexuality, we take what remains of him and treat the defect as if it did not exist. A hundred or five hundred years ago, when there were many fewer people than today, eccentricities were relished both for their entertainment value and for the evidence they gave of the plenitude and variety of human nature. Today there is not leisure or inclination to delight in the bizarre, and anyway it makes us uncomfortable.

The eccentricities that might be called complexes, particularly one's own, are treated differently. So much popular psychiatry has become current that such complexes have all been classified and catalogued for the layman. With this, they have of course been labeled as ills that can be treated professionally and, ideally, disposed of because they prevent the individual from functioning successfully. As they assume the status of clinical ills, they also become agents for whose acts the individual need not hold himself personally responsible. The self lives and struggles locked to its neurosis, but doctrine says that the lock can be broken, that it *should* not be a part of the self; it can be sloughed off and the "real" self restored to health and happiness. If this is true, then inescapably the neurosis is an aspect of the environment; it is an ill of a certain class, which has been named and explained; it was not born with the self; it is just like the ill that besets many other people; clearly it is an expression of the environment from which the free self will, it is hoped, some day be able to escape.

If the individual is led to think of his own psychological problems in this way, he will obviously think of others' in the same way. As we know, problems of this sort are discussed between chance acquaintances at a cocktail party; adolescents explore them together; a college freshman leaving a classroom was heard to remark to her friend, "I did badly on that test: I was feeling hostile to my mother this morning." Plainly the eccentricity is no longer the old bit of Adam. Now it lurks glowering threateningly somewhere in the penumbra of consciousness, apart from the self; it is in a group of items classified by science. A most important consequence of this change is that, since asocial conduct is usually impulsive and certainly unreasonable, moral responsibility for one's conduct is less frequently assumed, less frequently considered. Attention is concentrated on the self that has been damaged and continues to be threatened by forces in the environment. These lurking neuroses, furthermore, keep the self from direct contact with the outer world, since it perforce acts through them; and thus the self cannot be held accountable for actions that are forced upon it by them, even performed by them. My theme being the relation of characterization to plot in the novel, the fact that crucial actions may be performed by an alien force using the self, which the self does not acknowledge, is of tremendous significance for the novelist. Trying to make modern man show and find himself in a critical decision, he discovers that a completely new actor has entered the classical conflict. His hero is in the clutches of a force that acts through him; the character's problem is to escape from this alien force before he has been compelled to do something that will destroy him. The struggle is so unfair, so bewildering, that one's sympathy is with the hero, whose very thinking powers are distorted by the monster that has "possessed" him. The departure of the eccentricity into the environment leaves the self a diminished thing.

The massive drift toward the organization man is a third element that dilutes individuality. The man in the gray flannel suit, the beatnik, the young engineer, the sleek receptionist, and the rising politician are types before they are people, and we think of them merged with their surroundings and engaged in typical activities. Identified with their environments, such people do not appear to be individuals, and we prefer to accept them as types because we sense that there is not enough difference between them to make them worth the trouble of knowing better. The brassy products of Madison Avenue — the sun-tanned vacationers hot off the airplane, the users of the latest detergent, the happy motorists, the grinning dispensers of gasoline, the lady luxuriating on a supersoft mattress — have become aspects of the swarming commercial hive, exponents of buyer activity, dollar-givers in the cash line, and joyous consumers. They do not live with the basic, even tragic personal problems of a century ago because it is assumed that people with plenty of the world's goods are so busy consuming them that they do not think of anything else. Of course I exaggerate; we do know that everybody has serious problems that are not satisfied in the supermarket; but the swarm of happy buyers inhabits a world of material things that do not enrich the inwardness of the speculative life. Nor of course do the public images of people-supporting-the-economy suggest the depths of personality that we associate with Shakespeare and Sophocles. The mere quantity of such happy buyers makes us regard them superficially. And happy buyers demand happy, tireless producers; so the system tends to overshadow the individual, whose working life is more important to the common weal than his private soul.

It has been a cliché to speak of the "anonymous hordes" of illiterate serfs and peasants in the past. Today the worker is increasingly subordinated to the job because his life is so closely identified with it. Not only all union members but also clerks and young executives have become linked into a system of production and distribution that insists upon daily work from all. Once upon a time a man could go off into the woods for a month. Today New York City imports 7,000,000 pounds of meat every day, and the New Yorker sees in such a statistic his utter dependence upon the wheels that roll daily into the city. Let any substantial number of bodies neglect their jobs and chaos would follow hard thereafter. Or let the same number stop buying and the same chaos would follow. In this context we cannot afford to think of people as essentially independent or free. The world is too much with us for that. It would be easy to reply, since I have quoted Wordsworth, that

"It has always been," but a truer perspective sees that Ahab and Man-fred are now waiting for Godot.

I have tried to suggest in the preceding pages how the modern image of a character has become both confused and complicated because the focus of our lens has blurred. Science has discovered and explored the unconscious and then obscured the boundary between the conscious and the unconscious — and hence has made us increasingly unsure of whether a responsible and intelligent will controls our actions. Com-parative religion and anthropology have forever dimmed the bright outlines of right and wrong. Modern society has become so many lev-eled that the writers do not accept its premises and their heroes do not *find* themselves in its central activities and preoccupations. Whether it be the popular image of success, the popular image of love, the popu-lar image of good entertainment, or the popular image of beauty, the modern artist or intellectual will not permit himself to be seen framed and focused in its dimension. He is trying to find himself outside such frames, and so the writer finds his hero without a background against which he can be truly seen. As man-in-general has become blurred, so has the individual character become indistinct among the welter of values and activities that flow past him and over him. There are so many factors written into the equation of character that we cannot always determine what the equation means. This may be unfortunate, in the sense that it destroys the traditional form of the novel, but it is surely an extraordinary change, which must be explored to the end.

Let us, then, go back into another world and reconsider what Aris-totle said about the place of character in a play. What we discover is quietly astonishing. He said that in a tragedy character is less impor-tant than plot. He defined a tragedy as *the imitation of an action*. Character, he said, is revealed by the action but is of lesser importance. But modern critics have rarely been willing to accept this dictum; they nod and pass by, for they are categorically positive that character is the axis of a serious fiction, whether it be novel or drama, and that the action turns about that character. With character the hub, they would suggest that various wheels of action could turn about that hub, their several planes revealing different dimensions of the character or realiz-ing different potentials. The assumption is that character is source and motive and cause of what happens.

The great shift of perspective is itself dramatized by the modern explanation of Aristotle's *hamartia*. Aristotle presented *hamartia* as an aspect or function of the action: the modern world reads it as a function of character. It will be rewarding to turn back for a moment and look at some of the bones in the skeleton of Aristotle's *Poetics* that has come down to us. He writes (in the Bywater translation) that "Tragedy is essentially an imitation not of persons but of action and life, of happiness and misery. All human happiness or misery takes the form of action; the end for which we live is a certain kind of activity, not a quality. . . . In a play . . . they do not act in order to portray the characters; they include the characters for the sake of the action." By "action" Aristotle means plot or fable. It is, he says, "simply this: the combination of the incidents or things done in the story; whereas character is what makes us ascribe certain moral qualities to the agents."

Aristotle notes two elements that contribute to characterization. One is "a habit of choice or way of reacting to a situation," as Lane Cooper puts it. Second, a character "must be made to think and reason in ways that will appear in [his] speech and action." One is moral bent or ethos, the second is intellect. We note immediately that these two qualities are described in connection with action; they have to do with making choices in situations that require them — not with what the character is but with what he does. Tragedy, Aristotle says, must have action but may exist without distinctive characters, and he adds that most Greek tragedies since Euripides are deficient in the element of character. An example will perhaps clarify the relation of action and character. The plot or fable (i.e., the action) is like the plan of a building. It may be constructed of marble or granite or cement yet be essentially the same building, but if the plan is changed the building is altered essentially. In short, tragedy is an imitation, not of what men essentially are, but of "action and life, of happiness and misery," things which exist in activity rather than in pure static being, and which therefore are imitated (or represented) in the actions of comedies or tragedies.

In the modern world character is foremost, and in making character the fountainhead of the tragic action, the modern critic and the modern reader have become familiar with the concept of the so-called tragic flaw. Much has been written about the concept, but the word "flaw" remains to indicate, in virtually every discussion, its inescapable meaning of a defect. Shakespeare's major tragic heroes have been summed up as men of heroic stature who are destroyed by events *which are set* *in motion* by such flaws. Hamlet's is indecision, Macbeth's is ambition, Lear's is anger, Othello's is jealousy, and Antony's is passion. No matter how earnestly these characterizations have been attacked — and they have repeatedly been called oversimplifications — the essential notion of a defect has not been abandoned. A recent book on *Hamlet*, for example, reinterprets the play to show that the hero's defect is rashness rather than indecision* and the reviewers did not question the nature of the critical undertaking even though they may have challenged the conclusion reached. The line of Shakespearean criticism climbs to a point with Coleridge, who made Hamlet the archetype of the modern Romantic spirit for whom the occasions of life were a trap rather than a release. I shall discuss this Hamlet in more detail in Chapter 3, for he is a key figure in the evolution of modern thinking about character.

When Aristotle, on the other hand, speaks of the change in the tragic hero's fortunes, he says, "The cause of it must lie not in any depravity, but in some great error on his part." He speaks also of a "defect in judgment or a shortcoming in conduct," but the main stress seems to be on "error." Error might seem close to flaw, until we look at Aristotle's explanation. Oedipus erred in ignorance and discovered his error later; Aristotle says this is one of the most effective tragic turnings. The hero may kill a relative and then discover the relationship; or he may do the deed knowingly but for a mistaken reason; or he may be about to do the deed of horror but be prevented by a last-minute discovery. This last Aristotle finds highly emotional and effective. The worst is when the hero is about to injure a blood relative and then desists, for the intention is disgusting, and no tragic pity ensues for the victim. In all these cases the action comes first and the hero reacts to what confronts him. It is the situation that evokes the conduct, and I think the unspoken assumption must be that the situation would be a test for almost any character. In some cases, as when the hero is about to kill a relative in ignorance, the situation would be tragic for any character, because the error would not have required any "flaw" of character at all. The importance of the action is further attested by the fact that the Greeks used the same plots over and over again. The dramatist was judged for his exploration of the moral and ethical values that might grow out of the age-old situation.

At first glance, the question of character and action may seem like

* Bernard Grebanier's *The Heart of Hamlet* (New York: Crowell, 1960).

the question of the hen and the egg — both are essential. But if we recall that Aristotle said a tragedy could be represented without characters, whereas the modern world thinks that character is the source from which action flows and that a given character could be represented and explored through several actions that the novelist might invent, we see that there can be a vast difference in the relative importance of these two elements.

The Greek fables that were used again and again have one striking element in common: they move through events that are profoundly and utterly central to the moral and ethical concerns of the Greeks. Such questions as burying one's brother or respecting the king; avenging an insult or honoring one's parent; avenging one parent at the cost of the other; obeying the gods or obeying the ties of family; serving the state or respecting one's parents; and so on through one story after another — these are issues than which nothing could be more fundamental to the beliefs, the values, the customs, and the social order of the Greeks. In an action turning upon one of these issues, the hero reacts in terms of his dearest and deepest beliefs; he makes choices which involve the things he holds most important in the world. Such problems encompass the hero and bring him to reactions and discoveries out of which character emerges. The events are by no means latent or implicit in the character: rather, they evoke character where previously there had been a self-contained or an unthinking man. They are not events which merely test a person; they bring out the human significance of a world, and the person defines himself and discovers himself as he searches between himself and his world for the answers to his problem. It is the action, then, that precipitates from the social ambience the hard realities of a life. I have dwelt upon this element of customs and values because it is here that plot and character meet. A plot is unthinkable without human motives and intentions; these must come from a society. The hero, in turn, must think and choose with concepts that relate to the moral and ethical forces that move in the plot. The reason Aristotle said that a tragic plot could be represented without character was that the conflict, the recognition, and the suffering *could* be experienced by the audience; but in general the hero takes form between the conflict and the audience because he is the focus of value, conflict, and decision, and in being so he takes shape as a character. We know him, then, because he embodies, he expresses, and he reacts to the basic values of his society.

Or so it was in Greece.

Since the time of those magnificent tragedies society has become so complex that one character cannot embody and act upon its central concerns. The plots that would be grand enough to make tragedies (for Aristotle insisted upon a fable of significance) are likely to be too simple today, too elemental, and even too serious for people who have lost their bearings in a sea of uncertainty. A further problem springs from the fact that great actions require great people and grand language. The heroic style has not been insisted upon without reason. But little people cannot mouth the grand style without grand thoughts in grand language. As we move into the modern world, we find people and problems fractured from the marble blocks of antiquity into glittering dust. The sense of human greatness is frustrated by the narrowness of the occasions that offer. Not that everybody wants to be a hero, but he wants to live among heroic occasions. In these new relations of character, values, and actions, the problems of the modern novel reveal the changing condition of modern man.

The formulations of Aristotle are so good that one has a sense of fatuity in rediscovering them. As if nothing new had been contrived in the past 2000 years! Yet I do not know how to improve on his identification of the two elements that make character: moral bent and intellect. The first is the way the person reacts to a situation and translates his reaction into action; the second is the way he thinks about himself and his situation. I have considered these two elements in relation to the fact that character is a function of action, that, like the quantum, it cannot be seen except in motion, where it is the motion rather than the thing itself that we see. Thus we assume the is-ness of character just as we assume the is-ness of the quantum, but we *see* them in action. This parallel is not perfect: we are all, I think, totally sure that a person *is* something even though he is not acting; and we must think that there is an essence to what he is that is not the mere afterimage (the blur of light in movement) of what he has done. Yet if we were to back up and look at this situation again, we might be hard pressed to explain how a person who had done nothing could have any character whatsoever. Does not his self accumulate, after all, as the sum of things done, of actions taken, which accumulate as memories and attitudes? Are not character traits really mannerisms that are known because they are done habitually, repeatedly? Such a mannerism may be a tic or a twitch, at its most rudimentary, and as such it is little but a movement; it may also be a mannerism of thought, an idea or a little cycle of explanation, which takes its importance exactly from the fact that its repetition makes it command a significant proportion of the lifetime of the individual. That is, if he spends a certain amount of time going over a certain path of reverie, this time cannot be employed in any other way and therefore it characterizes in the sense of *constituting the form* of a part of him. This formulation puts character in time, and since there is only a given amount of time, the way a person acts serves in a temporal way to make up the span and shape of his self. Thinking thus of time as a function of action, we are forced to see how action is essential to character.

The accumulation of little activities (i.e., mannerisms) makes the character who discovers and defines himself in the big acts that come from the crucial choices at the crucial places in the plot. I have stressed the point that these acts, big and little, are most comfortably meaningful for the reader when they occur in terms of the central values, customs, and manners of a society.

The step from moral bent to intellect is not a great one. Where the character thinks his act as he performs it, there is really no step at all; but some characters do a great deal of thinking, whether in conversation or soliloquy, which expresses their contemplative rather than their volitional selves. They think about their situations, their friends, their problems, their world, and their ambitions. They yearn, they fear, and they lust. Here is the area in which characterization might seem to be achieved apart from the plot. Speculation and conversation generally, in the novel, precede the establishment of the conflict and the rising action to which it leads, and these mental activities obviously serve to make the reader know the people whom he is going to follow through the plot.

But here again the same issues present themselves. Whether acting or thinking, character defines itself by virtue of *what* it thinks, which is what it thinks *about*; and here again the dependence of the action upon the social fabric of values, customs, and manners is exactly repeated. Whether during the action or before it begins, the characters must think about a world which, being a world of social and human relations, serves to define them in terms of their relation to it. Where the characters are completely identified with the central concerns of their society, as in *Pride and Prejudice*, what they think about flows along with what they do, relates completely to the problems that lead into the conflict, and so defines them by the particular mold into which their temperament pours the elements of the social gelatin. Where the characters are alienated or in fundamental conflict with the central concerns of society, their thoughts will range more widely but they will not be so clearly realized as individuals. It is in this latter area that modern fiction is found.*

* I must return for a moment to the concept of temperament — to our intuition that people compellingly and powerfully *are* something regardless of their acts. We "know" this from direct emotional, even visceral, responses that cannot be denied. The concept of temperament and the old classification that began with the physiological basis (sanguine, phlegmatic, choleric, melancholy — each springing from its humor) were accepted over many centuries, surely, because they reflected the common experience of people. Yet these qualities of the individual require an action of some magnitude if they are to appear more than mannerisms or, at worst, grotesques. The man who is merely sanguine achieves no meaning for us until he acts in the context of the important issues of a society.

This classification, by the way, has passed out of fashion today because it is no longer useful — and for an interesting reason. Man's emotional nature has become so profoundly tied to hormones, glands, traumata, and other scientific provinces that it has lost all touch with the idea of freedom, and yet it is still by some notion of personal freedom that we live and care. We are therefore most uncomfortable with a term like the old "temperament," for it comes to us out of a past when it was closely attached to notions of freedom and responsibility. So we do not use it in the old sense and have protected ourselves by giving it a new set of spiritual affiliations. Movie stars now have "temperament," which is equivalent to one of the commonest meanings of "spirit" today. A racehorse has spirit, too, but we must not speak of his "temperament"!

2 *Some Illustrative Versions of Melodrama*

ALTHOUGH the aphorism declares that actions speak louder than words, anyone who is seriously concerned with fiction and drama will probably insist that what characters say is more significant and more interesting than what they physically do, and he will go on to explain that words are deeds. When an author wants to display his people, he puts them together and sets them to talking. Such talk is action and interaction. The stream-of-consciousness is an interior dialogue in which the character talks to himself about himself and his world: it presents the mind in action. But, as we shall see, unless that mind faces important problems and reacts to them with decisions, little characterization will be achieved.

Words are certainly related to deeds, but they are not *necessarily* deeds — and herein lies the difference between what one says and what one does. Quite apart from physical action, the most important actions are decisions; these are deeds on the level of highest importance, for almost all action that affects the human condition proceeds from decisions. Decisions are revealed in words, but they occur only in a life-situation that requires a choice; in fiction such a situation comes in a plotted action and requires a context of significant social values. That is, the decision has to be about something socially, morally, ethically *important* or it will not take us far into a character.

The dependence of words upon deeds can be demonstrated in the lives of famous personages of the twentieth century. President John F. Kennedy spoke with impressive literacy, force, and conviction. His inaugural address rang with memorable, quotable passages that seemed to unite vision and determination. Their force was increased by the general knowledge that he had, in the war, been a hero. With the Bay of Pigs fiasco these words lost their force as the invasion of Cuba foundered on half-measures and ended in catastrophe. Then Kennedy's image was restored in the Cuba crisis of 1962, when he took action that was advised, carefully planned, restrained, and absolutely firm. No bravado before, no hysteria during, and afterwards neither boasting nor recrimination. There was the fact that Russia had withdrawn her missiles. I believe it was this sequence of problem and action that did most to crystallize Kennedy's reputation. Here the world could see what a man *did* in an ultimate crisis. The promise of his earlier words had been temporarily obscured, but now he had to show whether he could in action rise to the heights he had set for himself in eloquent speeches. He did so rise, and to no small extent it was those subsequent actions that made the eloquence in his earlier speeches. They were eloquent, in part, after the fact and because of the fact. Anybody could have uttered the closing sentences of his inaugural address, but only after he had acted on Cuba did those words achieve the ring of greatness.

Language and actions relate somewhat differently in the cases of two other great men of our time, who may profitably be compared with John F. Kennedy, namely Dwight D. Eisenhower and Adlai E. Stevenson.

Mr. Eisenhower has never been eloquent. When he spoke impromptu the phrases dangled and the verbs were abstract and confusing. One did not, frequently, know what he was talking about. When he spoke from a script the sentences were better but they were seldom memorable. One recalls only platitudes of virtue and patriotism. But Eisenhower *had* acted. As Supreme Commander of the Allied Forces against Germany in World War II, he had led us to victory and in doing so he had gained the respect and devotion of other great men. So his words always stood for more than they said; the character of the man had been expressed and established by his deeds-in-crisis; heard against that background the words reinforced the image of a man who was so great in action that inarticulateness became a virtue.

Adlai Stevenson's language was so far superior in wit, point, elegance, and power that it is cruel to compare it with Eisenhower's. His campaign speeches were memorable. His speech accepting the Democratic Party's nomination for the presidency in 1956 was one of the finest in American history. Through no fault of his own, however, Stevenson did not have opportunity for great action. At the same time he made some people uncomfortable by being witty when they wanted the action of leadership. Wit is playing with language rather than using it purposefully: to the practical man it may seem evasive or irresponsible, whereas in fact it is a display of intellect *beyond* the needs of the immediate practical problem. His wit lost him many votes to Eisenhower, whose inarticulate sobriety rested on its massive foundation of past action, while Stevenson's brilliant and sincere language had no such base. The point of these comparisons is not to depreciate Adlai Stevenson but to show how words take their substance and power from action, while without confirming action they lose weight and force until they may even become suspect.

The perennial appeal of biography reflects the desire to know what great men actually said. If the novel has been losing some favor in recent years, while biography continues to flourish, with increasing audiences, it may be because the actions in the novels do not satisfy the practical man's desire to understand images of success and responsibility in men who have acted significantly in the world of affairs in which he aspires to succeed. The images of greatness in Shakespearean tragedy, which we shall explore with some care in the next chapter, come to us as finer and truer than raw life; if those in the modern novel are distrusted by "practical" men it is because they are not involved in actions significant enough to engage the serious attention of such men.

In real life, we think we know character intuitively, for we generally get impressions of people that amount to more than could have been "said" in a brief conversation. We feel the impact of the whole person and get the sense of knowing something that is essential and beyond words. Our attitudes toward public figures grow in the same ways: we set their words beside impressions they make upon us through pictures (fixed or moving) and through the actual reactions of other public figures to them. With the drama and the cinema we are perhaps tricked into sensing characters even when characters are not created, for the personality of the actor has exactly the same ability to draw an intuitive response. People go to the cinema to see their favorite actor or actress *as a person*, and the role he or she is playing may have a hard time coming through. This unliterary, unaesthetic cult of personality could be denounced as frightfully destructive of the drama; but I am rather tempted to say that it is the poverty of the drama that allows the actors and actresses to dominate it. We know how these deities from the Hollywood Olympus are paraded before our society; we know how avidly details of their private lives are consumed; but if the dramatic art were vital enough it would dominate these tin dolls, and it would challenge them to *perform*. In this connection, it is ironic that the Italian motion pictures that have used unknown actors and settings of the starkest realism, trying to escape the debasing glamour of the star, have again and again given the effect of reportage. The actors are so "real" that the reviewers comment on the fact that they seem to be actual people — as if this were a virtue! They confuse the representative, or mimetic, truth of good art with the impression of actuality that tired people and bald tawdriness of setting seem to convey. Thus the glamour stars have conditioned us to look for real people in the cinema, and the Italian effort is thwarted into an unintended effect — unless the producers and directors themselves have been self-deluded by a cult of personality into a cult of actuality.

Character becomes a puzzle and a mystery when we try to separate the thing — or "essence" — from its act and thus fix and isolate it. This is where the Western mind's search for absolutes, for abstractions that rise above incidents (which happen rather than "are"), leads it into confusions. The character is what it does; and what it does depends upon what lines of action are open to it. We might thus finally conclude that character is the quality, the flavor, with which the individual acts, plus the locus of experience and responsibility for all the actions he has taken.

Another way to formulate the issue is with the concept of motivation, which also may resemble the assumed quantum that can be seen only when it moves. It may once have been natural to think only of what the individual did, and to react to him strictly as doer. But somewhere the idea of motivation came in, and increasing stress was put on the question of *why* the person did what he did. This why seemed to be the key to what the character actually *was*, behind what he did. But it was always elusive: hard to "see" except in motion, impossible to arrest and define as an entity. Establishing motivation is trying to attach the act to the self from which it proceeds; it is trying to make the act an expression of an already-existing self, which it assumes to be prior to the act rather than discovered or created in the act. Interest in motivation takes attention away from the act and points finally toward the contemporary dissolution of plot, toward the "story" in which nothing happens, toward — as we shall see in the final chapter — the character as un-character, unknowable because he has no issues, no decisions, no definition. But this is to anticipate the end of a long evolution.

If what the character does depends upon the lines of action that are open to it, we may nibble around the fringes of the problem by looking at some extreme cases. Let us begin with melodrama, where we traditionally assume that the action dominates character to the point where characterization is insignificant. Here the plot is likely to be made of a steady flow of suspenseful movement, that is, physical activity. The characters are so busy in flight, pursuit, and physical battle that they have no time for moral speculation and decision. So they move through actions in which the moral values and the social context are very simple.

The hero of our story is a rancher, let us say, whose cattle have been disappearing. He lives with a young impulsive wife and her old rugged father. Here then are three sets of traits — the hero is strong and brave; the wife is impulsive and undoubtedly righteous; the old father is crusty and stubborn. Perhaps the hero has a weakness of character, but more likely he has a flaw in his past. Let's say he has been in jail in another state. When the cattle of the region disappear in large numbers, the ranchers get together and demand strong action. The sheriff is secretly in league with the rustlers, but he is forced by popular pressure to deputize several of the ranchers and through them extend the feeble arm of the law. Our hero is chosen. He wants badly to refuse because of his devotion to his young wife, his concern over the troublesome father, and his unwillingness to get into the public eye where his past might be discovered; but Duty and the need to keep his wife's respect triumph, and he accepts the badge of deputy.

Action follows hard upon. The hero wakes in the night to hear the rustlers passing; he steals out to follow them and identifies their leader as the close friend of the sheriff. A snapping twig discloses his presence, and although he escapes the pursuit the rustlers recognize him. Since they have not caught the hero, the rustlers kidnap his wife and her father; and now our hero is faced with the painful dilemma of saving their lives at the cost of conspiring with the criminals or, perhaps, of exposing his past.

In such a situation the hero can make a deeply significant and meaningful choice if he is man enough to translate the physical situation into moral and philosophical implications as profound as that physical situation is horrible. He can search into the nature of crime; he can study the claims of social against personal loyalty; he can wonder whether it would be right to risk criminal involvement in order to save his wife; he can go on to consider the meaning of love, of truth, and of law. Conceivably he can, that is, although the possibility is infinitely remote because such profound implications would be as foreign to our hero as they would be to the social context in which we find him: this is a world of simple action and conflict, not one of profound moral speculation. The world, of course, is made by the writer. A Euripides or a Faulkner would find depths here or anywhere; but our hero has never had time or opportunity to engage in the sort of speculation that would raise him to tragic stature. He has not had time to talk or think about the meanings that could be present for him in his predicament. He cannot, consequently, respond to them. The best he can feel is a brutal desperation and bewilderment.

The action must and will be resolved by circumstance. The wife will escape; the old father will die of heart failure; the chief of the rustlers will be killed by a stray bullet before he can reveal the hero's secret. Better, the villain will be caught up by his own evil temper in a gunfight and killed by a man with a faster draw, just as he is going to tell on the hero. This is probable enough to satisfy the demands of suspense and the reader's desire to identify with the generous hero (who has not had time to evade or face his terrible dilemma); and it gives the reader the extra satisfaction of feeling a poetic justice in the villain's destruction. However the events work out, they will move so fast that the hero cannot be given time or occasion to react to them profoundly: the action thus flows over and submerges the character.

How does this action differ from the tragedy which Aristotle said could be represented without character? The answer lies in the significance of the action. The great tragic action moves through the heart of the society's values and beliefs. The western melodrama moves through *situations* of violence, fear, love, honor, and courage that do not *engage* the characters in depth and do not take them down into profundities of moral or philosophical speculation where they could achieve the dimensions of character that result from acting in terms of such issues. The great tragic action dramatizes such issues so forcefully that they stand out almost apart from the people who enact them.

It is a giant step from American westerns to Corneille's *Le Cid*, a classic of the classic French theater, yet the latter illustrates some of the points we have just been exploring. Mixtures of melodrama and more significant conflict are particularly instructive for our purposes because they offer the purest possible specimens for analysis: two stories or plays set side by side will have aspects of style and subject that complicate the analysis, whereas if the two levels of conflict can be observed in a single piece we have a much purer and simpler problem. This is what we find in *Le Cid*.

The action of *Le Cid* leads quickly into a noble conflict between love and honor. Rodrigue is a gallant prince. His old father asks him the question that permits him to define himself: "Rodrigue, as-tu du cœur?" And he replies on the instant, "Tout autre que mon père l'éprouverait sur l'heure." Anyone but his father would be challenged to a duel for asking whether he had courage. Satisfied by this reply, the father goes on to explain that he has been mortally insulted; he has been slapped — by the father of Chimène! Chimène is the beloved of Rodrigue, yet the insult to his father can be satisfied only by the death of the offender. The play develops with magnificent speeches in which Rodrigue explores his dilemma. If he kills her father, he can only expect Chimène to loathe and reject him forever; yet if he suffers the insult to go unpunished he will not be worthy of her love. His insight into the fearful consequences of his nobility grows as he faces his dilemma, and with the growth of insight comes a deepening of his character. Formerly he would have acted on the instant in a matter of honor — and acted heroically. Now he cannot act for some time, and the significance of his character grows as he plumbs the significance of the choice he must make. He rises to the famous lines:

> Percé jusques au fond du cœur
> D'une atteinte imprévue aussi bien que mortelle,
> Misérable vengeur d'une juste querelle,
> Et malheureux objet d'une injuste rigueur,
> Je demeure immobile, et mon âme abattue
> Cède au coup qui me tue.

Si près de voir mon feu récompensé,
O Dieu, l'étrange peine!   [I, vi]

Honor triumphs. Rodrigue kills the younger man who had slapped his father, and when he comes to Chimène to beg her forgiveness, she pours her recriminations on him as any daughter of nobility and spirit would do. The action was as loathesome as it was necessary and honorable, and it would appear that a hero who searched its meaning right through to the end would have been forced to question honor itself.

But at this point the action changes direction slightly. Emphasis is turned upon the living, upon the beauty and nobility of the love between Chimène and Rodrigue. As the scene comes to an end, Chimène confesses that she *still* loves Rodrigue; but any thought of marriage would be such an unspeakable blot on her honor, now, that the idea cannot be entertained.

Into this unbearable situation steps the *deus ex machina* in the shape of the king, who simply commands Rodrigue and Chimène to marry. A command from the king is the ultimate word in a chivalric society, and so the problem is solved. But with such a solution the hero and heroine turn into two paper-thin silhouettes, for they have ceased entirely to move through the splendid issues of love and honor that have tortured and enriched them up to this point. With their problem solved by the king, they have ceased thinking, ceased probing toward the decision that would, one way or another, have shown them entering into the deepest meanings of their plight and making those meanings a part of themselves. Thus a tragedy turns into a melodrama, and *as* it turns the characters lose the qualities that they have developed during the rising tragic action; with the falling action they too are deflated into empty shells. *

*Faithful readers of detective stories sometimes find themselves beginning one that they read five or ten years earlier. They recognize the long-forgotten friend in a few pages, for the situation is re-created in their minds. But, they say, they can never remember how the story ended. This typical experience can be explained if we look at the relation of action and character in the detective story.

The characters are usually presented over several chapters as one by one they tell their version of the crime, or react to it in ways that generate some doubt of their innocence, or reveal a growing complex of interrelations that may bear on the crime or lead to further violences. This method of presenting characters serves two ends: it spaces them out so that the reader can get to know them; and it involves them in activities that advance the plot. It is very important that the reader become interested in the characters to the point where he speculates on their motives and carefully

If it is possible for promising depth of characterization to shoal off into nothing as the action loses significance, can the opposite happen? Can trivial characters gain roundness and weight because a slight action becomes more significant? Yes, this pattern is to be found in Lillian Hellman's *Toys in the Attic* (1960).

The essence of the Southern problem, whether in Tennessee Williams, Faulkner, or Carson McCullers, is the discrepancy between the myth and the actuality. The myth of Southern gentility, culture, chivalry, and grandeur is so far from the brute violence of a slaveholding reality that there results a split world. And the split goes right down into the mind of the individual. It makes his life a wild tension between his grand idea of himself and the tawdry social and personal occasions in which he has to live and work. The split reveals itself in the fact that people from other parts of the country are forever seeking to discover what the South *is* — but the energy of their quest is nothing compared with the fascinated fixation of Southerners on the same question. (This problem is explored in Chapter 12.)

The hallmark of Southern character is the gesture of aristocracy. This is revealed in the emphasis on manners, on family, on social obligations, on the constant sense of one's class. The gesture, however, is made in a frayed coat: there is blood on its sleeve, and the platform totters symbolically over a rotting economy. The elegant language of social occasion seems to come from a mouth different from that which discusses politics. The aristocratic gesture expresses status; when it becomes the chivalric gesture it tends to be violent, inflamed, and intem-

analyzes the implications of what they say. Whether in experiencing heightening fear and suspense, meeting unexpected new violence (typical is the sudden death of the reader's top suspect), or engaging in the pursuit of a trail of discovery and interpretation, the reader participates in events that create character; they all have to do with "who did what, and why."

The difficulty of course is that the findings are all both confused and tentative. The conclusion, generally coming in a dazzling tour de force of intellectual analysis by the detective-hero, packed into three or four pages, reverses all the reader's expectations and cancels out all the conclusions about character that he had been enticed into forming. The "events" of the story fade and dissolve into a brand-new set of true facts. The scheming old lady is loving and eccentric; the silent butler is an earl; the friendly old gentleman is a paranoid poisoner; and so on. This canceling-out of what seems to have *happened* in the story, by a new set of "facts," gives the reader an intellectual satisfaction, but it destroys the story that has gone before. And thus that story and the final explanation blend into confusion and are soon forgotten. Only the initial situation will be recalled. The characters vanish because in fact they are destroyed by the redefinition of their actions, which comes so rapidly and abstractly that the reader cannot assimilate it.

perate; it may not be the same arm that wields the noose and the blow-torch, but gestures have a way of evading the eye that would fix them.

Lillian Hellman's play opens on the triviality of the frayed gesture. We see Carrie Berniers coming home from work and chattering to her sister, Anna, about a dozen disconnected matters. She gives the impression of a woman frivolous to the point of stupidity, selfish and whimsical to the point of being frightening, but withal so frothy in her latent (or is it superficial?) craziness that we take her as a sort of commentary on the Southern style rather than an agent to be watched and evaluated. She is a silly frustrated stagey old maid, living in bootless dreams of her younger brother, whose vicarious triumphs are seen even through her eyes to be hollow.

This is Carrie until she moves into the center of the action. But first there is a good deal of conversation and commentary which expresses so fatuous, so frivolous and gushy, so absurdly unrealistic a concern for the handsome, glamorous, wandering younger brother that the total superficiality of the family seems to be unassailable. Into Carrie's pathetic and frivolous conversation with her sister enters the fact that they had $2843 in their savings account, put aside for a trip abroad; Carrie reveals that she has just sent a thousand dollars to the younger brother, Julian — and we learn that he is the focus of these poor ladies' lives. He married a year ago and went to Chicago to buy a shoe factory with his wife's $10,000 dowry. Now he has been out of touch with his sisters for some time, and they are sure that once again he has lost his money and will come back to them needing help.

It presently transpires that Julian has been in town (New Orleans) for several days, under mysterious circumstances. He comes home, wrapped in mystery and evasion, with his timid and bewildered wife, Lily, and with amazing presents — spinet, refrigerator, gowns, furs, jewels, and tickets to Europe for Carrie and Anna. They are drearily sure that this is just more of his usual play-acting, to cover his failure, and will all have to go back to the stores. Julian, however, insists. He gives them the canceled mortgage on the house. He shows an envelope containing most of $150,000 in large bills. The sisters are dubious. The worthless brother — unlike all the worthless and foolish brothers in the world — is grateful; he is paying back years of shameful debt with a joy that he has dreamed of. Yet his sisters resent his riches.

The money is coming, they learn, from some strange dealings that involve another woman; Julian's young wife (who is a trifle queer) has been spying on him and fears that she is being deceived and will be deserted. Her mother appears, accompanied by her colored lover, Henry, whom she has taken because her wealthy husband hates her. The mother shows why Lily is queer: she treats her with contempt and dislike, unwillingly revealed but powerfully obvious. As the second act develops, we discover that Carrie is physically in love with Julian, jealous of Anna (who loves him in a different but also sick way), and jealous of poor Lily. Carrie has been eavesdropping and discovers that Julian's packet of bills is virtually blackmail. He has been told by the unhappy part-colored wife of another brutal rich man that her husband has to have a certain two acres of swampland in order to swing a big deal involving a railroad right-of-way. Remembering a long past affair with Julian, she went to Chicago to tell him and supplied the money to buy the land because she wants to share the profits in order to be able to escape from her husband.

Between the myth of gentility and the miasma of their real lives yawns the gulf in which we must assume that the people live. Up to this point we do not know them, really, because we see them performing more or less ritualized gestures of gentility-in-misery. Lily's mother is so strange that she must be nearly out of her mind; Carrie and Anna have made a life of sacrificing themselves for a worthless brother; Julian is hidden behind his schemes. But now Anna is packing suitcases for the voyage to Europe, and Julian has gone to town to meet his old friend and give her half of the money. Here Carrie makes the decision that crystallizes the dark fluid of their lives into glittering gems of horror. She cleverly leads poor Lily to telephone the husband of the defecting lady. He has her and Julian waylaid and horribly beaten by thugs, who slash the woman's face and take all the money. Julian's scheme was foolish and shameful, even if not legally criminal, but Carrie's action is a choice that takes the control away from the neurotic environment and enforces her will. I say that the environment is neurotic to indicate the attitudes by which, since Freud, we so often transfer individual guilt and eccentricity to forces in the milieu and even in the psyche that the "self" presumably does not control. Carrie appears a classic example of Southern primness, folly, and helplessness. She is not attractive, but she seems to have been forced by starved love and lack of opportunity to reach out for her younger brother and dedicate

herself to him. She is thus a cluster of fears and frustrations and proprieties, with hardly any controlling "self" apparent.

But then she acts, horribly sacrificing everyone in order to maintain
her frail tie with Julian. Here evil looks out of the frivolous void —
strong, conscious, capable evil that plans and acts with shocking efficiency. By her frightful action Carrie defines and declares herself; she
becomes responsible because she knows what she wants and plans how
to get it, willing to hurt other people as much as is necessary to gain
her end. However "neurotic" she or her society is, she *knows* what she
is doing and she does it.

Clearly the plot provides Carrie's opportunity, and until it came she
could not have known what she would do, could not therefore have
known what she *was to become* by doing it. No amount of description
or play of intellect could, I think, have made such wickedness even
potentially real; it had to find itself in the act. It came into real being
in the act.

A motion picture entitled *The Conjugal Bed* (1963) illustrates other
interesting aspects of our problem. In it, a pleasant fellow approaching forty marries a beautiful and luscious girl whose sexual demands
rapidly reduce him to such exhaustion that he contrives to "work late"
at his office — not for adventures but rather to escape from the lady's
irresistible concupiscence. After agonizing delays, the wife becomes
pregnant and the husband looks for a respite, but alas his undue exer-
tions bring on a heart attack. As he rapidly deteriorates, the wife takes
over the business, the money, and the direction of affairs. The husband dies shortly before the child is born, shattered by making love to
his wife after he has been away for two months at a rest home.

It is hardly necessary to say that the film is a farce. The interesting
point is that, without being dull, it is very depressing, for a reason to
which I shall return presently. The film is essentially a decoration
contrived around an idea. The wife, expressing her natural drive toward maternity, consumes her husband like a queen bee; she draws
the life from him and grows more vigorous and beautiful as she does
so. The queen bee analogy is decorated by the fact that the girl takes
over the money, the business, and control of the cluster of relatives
that swarms around the married pair, but this activity is presented in
a series of scenes that always show what has happened, not what is happening. The effect is to emphasize the fact that a natural drive is being

displayed rather than acts of intelligent choice. With each scene the wife appears more brisk, self-contained, and powerful; while the husband has always taken another step toward the grave. Yet because the wife can no more refrain from expressing her drive than the husband can resist responding to it, there is no willed action, no responsible choice even on the most comic level, and hence there is no sense of character forming or revealing itself as it responds to critical problems.

It is, thus, no accident that the film is a series of separated scenes in which *results*, stage by stage, are *displayed*. There is no willed action that takes the audience from one scene to the next, no movement, no sense of a process in which human choices are involved and displayed. Nothing anybody wills or decides, in short, accounts for what happens next; the love-making occurs with great frequency and causes everything else that follows, but it is a natural force, not a human choice.

In this series of scenes without acts of will, no character can emerge. The wife is beautiful and desirable. She continually arouses and seduces her husband. When she becomes pregnant she ignores and rejects him as some animals do. The heightened energy that she discovers does not bring her to any plans or decisions that would characterize her by involving her mind and heart. As I have said, we merely see her in the next scene taking charge, with more power and poise, of some new activity, but when we see her she has already moved into the new area — "naturally," not by plan or choice. On his part, the husband is a likable fellow who becomes exhausted, desperate, stricken, and dies without making a single choice or decision. All we know of him is that he has a pleasant face, and suffers. Even with the cinema's enormous resource of picturing the character, it cannot make this person either live or develop.

The film was described by critics as the story of a designing, wicked woman who laid her snare with heartless guile and then cruelly consumed the helpless prey. But that story was written from the critics' private lives: an open-minded viewer saw no character that he could either praise or blame, for he did not witness any moral decisions. It was abundantly apparent that the girl was driven by a passion as uncontrolled as her husband's; being young, she had twice his energy, and she drew strength from both passion and maternity. Nature enabled her to turn, when pregnant, from wild sensual indulgence to

broody expectancy without desire; the poor husband oscillated between satiety and frustration, as is also natural with men.

This is very funny, particularly in the realistic bustle of family life
that the Italian directors handle so skillfully, but it is very depressing
too because the decline and death of the husband are intimately and
vividly displayed. Heart disease is as independent of the will as desire,
and the poor fellow never has any chance to formulate a choice, let
alone make one. The viewer, furthermore, knows that life is not really
like this; that passion is involved with intellect and ideality; that no
woman is totally compelled by her urge to maternity; that no reasonable man would be destroyed by a young wife who loved as well as
desired him. These elements would have to be displayed in a plot that
brought them to life, however, and they are not in this film. And it does
the depressed viewer no good to realize that sexual activity is not, in
fact, debilitating but quite the contrary.

This film may be considered a version of melodrama of idea. The
notion of a natural force destroying the mate as the queen bee destroys
the male that fertilizes her is a notion that negates human will and
therefore freedom. The idea is the *motif* that is treated in a series of
tableaux. There is only as much characterization as can be inferred
from the *appearances* of the characters. Strictly, this is no characterization at all, although there may be some illusion of it which the observer supplies from his own fund of attitudes.

In Elia Kazan's film *America America* (1963) characters grow to remarkable roundness for a cinema because the action and the social
context provide the movement and the medium in which character
seems to flourish best. The story begins with Greeks and Armenians
living in Anatolia, in poverty and humiliation under their Turkish
masters. Living in caves and hovels, the people still dress with some
formality, carry on their religious devotions, and maintain the intense
loyalty of the family. In the family the father is absolute lord; the
women live for his pleasure and speak with his permission. The children are absolutely obedient. The father, in his turn, takes his responsibilities very seriously — not in this society by working but by presiding over the family, which is equivalent to holding together the thing
that is the very soul of its members.

Particularly as he might be judged by American standards, the father in this cinema appears at first ridiculous and perhaps even con-

temptible. He wears a fez, a cravat, and a black suit; lives in a desperate hovel with barely enough to eat; allows his family to feed and serve him. The rebellious boy who is the hero wants to escape to America from Turkish tyranny and insults. He is Greek, and the Greeks are treated much better than the Armenians, but they know that the Turks will turn on them when the occasion offers — that is, when the Armenians have been disposed of. When the Armenian church is burned in reprisal for some misbehavior in far-distant Constantinople, the boy explodes in rebellion. When his father rebukes him with a slap, then embraces him, the strength of the family is demonstrated. When the father decides that the boy shall take every cent and scrap of the family property and go to Constantinople to make his fortune and bring the family after him to a better life, he presents the decision with a gravity of judgment and responsibility that demonstrates the family unity in absolute and crucial action. In these incidents the father takes form as a man of love, dignity, decision, but also weakness: his faith in entrusting everything the family owns to the boy is touching, but also pathetic in its innocence.

The characters have defined themselves thus quickly because they are in an established social order, with rules, customs, forms, loyalties, beliefs. Under the Turk, their decisions are matters of life itself, and the quiet strength with which they undertake to entrust everything to the boy defines their characters in depth. On his way over desert and mountain to Constantinople, the boy is cheated, robbed, beaten, humiliated — again by a Turk. There he works at the lowest tasks, trying desperately, helplessly, to save enough for his passage to America. Defeated, robbed again, almost killed by the police, he goes to an uncle and through him is presently well dressed and working for a rich rug merchant who has four daughters. By now the boy is hard, unsmiling, tormented. Plans are made for him to marry one of the daughters, share the business and the prestige, and settle down in the bosom of a big happy loving family.

The daughter is described as unattractive, and in her first two or three appearances she is shy, reserved, even anxious-looking. But the marriage is arranged, and she seems to be strongly attracted to the unsmiling young man who is still a stranger to her. He, in turn, is tormented, for while he responds to the trust and warmth of his new circle, he cannot give up his almost frantic determination to get to

America. When the marriage settlement is discussed, he rejects the father's offer of 500 Turkish pounds; he wants only 110. We know that this is the price of passage to America — and so we know his unspoken intention; he will marry the girl and desert her.

Two brief scenes follow that are worth close attention. In the first, the shy girl talks with her adoring father. Although the family, like the boy's family back in the country, is absolutely dominated by the father, to the point where the women hardly say a word without permission, the girl is able to speak her heart. She senses a terrible secret in the boy's manner, and she is afraid of him — yet in love and willing to devote her life to him. Her father comforts and encourages her, with no belittling of her fear.

Soon after, he presents the young people with the key to an apartment which is to be theirs when they are married. It is a charming place, but the couple examine it under great constraint, the young man nursing in tormented silence the thought of what he has planned to do, the girl loving him and yet apprehensive. She begs his permission to ask him a question, after assuring him that her only wish is to do exactly what he wants her to do, to make him happy. He cannot answer, and the girl suddenly breaks out demanding that he "Say something! Speak! Speak!" She apologizes once or twice for speaking, and again for showing strong emotion; but she goes right on showing it, and she expresses herself with feeling and effect. Thus a character unfolds in expression before our eyes. Within the limits of her family life there is a rich texture of manners, beliefs, and conduct. These have given the girl a freedom that is unexpected until we see it in action. For if she has lived in a situation where freedom seems greatly restricted, she has within its confines found love, duty, and emotional growth. The scene in which she spoke her troubled heart so freely and openly to her father showed that the family ties were not bonds but connections over which full communication could flow. Now in the troubled scene with the boy, she reveals tenderness, intelligence, courage, and even humor. She makes no coy secret of the fact that she adores him and places the hope of her life on him, but she retains her dignity in the act of speaking. Her directness expresses her pride; even more, it expresses her confidence in herself and in her expectations. Like her father, like her family, she is strong, honest, forthright, happy; she is full of vitality. This rich and moving characterization is achieved in two short scenes because there is a rich social context and the character is confronted with a critical situation in her life. She succeeds, furthermore, in making the boy reveal his intentions. He tells her that he will probably never know another woman as good as she is; and she is able to accept her bitter disappointment with generosity and more love.

Personality is usually thought of as something that comes through in one's instinctive reaction to a new person. Personality is superbly expressed in the acting of Charles Laughton, or Peter Sellers, or Alec Guinness; and it makes an immediate impression that carries one back to the magnificent abundance of a Dickens character. There we have a sense of a person bristling with mannerisms, plastered with whims and fancies, rolling in mummery and eccentricity. This is the personality, and there can be no question that it comes out in appearance and speech very quickly with an actor and often almost as quickly in the first descriptive presentation by a novelist. This gives a sense of prior life, of the person coming into the story with a self, and with a past that has produced that self. This illusion (for it must be an illusion, since the character does not in fact exist until he appears in the novel) is enriched by devices of flashback or what is called retrospective dialogue in the drama, which take us from the present action back to the past where the character was compounded and generated. These are, then, devices that enrich the action by drawing a past (not the actual past) into it; we must remind ourselves, as we analyze, that this past did not in fact exist, and that it is therefore as much an illusion as the present action that we watch or read about.

Personality is either a face or a mask. The reader may not know whether it is a mask or not; and if he is sure it is a mask, he may not know what lies behind it. The character is not sure either. If his personality is a mask, is it viable? Can he maintain it under new pressures? In one action the character may abandon his mask and reveal himself. In another he may discover his "real" self. In another he may grow from his mask into a new self. Or he may be destroyed because his mask is not viable, not adequate to new occasions. It seems generally safe to say that the personality may reveal the character, which may or may not, then, be "hidden" behind it. The event (in other words, the action) will show us: the character will evolve, grow, succeed, fail, reveal, or merely verify itself.

The question of the "real" self as opposed to the public self, or mask, is one of the central problems of character — indeed of man. This self ranges from the happy simple state (if it ever existed) when people were simply and only what they appeared and did, to the existentialist dilemma where the hero does not know for sure that he is, let alone what he is. The first state may evoke melodrama, whereas the latter demands an un-action or un-plot because even the author cannot commit himself to the extent of letting something serious happen. After all, what is serious enough to believe in?

Between these extremes come the manners of an ordered society, the gestures of aristocracy, and all the other patterns that have participated in the definition and display of character. The contest between man and mask has been explored in poem after poem by William Butler Yeats, who saw it as the essential problem of character. His formulation rests upon a notion of what a person essentially *is*. Viewed in my perspective of plot, which assumes that it is the action that produces the character, the tension of mask and man, we may say, is dramatized in the problems and conflicts that emerge from the tension between myth and actuality.*

---

* Cyrus Hoy, in *The Hyacinth Room: An Investigation into the Nature of Comedy, Tragedy, and Tragicomedy* (New York: Knopf, 1964), explores his thesis that "the fundamental basis for all valid dramatic literature" is to be found in the conflict between illusion and actuality, or myth and reality. My problem of characterization involves this conflict — and particularly the nature and the size of the gap between illusion and reality; but it will also take us into many sorts of situations where the conflict is not joined, where the illusion is rejected, or where the actuality itself is treated as illusory.

It is unfortunate that Yeats, who wrote so much about this question of character, should have used the terms "character" and "personality" with meanings almost exactly counter to mine. He says that "Character is the ash of personality," because personality is the deep elemental core of man, whereas character takes form in eccentricities and circumstances. Personality grows from the passion of tragedy, whereas comedy is the clash of character. "Juliet has personality, her Nurse has character." He is close to the Aristotelian point in saying that tragedy is essentially the conflict of passions, possibly even to the exclusion of personality, whereas comedy, being passionless, objective, and realistic, develops characters. See *The Autobiography of William Butler Yeats* (New York: Macmillan, 1953), p. 286.

I believe that the common usage has passed Yeats by here and that we now generally use "character" to designate an ethical core of man (cf. Emerson's famous "Character is higher than intellect"), "personality" to indicate his masks and mannerisms.

PART II

A Crux and
a Classic

ARISTOTLE said that character was composed of intellect and ethos, these being the areas in which a person manifested the flavor of his individuality. In the Greek tragedies the action was so strong that it had a life of its own: the *story* of the House of Atreus stood there dominating its actors, ignoring them. Thus Aristotle seems to have been impelled to seek out qualities of mind and judgment that identified the persons in one of these great actions apart from the fated deeds that they performed in the story, deeds that were going to take place inevitably and almost independently of the actors who might be enlisted in a particular drama to perform them. Aristotle identified intellect and ethos as giving such actors individuality. Today we can see that the substance of both speculation and moral choice is to be found in the action, and that when a person thinks without making significant choices he will not define himself firmly, he will not know himself — whereas the Greek tragic hero was on the other end of this problem: he had the tremendous action but not necessarily the occasion for small talk or the evincing of mannerism.

In the following two chapters I shall deal with two works that seem, on first glance, to be totally different, in order to show that they both respond to analysis based on the assumptions I have presented. They are *Hamlet* and *Pride and Prejudice*.

To search incessantly into the mystery of what Hamlet *is* in order to understand why he speaks and acts as he does leads us, I believe, to ask all the wrong questions. But if we assume that Hamlet is an ideal prince and then turn our attention to the action to see what happens to him, we are asking an entirely different set of questions that will enable us to take seriously every incident in the play. Instead of a glittering string of soliloquies, we have a most compelling story in which the hero finds himself in one situation after another that puts unforeseen demands upon him, that calls for decisions he is not ready to make, and that evokes responses which he has never experienced before. His character forms and reveals itself in this complex, this packed, this intense action. I shall try to explicate the play from this point of view.

The great irony of *Hamlet* is that the *inaction* that pervades the action has inspired the modern notion of a hero whose whole character exists in a paralysis of speculation, indecision, and anguish quite apart from the story in which he appears. We are still watching and enacting the consequences of this great reversal.

In *Pride and Prejudice* we have a story that flows so brightly and steadily, while its characters live so completely in its situations, that it serves as a classic example of the fusion and interdependence of character and action.

3   Hamlet *as Action*

I SHOULD like to try to discuss *Hamlet* to make some fundamental points about characterization in the terms I have been exploring. One hesitates to propose anything new on a play about which "everything" has been said; but I am impelled to it by the fact that *Hamlet* is crucial to the emergence of modern notions about character in fiction. If there have been something like three thousand books and articles published on the play since 1900, it is because (and here I can make one statement without qualification) the character of Hamlet continues to puzzle us and everything written seeks to throw some new light on the mystery.

In general, the critical contest has been between those who would explain the play by finding the key to the mystery of Hamlet's character and those who would reduce it to melodrama and spectacle. A third team of critics dabbles in philosophical problems, but these do not greatly affect the tides of the major battle. In the main contest, those who explore the mystery of the character make it the source of the action, whereas those who have insisted on the primacy of the action generally say that the problems of motivation and character in the hero disappear if we consider the play as a rapidly moving, even melodramatic spectacle of bloody violence and revenge. I should like to look at one or two of these exegeses and then try to look at the play in a completely fresh way.

The general terms of the contest, suggested above, are illustrated in

an introduction to *Hamlet* by my revered teacher O. J. Campbell.*
His own position and his definition of the opposition are equally interesting. He begins by dismissing as the "speculations of subjective
critics" such notions as that "Hamlet was . . . a brooding 'philosopher
of death, a scholar of the night.' The modern variant of this idea is the
notion that in Hamlet the desire to die has triumphed over the desire
to live. Other commentators have assumed that Hamlet's grief has
paralyzed his will, so that he is ever at the mercy of a mind involved
in ceaseless debate with itself. Still others," he continues, "explain
Hamlet's difficulty as the revulsion of a sensitive nature against the
violent revenge which the ghost has ordered him to take." The corrective to misguided modernism is to "search the contents of the Elizabethan mind." There we find that Shakespeare's audience had a much
more precise notion of "melancholy" than we have. "It was the name
given to a nervous malady described at length in all the household
medical handbooks of Shakespeare's day, and Elizabethan doctors were
making careful attempts to observe and describe its symptoms." Since
in the seventeenth century people in such conditions were not confined or even treated, "many cases of pathological melancholy were at
large in Elizabethan society and easily recognizable by anyone interested in human personality." In Hamlet's case, the "rhythm of his
malady" is so timed that "at every crucial moment he finds himself in
the grip of emotions which fit him least to deal with the situation con-
fronting him . . . With each new revelation of this irrepressible conflict Hamlet's inner tension mounts until at the final catastrophe his
tortured will explodes in a wild frenzy of unconsidered action." Professor Campbell has elsewhere elaborated his theory with the term
"manic depressive" to label the malady from which Hamlet fails to act
when he would most profit by acting, and acts on impulse when he
should have kept his peace and his counsel.

Professor Campbell acknowledges that many students of the play
would reject his interpretation as reducing a great drama to the level
of a case history of a sick psyche. They would say that Shakespeare intended to give his characters just enough individuality to perform the
deeds in "an exciting story of revenge." While he acknowledges that
this emphasis is a good corrective to the sort of subjective speculations

*O. J. Campbell, *The Living Shakespeare* (New York: Macmillan, 1949). The quotations are from pp. 744 and 745.

mentioned above, he believes that "carried too far it puts *Hamlet* on the same level as scores of other Elizabethan melodramas. Something very serious is the matter with Hamlet, and the full meaning of the great tragedy will never be clear until critics discover in the drama a conscious artistic design like the one sketched above." So either "something very serious is the matter with Hamlet," or the play is a melodrama of violent revenge. I know that this account of Professor Campbell's interpretation is somewhat reductive, but I think I have not done violence to the main outlines. It is perfectly clear that he considers the mystery to be in the character of Hamlet — in what he essentially *is* as a man, which accounts for how he acts in the play; and he sees the alternative as tending to reduce the hero to a simple figure in a melodrama on the order of the heroes of American westerns described in Chapter 2.

Even if *Hamlet* is not a case history of a diseased mind (although the term "manic depressive" makes Hamlet dangerously close to being one, in spite of the disclaimer), we must acknowledge the intrusion here of modern psychological concepts of the sort that reduce the self by classifying its eccentricities and putting them in pigeonholes where they are seen as items in the environment. The struggle of the diminished self with its environing neuroses is a mystery of exploration and understanding rather than a dramatic action. Pushed far enough, it becomes the story of a naked eyeball suffering the cold winds of the world, absorbing agony while it fights to keep from freezing into a permanent trance of horror. If Hamlet is the beginning of this transformation, he is so, I would suggest, only as seen in the perspective of hindsight; and yet I will try to show that he must have been seen in his own time as adding a new element to the idea of man. When Pepys wrote in his diary that it was the best play and the best part ever written, he must have been responding to something that, even after 1660, was still startlingly new.

I think we can identify this element, but let us for a moment consider the range of critical opinion: Lily Bess Campbell finds Hamlet a medical case of "sanguine adust"; the great Kittredge insists there is no delay but only problems Hamlet must solve (i.e., the ghost) and opposition he must outwit with feigned madness; Bernard Grebanier, after a lifetime of study, declares that Hamlet *never feigns madness*; E. E. Stoll reduces the play to a hasty, opportunistic adaptation of an old play, in which revenge predominates and the hero is not to be analyzed but only watched as he flashes from scene to scene in a wild, melodramatic plot.*

Before we succumb to the temptation to write off the action of *Hamlet* and say that Shakespeare was using tag-ends of old plots while he wrote poetry to express the romantic despair of a new, autobiographical hero, it is worth glancing at the plots of the other major tragedies which Shakespeare was writing during the years before and after *Hamlet*. In every one, the action is of dominating importance, even while it serves to bring out character and, in the process, the poetry which expresses the characters' quality of mind. In *Julius Caesar* the story is everything. Its theme moves around the problems of sovereignty and leadership and ambition; it moves through a famous story which has been retold a thousand times. What the characters become appears in their reactions to great challenges and final decisions; and their importance is writ large on the pages of history. *Othello* is an overpowering story; what the hero *is* cannot be conceived apart from the particular action of this play. Indeed, before this action he was a great soldier and a tremendous leader of men. A towering hero, he carried the simplicities of heroism, for he lived on a battle-stage where he saw his own actions against a prodigious and majestic backdrop. The warrior's simplicity entranced Desdemona and infuriated the subtle Iago, under whose management the plot moves into a labyrinth of horror where the Moor rages, struggles, and destroys even while he cannot find his way from turning to turning. It is what Othello *did* that he talks about in the great speech that ends with his suicide. It is what he did, beside which what he previously *was* is as nothing, for he has become the creature of his horrid act — a new and terrible creature who cannot undo his ghastly mistake.

There are two time schemes in *Othello*. To achieve the psychological intensity and the headlong rush that keeps the hero from having time to step aside and think, Shakespeare has packed the action into thirty-six hours after the arrival at Cyprus; but to allow for the probabilities of moral growth, that is, to make the canker of suspicion grow to a

---

* See Lily Bess Campbell, *Shakespeare's Tragic Heroes: Slaves of Passion* (Cambridge: The University Press, 1930); George Lyman Kittredge, *Shakespeare's Works* (Boston: Ginn, 1936), notes; Bernard Grebanier, *The Heart of Hamlet* (New York: Crowell, 1960); E. E. Stoll, *Art and Artifice in Shakespeare* (Cambridge: The University Press, 1933).

cancer of jealousy, takes more time, and for this Shakespeare has provided a series of clues that stretch the same events out to three weeks or so. No member of an audience would ever disentangle the two sets of time clues at a single performance. An actor could perform the part without realizing that they were there. But the artistic depth and validity produced by them is one of the great wonders of the play, as it is of Shakespeare's craft. Within a single action he has evolved the sort of moral and psychological density that comes from the double plot in *Lear*. The subtlety and ingenuity of this construction reveals so profound an insight into the function of the action that I do not see how we can turn from it to *Hamlet* and say that Shakespeare was not really interested in what happened — or that he did not dare to meddle with legendary events that his audience would insist upon seeing unchanged. No audience of spectators over five years old could be so rigid.

Not until *King Lear* does Shakespeare venture to make the plot grow from the character of the hero. There he does, and with the surest hand that he was ever to show, making an action of cosmic dimensions grow out of the strange mixture of vanity, fatuity, and trust in the bosom of a monarch who has but slenderly known himself because he has been insulated by the sheer mass of his authority from his court and his family. Starting with his initial folly, Lear is plunged into a nightmare which puts out the light of his mind before it has purged him of his vanity and his overweening authority. I think everyone feels that *Lear* is Shakespeare's most powerful play, his profoundest search of the human heart. This greatness is achieved because he begins with a king whose first speech involves him in an action of tremendous significance — and from the initial folly a flood, an ocean, a world, a cosmos of evil pours over him and crashes on to engulf the characters in an action that is, in one way or another, final for them all. It takes two plots to explore the physical blindness of Gloucester beside the intellectual blindness of Lear. When the turmoil has passed and the king has regained contact with humanity, the depths of human suffering have been plumbed and agonies of self-knowledge have been realized. The force of the action is hinted in Albany's closing couplet:

> The oldest hath borne most; we that are young
> Shall never see so much, nor live so long.   [V, iii, 325–26]

I say "hinted," because no words can begin to describe it.

In *Macbeth, Antony and Cleopatra,* and *Coriolanus* the actions continue to be grand, involving issues and conflicts that challenge and define their heroes. Macbeth is not merely ambitious: he is caught up in a temptation as compelling as it is horrifying, which unveils the inmost mysteries of man's contradictory nature, where rational good forever struggles with impulsive evil. As the action moves into the very sovereign heart of the body politic, and moral darkness rises to disrupt the wholesome state embodied in its gentle king, so within Macbeth these forces engage in a conflict of appalling depth and intensity and he becomes as full and great as this action. The supernatural itself is called upon to figure forth the immensities of his spiritual turmoil.

Antony and Cleopatra does not have the cosmic dimensions of *Lear,* contained within a single spirit, but it moves in a larger world than any other play. Rome, Athens, Alexandria — the whole Mediterranean world, indeed the whole civilized world — become dazzling baubles well lost for the exalted and devastating passion that consumes while it glorifies the heroes. Armies are betrayed, fleets of warships abandoned, kingdoms tossed aside to dramatize the relation between Antony and Cleopatra. She uses these elements to describe him:

> His face was as the heavens; and therein stuck
> A sun and moon, which kept their course, and lighted
> The little O, the earth. . . .
> His legs bestrid the ocean; his rear'd arm
> Crested the world: his voice was propertied
> As all the tunèd spheres, and that to friends;
> But when he meant to quail and shake the orb,
> He was as rattling thunder. . . .
> > in his livery
> Walk'd crowns and crownets; realms and islands were
> As plates dropp'd from his pocket.   [V, ii, 79–93]

And when such a one dies,

> > O sun,
> Burn the great sphere thou move'st in! Darkling stand
> The varying shore of the world!   [IV, xv, 11–13]

Only with such a world backdrop could Shakespeare have glorified a destructive passion, a fading hero, and a sensual and imperious woman. And it is more than a backdrop: it is the substance of the action against which the demands of the passion are measured and revealed. Without these imperial choices the story would not rise to its imperial theme. Repeatedly in the play the characters are defined through their choices in situations of extraordinary importance: when Antony flaunts Caesar, when Cleopatra flees from the sea battle, when Antony flees after her, when he has to ask Eros to kill him, when Cleopatra refuses to come down from the monument, and when she makes her choice of death rather than deal with Caesar, the characters grow into their worldly and world-dominating richness. Thus we see Cleopatra's character as made of her thoughts about and her reactions (i.e., decisions) to these grand situations. She has her being, she becomes herself in these events. She is woven of the strands in this fabric of setting and action.

Likewise in *Coriolanus* we see an action that brings military heroism into violent confrontation with the demands of plebeian democracy — and the hero advances into a situation where he has to break the ties that gave his military leadership its meaning. Coriolanus emerges into choices and deeds that shatter his identification with state, with self, with family; and yet the state and the family still sway on his decisions. We no longer respond to this play very successfully because physical heroism no longer confers utter greatness: two world wars have shown us that valor may appear at any level of society and that valor does not make for ultimate greatness. But we can appreciate the fact that the action of *Coriolanus* is everything; it brings the hero into new realms of the spirit; it makes him realize and enact implications of his position that could not have existed apart from this action. Again, what Coriolanus becomes is not implicit in him unless he is involved in the action of the play; it is the action that makes the emerging man.

The more we look from one great play to the next, the more difficult it becomes to sustain the notion that plot was not important to Shakespeare. If we take the proper perspective, however, we see that Shakespeare used old and famous stories precisely because plot was so important to him. It was only with important actions that he could generate important characters, and such important actions cannot be invented out of nothing; they must be drawn from the deepest springs of the society.

I propose that we should look at *Hamlet* as primarily the imitation of an action. Then instead of wondering "what is the matter" with the hero, we shall be able to start with the simple and indeed the engaging assumption that nothing at all is the matter with him. Starting on this ground brings us the inestimable satisfaction of being able to believe what another important character says when she describes him. Everybody knows Ophelia's description, which is about as forceful and unequivocal as it could possibly be:

> O what a noble mind is here o'erthrown!
> The courtier's, soldier's, scholar's, eye, tongue, sword,
> The expectancy and rose of the fair state,
> The glass of fashion and the mould of form,
> The observ'd of all observers . . .
>   that noble and most sovereign reason
>   [III, i, 158–65]

Speeches of this sort are an extremely familiar convention of drama to establish the "official" view of a character. When they are so eloquently full and precise, they are there for the audience's information. The point is further supported by the fact that Ophelia is speaking only to herself, since Hamlet has just stormed offstage and the king and Polonius have not come up to her yet. She is not concealing or probing or manipulating, but speaking her heart. Nothing in the play gives any sound reason for doubting this speech. Ophelia is not mad yet, and she certainly knows Hamlet well enough to speak with authority about him. That Shakespeare should give her so eloquent a speech is in itself evidence that she is to be seen as capable of such eloquence (as Polonius and Laertes, who also comment on Hamlet, are not, the one being fatuous and tedious, the other pompous and fulsome), and it seems equally obvious that the eloquence implies intelligence and insight. Ophelia of course is mistaken in thinking Hamlet mad at this point. In her distress and innocence she is as easily taken in by his subterfuge as she is intimidated by his violence. But this innocence is our assurance that she speaks without subtlety and expresses the general and "official" view of Hamlet.

Her speech tells us in the plainest terms what Hamlet *was*. She has described the ideal Renaissance prince and we must start by accepting this as fact. The ideal prince was as far as anyone could be from having "something the matter" with him. He was the model of courage, decision, manners — the mold of form, the expectancy and rose of the fair state. This character has been so firmly established by Hamlet's early conduct that Polonius and Laertes characterize (and damn) themselves by their suspicions of him. The ignobility of their advice to

Ophelia condemns them in the speaking of it. Hamlet needs no defense from such contemptible charges. His essential nobility and honor have already been made clear by his appearance, his speech, the deference of Marcellus and Bernardo, the loyalty and respect of Horatio, and the fact that they go straight to him with the dangerous story of the ghost. These early impressions are fortified by the magnificent courage and intelligence of his confrontation of the ghost in Act I, scene iv, as they have already been strengthened by the respect for him shown by Claudius and Gertrude in the court scene at the king's first audience. In this scene, and in later discussions of the errant prince, Claudius, Gertrude, and Polonius never say that Hamlet *was* queer, or inadequate, or too intellectual; rather, they all speak of the change that has overtaken him and wonder what it means. Much later in the play the same notions of Hamlet's nobility are expressed. Claudius complains to Gertrude of the people's love — "He's loved of the distracted multitude" (IV, iii, 4) — and he tells Laertes that Hamlet is "remiss,/ Most generous, and free from all contriving" (IV, vii, 135–36). The belief that Hamlet is the ideal prince is universal; it is assumed in every reference to his change or his "madness." Ophelia's account of his coming in muddy disarray, shaking his head and looking at her accusingly (II, i), conveys her shock and fear at the change in her lover.

The hero is the ideal prince at the beginning. The play's the thing — that is, the plot does not express and grow from Hamlet's peculiar character; rather it is the plot that brings about his problem and his complex series of reactions to it. In saying that plot is the prime mover, I do *not* intend to suggest that the play is a melodramatic tragedy of bloody revenge in which there are many unorganized remnants from earlier bloody plays — or that Shakespeare slavishly followed his sources merely because they contributed to the violence and excitement. (This view makes the plot unimportant and the character created by the poetry.)

The plot should be taken much more seriously — and it will be taken seriously if we adopt the view that it accounts for, indeed produces, the subtleties and complexities of characterization that appear as it unfolds. Then instead of an amorphous modern intellectual (or a high-level beatnik) imposed upon a patchwork fable scrambled hastily together from Saxo Grammaticus, Belleforest, and Thomas Kyd (I say "scrambled," yet these are also represented as authorities whose fables had to be slavishly followed lest the audience rebel, although it is never made plain how three conflicting sources could all be respected at the same time), we shall have an extraordinarily complex plot that generates an extraordinarily complex hero, step by step, as he moves through it. If plot were thus of absolutely first importance — which it was — Shakespeare would have given most careful attention to it. He would have scrutinized it item by item in order to make every incident work into the developing situation and character of his hero. I assume that Shakespeare was responsible for every detail in the final plot. I am not willing to concede that anything in *Hamlet* was forced on Shakespeare by the fictitious authority of a story that his audience would not allow him to change — or by any grand heedlessness of consistency or relevance on Shakespeare's part.

I have seen a good many performances of *Hamlet*. In every one the hero has become dissociated from the plot by Act III. Thereafter he ponders, postures, and performs, but he does not seem to know which of the fifty Hamlets of criticism he is. As the end approaches he becomes less and less aware of what he is saying, until sometimes he lapses into a sort of sleepwalking declamation, going through a set of motions that are not connected by a developing action but rather appear as set pieces or famous little vignettes with fine speeches. Part of the trouble lies in the length of the play and the fact that big chunks are omitted in performance without proper transitions, so that at worst the play becomes a series of soliloquies; part is that the language is so magnificent that the purple passages overpower the actor; but basically the trouble is that the actor has these fifty Hamlets milling around in his brain and they are all Hamlets of various critics' contriving rather than Hamlets caught up in a formidable, dominating series of events. The actor's grip on his role steadily weakens, until the final catastrophe is endured by an audience somewhat listlessly waiting for "Absent thee from felicity a while . . ." and "Good night, sweet Prince, and flights of angels sing thee to thy rest."

The condition that establishes a dynamic and organic relation between Hamlet and the action is that he finds himself in a situation where *he does not understand his own reactions*. It must be shown that Hamlet is the most baffled and bewildered character in the cast. How does this come about? Plot and character meet, as we have seen, in the interplay of values, manners, and customs which is the design and substance of the social fabric. The subject of *Hamlet* is at the center of this design. It is the question of sovereignty, which is to say it is the principle that makes the state and holds it together — the life and mind of the body politic. The king is, according to the powerful symbol of medieval and Renaissance polity, the head of the body politic. Cut off that head and the state is naught. It is the source of order or "degree"; "untune that string" and chaos is come again. Sovereignty is the initial concern of any Renaissance historian; it is the central concern of most. It is the subject of Shakespeare's history plays: what happens when the string of order is untuned by the murder of a king or the usurpation of proper succession? The theme attracted Shakespeare again and again. "For God's sake, let us sit upon the ground/ And tell sad stories of the death of kings," wailed Richard II, in a play that many critics feel to be a trial run for *Hamlet*.

Before Hamlet knows anything of the ghost, he is presented, in the second scene, garbed in solemn black, brooding on the fringe of the gay company that has assembled to bask in the first sunshine of the new sovereign. Claudius is strong, confident, masterful. He offers thanks to his followers, makes a virtue of his hasty marriage to Gertrude, dispatches a few items of important business — and then turns to his most serious problem, Hamlet, who is lurking somberly on the edge of the gathering. The first speeches are electric:

CLAUDIUS: But now, my cousin Hamlet, and my son, —
HAMLET: *(aside)* A little more than kin, and less than kind.
CLAUDIUS: How is it that the clouds still hang on you?
HAMLET: Not so, my lord, I am too much i' the sun.

[I, ii, 64–67]

What strikes one most forcefully here is that Hamlet is out of the act; he has no role; where everyone else is participating in the new order of sovereignty, he is apart and aside, glooming on the edge, not fitting into the drift or spirit of the occasion. The ideal prince is a man of action: he translates the thought into the deed on the instant in a manner exemplifying his readiness, his courage, his leadership. Here Hamlet's aversion for Claudius, which alone would not disturb his princely dedication to sovereignty, is exacerbated by his doubts about his own status. He is both son and nephew — and neither; he is chief mourner except for Gertrude — and she paradoxically has become chief celebrant; he is witness to luxury, incest, and wassail — and yet there is no proper position from which he can positively *act*. Sovereignty is firm and confident; only Hamlet does not know where he stands.

His two replies quoted above, which are his first words in the play, have been subjected to exhaustive analysis. A dozen meanings have been found in them — and properly so, for they are supercharged, exploding from a brilliant intelligence under the tension which characteristically in Shakespeare produces a flood of puns or turgid mixed images. Only Shakespeare, I think, has been able so magnificently to represent the energy of the powerful mind under extreme stress. With his rebellious garb and his eruption of puns, he declares himself totally apart — and without a part. As the scene continues, he becomes more incisively rude, and in his next speeches he actually foreshadows the notion that, having no proper part, he must invent a role:

> HAMLET: Ay, madam, it is common.
> GERTRUDE: If it be,
>   Why seems it so particular with thee?
> HAMLET: Seems, madame! Nay, it is; I know not seems.
>   'Tis not alone my inky cloak, good mother,
>   Nor customary suits of solemn black . . .
>   These indeed seem,
>   For they are actions that a man might play;
>   But I have that within which passeth show,
>   These but the trappings and the suits of woe.
>   [I, ii, 74–86]

Lurking on the edge of the company has given him the sense of alienation which comes out in the phrase "a man might play." It is the familiar sense of unreality that comes to an observer who is partly in and partly out of the scene that he observes. For Hamlet it is a baffling and an exasperating experience, which produces in him tension and violence of speech. At this point Hamlet must not be seen as aloof, superior, or intellectually detached. Nor is he sick with melancholy. Quite the contrary, he is emotionally engaged in the situation but baffled by his inability to do anything meaningful. This must be a new sensation for him, and its newness accounts for the violence to which his bewilderment gives rise. Inability to match the deed to the thought is something that the glass of fashion and the mold of form, the observ'd of all observers, never dreamed of suffering. The ideal prince will think deep thoughts, but these thoughts will not inhibit action or replace it.

It is therefore not Hamlet's nature but the situation that evokes these violent, exasperated speeches. It does, of course, require a certain kind of man to respond so; the point is that the response is produced by the situation and would never have come without this particular situation. The following soliloquy — "O, that this too, too sullied flesh would melt" — not only specifies what is most on Hamlet's mind (his mother's hasty and incestuous marriage) but also reveals the element of theatricality generated by suppressed emotions and inability to act; and when Horatio enters a moment later with news of the ghost, Hamlet suddenly comes alive, delighted to join thought and deed as he asks searching questions and instantly plans to watch that night with Horatio and the soldiers.

Before Hamlet talks with the ghost, he hears the cannon bruiting the king's carouse and comments on the unwholesome excesses of his land:

> This heavy-headed revel east and west
> Makes us traduc'd and tax'd of other nations.
> They clepe us drunkards, and with swinish phrase
> Soil our addition . . .   [I, iv, 17–20]

The speech tells us what, after his mother's hasty marriage, troubles Hamlet most; the drunkenness in Denmark is a second form of moral deterioration. His distress is redoubled by the ghost's disclosure. In a state of tremendous excitement, he twice begins to reveal to his companions what the ghost has told — and twice he catches himself in midsentence and retreats into "wild and whirling words." From this acting, he turns to the business of demanding a solemn oath of secrecy, which is interrupted by the ghost speaking under the platform. This sets Hamlet off into more extravagant play-acting by which he dissembles both his knowledge and his feelings; and he ends the scene by telling his companions in mysterious terms that he will be doing strange things, that he may "perchance hereafter . . . think meet/ To put an antic disposition on," and that they must not give him away.

Before the ghost's revelation, Hamlet had had time to think about the question of sovereignty as he saw it incarnate in Claudius and Gertrude. He had also thought about play-acting. Now personal danger, uncertainty about the ghost's message, and the knowledge that for better or worse Claudius *is* the state make him retreat from a situation in which he has no role to the feigning of an antic disposition —

or madness — in which he can maintain the intolerable dilemma of having to act and not being sure enough to act — or not being able to make himself act. Many forces are in tension. Pulling one way are respect for sovereignty, a disinclination to violence, a sense that more is wrong than murder, possible doubt of the ghost, and the earlier speculation that has begun his detachment; pulling the other way are murder and the filial duty of revenge. Of course there are more, many more, which have been set forth by a long line of distinguished critics, but what it boils down to — and it has to be boiled down to be stage-able — is that Hamlet is put in a situation where he cannot act, where as an ideal man of action he is bewildered and furious at his inability to act, and from which he escapes into the invented role of madman. This role gives him time for speculation which increases his detachment; it requires antic conduct which works with the tensions produced by his frustrations; it keeps him in the presence of the murderer-sovereign, which exacerbates his guilt.

Most extraordinary is the manner in which Shakespeare has contrived so that his hero has *acted* himself into this state — first in solemn black, then in theatrical soliloquy, and then in wild and whirling responses to old Truepenny calling "Swear!" from the cellarage. The state of vexation and uncertainty in which he finds himself is expressed by his closing words to this remarkable act:

> The time is out of joint; — O cursed spite
> That ever I was born to set it right!
> [I, v, 188–89]

A superb verbal touch is that Hamlet uses the image of a bonesetter, which he certainly is not.

The key to a performance that will allow the plot to dominate, as it should, will be that Hamlet constantly shows that he is *changing* under the impact of events which have effects on him that he does not understand. If this failure to understand his own responses is properly rendered, the actor-hero will come through as a man discovering himself under totally unforeseen pressures and evolving under them into a new sort of man. The action stays a step ahead of Hamlet, all the way to the end.

The most powerful confusion forced on Hamlet by the action is the madness, which slips back and forth over the lines between clowning, exasperated fury, and hysteria. He is clowning with Polonius and

Osric, he is furious with Ophelia and Gertrude because his assumed madness has got between him and them, and he goes just over the edge when he rants at Ophelia, kills Polonius, and jumps into the grave with Laertes. These shadings must be seen in relation to each other. The feigned madness comes out of the first tension with the ghost, *after* the days of brooding over the real ambiguities of sovereignty and kinship which make Claudius outside the law because he *is* the law and further because Hamlet is the son and nephew of Claudius. The feigning begins, indeed, as a wild compulsion. It becomes a habit and a safety valve. And it becomes a trap. People look askance at him just when he wants to be taken most seriously; so he cannot communicate, and so he jumps from one role to the next. In the second state — exasperated fury — he is well on the way to the third, where he will endanger himself and his program with conduct that is irrational if not mad. Surely it is the uneasy sense of being looked at askance that motivates his long speech to Horatio before the Mousetrap scene.

These drifts between clowning and hysteria must be seen as functions of the plot; that is, they are not inherent in Hamlet but forced upon him by the developing situation, and he must show himself to be repeatedly surprised by what he does. This is what makes character grow out of the action. It links hero and event in an exciting and wonderfully interesting sequence. It makes every detail in the action important, but only if Hamlet is as tense and curious as the audience about what will happen next. I suspect that twentieth-century attitudes make it extravagantly difficult for us to see the play this way. Drugstore Hamlets are a dime-a-dozen today because so many people do not know what is important in the world. The common question today is "What should I want, and why?" In this context uncertainty and indecision are more common than resolution and confidence. How many of T. S. Eliot's memorable lines rest just on this theme!

> April is the cruellest month, breeding
> Lilacs out of the dead land, mixing
> Memory and desire . . .
>
> I will show you fear in a handful of dust . . .
>
> I can connect
> Nothing with nothing . . .
> [*The Waste Land*]

Ironic juxtapositions abound as commentaries on this condition:

> Gloomy Orion and the Dog
> Are veiled; and hushed the shrunken seas;
> The person in the Spanish cape
> Tries to sit on Sweeney's knees . . .
> ["Sweeney among the Nightingales"]

In this modern world it would be hard enough to imagine Hamlet's state as utterly new and bewildering even if we were not all familiar with the story; being familiar with it, we find it immeasurably more difficult to experience the suspense that brings meaning to the action. But we must try if we are to see what the play meant to the Elizabethans. Everything, in fact, depends on the actor; if he really feels his part he will be able to convey it, no matter how old the story is. We must see the roles as becoming forces upon Hamlet with which he is unable to cope because he cannot stay the passage of events as they come flooding over him.

If Act I sets the stage and establishes the conflict, Act II develops that conflict. In criticism and in performances of the play, Act II is the prime source of confusion. A good deal of time has passed, the hero has changed, the action drags, the digressions mount, and the critics really dig in. What is actually happening is that Hamlet, having adopted a role in order to conceal his doubts, his tensions, and his *consequent* reluctance to act against Claudius, has got himself into a melancholy and speculative paralysis. His real part as prince of the realm having been destroyed by murder and incest, he has adopted the role of madman. Playing his role has further dissociated him from his true role of prince. He becomes, not mad of course, but increasingly detached in spectatorship. Once having stepped out of his first self — for whom noble action would be instantaneous — he finds that delay and speculation possess him; and the more he observes and speculates, the more complexities he sees.

He tries, for example, to explore Ophelia's heart by appearing to her as a madman, disheveled and muddy. What he sees in her eyes adds a heavy stone to his burden of doubt. It was a diversion and a distraction, a trying-out of the power derived from a concealing role; but the consequences are shaking. Ophelia, terrified and speechless, seems to be concealing something herself: a new element of doubt thereafter confuses his speculations.

As the complexities grow, the temptation to go on observing and speculating becomes stronger; but with delay the tension from his failure to act becomes increasingly painful until it exacerbates him to sudden violence. The violence itself becomes a refuge because it enables him to play the mad role at the same time that he releases his pent-up wrath and exasperation. He taunts Polonius (while revealing alarm at the discovery that Polonius is probing him) with ambiguous remarks upon corruption and sovereignty:

> HAMLET: For if the sun breed maggots in a dead dog, being a god kissing carrion, — Have you a daughter?
> POLONIUS: I have, my lord.
> HAMLET: Let her not walk i' the sun. Conception is a blessing, but not as your daughter may conceive. . . .
>
> [II, ii, 181–85]

It may be noted at this point that there is no need at all for Dover Wilson's elaborate emendations of the stage directions, to make Hamlet overhear Polonius planning to "loose [his] daughter to him," for Hamlet's suspicions have had plenty of time to develop since he tried to read Ophelia's thoughts.* "There's no art," says Duncan in *Macbeth*, "to read the mind's construction in the face," but Hamlet has not learned this truth yet. Hamlet's attitude toward Ophelia would not harden into violence so quickly; she has been part of the corrupt setting since the beginning of the play.

A moment later he runs circles around the prying Rosencrantz and Guildenstern, whose clumsy attempts to discover the cause of his distemper merely serve to expose the fact that they are pawns of Claudius. It is therefore the highest dramatic irony that the duplicity of these sycophants, probing Hamlet's assumed role, should no sooner be discovered than they tell of the players newly arrived — and Hamlet is thrust into further contemplation of play-acting. The idea of the detached actor-observer began as an impulse; it grew with the wild foolery after the ghost's appearance and the successful attempt to frighten Ophelia; and now fortune draws Hamlet into it to the point where it becomes more real, more compelling than his business of revenge. The Player's recitation of the speech from "Aeneas' tale to Dido" moves Hamlet profoundly. Many critics have treated this speech as a parody

* See John Dover Wilson, *What Happens in Hamlet* (New York: Macmillan, 1935), p. 108.

of Marlowe or Kyd, meant to be somewhat ludicrous. Nothing could be more inappropriate to these climactic moments of the action. I find it an absolutely superb speech and a deeply moving one. It is archaic and therefore a bit rigid, of course, but Shakespeare, who almost certainly wrote it himself, would want it to be different from the "real life" language of his own characters. That is, if his poetic language is an imitation of real life, then the language of the players-within-his-play must be a step further removed from common speech. Illusion within illusion must define itself by a difference in form. Indeed, this is fairly simple compared with the passage wherein the boy actor playing Cleopatra complains that if "she" is carried to Rome by Caesar "she" will be mocked by boy actors:

> the quick comedians
> Extemporally will stage us, and present
> Our Alexandrian revels; Antony
> Shall be brought drunken forth, and I shall see
> Some squeaking Cleopatra boy my greatness
> I' the posture of a whore.
>
> [V, ii, 216–21]

Let no one say that Shakespeare was not aware of these subtleties!

Harry Levin even proposes that the Player's speech be seen as a carefully wrought mirror image of Hamlet's following soliloquy.* Both involve the slain king and the mourning queen, Hecuba passionate, Gertrude seemingly indifferent. The Player describes action; Hamlet talks instead of acting. The Player curses Fortune; Hamlet curses himself — and so on. Most brilliantly conceived is the contrast between the Player's fustian dramatization of the theatrical, which moves him to tears, and Hamlet's "realistic" commentary on himself, which surely rises to a shriek with

> Remorseless, treacherous, lecherous, kindless villain!
> O, vengeance!   [II, ii, 609–10]

The ironies latent here would be best realized if the Hamlet-actor actually lost control, tore the passion to tatters, and became more involved in his performance than the Player had just been in his, the point being that the true artist in performance must maintain a certain objectivity in order to bring out the emotions in his part. If he lets himself experience these emotions, he will be worn out and his

---

*See Harry Levin, *The Question of Hamlet* (New York: Oxford University Press, 1959), pp. 156ff.

acting will fail. Hamlet is feigning but has become so involved that he has lost the objectivity of true feigning: the play-world has become in considerable part his real world.

This magnificent contrivance brings the interpenetration of drama and "reality" to the point where the audience itself is involved in the uneasy footing. It shares some of Hamlet's doubts. Earlier in Act II he confounded Rosencrantz and Guildenstern with teasing ambiguities over the question of dreams and reality:

GUILDENSTERN: Which dreams indeed are ambition, for the very substance of the ambitious is merely the shadow of a dream.
HAMLET: A dream itself is but a shadow.
ROSENCRANTZ: Truly, and I hold ambition of so airy and light a quality that it is but a shadow's shadow.
HAMLET: Then are our beggars bodies, and our monarchs and outstretch'd heroes the beggars' shadows . . .
[II, ii, 263–70]

Now he is caught up in the thing itself.

There is far more method in his madness, furthermore, than just filling out a long act with a contribution to the War of the Theaters. It is right here that Hamlet's preoccupation with acting begins to carry him so far that he cannot come back, but I must repeat that the *plot* brings the players on the scene, and it is in the plot that Hamlet finds with them an occasion for doing something direct and specific in the way of his revenge. The irony is that he is carried further and further into the realm of illusion. What came to him from a ghost he will now have re-enacted by the players, so that the real problem is wrapped in layers of dramaturgy which inevitably blunt the bright edge it should have. And as he becomes entangled in his contrived roles and plots, he frets and rages at himself and his situation; in the great soliloquy ending Act II ("O, what a rogue and peasant slave am I!") he first wonders what the Player would say if, instead of Hecuba, he had

the motive and the cue for passion
That I have? He would drown the stage with tears
And cleave the general ear with horrid speech,
Make mad the guilty and appal the free . . .
[II, ii, 587–90]

He is now thinking in terms of the stage and its actors, and after accusing himself of the abominable sin of cowardice, he comments on the fact that he is speaking instead of doing, which is another way of saying that he has escaped into his assumed role. And this is not all; his next step is to repeat his plan for the Mousetrap. Having ended Act I with the grotesque metaphor of a bonesetter, he ends Act II acknowledging that he has become a director:

> The play's the thing
> Wherein I'll catch the conscience of the King.
> [II, ii, 633–34]

The scene that follows is controlled by the elements that have been developed. Play-acting, and thinking about play-acting, where illusion and reality are united and confused, compelled to feign madness until the evening's performance, exacerbated beyond bearing by the delays and cross-purposes in which he has become entangled, Hamlet first speculates on mortality and suicide — and then turns in half-real and half-feigned mad fury on Ophelia. He is now indeed caught in the role he has contrived, to the point where he can act only through it — and where his conduct adds to the suspicions of the spying Claudius and begins to close the net that will carry him to England. This role is now necessary to his preservation but intolerable for the ideal prince. It is an image of the predicament of modern man as he slips from the "certain certainties" of the divine and feudal state into the agonies of moral relativism that inescapably accompany detachment and speculation. While his intellectual world grows, the straitjacket of his role tightens about him. Small wonder that he should lash out with bitter speeches: his tongue is his only weapon. And rather than speculate about exactly when in the Nunnery scene Hamlet becomes aware of the king and Polonius eavesdropping, we should realize that his struggle is, primarily, with the situation into which he has slipped; this makes him lash out at Ophelia, and when he discovers the two spies he can only lash out more furiously from his mad role and increase their suspicions. He has already lost control of the situation; the next scenes will bring climax and consequences.

Scene ii begins with a necessary breathing spell after the violence of the Nunnery scene, but it is not wasted. Hamlet's advice to the players dwells on the excesses of false art — on the actors who tear a passion to tatters, the clowns who "laugh to set on some quantity of barren spectators to laugh too, though in the mean time some necessary question

of the play be then to be considered" (ll. 45–48) — and on the ideal of
holding the mirror up to nature, "to show virtue her own feature,
scorn her own image" (ll. 24–25). He is also ironically throwing light
on the predicament of one who has exchanged the image for the
actuality. Like Alice in Allen Tate's poem, he has passed through the
looking glass and shattered the real world:

> Turned absent-minded by infinity
> She cannot move unless her double move,
> The All-Alice of the world's entity
> Smashed in the anger of her hopeless love.
> ["Last Days of Alice"]

In the speech to Horatio he makes a great effort to justify the Mousetrap and even speaks as the ideal prince in commanding him to "Even
with the very comment of thy soul/ Observe mine uncle" (III, ii, 84–85).
But this comes after he has revealed his sense of isolation by describing the man he ought to be but no longer is:

> and blest are those
> Whose blood and judgment are so well commingled,
> That they are not a pipe for Fortune's finger
> To sound what stop she please. Give me that man
> That is not passion's slave . . .
> [III, ii, 74–77]

In the context that has grown through the plot — the ideal prince
trapped in play-acting not so much through weakness as through the
combination of circumstances operating on his special virtues of idealism and intellectuality — the Mousetrap scene epitomizes the situation
while it is the very substance of the plot, for there we see the crisis of
action and character as they have become entangled. Hamlet must
direct his play, calculate its effect, and also carry on with his own play
— but in fact he is involved in several "plays" by now. He is a mocking
and frightening lover to Ophelia; he is mad with love to Polonius,
mad with (perhaps) ambition to the king; he is a rational truth seeker
to Horatio; and he is all these things plus a philosopher and a
producer-director to the audience. He is also caught in the scene he
has set, which includes Claudius, Gertrude, the court, and the archaic
performance of *The Murder of Gonzago.*

The strange repetition in having the dumb-show before the spoken
play — for which scholarship has found no precedent* — must be sig-

---

*Dover Wilson discusses this fact at length in *What Happens in Hamlet.*

nificant. Let us not, at this crucial point, try to argue that Shakespeare nodded, or that he has been misrepresented. The dumb-show is in the Second Quarto as well as the Folio. It must be essential to Shakespeare's plan and plot. Philosophically, it adds a layer to the several layers of unreality that have been developed and projected: there is play within play within play. Practically, the repetition is needed if we are to follow Hamlet into all the relationships that have grown up about him. Particularly if the play is presented as an imitation of an action, the complexities of Hamlet's character will appear in what he does as he *acts* his relations to the others and further finds himself in each act. As each moment and event add something to Hamlet's character, he must be acted as *discovering* himself, and he must be more surprised by his conduct than the audience is. This is asking a good deal, but it indicates the direction that should be taken in the staging in order to put the emphasis of the performance on the events (which of course include the relationships, the ideas, and the values involved) and show that as they take place the characters respond to them.

Well, one may reply, it takes a character to do something, since all that happens is what people do. Yes, but especially in *Hamlet* it is common to see the hero displaying himself, reciting Shakespeare, and regarding the stage and the rest of the cast as foils to his performance. The importance of shifting the emphasis to the action is that doing so brings more effective forces to bear on the hero.

The Mousetrap scene must show Hamlet trying almost desperately to play all his roles at once. He must direct the players, who may overdo it and "give all away." He must "use" Ophelia somehow in order to confuse Polonius and those who think he is mad for love, while he also vents his wrath in sarcasm because he is not sure what he thinks of her or how much he needs her. It is because of such conduct — in which only a part of his attention comes to focus on her — that he can contribute to her distraction partly by heedlessness and partly by an explosive rather than an intended cruelty. He must watch Gertrude, whom he suspects of complicity in the murder and whose lecherous compliance disgusts him; here, again, his responses are more heedless than reasoned. Attempts to carry out Dover Wilson's suggestion that Hamlet is, to the court, mad with ambition, have not been successful; yet the idea is unmistakably present in his own words, "This is one Lucianus, nephew to the king," describing the poisoner. Either this is a planned threat to poison Claudius in order to convey the theme of madness-from-ambition or it may come as an impulsive exclamation, unplanned and as dangerous to his cause as his wild words in the Nunnery scene. Of all his tasks, Hamlet's most urgent is that he watch Claudius, even though he has assigned this duty to Horatio. There must also be time for the audience to observe Claudius in various states of boredom, infatuation, anxiety, and terror.

To convey this tremendous complexity of action, illusion, and perception, two performances are scarcely enough. If the dumb-show is omitted, it is because the director does not have anything to "say" through it, and that will be true if he does not take the plot seriously because he is tracing everything to "what is the matter" with Hamlet. It would be a great challenge to a director to convey the three-level phantasmagoria of reality and illusion, where the stately court is a false front and the archaic play is the starkest actuality. This confusion of illusion and reality might be portrayed with lighting. It could have been rendered on Shakespeare's stage if one group of actors were stiffly artificial and the other the opposite. Thus the Mousetrap players could talk their quaint verse but act like contemporaries, whereas Claudius and the court could appear like cardboard figures while speaking their "real life" English. I think we tend today to underrate the poetic and expressive subtleties that must have been easy to the Elizabethan-Jacobean stage. There was a relatively small community; the actors worked together month after month; the sensitivity to language was certainly more richly cultivated than it is today where there are so many other media of communication; the greatest poet of our language, at the very apogee of an exploding art form, was working with complexities of language and imagery which must have been rendered with subtleties of acting and staging that we do not see in the clumsy models and pictures of the Globe Theater that we know. All this would have to be presented with exactly the right balance between the bewildering action and the reactions of Hamlet. Trying to manage all his roles and his inquiries, trying to understand what is happening around him, the prince is caught up in a fury of activity. That he is not completely confused is a tribute to his great courage and intelligence, but he is far, far from being in control of the situation.

Right after the Mousetrap, when Claudius has run off in panic and

Hamlet has danced a triumphant jig, the interview with Rosencrantz and Guildenstern follows naturally enough. Hamlet has to contain his wild exhilaration and conceal his intentions. And Shakespeare has to give some relief from the tension built up with the climax of the Mousetrap; he knew that tension would at a point give way to laughter if it were not relieved, and he had an instinct for timing his relief in a manner that advanced or enriched the action. The entrance of these two time-servers shows that the forces against Hamlet are gathering and that he is so much in disfavor that these upstart courtiers dare to speak severely to him. At no point in the play, perhaps, does Hamlet jump about so in language and manner: he pours out puns and veiled attacks; he feigns madness most energetically; and yet he must also use the recorder for a thinly veiled censure of these impertinent upstarts who are so obviously trying to sound a man who is worlds beyond them. Worlds beyond, yet confused enough to reveal his intensity and his intelligence at the very moments when he is also letting off steam in his wild foolery and feigning madness to the top of his bent! The scene is an extraordinary epitome of the action thus far; and the short concluding soliloquy, directed so fiercely and confusedly, beginning with "Now could I drink hot blood,/ And do such bitter business as the day/ Would quake to look on," and in the next sentence directing all this to his mother along with an injunction "O heart, lose not thy nature . . . speak daggers to her, but use none" (III, iv, 408–14) — this shows the accumulated fury and confusion of a man who is far from being in control either of himself or of the situation.

If the Mousetrap were handled as I propose, the mystery of the following prayer scene would clear itself up. The impact of the former would account for Hamlet's being unable to come to terms with his opportunity when it offered itself. It comes too soon, and there is far too much on Hamlet's mind when it comes. One might say that the walls have hardly stopped whirling around him. He has been transported into a world of thought, and the poor figure of Claudius at prayer is a dim gray shadow on the fringe of this inner light. Hamlet must be shown struggling to believe in its reality, and his soliloquy must show how his created imaginings put him into such a detachment from the living Claudius that he must invent the pretext for passing him by and going on to his mother in her closet. There the rupture of illusion-reality takes a form with which he thinks he may be able to cope. And it is not improbable, psychologically, that an individual would organize his scattered forces by bringing himself somewhat violently to bear on a single "manageable" issue. This is what Hamlet does in going to his mother. He will wring her heart and make her see the true moral image of her conduct. But again events take command. Polonius stirs behind the arras, and Hamlet is galvanized into action. Having killed Polonius, he is again beside himself with the intensities and complexities of the situation.

He is, indeed, so carried away by the violence generated in killing Polonius that he goes on and on in his attack on Gertrude until the ghost himself intervenes to protect her. Here the confusions of illusion and reality multiply with a vengeance. The outraged spirit of Hamlet's father comes back a second time to protect the incestuous queen who has figured so largely in the court life that dismays Hamlet. And here Hamlet learns not only that Gertrude was innocent of any part in the murder of her husband but also something of the utmost importance — namely, that the ghost is genuine.

Three centuries of critics have explored the question whether the ghost is "a spirit of health or goblin damned," and from a hundred angles. At one extreme it is dismissed as a trivial matter; at the other extreme it is *the* question that accounts for Hamlet's delay. I think Hamlet believed the ghost when he first saw it but came to doubt it as he doubted everything when the tensions and contradictions in his situation became overpowering. When the ghost intervenes to protect Gertrude, he proves beyond any doubt that he is indeed the ghost of the dead king. Only the true spirit would show such tender concern for his lost and faithless wife. Yet this important proof has been largely ignored by the critics — because they are no longer interested in the action. The question of "what is the matter with Hamlet" comes to a dead end, a paralysis, with the prayer scene, and the play seems to break in two at that point for the psycho-philosophical critics. The arguments for sparing Claudius are too horrible, so horrible that many critics have been reduced to saying that Hamlet must spare Claudius in order to permit a fourth and fifth act! Not knowing why he fails to kill Claudius, they have no bridge to the next scene, in the queen's closet. The "action" has become only a patchwork assembled to give Hamlet a stage for ranting over the praying king and, presently, the obtuse and libidinous queen.

But if the action is taken seriously we can see the complexity of event and reaction that Shakespeare has contrived. From the dim praying king, Hamlet goes to the guilty queen. Killing Polonius, he is himself spurred to fury. The ghost comes to protect the queen and, as he says, "to whet thy almost blunted purpose," and for a moment he does succeed in bringing Hamlet back to a more controlled and reasonable disposition. But right here another factor comes to bear: the queen thinks Hamlet is indeed mad, because she does not see the ghost, and the exasperation of trying to convince Gertrude that he is not mad, so that he can bring her thoughts back to her own guilt, raises him immediately to a new pitch of fury. He goes on and on with his lecture, but between the queen's terror of his violence and her desire to ignore his "mad" reproofs he has lost what slight control of the situation he might have gained. He is right, and his words are wonderfully eloquent, but Gertrude has neither the desire nor the ability to see this rightness through the chaos of violence in which she is plunged. We don't carry on a quiet talk about morals while the body of a murdered counselor is lying, still warm, a few feet away. Yet Hamlet has not time to wait for a calmer hour; he must make matters worse by driving ahead, and his very lucidity only furthers the queen's bewilderment.

Interpreters of the first scene in Act IV have a way of assuming that Shakespeare has not written what he intended and so must be "explained." If they want to argue that Hamlet has convinced Gertrude of his sanity in the previous scene, they then claim that Gertrude is pretending in this scene; but elsewhere they tell us that Shakespeare frequently gives the most explicit stage directions right in the dialogue. He does, and nowhere are these directions more precise than here. Claudius says, "There's matter in these sighs, these profound heaves;/ You must translate; 'tis fit we understand them" (IV, i, 1–2). Sighs and profound heaves do not describe terror but sorrow — nothing else. Gertrude is heaving deep, sorrowful sighs because she knows now that Hamlet is mad. And she is saying exactly what she believes when she says he is

> Mad as the seas and wind, when both contend
> Which is the mightier. In his lawless fit,
> Behind the arras hearing something stir,
> He whips his rapier out, and cries, "A rat, a rat!"
> And in his brainish apprehension, kills
> The unseen good old man.   [IV, i, 7–12]

This is no time — and there is not that much room in the drama — for a whole new set of speculations about Gertrude's motives, or about her pretending now in order to protect Hamlet from the king's wrath. She has not been convinced; she has not come over to Hamlet's side; simple-mindedly as always she has reacted as almost anyone would react when a son raves and raves and then sees a ghost that isn't there.

The point of this scene is that Hamlet's roles have taken over. He has spoken with brilliance, deep feeling, and great lucidity. The audience understands him perfectly. It must also be allowed to understand that Hamlet has completely and utterly failed to get his message across to his mother. This is the final irony and the final step in his isolation: his mother loves him, and yet she has not "heard" a word that he has said to her. Grieving deeply, she only wants to get him out of the country, and she utters no word opposing Claudius's decision to send him to England. Claudius, of course, knows better; he understands Hamlet almost as well as the audience does. He certainly grasps the practical aspects of the problem, and he acts instantly to get Hamlet out of the way. In fact, the communication between Hamlet and Claudius has always been pretty accurate. When Rosencrantz and Guildenstern appear to put Hamlet, in effect, under arrest (IV, ii), he feigns madness to the top of his impudent bent, even while letting the audience feel his confusion, his justified rage, and his desperation at having worked himself into a situation where he cannot act — to say nothing of his having thought so much about it that he has got out of the way of acting. But when these rascals bring Hamlet to the king, there is a real moment of truth: between the pass and fell incensed points, the mighty opposites look one another in the eye with total, but secret, understanding:

> CLAUDIUS: . . . The bark is ready, and the wind to help,
>   The associates tend, and everything is bent
>   For England.
> HAMLET: For England?
> CLAUDIUS: Ay, Hamlet.
> HAMLET: Good.
> CLAUDIUS: So is it, if thou knew'st our purposes.
> HAMLET: I see a cherub that sees them.
>   [IV, iii, 46–50]

Such directness is now neither irresponsible nor a luxury, for Claudius has already signed the order for Hamlet's death. This moment of truth is the lowest ebb of the hero's fortune up to this point; now, in whatever role, he has lost not only the initiative but also his freedom of action. And almost his life.

In the rest of Act IV and the first scenes of Act V, we have a typical Shakespearean device: the action slows down and spreads out, so that the audience has time to assimilate the meaning of what has happened and become ready to receive the full impact and meaning of what follows. If we have followed Hamlet up to this point, we have seen an ideal Renaissance prince becoming entrapped by situations and responses to them that make him detached, speculative, philosophical — and also alienated among his unstable, unpractical roles — and also exasperated and violent both because of his inability to act and to communicate and because of seeing himself performing in a manner that is totally surprising to him.

Now with the fourth-act expansion and relaxation, we have time to grasp and feel what Hamlet has become: he has become wiser and deeper. He does not feel quite so close to his burden of revenge; he is not hemmed-in and exasperated; and he is thinking of man in larger dimensions than he could have before. This summary is of course a barren thing beside the wonders of Shakespeare's poetry; it is meant only to indicate what the audience will feel if the performance has brought it up through a consistent action in which the character has developed so that he *thinks* his lines instead of merely reciting them.

If Hamlet is more objective, he is also more removed from the immediate pressure of bloody revenge: the examples of a drunken, lustful king and a complaisant mother are not before his eyes. Yet the problem remains. The ideal prince is still burdened with his grisly duty, which honor enjoins as severely as it ever did. And Hamlet still knows, still accepts it, but with the great difference that is expressed in his humorous and philosophical attitude toward the gravediggers. He has placed the warring elements in a perspective, not of resignation but of wisdom, the depth of which makes the contrast between Hamlet and the twentieth-century hollow man appear vast indeed. Today's hero would continue to doubt everything, and the story would end in guilt and despair, with perhaps some adventitious affirmation of the essential dignity of man. I say adventitious because although deeply felt it would not have been realized in the action. Hamlet's insights do not make him doubt the essential values of his world. If he has lamented being its scourge and minister, yet he has accepted the task and has now grown more convinced of its dignity and importance. The cost of such wisdom is that he returns to Denmark not knowing how the forces against him will be organized.

And of course the facts soon fly at him thick and fast. When he sees Ophelia being buried with maimed rites and the crass Laertes beating his breast in the grave, his wild roles take instant possession, and an ultimate epitome of his feigning-mad-furious-hysteria occurs. Never was Hamlet so earnestly idealistic, never does he appear more insane to the others, and never does he play more openly into the hands of his enemies. What he has lived through in the previous acts is now a part of him that he cannot slough off. Nor can the profounder wisdom and insight, once gained, stop the various counter-movements he has set in motion in the costly process of gaining them.

He reaffirms his clear knowledge of his duty:

HAMLET: Does it not, thinks't thee, stand me now upon —
          He that hath kill'd my king and whor'd my mother,
          Popp'd in between the election and my hopes,
          Thrown out his angle for my proper life,
          And with such cozenage — is't not perfect conscience
          To quit him with this arm? And is't not to be damn'd
          To let this canker of our nature come
          In further evil?
HORATIO: It must be shortly known to him from England
          What is the issue of the business there.
HAMLET: It will be short; the interim is mine,
          And a man's life's no more than to say "One."
                                                  [V, ii, 63–74]

and a few moments later balances this with the moving fatalism of a speech in which he shows that he is now caught in a grand action which he may not be able to dominate — or even survive: "Not a whit; we defy augury. There's a special providence in the fall of a sparrow. If it be now, 'tis not to come; if it be not to come, it will be now; if it be not now, yet it will come; the readiness is all. Since no man has aught of what he leaves, what is't to leave betimes? Let be." (V, ii, 230–35.)

From this level of humor, wisdom, and acceptance, Hamlet goes into the final catastrophic action where he acquits himself magnificently. Here, finally, the mocking, the feigning, and the uncontrolled fury are absent. He reaches the top of his princely greatness in matching the combined trickery of Claudius and Laertes — matching only, for mastering it would be too much to expect.

I have not discussed these latter scenes in great detail because in them the power and dominance of the plot is absolute, overpoweringly so in the final scene; and if the audience has been taken along with a consistent, growing Hamlet up to the middle of Act IV, there is little fear that the interpretation will go astray thereafter. Indeed, the character developed will cast a dazzling light on the closing action. Throughout this discussion I have touched very lightly on the satiric humor, the good nature, and the verbal brilliance of Hamlet — not because these do not contribute enormously to his personality and to our pleasure in the play, but because I have tried to restrict myself to the particular problem of the relation of characterization to plot. The constant relation of ethos and intellect cannot be missed.

We have assumed a framework in three stages: first, when only the deed mattered; second, when a motive was assumed behind the deed; and, third, when the hero could not be adequately expressed or represented in any deed. It should be noted that the first category includes the possibility of enormous complexity of *response* to a situation. Oedipus, for example, discovers and reveals himself in extraordinary complexity as he responds to situations that presented themselves to him unplanned, unsought, unwilled. Oedipus, therefore, falls completely into the first category; and Hamlet may be seen in the same perspective, for the situations are not of his making or desiring. With Iago we move into the second category, for Iago directs and *manages* the action, which is therefore a product of his will. The motive (that he has been passed over in favor of Cassio?) does not adequately explain the monstrousness of his performance, and so the audience is taken into speculations that suggest a variety of possible motives — motives prior to the action and apart from it. *Hamlet* calls for no such speculations.

4 *Jane Austen's Minuet*

THE PROBLEM of *Hamlet* has grown and grown since the seventeenth century *pari passu* with the post-Renaissance dissolution of certainty. It is no accident, however, that the alienated Hamlet was not deeply explored until the Romantic movement. When that phenomenon burst upon the intellectual front it redefined man as "a god in pain," in Keats's phrase, a creature for whom the occasions of reality were mean, stifling, and inadequate and whose spirit must revolt against the narrow mold that contained it. With this new spirit the assault on the bases of society itself begins. While Coleridge reaches for Xanadu, Wordsworth seeks truths in pure natural man — a fiction, of course — and Byron conducts the flamboyant pageant of his bleeding heart over the deepest taboos and then outside of his native world into new domains where his wild revolt finds expression in poetry and exploit. Wordsworth embraces the French Revolution, Coleridge plans a new transcendental community in America, and Shelley throbs between the necessity of atheism and the Greek ideal. The Romantic movement brings an incomparable burst of lyric poetry, expressing its rebellion; but the novel and the drama inevitably fell behind because, as we have seen, these genres were not suited to rebellions against the basic values of society. They could not be, since they were *made* out of those basic values. It is in the lyric that the individual expresses the Romantic yearning to understand or to escape and even to destroy.

In the eighteenth century the lyric was infinitely subdued, sentimentalized, and pious because wild rebellion was not the order of the times. Excepting the Romantic Blake, the poets Miltonized and Pope-ized in formal couplets. The Gothic *frisson* of a Thomson or a Blair was decorative, like the popular Gothic ruins in wealthy gardens. Even the revolutionary trends were ushered in under the auspices of pure reason. For the novel, it was a time when plot and character could grow in a perfectly balanced compost of manners and values.

Pride and Prejudice is exemplary, for in it we can see how this per-fect fusion is expressed. Here character and plot live in the design of manners, customs, and values which make the social fabric. At the cen-ter of *Pride and Prejudice* is a society firmly and rock-solidly based on status, manners, education, which in turn all rest on wealth. These elements are absolutes, but they are not constants, and they do not presuppose each other in constant quantities, relations, or depend-encies. One may be rich with no education or manners. One may be poor with fine manners and good taste, but this is unlikely. One may have fine manners but little culture. Good hearts and bad hearts go with good minds and bad minds — and vice versa. The kind may be rich or poor. People of fine old families may be rich or poor, and well educated or not.

The ideal is to have family, education, manners, and of course wealth. With these, goodness is desirable also, and it is recognized where it appears. Granting that all these elements are variable, status comes first, and it depends upon wealth. It may, to be sure, depend to a considerable extent upon family, but it cannot be maintained with-out wealth.

Status is displayed by comfort and breeding. Both are dependent upon wealth, and although wealth does not guarantee them it is likely to produce them to the degree that the people in question have intel-ligence and talent — and perhaps some goodness. Since the society is unquestionably oriented toward these values, "everybody" naturally seeks them. Status, to repeat, is displayed by comfort and breeding. The word "displayed" is crucial here, for the display of status is what the people, in their various fashions, do. They live in their houses or manors; ride in their carts or carriages; go to teas and musicals and dances; perform and converse according to their accomplishments. Women bear children and men conduct affairs, too, and life goes on; but it seems to be status that makes them feel good and that puts them in the way of being cultivated and elegant and kind. It may be assumed that family plus the application of a talent would produce a good life and a respected one. So they would. So would also elegant manners displayed in elegant entertainments. It is among these permutations and combinations of the elements that people move with what freedom there is and so individualize themselves.

Beside the display of status goes the acquisition of status — by inheritance or by marriage. By education too, of course, but this is made possible by wealth, the *sine qua non* with which one is born or which one acquires by marriage. The society is so tightly organic that it shows its life from any angle: the display and the pursuit of status go on together all the time, with the usual modulations decreeing that at one end of the scale some need only display their holdings, whereas at the other end some have time and strength only to pursue. But these extremes really serve to bound the society, and the people are generally engaged in both the display of what status they have and the pursuit of what more status they seek. What one has, indeed, determines just how high he may reach, so that displaying is usually a way of pursuing. It indicates what one has a right to covet.

It has been pointed out by a close textual critic that the language of Jane Austen's *Persuasion* turns upon versions and metaphors of property, money, and interest:

We are in a world of substance, a peculiarly material world. Here, indeed, changes are usually named *"material* alterings" — for example, in "style of living" and "degree of consequence." Perhaps the word is used most tellingly in the phrases "a face not materially *disfigured"* and "a material difference in the *discredit* of it"; for *figure* and *credit* suggest the two large areas of metaphorical interest — arithmetic and business.

Time is *divided,* troubles *multiply,* weeks are *calculated,* and even a woman's prettiness is *reckoned.* Thus, one's independence is *purchased*; one is rendered happy or unhappy; one is on *terms,* friendly or unfriendly, with others. Young Mr. Elliot has "nothing to *gain* by being on *terms* with Sir Walter," but Lady Russell is convinced that he hopes "to *gain* Anne" even though Anne cannot "know herself to be so *highly rated*." We are asked to "take all the charms and perfections of Edward's wife upon *credit*," and "to judge of the general *credit due*." Captain Wentworth thought that he had *earned* "every blessing." "I have *valued* myself on honourable toils and just *rewards*."
. . .

Moral qualities are persistently put in economic figures: Mary "had no *resources* for solitude" and she had *inherited* "a considerable *share* of the Elliot self-importance." Love, likewise: if Elizabeth is hoping to be *solicited* by baronet-blood, Anne has had to reject the "declarations and proposals" of an improvident sailor. "Alliance" is a peculiarly appropriate word for such prudential arrangements as these, and at the end of the novel, when "the engagement" is *"renewed,"* one sees bonded documents. Anne need no longer suffer those fits of dejection in which she contemplates others' *"prosperous* love," for hers at last has prospered, too.*

The society is fixed in structure as well as status. This is equally if not more true in *Pride and Prejudice*, where there does not seem to be any avenue to rapid wealth — except marriage. In the country society the wealth is largely inherited, and it ranges from miserable pittance through modest elegance to real opulence. If we consider in what terms the characters emerge, we shall find that it requires attention to the action to understand them truly.

The first sentence announces the values I have just noticed: "It is a truth universally acknowledged, that a single man in possession of a good fortune must be in want of a wife." When Mrs. Bennet learns that Netherfield Park has been rented by a Mr. Bingley, she immediately marks him down for one of her five daughters; but she is sarcastically handled by Mr. Bennet when she asks him to call and pay family respects to the new tenant. The chapter concludes with a vignette of characterization that launches the story: "Mr. Bennet was so odd a mixture of quick parts, sarcastic humor, reserve, and caprice, that the experience of three-and-twenty years had been insufficient to make his wife understand his character. *Her* mind was less difficult to develop. She was a woman of mean understanding, little information, and uncertain temper. When she was discontented, she fancied herself nervous. The business of her life was to get her daughters married; its solace was visiting and news." (Chapter 1.†)

At the first ball, Jane, the eldest Bennet daughter, is favored by two dances with Mr. Bingley, the other girls are passed from hand to gay hand, but the clever Elizabeth is slighted by Mr. Darcy, the handsomest and richest man present, who is introduced in this manner: "Mr. Darcy soon drew the attention of the room by his fine, tall per-

---

* Mark Schorer, "Fiction and the 'Analogical Matrix,'" *Kenyon Review*, Autumn 1949, pp. 539–60.

† Here as with novels discussed later for which there are many editions I note chapter, rather than page, after the quotations. For other novels, the page references are to the first American edition.

son, handsome features, noble mien, and the report which was in general circulation within five minutes after his entrance, of his having ten thousand [equal to $100,000] a year." (Chapter 3.) Because he slights the local girls, Darcy is quickly judged a detestable boor, whereas Bingley is everything a gentleman should be. Thus in a flash are the financial prospects translated into moral values. The unattainable wealthy man is a boor, the available one a gentleman. Mrs. Bennet may appear ridiculous in the incautious haste of her conclusions, but the beautiful Jane is not far behind and shares similar views in private with Elizabeth. The girls show much more taste in this discussion than their mother, but every word they utter relates to the same status, prospects, and people, and they begin to define themselves quite clearly by their reactions and evaluations. Elizabeth has no immediate reason to approve of Bingley; so she can be more critical than her sister.

Jane Austen's tone reveals with extraordinary delicacy the relation between status and values as she describes the sisters of Mr. Bingley and comments on them: "They were rather handsome, had been educated in one of the first private seminaries in town, had a fortune of twenty thousand pounds, were in the habit of spending more than they ought, and of associating with people of rank, and were therefore in every respect entitled to think well of themselves, and meanly of others." (Chapter 4.) Only in the diminished cadence of the last phrase does she reveal the area of friction and soreness in her world, the area where the necessities of status confront true goodness and true purity of human intercourse; it is in this area that individuality appears, but it appears always *in terms of* the social exigencies. With his ample wealth, Darcy is clever and "at the same time haughty, reserved, and fastidious, and his manners, though well-bred, were not inviting." Elizabeth is also clever — and proud. So the problem and conflict develop: it is a test of the manners of the society whether she and Darcy will be able to come together to their mutual benefit.

Understanding develops when the eldest, Jane, is taken with a severe cold because Mrs. Bennet insists that she ride horseback to visit the Bingleys, in spite of threatening rain. If she were to use a carriage, reasons Mrs. Bennet, she could return the same night; but a-horse, she will have to spend the night. So the avid mother risks the girl's health — and Jane is drenched and becomes so ill that she has to stay a week. Thus Mrs. Bennet's greedy stupidity defines itself and acquires moral dimensions through action. Elizabeth walks over to see Jane, and she too stays over. Now there is time for a leisurely social expansion: Darcy remains aloof; Miss Bingley makes a fool of herself flattering him and criticizing Elizabeth whenever she is out of the room; Darcy is increasingly taken by Elizabeth's sincerity and wit. Levels of snobbism are deftly portrayed, as when Sir William Lucas tries to impress Darcy: " 'I had once some thoughts of fixing in town myself — for I am fond of superior society; but I did not feel quite certain that the air of London would agree with Lady Lucas.' " (Chapter 6.) Or when Miss Bingley assails his reserve in these terms:

"I can guess the subject of your reverie."

"I should imagine not."

"You are considering how insupportable it would be to pass many evenings in this manner — in such society; and indeed I am quite of your opinion. I was never more annoyed! The insipidity, and yet the noise — the nothingness, and yet the self-importance of all those people! What would I give to hear your strictures on them!" [Chapter 6.]

These passages occurred before the visit; during it Elizabeth and Darcy come into closer contact by matching wits over the values and qualities that are basic to the social flow of their lives. Mr. Bingley, for example, confesses that he writes carelessly:

"My ideas flow so rapidly that I have not time to express them — by which means my letters sometimes convey no ideas at all to my correspondents."

"Your humility, Mr. Bingley," said Elizabeth, "must disarm reproof."

"Nothing is more deceitful," said Darcy, "than the appearance of humility. It is often only carelessness of opinion, and sometimes an indirect boast."

"And which of the two do you call *my* little recent piece of modesty?"

"The indirect boast; for you are really proud of your defects in writing, because you consider them as proceeding from a rapidity of thought and carelessness of execution, which, if not estimable, you think at least highly interesting. The power of doing anything with quickness is always much prized by the possessor, and often without any attention to the imperfection of the performance. . . ."

When Bingley tries to refute the accusation, Darcy counters by challenging his earlier remark that if he resolved on quitting Netherfield he would be gone in five minutes: " 'If, as you were mounting your horse, a friend were to say, "Bingley, you had better stay till next week," you would probably do it, you would probably not go — and at another word, might stay a month.' " Elizabeth defends Bingley by attributing this to good nature; Darcy rejoins that it would be done by Bingley merely on whim and without serious reason. She says:

"To yield readily — easily — to the *persuasion* of a friend is no merit with you."

"To yield without conviction is no compliment to the understanding of either."

"You appear to me, Mr. Darcy, to allow nothing for the influence of friendship and affection. . . ." [Chapter 10.]

In a few more sentences the discussion has cut so deep below the surface of motives, and has become so involved with logic, that it must be abandoned.

What I have quoted and paraphrased at some length here is representative; the formal manners and slightly elevated speech, the concern for a rational as well as a humane basis for conduct, the status-bounded perspective on social intercourse, and the mutual esteem that grows from the mutual exercise of wit — all flow out easily and naturally while at the same time they advance the plot. Character is so perfectly woven into the social fabric that a thread of one is a thread of the other: the society consists of these elements, and in speaking them the characters define themselves. Every word enriches character, advances the plot, and delights and amuses us with revelations of the wide range of motives, pretenses, maneuverings, and foibles that are possible within this apparently limited social context.

Looking at these qualities, we realize that this "limited" social context provides the richest possible characterization — and the *easiest* — because nothing is wasted. Every light word tells, and Jane Austen astonishingly evokes more density of character in a few pages than some highly practiced and intellectual modern novelists can achieve in hundreds. Dealing not with characterization but with another facet of the same jewel, the inseparable problem of form (since form is plot), Marius Bewley has noticed the same qualities in a passage so apt and succinct that it must be quoted: "Jane Austen, to take the ideal example, was able to move progressively into her values in the course of any given novel, to reveal them in the very circumstances of her story, in the inflections of her characters' speeches, or the way they wore their inherited manners. Her values *pre-existed* in the materials and conditions of her art, even if it took her genius to reveal them. Her art is essentially an art of ironic illumination, of revealing in a

new light what had been there all along."* Well, it *seems* to have been
there all along, perhaps because genius has given it such brilliance of
form and unity of texture. But this apparent naturalness and inevi-
tability is characteristic of the work of great genius.

The Bennet family has a serious financial problem in that their
estate is entailed, in default of a male heir, to a cousin of Mr. Bennet,
a Mr. Collins, who has recently been ordained. Should the father die
suddenly, they would all be summarily ejected in his favor. A letter
from the hitherto-unknown Mr. Collins proposes a visit to the family.
It is a pompous letter, and five successive comments on it reveal in
turn gentle amiableness, cleverness, cynicism, pomposity, and vulgarity:

"Though it is difficult," said Jane, "to guess in what way he can
mean to make us the atonement he thinks our due, the wish is certainly to his credit."

Elizabeth was chiefly struck with his extraordinary deference for
Lady Catherine [his patroness, on whose property his meager "living"
is], and his kind intention of christening, marrying, and burying his
parishioners whenever it were required.

"He must be an oddity, I think," said she. "I cannot make him out.
— There is something very pompous in his style. — And what can he
mean by apologizing for being next in the entail? — We cannot suppose he would help it if he could. — Can he be a sensible man, sir?"

"No, my dear; I think not. I have great hopes of finding him quite
the reverse. There is a mixture of servility and self-importance in his
letter, which promises well. I am impatient to see him."

"In point of composition," said Mary, "his letter does not seem de-
fective. The idea of the olive-branch perhaps is not wholly new, yet I
think it is well expressed."

To Catherine and Lydia, neither the letter nor its writer were in
any degree interesting. It was next to impossible that their cousin
should come in a scarlet coat [i.e., as an officer], and it was now some
weeks since they had received pleasure from the society of a man in
any other color. [Chapter 13.]

Mr. Collins, who turns out to be a paragon of fatuity, comes not
only to admire the house and furnishings that he will inherit, but also
to find, perhaps, a wife among the Bennet girls. When Mrs. Bennet
advises him that Jane is virtually married to Mr. Bingley, he shifts his
attentions from the beautiful Jane to the lively Elizabeth without
missing a beat, and almost overwhelms her with painfully unwelcome

*Marius Bewley, *The Eccentric Design* (New York: Columbia University Press,
1959), p. 15.

attentions which obtusely continue in spite of Elizabeth's efforts to make it plain that they are not welcome.

The counter-action begins with a memorable dinner party and ball at Mr. Bingley's fine house. Mrs. Bennet runs on and on in a loud whisper over her joy and triumph at the imminent (she thinks) betrothal of Jane and the host. Mary thrusts her stuffy self forward and bores the company with dreary song. Mr. Collins forces himself upon the supercilious Darcy. Mr. Bennet facetiously tells Mary, " 'That will do extremely well, child. You have delighted us long enough.' " (Chapter 18.) At the protracted goodnights of Mrs. Bennet, Elizabeth is almost paralyzed with mortification, for everyone in her family except Jane has deserved the unconcealed disdain of the Bingley sisters — and perhaps except Mr. Bennet, who maintains his own detachment and to whom the whole evening is richly amusing.

Mr. Collins's formal proposal follows on the very next day. It is not possible to present — except in Jane Austen's own language — the abysses of complacent bad taste into which he plunges. Having given the most fatuously ungracious reasons for electing to favor Elizabeth with his hand, he concludes, " 'This has been my motive, my fair cousin, and I flatter myself it will not sink me in your esteem. And now nothing remains for me but to assure you in the most animated language of the violence of my affection.' " (Chapter 19.)

From this point the plot is handled with such ease that it seems inevitable. The Bingley sisters depart for London, and the unmarried one writes Jane a letter calculated to destroy her hopes: they will be gone all winter; she thinks Mr. Bingley will marry Georgiana, Darcy's sister; and she hints that she herself will marry Darcy. Mr. Collins in the next breath runs down the street and proposes to Elizabeth's good friend, the unattractive Charlotte Lucas, "who accepted him solely from the pure and disinterested desire of an establishment, [and] cared not how soon that establishment were gained. . . . Mr. Collins, to be sure, was neither sensible nor agreeable; his society was irksome, and his attachment to her must be imaginary. But still he would be her husband. Without thinking highly either of men or of matrimony, marriage had always been her object; it was the only honorable provision for well-educated young women of small fortune, and however uncertain of giving happiness, must be their pleasantest preservative from want." Mr. Collins will carry Charlotte off to his residence on the domain of Lady Catherine de Bourgh, who in turn is a relative of Darcy's.

While this new wine is fermenting, there is time for discussion of the situation in which, under stress, the characters explore their world and reveal themselves more profoundly. Jane defends Charlotte's acceptance of Collins, but

"Nay," said Elizabeth, "this is not fair. *You* wish to think all the world respectable, and are hurt if I speak ill of anybody. *I* only want to think *you* perfect, and you set yourself against it. . . . There are few people whom I really love, and still fewer of whom I think well. The more I see of the world, the more am I dissatisfied with it; and every day confirms my belief of the inconsistency of all human characters, and of the little dependence that can be placed on the appearance of either merit or sense. . . ."

"My dear Lizzy, do not give way to such feelings as these. They will ruin your happiness. You do not make allowances enough for difference of situation and temper. Consider Mr. Collins's respectability, and Charlotte's prudent, steady character. Remember that she is one of a large family; that as to fortune, it is a most eligible match; and be ready to believe, for everybody's sake, that she may feel something like regard and esteem for our cousin." [Chapter 24.]

The formality of their manners covers most occasions and softens their harshness; but their formal language is not inadequate to sustain explicit discussions of problems, fundamentally searched and penetrated often more sharply and clearly than later periods have been able to do. Certainly the intimate connection between the language and the social context in which they live and think makes every discussion enrich characterization even as it advances the plot. We rapidly get to know the texture of discourse and the contents of the minds as well as the quality of sensibility of Jane and Elizabeth. Unlike many modern characters, struggling to find themselves, these girls are never at a loss for the right word, and they know exactly what they want to say; so they truly express and disclose themselves in their talk.

Elizabeth's discussion with Jane prepares us for the former's visit to her old friend, in which we plumb one of the abysses of this society. We find Mr. Collins outdoing himself in fatuous proprietary condescension over his house and gardens, and in nauseating servility to the gross and heartless arrogance of his patroness, Lady Catherine de Bourgh. Poor Charlotte is trapped by her choice in a nightmare that promises no awakening. Here, firmly and calmly presented, is a life of quiet desperation, from which, as Thoreau also said, "only death can set her free." How does she face it? Quietly, bravely, and with dignity; no histrionics ruffle the polished surface, but its placid reflection does not prevent the observer from seeing clearly through it and down into the depths of her plight. The comic tone is such that the despair is not even revealed. With such limited choices, people really did make the best of a bad situation.

After her first rebuff by Darcy, Elizabeth has met a young officer named Wickham in the nearby town where her giddy younger sisters like to stroll. Wickham is *persona non grata* to Darcy, for reasons Darcy does not deign to discuss; but Wickham spreads the tale that Darcy has cruelly failed to fulfill certain promises of support and patronage made to him by Darcy's late father. To this evidence of ill-nature chance adds the abominable information that it was Darcy who persuaded Bingley of the impropriety of marrying one so poorly connected as Jane Bennet! It was Darcy who was behind the Bingleys' removal from Netherfield Park. It was Darcy, then, who had caused Jane's broken heart and spoiled Bingley's chance of happiness with her.

Hard upon this shocking discovery comes Darcy himself, who informs Elizabeth that against judgment, propriety, and interest he has fallen irrecoverably in love with her and wishes her hand in marriage. But, "His sense of her inferiority — of its being a degradation — of the family obstacles which judgment had always opposed to inclination, were dwelt on with a warmth which seemed due to the consequence he was wounding, but was very unlikely to recommend his suit." (Chapter 34.) It precipitates, rather, a battle royal. When Elizabeth says that she never sought his good opinion and trusts his attraction will soon fade, Darcy taxes her with incivility. When she says that the indifference of her feelings toward him has been turned to earnest dislike by the fact of his destroying her sister's happiness, he replies that he has been kinder toward Bingley than he is now being toward himself. And when, now boiling with indignation, she accuses him of cruelty toward the unfortunate Mr. Wickham, he charges her with reciting these incidents to conceal the hurt to her pride " 'by my honest confession of the scruples that had long prevented my forming any serious design. . . . Could you expect me to rejoice in the inferiority of your connections? — to congratulate myself on the hope of relations, whose condition in life is so decidedly beneath my own?' " (*Idem.*)

In this furious dialogue, the union of moral and status values is as fascinating as it is intimate. Elizabeth puts goodness first, but her whole moral self and spirit are drawn to Darcy with a magnetism whose power is attested by the brilliance of the sparks it emits on contact. The magnetism operates next morning to take her for a walk by the "park," so that Darcy, who has been waiting, can hand her a long letter of explanation and amplification.

Concerning Bingley and Jane, Darcy in his letter sharpens his charge in a manner to pit Elizabeth's ambition against her family loyalty: " 'The situation of your mother's family, though objectionable, was nothing in comparison of that total want of propriety so frequently, so almost uniformly betrayed by herself, by your three younger sisters, and occasionally even by your father' " whereas " 'let it give you consolation to consider that, to have conducted yourselves so as to avoid any share of the like censure, is praise no less generally bestowed on you and your eldest sister.' " (Chapter 35.)

Then he insists that he believed Jane to be quite indifferent to Bingley, so that his only guilt has been for conspiring to conceal from Bingley the fact of Jane's presence in London, where she has been visiting her aunt, for the past several weeks.

As for Wickham, Darcy disposes of his claims and discredits his lies so effectively that he draws credit upon his own discrimination and forbearance. Angry as she still is at his renewed attacks on her family (i.e., her status), Elizabeth is so impressed by his judgment and honor in handling Wickham that we can see her ever so reluctantly entertaining the first faint glimmerings of an insight into the thought that Darcy's pride may be justified, that his status, in short, is total, being composed of family, wealth, manners, breeding, and goodness. It takes her some time to assimilate the lesson; when she does, the language of her reflection unites the operative forces metaphorically: "she considered that Jane's disappointment had in fact been the *work* of her nearest relations, and reflected how *materially* the *credit* of both must be hurt by such *impropriety* of conduct." (Chapter 36, italics added.)

The Bennet children have an aunt and uncle, Mrs. and Mr. Gardiner, who are people of manners and substance. With them Elizabeth visits Derbyshire, where the splendid Darcy estate is to be found, and here by the help of a very little luck and a good deal of unconscious design, she meets Darcy again. Now he is all manners, cordiality, and attention. The Gardiners respond to his invitation with a decorum that pleases Elizabeth to the roots of her pride. Under these new auspices the magnetism flows back and forth between Darcy and Elizabeth over golden strands. The sparks cease to fly, both parties relax under the warm currents of landed opulence and responsive decorum, and fulfillment is only a step away.

Only a step. Just when Darcy has marked the passing of their differences by inviting Elizabeth to the manor — and the social context of this action is significant — comes news of social action on another front that crushes her hopes once more: her youngest sister, Lydia, has eloped with Wickham. And not only eloped; disappeared, and unmarried. Elizabeth rushes home, where Mrs. Bennet has taken to her bed, while Mr. Bennet and Mr. Gardiner converge on London to search for the missing pair. Reactions to the catastrophe vary predictably according to the temperaments that express them. The jewel is from the unspeakable Mr. Collins, whose letter of condolence soon reaches this sentence: " 'Lady Catherine and her daughter . . . agree with me in apprehending that this false step in one daughter will be injurious to the fortunes of all the others; for who, as Lady Catherine herself condescendingly says, will connect themselves with such a family? And this consideration leads me moreover to reflect, with augmented satisfaction, on a certain event of last November; for had it been otherwise, I must have been involved in all your sorrow and disgrace.' " (Chapter 48.) Sinking under the disgrace, the family finally gets word that Mr. Gardiner has found the runaways and persuaded Wickham, in return for payment of his debts and a generous settlement, to marry Lydia.

Under these stresses the characters discover further levels of themselves. Mrs. Bennet bounces out of bed, disposing of the crushing obligation to Mr. Gardiner, who has presumably given his own money to Wickham for the settlement: " 'Who should do it but her own uncle? If he had not had a family of his own, I and my children must have had all his money, you know; and it is the first time we have ever had anything from him, except a few presents.' " (Chapter 49.) She dances with joy at the prospect of a daughter married — and at sixteen! — and begins planning a trousseau and celebration with no thought of the social catastrophe (let alone the moral guilt) so narrowly averted. Kitty shrieks over the excitement. Mary's polysyllabic sententiousness becomes grotesque. Jane continues to search for a ray of light. Elizabeth cuts straight down to the issues: " 'That they should marry, small as is their chance of happiness, and wretched as is his character, we are forced to rejoice. Oh, Lydia!' " (*Idem.*) Then Mr. Bennet puts his foot down hard, for the first time, refusing either to receive the newlyweds or to give Lydia a penny for clothes.

Elizabeth presently learns that it was Darcy who found the elopers in London and who gave the money that persuaded Wickham to marry. His "motive" makes a delectable confection of native ingredients: he feels "responsible" in not having explained his disapproval of Wickham; he feels compassion for the foolish Lydia; he loves Elizabeth and chooses to protect his *interest* in her heart and status by protecting her sister's reputation. Moving amidst the appalling vulgarity of Mrs. Bennet and her younger daughters, and the intelligent, urbane irresponsibility of Mr. Bennet, Elizabeth rises toward higher levels of cultivation and status. Love conquers all so prettily that there appears to be a good deal of freedom, and though worlds apart Lydia and Darcy can become relatives. Jane Austen even pauses to tell us that gratitude and esteem may be better foundations of "affection" than love-at-first-sight. Elizabeth learns to love Darcy as she experiences the solidity of his manners, the security of his consideration, and reflects on the shallowness of her attraction to Wickham, which was based on nothing but his appearance.

This detailing of the main flow of the plot is the merest skeleton of the story, and yet in a way it serves because the whole novel is so completely of a piece, so densely uniform in texture that any part will serve as a sample of the whole. What one must notice in the situations described and the passages quoted is that everything anyone says is directly and exclusively connected with the spectrum of values grading from wealth to goodness, as we have observed them. Nobody says anything at all that does not relate to these values, that does not bear upon the forthgoing activities that spring from their pursuit and display, and that does not in some way reveal his status in this society whose components they are. One's continual delight in reading the novel stems from the fact that every passage not only advances the plot but also reveals new intricacies, new inter-entanglements, new patterns of these components.

Everything done and said makes kaleidoscopic designs within a bounded frame and out of known elements. The image of a kaleido-scope is organic: definite parts and controlled space. One senses the quality of mind, spirit, and feeling that makes the character at any moment because he is familiar with the parts and has a sense of the possibilities; the pleasure comes from the fact that the patterns are never exhausted, and their symmetry and charm grow with the definite-ness of the parts. Elizabeth speculating on Darcy's motives, wondering how far she may trust the evidence of his attraction toward her, against her knowledge of his pride-in-status and her own history of impudence to him, evolves moral overtones which are facets of her personality; we *know* her as she entertains these thoughts. What we know of her is made of the quality of these thoughts as she expresses them, and we know her so well that we feel ourselves to be within the circle of her problems as she works with them. There is a grand scene, for example, when the loathsomely overbearing Lady Catherine de Bourgh calls upon Elizabeth and tries to force her to promise not to engage herself to Darcy. Elizabeth stands up to the old harridan with courage and poise — and the confrontation serves to let Darcy know, through his aunt, that Elizabeth has refused to affirm that she still scorns him. This knowledge gives him courage to propose anew, and so her ladyship brings about her own discomfiture.

Mr. Bennet requires special attention, because he offers the best example in the novel of the dependence of character on plot. If he is taken out of the action, he is an urbane, witty, and delightful man. We see him on the sidelines or retired into his study, making deli-ciously ironic remarks about the follies of his daughters and trying to evade the boredom of association with his shrill, pretentious, and stupid wife. This is the attitude that a great many readers have taken toward him — and it is an attitude that carries with it a problem: he is so far superior to Mrs. Bennet in decorum, intellect, and cultivation that one wonders how he came to marry her. Is Jane Austen napping here? Has she, perhaps, inserted this sophisticated wit in order to have a mouthpiece for her own most refined observations? Could such a man have married Mrs. Bennet? This clever man misleads the twentieth-century reader particularly because he understands and ap-preciates Elizabeth so well. She is our favorite, and apart from her father nobody is clever enough to value her properly; hence we are likely to accept him as *the* ideal observer.

But if we look at his part in the action — as Jane Austen surely intended us to do — we find a far more significant and organic character. There is abundant evidence, from one end of the book to the other, that Mr. Bennet is a prime force on events. He is responsible for the disorder in the family, for the vulgarity of the younger sisters and the humiliating aggressiveness of his wife. With his first two daughters, Jane and Elizabeth, Mr. Bennet must have acted as the proper head of the household, so that the girls were constantly under his instruction and example — and so that Mrs. Bennet was to the same degree controlled by his presence. With the third daughter, Mary, Mr. Bennet began his withdrawal. Mary responded by becoming a bookworm, with a learned manner and an insufferably pompous way of talking; these were her defenses against the superior attentions that her elder sisters had received. The next two girls then came into a family where the father had increasingly withdrawn from responsibility. Their mother, as a consequence, became increasingly disorganized, panicky at the thought of all those daughters to marry off, and aggressive. She did not have a great deal of depth to begin with, but with consistent help and guidance from her husband it would have sufficed because she would have developed under his tutelage. Instead, she has deteriorated under the pressures. Thus it is her frantic vulgarity and the indecorous conduct of Kitty and Lydia that make the problem in the action, for they exacerbate the pride of Elizabeth and the disdain of Darcy.

This account of Mr. Bennet's role is verified every time he appears, and it is sustained with meticulous consistency by the author. I can illustrate by reference to a handful of passages taken almost at random. At the first ball at Bingley's, where Elizabeth is humiliated to see her mother and sisters making fools of themselves, "Darcy said nothing at all. Mr. Bennet, in equal silence, was enjoying the scene." (Chapter 18.) When the Bingleys depart for London without saying good-bye, " 'So, Lizzy,' said he one day, 'your sister is crossed in love, I find. I congratulate her. Next to being married, a girl likes to be crossed in love a little now and then.' " (Chapter 24.) He is "partial to Wickham" through carelessness. Insulted by Darcy, Elizabeth thinks of "the unhappy defects of her family . . . They were hopeless of remedy. Her father, contented with laughing at them, would never exert himself to restrain the wild giddiness of his youngest daughters;

and her mother . . . was entirely insensible of the evil." (Chapter 37.) At the critical point, Elizabeth speaks out, begging her father not to allow Lydia to go off to Brighton: " 'If you, my dear father, will not take the trouble of checking her exuberant spirits, and of teaching her that her present pursuits are not to be the business of her life, she will soon be beyond the reach of amendment. . . . In this danger Kitty is also comprehended. . . . Vain, ignorant, idle, and absolutely uncontrolled! Oh! my dear father, can you not suppose it possible that they will not be censured and despised wherever they are known, and that their sisters will not be often involved in the disgrace?' " (Chapter 41.) Mr. Bennet turns this solemn protest aside with a comforting laugh and the assurance that no stain can rub off on Jane and her. A few pages later the charge is spelled out in the plainest terms: "Elizabeth, however, had never been blind to the impropriety of her father's behavior as a husband. . . . that continual breach of conjugal obligation and decorum which, in exposing his wife to the contempt of her own children, was so highly reprehensible. But she had never felt so strongly as now the disadvantages which must attend the children of so unsuitable a marriage, nor ever been so fully aware of the evils arising from so ill-judged a direction of talents; talents which, rightly used, might at least have preserved the respectability of his daughters, even if incapable of enlarging the mind of his wife." (Chapter 42.)

After the catastrophe of Lydia's elopement, he has the grace to acknowledge responsibility: " 'Who should suffer but myself? It has been my own doing, and I ought to feel it,' " but in the next moment he turns all into a joke: " 'No, Lizzy, let me once in my life feel how much I have been to blame. I am not afraid of being overpowered by the impression. It will pass away soon enough.' " (Chapter 48.)

After the crisis has passed and the happiness of Jane and Elizabeth seems inevitable, Mr. Bennet makes a great many witty comments and contributes charmingly to the happy atmosphere into which the story expands, and since nobody holds a grudge in a comedy he enjoys the general beatitude attending his two daughters' splendid matches. This is the final impression. At the other end, his activity in the story is considerably delayed, until the characters of Mrs. Bennet and her daughters have had time to display themselves elaborately. By then the reader's emotions are so sharply engaged that he may pass Mr. Bennet by without thought. I suspect this is what accounts for the fact that his organic characterization through the plot has not been given its due. Yet he is one of the dimensions that make Jane Austen's book continually re-readable.

And now, how profound is the characterization in this novel? To answer this question one must understand that not everything has to be told about each character, and so we know more of any character in the book than is specifically shown about him. Social display occupies the largest part of the lives of all these people, and while amusing themselves they are also enjoying their status or worrying about their pursuit of it. Taste operates on these elements and is reflected in the same sentences that refer to status and aspiration. For example, Mr. Collins is fawningly rapturous at being noticed by Lady Catherine de Bourgh. He puts so earnest and so stupid an importance upon it that he describes her rudeness as kindness and her effrontery as condescension. He is so status-hungry that he must stand and soak up with his eyes every path and tree on his property, and his energetic gardening expresses his need to feel and handle the earth of his estate. The same physical greed for the materials of status is expressed in his speech and writing: he rolls out unctuous periods as if each one were a pat of butter, a golden coin, a polished ivory statuette, or a glistening walnut newel. The consciousness which engages in this sensuous enveloping and gobbling of the luscious fruits of status is as amoral as a baby with a pot of jam. It is equally insensitive to what other people feel because it lives in sensations rather than responds to ideas of value or goodness. Mr. Collins does not mind turning from Elizabeth to Charlotte Lucas with proposals of undying passion, even while he dumbly senses that these are currency in a transaction that will bring to him another material possession to gloat over. We have, then, the substance of Mr. Collins's mind and the texture of his thought. We know that he thinks in exactly the same elaborate phrases with which he talks and writes.

He delights Mr. Bennet because he is something of a curiosity in this respect. Being delighted thus, Mr. Bennet reveals a capricious sensitivity to shades and flavors of character. It is also irresponsible, this sensitivity, because he reacts to the whimsical delight of a person or a situation rather than to its ethical implications. His humor has become an instrument of evasion as well as a mode of perception. He has joked his way out of contact with his family. The formal manners of the society make such evasion relatively easy.

The four sisters of Elizabeth Bennet are evoked with bold economy. The screaming vulgarity of Lydia and Kitty comes out with a few sentences as they speak of men, clothes, parties, and journeys with equal violence and insensitivity to the feelings of others. They recognize the marks of status with no thought for their meaning. They are energetic (alas, tireless) and gay, with a vulgar relish for life. Whereas they disgust their father, he means little to them. Mary is reduced to a comic pedant. She produces elaborate comments on the moral niceties of every situation — but their verbal elaborateness is no instrument of depth. If one pauses to speculate on Mary he sees a girl who has adopted a manner which will be comic until it shrivels her into a grotesque. Jane has beautiful manners, natural dignity, and some taste. Only her intelligence is limited, and her mind is full of sentimental clichés.

To get the whole of Elizabeth one has to follow her through the book, where her pride and sharpness of tongue reflect and balance her intelligent wish for a better life than is to be expected under the parental auspices she suffers. Her moral earnestness, her good manners, and her kindness do not ever lead her to question the society in which she lives and moves. It does not confine her if she has no notion of anything fundamentally different. Rather it provides the materials out of which her spirit has been fashioned.

It is especially interesting to consider the fact that Jane Austen does not seem to be particularly intense about characterization, as a special enterprise. She is obviously interested in her people — her characters — but she is even more concerned with her *story*. The action dominates the novel. Indeed the action unrolls without great stress on crucial acts of will; this is because the people act *what they are*, continually, rather than making acts of will at particular crucial moments. Under stress they reveal or discover qualities that are usually concealed, but these are generated in response to the intensities arising from the action, rather than themselves bringing about intense moments or situations. We do not, for example, see Lydia making a catastrophic decision to elope with Wickham. Rather we assume that she acted what she was, without any special moment of choice. With her unschooled avidity, she did not think, but by her conduct before and after the event she makes her action seem inevitable.

Jane attracts Bingley and falls in love with him as naturally as a fish swims. She lives eagerly through the experience, suffering agonies of dignified silence when she is jilted, but she never seems to make any particular occurrence *happen*. She just lives her social life as her social self, flowing with the occasions and confusions that appear.

Darcy's generous pursuit and redemption of the elopers is learned later, not observed. The point of view, which remains with Elizabeth, generally gives the reader information only as it comes to her, and this might prevent our watching Darcy decide what he will do; but the total effect of people acting their whole selves is rather a by-product of the dominating plot. Elizabeth does not ever dramatically choose so much as she acts out decisions that have grown slowly in her mind. She does specifically reject Darcy, but she is bouncing with indignation at the time and certainly does not see herself as making a choice. At one point she does act. She draws him out — and at a most well-chosen moment — by speaking of her gratitude for his aid with Lydia and Wickham. This is just enough to give him confidence to renew his proposal; but even here it is conduct rather than decision that we witness, for by this time the match was inevitable and the only question was how the lovers would perform the rituals of declaration.

We have in *Pride and Prejudice*, then, a fusion of action and character. The people exist in the onflowing movement of their society. They can almost be said to have no being apart from that movement, which they are. The movement is the material of which they are composed. We see what they *do*, always with reference to that social flow, and only with reference to it. It is a minuet:

> O body swayed to music, O brightening glance —
> How can we know the dancer from the dance?

PART III

Characterization
in Symbolic
Journeys

I SHOULD like to let the example of Jane Austen stand for the works
of such great storytellers as Fielding, Thackeray, Dickens, and Trollope. For all their differences, they are spun from the same yarn. The
novel of manners could be what I might call "ideal" only in writings
of the eighteenth and nineteenth centuries. Before then, the novel had
not been perfected; afterwards the manners did not prevail over the
whole body of society. The genre continues, of course, even now, but
it is generally a minor expression, particularly in the American novel.

Before we come to the impact of naturalism, which expresses itself
in the restless searching of novelists for new forms that do not depend
upon the decisive functioning of the free will at critical moments in
the plot, we have a form of long standing that does not resemble the
dramatic novel. This is the symbolic journey. It goes back to the *Odyssey* and includes a long tradition of episodic and picaresque romances.
It has grown into a form that serves for themes of observation and dis-

covery where such concerns take precedence over the problem and conflict of the novel of manners. Conrad's "Heart of Darkness," Melville's *Moby-Dick,* Hawthorne's "Young Goodman Brown," Mark Twain's *Huckleberry Finn,* and Katherine Anne Porter's *Ship of Fools* use the journey as at once a form and a symbol. Their journeys penetrate into darker and darker regions which correspond to states of mind and to conditions of man. The voyager makes a journey into his own spirit as he penetrates the human conditions that are both physically and symbolically represented. Observation and discovery, although enacted apart from the typical social setting, become social, psychological, and even philosophical. In such journey forms, the characters' choices are not crucial in moving the plot, for the "plot" is a pattern formed in the author's mind.

Except for the first chapter, the order in this part is chronological. I have chosen to take up "Heart of Darkness" first, however, because it is an especially instructive example of characterization under the symbolic form of a journey. The story has a great theme, and although laid in darkest Africa it draws upon the basic values of Western culture. Since the action cannot physically move through the society in which these values live, it must be rendered through the mediating intelligence of a narrator whose intellectual range transcends physical distances. The society is present and lives in his mind. The consequences for characterization illuminate what obtains in the four other works treated in this part.

5   *To the Last Outpost of Evil*

CONRAD'S narrator in "Heart of Darkness" (1899), Marlow, begins his story on a sailing ship anchored in the Thames Estuary, waiting for the tide to carry him and his friends down to the sea; he begins with a thought for old England and some Roman soldier yielding to the fascination of the abomination as he struggled with himself in the dark forests of a barbarous clime. He cryptically outlines the story he is going to tell: "The fascination of the abomination — you know, imagine the growing regrets, the longing to escape, the powerless disgust, the surrender, the hate." The problem is whether one were man "enough to face the darkness." Or would he "in some inland post feel the savagery, the utter savagery, had closed round him — all that mysterious life of the wilderness that stirs in the forest, in the jungles, in the hearts of wild men. There's no initiation either into such mysteries. . . ." (Chapter 1.)

Beginning with this philosophical drift, the story quickly takes on perspectives of time and distance, for it is to be a tale of Marlow's youth and a journey up the Congo into the heart of the Dark Continent. Each incident and character furthermore represents an aspect or a stage of Marlow's penetration into the mystery for which there is no initiation — the mystery of man's capacity for evil.

In the foreground of the story, Marlow is characterized entirely by intellect rather than ethos. The adventure took place a long time ago, in his youth; he now narrates it in the first person, conveying what he felt then and what he thinks about it now, giving the play of his mind

93

over the events and the idea that takes shape around them. For "to him the meaning of an episode was not inside like a kernel but outside, enveloping the tale which brought it out only as a glow brings out a haze." (Chapter 1.) The play of Marlow's intellect is humorous, self-deprecatory, even facetious, alive with vivid recollections of sights, sounds, and sensations. These aspects of the way Marlow tells his story invest it with certain complementary qualities — it appears at the end of a longish perspective; it has a dreamlike remoteness; and it is instinct with speculation and meaning. Here on this level the relation of character and action has a special interest: the *subject* of Marlow's play of intellect gives it a seriousness and an importance that it could not have with a trivial subject. The subject is an action, too, and so the play of intellect has a tightening series of incidents to which it can respond. It thus evolves ethical speculations which if not acts of choice are later responses to people and situations carrying far more moral involvement than they could if the subject were trivial, anecdotal, or merely topical. Conrad represents Marlow as profoundly involved, almost grappling with the great subject that he is trying to reproduce in its full ethical roundness. The action of the story itself is not so much suspenseful and dramatic as revelatory: we are insulated from suspense by Marlow's play of intellect over his past. His decisions are not so crucial as what he observes in the other people.

The intellect, then, is playing over significant events which it evaluates morally as well as discusses with interest and humor. Thought *represents* action — and the more so because Marlow was himself the central observer. Yet the commentator is exclusively intellectual only until he has with his curiosity and intensity carried the reader past his first reluctance to become involved in so agonizing an enterprise as the penetration of ultimate evil. The intellectual filter and the perspective of time continually make the story more absorbing, more gripping than would seem possible.

The forces that keep men from ultimate evil are laid out and represented in orderly sequence. "Efficiency" and "the idea" are offered by Marlow as justifications of colonialism, which is otherwise evil. They redeem it, he says, but the Congo is not so redeemed. His first contact is in the office of the anonymous Company, presumably in Brussels or Antwerp, where he is struck by the "dead silence" of a "whited sepulchre," an office presided over by two women significantly knitting like the Fates. There was a map; he was going into the "yellow. Dead in the centre. And the river was there — fascinating — deadly — like a snake." There are also the director, who deals with him in about forty-five seconds, and a seedy doctor who measures his head with "a thing like calipers" and advises, "Avoid irritation . . . '*du calme, du calme.*'" (Chapter 1.) Here are apathy, desuetude, and remoteness from evil.

He visits his aunt, who talks about ideals and provokes him to remark, "It's queer how out of touch with truth women are. They live in a world of their own, and there has never been anything like it, and never can be." The trip out to Africa suggests a "sordid farce acted in front of a sinister back-cloth," keeping evil at bay by ignorance and comedy. At the Outer Station, thirty miles up the Congo, he sees cruelty, waste, "a flabby, pretending, weak-eyed devil of a rapacious and pitiless folly." (Chapter 1.) He watches a senseless blasting of the mountainside; then looking about him in the green sun-dappled shade he presently discerns black shapes crouching, lying, sitting among the trees. They have been brought there to work on legal time contracts, and now they are quite free — to die. They are wasting away from starvation, disease, and acute misery.

In sharp juxtaposition to these wretches, Marlow meets a man who is resisting the fascination of the abomination, out here away from the restraints of society, by fastidiousness: starched collars, "vast cuffs," brushed hair, "snowy trousers," and "varnished boots." This is the manager, also the Company's chief accountant, who keeps his books, hating the blacks for interrupting his concentration on his columns of figures. He mentions Kurtz, an agent in the farthest depths of the jungle who is sending back as much ivory as all the others together.

Two hundred miles farther inland, Marlow finds the Central Station and its manager. Here the "flabby devil" of greed presides. The manager maintains his post by the vigor of his constitution, his ability to "inspire uneasiness," and the mystery of some inner strength that might be inner emptiness. "Such a suspicion made one pause — for out there there were no external checks." Marlow is charged with repairing the steamer that he is to pilot into the hinterland, where Kurtz, who is manager of the Inner Station, appears to be in trouble. In the prevailing atmosphere "of imbecile rapacity," Marlow keeps hard at work, for work is a substitute for the "external checks" provided by a social order. And into the miasma of imbecile rapacity in which he works there comes a glimmer of hope in what he learns about Mr. Kurtz. Everybody talks about him in guarded tones of fear, envy, and caution; but one rascal says, "He is an emissary of pity, and science, and progress," and Marlow is curious to know "whether this man, who had come out equipped with moral ideas of some sort, would climb to the top after all and how he would set about his work when there." (Chapter 1.)

The steamboat repaired, they go up the river, into the heart of darkness, back into "the night of first ages," which nevertheless are still in the heart of man. The savages dancing and howling on the shore "thrilled you . . . [with] the thought of their humanity . . . of your remote kinship with this wild and passionate uproar. Ugly. Yes, it was ugly enough; but if you were man enough you would admit to yourself that there was in you just the faintest trace of a response to the terrible frankness of that noise, a dim suspicion of there being a meaning in it which you — you so remote from the night of first ages — could comprehend. And why not? The mind of man is capable of anything — because everything is in it, all the past as well as all the future. . . . Let the fool gape and shudder — the man knows, and can look on without a wink. But he must at least be as much of a man as these on the shore. He must meet that truth with his own true stuff — with his own inborn strength. Principles won't do. Acquisitions, clothes, pretty rags — rags that would fly off at the first good shake. No; you want a deliberate belief. An appeal to me in this fiendish row — is there? Very well; I hear; I admit, but I have a voice, too, and for good or evil mine is the speech that cannot be silenced." (Chapter 2.)

At this point the intellect of the character, the theme he is presenting, and the unfolding action become slightly tangled. Marlow has affirmed a noble belief in his "own true stuff . . . his own inborn strength" as the power that will enable him to resist the fascination of evil. Very well, but a few lines later, when he is challenged by one of his auditors with having uttered "fine sentiments," he replies, "Fine sentiments, be hanged! I had no time. I had to mess about with white lead and strips of woolen blanket . . . on those leaky steam pipes." The action presumably will tell us whether Marlow discovered the inborn strength required to meet the situation, or whether he was just too busy to respond to the grisly appeal of the savages, but at this point he has in one breath declared the fine sentiments and in the next made fun of them. It would appear that the author spoke in the first instance, and his character in the second; the intellect of Marlow is not, therefore, directly related to the situation. The characterization slips a cog, illustrating again its ultimate dependence on the action; that is, where such sentiments were confronted with a situation in which a choice had to be made, there would be no such uncertainty about the character.

Evil is avoided by the presence of the policeman, by decorum, by work, even by the brutal commercialism of the traders. Going up the river, Marlow discovers that the cannibals who have been hired to cut wood are starving. Their hippo meat has spoiled; they cannot eat the nine-inch pieces of brass wire which they are given regularly as wages. Yet they do not turn upon their employers and eat them. Why not? Some *restraint* in recognition of an obligation holds them back. It is a mystery, but there it is.

Marlow finally gets to Kurtz and discovers that this man of ideals has given himself totally to the fascination of the abomination. He has made himself into a god to be worshiped by the wild natives of the heart of darkness. He has even participated in rites too obscene or disgusting for Marlow to describe. He does mention a row of human heads impaled on stakes, looking *in* to Kurtz's house, a beautiful savage woman imploring the intruders to leave, and Kurtz, a soul gone mad, a hollow voice, speaking of " 'My intended, my ivory, my station, my river, my —' everything belonged to him. . . . The thing was to know what he belonged to, how many powers of darkness claimed him for their own. . . . He had taken a high seat amongst the devils of the land — I mean literally." (Chapter 2.) Even though dying of fever, Kurtz steals off in the night to attend one more ceremony and be worshiped again. But he is not only being worshiped: he has enlisted his worshipers into a small army with which he has terrorized the surrounding tribes and plundered them of their ivory. His intelligence is perfectly clear; only his soul is mad. "I saw the inconceivable mystery of a soul that knew no restraint, no faith, and no fear; yet struggled blindly with itself." Kurtz has shrunk to a voice, eloquent, magnificent, and utterly depraved — only a voice resonating, echoing the spiritual void within. "The shade of the original Kurtz frequented the bedside of the hollow sham . . . But both the diabolic love and the unearthly hate of the mysteries it had penetrated fought for the pos-session of that soul satiated with primitive emotions, avid of lying fame, of sham distinction, of all the appearances of success and pow-er." (Chapter 3.)

Marlow's moral reaction to Kurtz is dramatized in his relations to other characters who know him. The first is a young Russian adven-turer, blue-eyed, innocent, wandering through the forest in rags and patches that remind Marlow of a harlequin. The Russian explains the sudden attacks of the savages on the steamer as it approaches the Inner Station: " 'Why did they attack us?' I pursued. He hesitated, then said shamefacedly, 'They don't want him to go.' 'Don't they?' I said, curious-ly. He nodded a nod full of mystery and wisdom. 'I tell you,' he cried, 'this man has enlarged my mind.' He opened his arms wide, staring at me with his little blue eyes that were perfectly round." (Chapter 2.) The Russian is, as Marlow says several times, a fool. He cannot be deep-ly touched by evil. A moment after Marlow has recoiled in angry horror from his attempts to describe the "ceremonies used when approaching Mr. Kurtz," the Russian explains that the heads on the stakes were "rebels," and that " 'You don't know how such a life tries a man like Kurtz . . . There hasn't been a drop of medicine or a mouthful of invalid food for months here. He was shamefully abandoned. A man like this, with such ideas. Shamefully! Shamefully! I — I — haven't slept for the last ten nights . . .' " (Chapter 3.)

The rapacious manager of the Central Station speaks only of the "unsound methods" used by Kurtz, which have closed the district to further exploitation. Marlow comments, "It seemed to me I had never breathed an atmosphere so vile, and I turned mentally to Kurtz for relief." In this "choice of nightmares," as Marlow calls it, the moral insanity of Kurtz is somehow preferable to the moral imbecility of the manager. On the night of these thoughts Kurtz arises from his bed and crawls, actually and symbolically, through the grass toward a fire where the natives are chanting and beating their drums. Marlow cuts him off thirty yards from his goal. " 'You will be lost,' I said — 'utterly lost.' . . . I did say the right thing, though indeed he could not have been more irretrievably* lost than he was at this very moment, when the

---

* I would call this sentence to the attention of anyone who is tempted to think that Kurtz in some measure redeems himself by the insight expressed in his dying breath: " 'The horror! The horror!' " Kurtz, totally lost, is an object of moral and intellectual speculation. The manager from whom Marlow turns toward Kurtz as

foundations of our intimacy were being laid — to endure — to endure — even to the end — even beyond." (Chapter 3.)

Marlow's insight responds to the electrifying moment of Kurtz's death: "Oh, I wasn't touched. I was fascinated. It was as though a veil had been rent. I saw on that ivory face the expression of sombre pride, of ruthless power, of craven terror — of an intense and hopeless despair. Did he live his life again in every detail of desire, temptation, and surrender during that supreme moment of complete knowledge? He cried in a whisper at some image, at some vision — he cried out twice, a cry that was no more than a breath — 'The horror! The horror!' " (Chapter 3.)

The puzzle of the story is not that Marlow says Kurtz was a "remarkable man." He was indeed remarkable in the loftiness of his ideals, the range and penetration of his intelligence, the unspeakable depths to which he sank, and finally in the fact that at the end he "had something to say. . . . He had summed up — he had judged. 'The horror!' " The puzzle is that Marlow feels some affinity, some loyalty to Kurtz and finally lies for him to his "intended," a "thunderingly exalted" lady who cherishes Kurtz's memory as if he were a god. With muttered ambiguities Marlow gives her Kurtz's papers, and " 'His end,' said I, with dull anger stirring in me, 'was in every way worthy of his life.' " He simply could not tell her the truth. "It would have been too dark — too dark altogther." (Chapter 3.) He also lied by implication in not telling the world about Kurtz. And this lie by Marlow was a judgment of the world. Better unspeakable degradation with the intellectual victory, at the end, of insight and judgment than the imbecile rapacity of the traders whose only comment was that Kurtz had ruined the district for trade by his "unsound methods."

It is tempting to say that Marlow sees Kurtz as having explored these depths of evil in his stead, somewhat as Leggatt in "The Secret Sharer" protects the narrator by absorbing the current ration of bad luck and failure that the unknown gods of destiny have set out on that day for Man — but this is not made clear enough. What happens is, perhaps, only "the fulfilment of one of those ironic necessities that lurk in the facts of human existence." (Chapter 3.) It is also terrifying as an insight, an ultimate insight into the *human* capacity for evil.

"the nightmare of my choice" is less evil, perhaps, but more an object of revulsion than speculation. Is Satan himself redeemed by the intelligence that accompanies his pride?

This terrifies Marlow, and it is something that he cannot reveal to a fool, a scoundrel, or a thunderingly exalted person. I do not believe that Marlow came even distantly close to such evil. He knew restraint; but at the gray point of death he had nothing to say, whereas Kurtz did. Marlow could understand the fascination of the abomination and thereby plumb a new depth of man's potential capacity. Like the organization of the narrative itself, this insight is a matter of intellect; it searches, explores, even relishes the widening of experience that the mind of man is capable of. The journey up the Congo is finally a journey not into darkness but of illumination, for every detail of the story is organized to lay out for the mind the physical conditions and the human qualities that must meet in order to achieve the ultimate degradation.

The idea upon which the story is organized provides a discipline that liberates rather than confines. The capacity for evil is presented in rather abstract language (unspeakable degradation, abominable terrors, abominable satisfactions, etc.), but the character of Kurtz is tied in to concrete matters: the heads on the poles, the barbaric woman and the exalted "intended," the grieving savages, the crawl through the night toward the place where he might be worshiped again, and the final words, " 'The horror! The horror!' " Yet even so the characterization of both Marlow and Kurtz is abstract, moral, intellectual. Character is dominated by probing intelligence, bounded and defined by it; even Marlow's disgusts are moral and evaluative rather than passionate.

Conrad deliberately carries us away from society in order to deal with his people in situations where they are free from the dulling confines of routine, manners, and security. He wants to see how people will act when they are on their own. Anyone who is contained in the norms of his society does not interest him except insofar as he is taken apart away from it and put to some free test. A journey up the Congo is at first glance exceedingly remote from, say, the comforts of London. It does not follow the ordinary pursuits of people seeking or displaying status, but it is nevertheless firmly rooted in the society of middle-class England toward the turn of the present century. It is probing the uncertain area between the myth of that society's values and morals, and the actuality of their meaning. Honesty, thrift, industry, humanitarianism, and decency are certainly among the central values of the

Victorian affluence or its counterpart across the English Channel in Western Europe. In the snug confines of daily tea and trade these values seem to organize human intercourse on a fairly high level, but when the people who represent them are taken out beyond the frontiers, the *values* are tested rather than the "essential" people. For the people are what the society has taught them to be, and their drives and ambitions are expressions of their society's goals. Thus the manager of the Central Station is purely expressing the commercial drive; the Russian is Romantic and individualistic; Kurtz is humanitarian, progressive, idealist. We know the types at home where they grow, but when we follow them into the heart of darkness they suddenly burst into flowers of evil: industry becomes cold greed; idealism and progress become a naked insane lust for power; adventure becomes irresponsibility. The worst of course is idealism becoming a lust for power, in Kurtz, because the gulf between myth and actuality is so wide there, and one must wonder about the connection between such extremes. It is this: idealism that seeks out the most remote spot on earth, where there are people and "savage customs" to suppress, reveals the danger latent in a society that undertakes to manage and change people into patterns abstractly formulated. What bursts in the Congo must be a tension in London or Brussels that does some violence to the human beings who embody it. It will be controlled by wisdom and restraint, the qualities that philanthropy and idealism assume but do not always enjoy, because the abstract patterns of idealism are very rigid; they assume a proper form that man should take, that he must take; and they do not accommodate the complex social and personal problems of the (perhaps savage) people who fail to embody these rigid ideals. Hence the humorless intolerance and impatience that characterize so many "operators" on the body politic. Hence also the ease with which they slip from pattern to pattern.

The action of "Heart of Darkness" is retrospective, held at a distance in time so that the cool light of intellect can play over it. It is also symbolic, in that it is presented to test, in several representative individuals, the excess of a *quality*. Particularly it explores and elucidates the phenomenon of idealism tainted by lust for power and, to some degree, by commercial greed, since the idealism of colonial nations is often directed at the people they are exploiting. In these intellectual perspectives we see modern man in new frames of reference. Through the course of Western history he has elaborated systems of values that become more abstract as they are imperfectly reflected in more complex social patterns. Finally they break loose from social reality and become obsessions of individuals who are alienated by and into such excesses as Auden understood in a Hitler:

> Grave the vision Venus sends
> Of supernatural sympathy,
> Universal love and hope;
> While an abstract insight wakes
> Among the glaciers and the rocks
> The hermit's sensual ecstasy.
>   ["Lay Your Sleeping Head, My Love"]

Whether the fault is with the nature of man or is a consequence of the exploding size of our world, the normative *activities* of society are no longer enough to contain and account for a person who penetrates into its abstractions. Society does not provide a dense usable medium (as it does for Elizabeth Bennet) in which its values concretely live. So the individual is "liberated" by them into a partial void, where he must test himself and his values in circumstances that offer too little guidance and protection. Here the dark side of man is forced into the open, while he is tried under circumstances more uncertain (if not more difficult) than any that man has known before. New prospects — if not new achievements — of human dignity are revealed by Conrad.

The major characters, especially Kurtz, are identified by the excess that overwhelms and possesses them. The adventure of Marlow explores the human heart, the source of this excess, in a sequence of mounting intellectual disgusts. He shows how he felt and thought, yes, but the stress is on the intellectual ordering of the experience. Insight provides the excitement of each new step into a deepening moral and intellectual experience. It is not character that emerges from a conflict, then, but intellectual insight from an experience. The values, customs, manners of the society are reviewed and explored more than they are seen as the substance in terms of which character defines and expresses itself in conflict.

Both Kurtz and Marlow have explored the fascination of the abomination, Kurtz sensually, Marlow intellectually. The two experiences are complementary, as if it required two people, two enterprises, to round out the human capacity to feel and to know itself through them. This device of exploring a character represented by two or more different aspects of itself brings us to the threshold of a time when man is seen as so complex that no single "plot" can reveal him completely.

The intellectually conceived symbolic pattern of "Heart of Darkness" constitutes not so much a plotted action as an organization, an arrangement of intellectual analysis in concrete terms. In this analytical arrangement, Kurtz and Marlow are two halves of the single persona who penetrates and understands ultimate evil. Characterization is subordinated to a generalized, speculative analysis of an idea about man. It is true that the idea is embodied in people-in-action, but the symbolic structure moves the stress from character to theory, from plotted action to an experience and an insight.

6   *Quest for the Antagonist*

THE ultimate journey into darkness in American literature is still *Moby-Dick* (1851). To be sure, it is not as dark as Melville's *Pierre*, but it demands treatment in this part because it is so beautifully akin to our four other explorations into ideas — ideas about good and evil, ideas which dictate the form and dominate the characterization. Call me Ishmael, says the narrator, who acknowledges that when he gets the "hypos" he goes down to the sea in a ship and sets out to explore in some new fashion that epitome, that symbol of the outrageous strength and inscrutable malice sinewing the mask of evil that may indeed be the face of God.

Whereas Conrad's problem in "Heart of Darkness" was the contest between Western progress, humanitarianism, and idealism and the capacity for evil in the inmost heart of man, Melville undertook a longer and profounder voyage: he was exploring the incarnation of an omniscient and omnipotent God in the physical world of man and nature where alone, for all practical purposes, that presumed God was to be met and measured. Was there a God? Was he wise; was he good? If he were wise and good, whence came the monstrous proportions of evil in man and nature? The quest is described in Captain Ahab's famous speech: " 'All visible objects, man, are but as pasteboard masks. But in each event — in the living act, the undoubted deed — there, some unknown but still reasoning thing puts forth the mouldings of its features from behind the unreasoning mask. If man will strike, strike through the mask! How can the prisoner reach outside except by thrusting through the wall? To me, the white whale is that wall, shoved near to me. Sometimes I think there's naught beyond. But 'tis enough. He tasks me; he heaps me; I see in him outrageous strength, with an inscrutable malice sinewing it. That inscrutable thing is chiefly what I hate; and be the white whale agent, or be the white whale principal, I will wreak that hate upon him. Talk not to me of blasphemy, man; I'd strike the sun if it insulted me. For could the sun do that, then could I do the other . . .' " (Chapter XXXVI.)

The quest itself was so blasphemous in the mid-nineteenth century that Melville had to wrap it round and round with layer upon layer of jocular hint, evasive double-talk, and quick shifts of position. These have made it possible for generations of readers to see almost anything they want in the book, and to quote chapter and sentence in support. But all these stylistic devices merely enrich the unmistakable total drift of the work if they are seen in the essential perspective of its large unity. To look at just one example: After the scene on the quarter-deck in which Ahab announces his purpose, with the speech I have just quoted, there are two long chapters entitled "Moby Dick" and "The Whiteness of the Whale" that explore and universalize the White Whale to make him a symbol of everything unknown and feared in nature. In the course of developing these ideas, Melville establishes a symbolic opposition of land and sea, according to which the land stands for safety, security, conformity, orthodoxy, and so on, while the sea stands for the hidden, the secret, the half-known world where the other side of reality is shown and where alone one may find the full truth. Landsmen thus become conformists; mariners are those who speculate, search, and ask ultimate questions. A few short chapters later (Chapter XLV), Melville works this symbolism up to a pitch of eloquence and enthusiasm in which he affirms, "So ignorant are most landsmen of some of the plainest and most palpable wonders of the world, that without some hints touching the plain facts, historical and otherwise, of the fishery [which Melville is piling up in chapter after chapter], they might scout at Moby Dick as a monstrous fable, or still worse and more detestable, a hideous and intolerable allegory." Missing the irony, more than one serious critic has quoted these lines as final proof that *Moby-Dick* cannot be allegorical; whereas in fact that is exactly what, at this point, Melville is telling us it *is*.

The work is symbolic and allegorical from one end to the other. Its greatness rests upon a massive foundation, which is the fact that the whale is so wonderful a symbol for the undertaking: the whale in actual fact embodies all the ferocity, the mystery, and the outrageous strength, on the one hand, against its usefulness and abundance, on the other, that make it the perfect symbol of the mask that either *is* or *hides* ultimate truth and against which man must hurl himself if he is to get at it at all. What Melville is plainly saying is just this: the whale is ferocious, beneficent, unknowable in actual fact, and thus *is* what it also symbolizes. Only if we take an allegory to have a "hidden" meaning, to which one has to have a private key, can we perhaps say that the novel is not allegorical but symbolistic. I do not believe that Melville made such a distinction. He was, rather, concealing somewhat the too-obvious symbolism of his shocking theme. If we think of the hunters of Moby Dick as seekers who are trying to get through the surface to the ultimate truth about reality, we can appreciate the perfect symbolism of the following sentence: "Judge, then, to what pitches of inflamed, distracted fury the minds of his more desperate hunters were impelled, when amid the chips of chewed boats, and the sinking limbs of torn comrades, they swam out of the white curds of the whale's direful wrath into the serene, exasperating sunlight, that smiled on, as if at a birth or a bridal." (Chapter XLI.)

Here the mystery is insoluble, for if one gets to the center for a close look he is torn to pieces; yet just a few yards away is the same nature's serene, exasperating sunlight, smiling on as if at a birth or a bridal. The quest into this mystery, furthermore, is also a quest into the human microcosm of which nature and the cosmos are the great image: we shall finally discover that the same answers apply to both.

The problem of this book could hardly be farther outside the comfortable milieu of the novel of manners; nor could its characterization. The latter is almost totally dependent upon the ideas that Melville seeks to embody in his people; so characterization is partial and intellectual and even programmatic: characters enter and exit when what they stand for is needed or not; otherwise they are pawns in the great game that Ahab is playing with the Mask. It is therefore a remarkable tribute to the vigor of Melville's style that he is able to describe his characters in a way that brings life and reality to them. He gives them personality for the moments when they are in the foreground; when they retire, they also fade out as characters or forces because they do not act in any plot conflict.

Since the problem of the novel is the nature of Ahab's antagonist — whether It is good, evil, indifferent, nonexistent, or some unknown Else — it is obviously not possible to give Moby Dick a firm character that will act consistently, or even a preliminary personality that will enable one at least to recognize him. In the symbolistic development of the materials of the story, it is suggested that Moby Dick is immortal, ubiquitous, and also totally imaginary! If the conflict cannot be between Ahab and an understandable antagonist, it must be elsewhere. Like Conrad with a comparable problem, Melville chose to establish the conflict within the mind of his hero. To this end he had Ahab go through four distinct stages of intellectual (even religious) orientation, which constitute four major attitudes toward ultimate reality as embodied in and, later, symbolized by Moby Dick. Each stage is brought about by actions or conditions of some sort in the physical world, although they are not always actions by Moby Dick. Let us examine these stages and see whether they provide action — or plot — that is adequate to characterize Ahab and discover and define the meaning of the novel.

Well before the opening of the novel, Ahab had studied and thought. Captain Peleg describes him to Ishmael in a celebrated passage: " 'He's a grand, ungodly, god-like man, Captain Ahab; doesn't speak much; but, when he does speak, then you may well listen. Mark ye, be forewarned; Ahab's above the common; Ahab's been in colleges, as well as 'mong the cannibals; been used to deeper wonders than the waves; fixed his fiery lance in mightier, stranger foes than whales.' " (Chapter XVI.) The mightier, stranger foes can, surely, only be ideas, which likewise are the only "deeper wonders than the waves." The nature of these ideas is hinted by the "prophet" Elijah, a few pages later, in a series of obscure questions which Ishmael dismisses as gibberish. " 'What did they *tell* you about him?' " he demands. " '. . . nothing about that thing that happened to him off Cape Horn, long ago, when he lay like dead for three days and nights; nothing about that deadly skrimmage with the Spaniard afore the altar in Santa? — heard nothing about that, eh? Nothing about the silver calabash he spat into?' " (Chapter XIX.) A calabash is a gourd that is dried and used as a pitcher or drinking vessel. In this context, a silver calabash before an altar would be a vessel in a Catholic church, probably used in the mass. Ahab became involved in the deadly scrimmage with the Spaniard because he had rudely desecrated this sacred object by spitting into it. The Spaniard, a pious Catholic, attacked Ahab for his action, which was the expression of the passionate religious conviction of a nineteenth-century New England Protestant. To him the Catholic Church was the embodiment of error and evil, the Inquisitorial force that had caused the Reformation and in so doing generated a zeal that had moved on to express itself in puritanism. Ahab's deep thoughts were centered upon the ultimate questions of religion, and at this point he was a dedicated Protestant.

We must make a great jump here, for Melville was moving along the edge of blasphemies so appalling that he did not want — probably did not dare — to be explicit. Indeed, this is the key to the whole book: the jocular evasion and the double- and triple-talk are the instruments of an investigation too impious to be directly exposed. Melville gave enough answers so that he could not be absolutely held to any one that would damn him in the eyes of his society. Calvinism emphasizes the greatness and the justness of God. He is stern; he is mysterious, unknowable; but he is just. Whatever happens to man, the New England Primer tells us, he deserves: "In Adam's fall/ We sinned all." What seems difficult or harsh in the world is an aspect of man's error and corruption. Nothing man can do by way of penance or penitence will cancel one jot of his infinite sinfulness — infinite because it is the mark of his rejection of God's infinite Grace. One of the documents that shored up this frightening theology in a time when men were beginning to toy with the pleasanter idea that man was essentially good and the culprit was history or civilization was Jonathan Edwards's *On the Freedom of the Will* (1754). Edwards proved with devastating logic that man did not have free will, hence could not deserve any reward for pious acts or good conduct, and hence could not earn any forgiveness from God. This forgiveness, when it came, was of God's totally free Grace, not of man's earning.

These ideas turned many readers away from Calvinism to a happier theology. By the mid-nineteenth century America had moved a long way in the romantic quest that was to find man the measure of all things, but the Calvinist tradition was still powerful. It still held Hawthorne, for example, whose *Scarlet Letter* (1850) shows that sin is permanently warping. It shows at the same time that Hawthorne did not accept this truth eagerly or happily, as earlier Calvinists certainly did, but sadly and bitterly. It is the nature symbolism in *The Scarlet Letter* that expresses warmth and beauty and humanity — even while Hawthorne makes it clear that nature is the source of sinful impulse. In July 1850, when he was halfway through *Moby-Dick*, Melville read Hawthorne's *Mosses from an Old Manse*, and wrote an exuberant review of it. In August he met Hawthorne, talked and talked with him, and then drew back and set about writing his book all over again. Its publication was delayed many months. Melville dedicated the novel to Hawthorne, who wrote him a letter about it that delighted him so that he replied, "A sense of unspeakable security is in me this moment, on account of your having understood the book. I have written a wicked book, and feel spotless as the lamb. . . . I would sit down and dine with you and all the gods in old Rome's Pantheon." Hawthorne did not doubt the Calvinist theology; he did not doubt that sin was permanently warping; but he took a sad and doubtful view of the Providence that ordained it thus. Drawn to Hawthorne, pouring his heart out to him and Sophia in long nights of talk during the summer of 1850, Melville must have voiced his doubts about the goodness of the God that presided over human destiny. If he wrote (more important, rewrote) a "wicked book," it was because it embodied these doubts. And what more natural than that he would dedicate it to the man who shared the thoughts that led him into his greatest burst of creative power. Melville did not turn from Calvinism to romantic optimism but to fierce rebellion against the stern old God of his forefathers.

These facts guide us to see that it is most probable that Ahab's speculations were about these very same problems of good and evil and the nature of God. It is difficult to imagine, in view of Melville's relation with Hawthorne and his unguarded description of a "wicked book," what *else* Melville could have had on his mind as he addressed himself to rewriting a novel that was virtually finished. These ideas carry the devout Protestant who spat into the Catholic chalice on to his second stage, indicated in Elijah's other question, quoted above — " 'nothing about that thing that happened to him off Cape Horn, long ago when he lay like dead for three days and nights[?]' " What happened was that he was struck by lightning, under strange circumstances, which are in fact revealed many chapters later in the story.

To one who has come to doubt the total goodness of God but who does not want to turn against him, a logical step is to turn to Zoroastrianism, which believes in two gods, two equal powers, representing good and evil, in ceaseless contest for control of the cosmos. The god of good is Ahmazd; the god of evil is Ahriman. The one is identified with light, the other with darkness. They are independent and equally powerful; their warfare is incessant. Ahab has brought a strange dark harpooner named Fedallah on the present fatal voyage; and he later tells that it was Fedallah who had earlier instructed him in Zoroastrianism. Fedallah is a "Parsee," that is, a Persian Zoroastrian living in India. Many chapters later, Ahab addresses the corposants (or St. Elmo's fire) by putting one foot on Fedallah, grasping the lightning chain in his hand, and exclaiming: " 'Oh! thou clear spirit of clear fire, whom on these seas I as Persian once did worship, till in the sacramental act so burned by thee, that to this hour I bear the scar . . .' " (Chapter CXIX.)

Worshiping Ahmazd in the fire of lightning, Ahab was struck by that lightning. The scar is noticed by Ishmael when he first comes on deck: "Threading its way out from among his grey hairs, and continuing right down one side of his tawny scorched face and neck, till it disappeared in his clothing, you saw a slender rod-like mark, lividly whitish." And the clue is given: "It resembled that perpendicular seam sometimes made in the straight, lofty trunk of a great tree, when the upper lightning tearingly darts down it, and without wrenching a single twig, peels and grooves out the bark from top to bottom ere running off into the soil, leaving the tree still greenly alive, but branded." (Chapter XXVIII.)

Thus struck and branded, Ahab "lay like dead for three days and nights." When he recovered, he was struck a second time: the whale, symbol of nature's bounty, source of heat, light, and food — and not any whale but the White Whale, Moby Dick — reaped off his leg with one slash of his sickle jaw. One such assault Ahab might have taken as evidence that not all fire was Ahmazd, but two assaults in succession, one coming from the object worshiped, the other from nature's bounty, were too much. Ahab was weeks recovering from the second assault, and he went through a fire of anguish while doing so. He emerged convinced that the Power in control of the cosmos was malign. Not careless, not indifferent, but actively malign. He does not know whether it is intelligent, but he has felt its power and sensed its malice, and he is mad for vengeance. Ahab is in this third stage when he appears in *Moby-Dick*.

This sort of antecedent action functions like description or retrospective dialogue to give the character a momentum that projects him into the present situation. It is more effective than description because it gives the character shape and tension in a conflict: we see what he has been doing that accounts for his condition and his attitudes when we find him at the beginning of the present action. This momentum is greater than what can be provided by a reverie, or a description, or even a conversation, although these latter, successfully handled, can accomplish very much the same effect. And for all its energy, this presentation still reveals Ahab by hearsay and exposition rather than directly and dramatically.

Ahab continues in his third stage through most of the novel. In the tremendous "Quarter-Deck" chapter (XXXVI) he explains his wild purpose in such exciting terms that he is able to carry the crew with him. Even Ishmael acknowledges that he was caught up in the fierce emotion — "Ahab's quenchless feud seemed mine" — and the three savage harpooners seal the pact in their blood: they will chase Moby Dick to the ends of the earth if need be. Now through the central part of the story there is a great deal of incidental activity mixed with many passages of information about whaling that usually end with a paragraph or two of symbolistic extension which grows straight out of the physical circumstance and relates, more or less, to the problem of the main action. The bulk of this material does not concern or directly involve Captain Ahab, but extends the reader's sense of the ominous mystery symbolized by the sea. These passages continually feed one's fear that Ahab is indeed mad. A chapter on brit, for example, which is the food of the right whale, modulates into a reminder of the dark power of the sea; landsmen are ignorant of it, and even mariners through familiarity forget its awfulness: "for ever and for ever, to the crack of doom, the sea will insult and murder him, and pulverize the stateliest, stiffest frigate he can make; nevertheless, by the continual repetition of these very impressions, man has lost that sense of the full awfulness of the sea which aboriginally belongs to it." (Chapter LVIII.) That is to say, the terrors of the unknown are too easily forgotten by man because he will not trouble himself to face them. A few paragraphs later the exposition carries from the treacherous ferocity of the whelming sea, with its universal cannibalism, on to the analogy with man: consider this appalling power, "and then turn to this green, gentle, and most docile earth; consider them both, the sea and the land, and do you not find a strange analogy to something in yourself? For as this appalling ocean surrounds the verdant land, so in the soul of man there lies one insular Tahiti, full of peace and joy, but encompassed by all the horrors of the half known life. God keep thee! Push not off from that isle, thou canst never return!" (*Idem.*)

So Ahab's problem becomes the reader's problem. Through these expositions, and the nine gams (to be discussed presently) by which the slender action is sustained, Ahab's mad rage softens somewhat. The voyage is long; the crew and mates are under control; Ahab has faced down Starbuck's ineffectual rebellion, but not without feeling some pity for him; and the little Negro cabin boy, Pip, driven out of his mind by terror when he jumped from a whaleboat fastened to a whale, has brushed his heart with love. Out of these incidents and expositions Ahab comes into his final stage, in which he accepts the fact that reality is an impenetrable fusion of good and evil.

Described in these terms, Ahab appears to be a character developing in action; but it is not that simple. Ahab is not the continual center of the action because very much more than half of what happens is known through the exploring and discussing voice of Ishmael, and even the passages in which Ahab's "purpose" is explored are often discussions *about* Ahab rather than dramatizations of his thoughts. In one place the mystery of his "madness" will be heightened when Ishmael explains that when he burst from his cabin in a nightmare, it was his "eternal, living principle or soul," for the time being "dissociated from the characterizing mind" that "sought escape from the scorching contiguity of" his frantic purpose, which had full possession of his conscious mind. (Chapter XLIV.) Or he speculates that Ahab's "mad" purpose has stormed the fortress of his sanity and turned all its guns upon his crazy goal. When Ishmael falls asleep at the tiller, during the trying-out of a whale, and awakes faced about with the ghastly impression "that whatever swift, rushing thing I stood on was not so much bound to any haven ahead as rushing from all havens astern," he goes on to warn man against staring into the fire (of evil) until he is hypnotized into thinking it all reality. He explains that

"there is a wisdom that is woe; but there is a woe that is madness" —
and then again he neutralizes this by suggesting that Ahab is like a
Catskill eagle, diving "into the blackest gorges," for "even in his lowest
swoop the mountain eagle is still higher than other birds upon the
plain, even though they soar." (Chapter XCVI.) Higher here may
mean nobler, or closer to truth; so the "woe that is madness" may be
justified by the nature of reality. The same ambiguous thought appears in the chapter on little Pip, who lost his mind from fright. "He
saw God's foot upon the treadle of the loom," down deep in the sea of
reality, and he spoke to it and knew it, "and therefore his shipmates
called him mad. So man's insanity is heaven's sense," and wandering
from mortal reason, man comes "at last to that celestial thought, which,
to reason, is absurd and frantic." (Chapter XCIII.) The thought is not
specified, but one cannot miss the suggestion that what drove Pip out
of his mind was his glimpse of some essential horror in "God's foot
upon the treadle of the loom," making the world what it is.

Thus instead of Ahab at the center of the action, we are given expositions that raise questions, always questions. Is Ahab mad? Is the world
good or bad? Is there a benign Providence? How many frightening
questions should a wise man ask? What will Ahab finally do? Mysteries
multiplied and compounded, circling about the moody ferocity of
Ahab, bring us at long length to passages in which he darkly reveals
his fourth stage. It is not long after he has by sheer will faced down
Starbuck, threatened him with a musket, and defied his reasonable
demand that the casks be lifted from the hold and the water pumped
out so that a leak can be found and stopped. He faces Starbuck down,
then reverses himself and responds to the reasonable demand. "It were
perhaps vain to surmise exactly why it was, that as respecting Starbuck, Ahab thus acted. It may have been a flash of honesty in him;
or mere prudential policy which . . . imperiously forbade the slightest symptom of open disaffection" that might later interfere with his
purpose. (Chapter CIX.) After this ambiguous flash of humanity (or
reasonableness), Ahab speaks in his own voice to a dying whale that
turns his head to the sun while expiring. "He too worships fire," and
the observation distresses Ahab, for it makes him for a moment fear
that nature worships light and by so doing proves the dominance of
good. " 'Oh that these too-favoring eyes should see these too-favoring
sights.' " He feels the pull to believe and doubts his ability to resist it.

Here on the sea, uttermost symbol of reality, here " 'beyond all hum of human weal or woe; in these most candid and impartial seas; where to traditions no rocks furnish tablets,' " here, that is, where truth shines forth free from custom, tradition, and frail hypocrisy, " 'here, too, life dies sunwards full of faith.' " But the whale dies, nevertheless, and in death turns the other way. " 'In vain, oh whale, dost thou seek inter-cedings with yon all-quickening sun, that only calls forth life, but gives it not again. Yet dost thou, darker half, rock me with a prouder, if a darker faith.' " It is faith in himself, seeking a deeper truth. In terms of the persistent symbolism, he is " 'Born of earth, yet suckled by the sea . . . ye billows are my foster-brothers!' " (Chapter CXVI.) He has grown through the world's traditional pieties to that higher vision which sees man as the measure of good.

In order to maintain his ascendency over the crew, Ahab defies the St. Elmo's fire (cones of static electricity pallidly glimmering from the ends of the spars, which bode evil) by invoking it and identifying him-self with it. He grasps the lightning chain, places one foot on the back of the kneeling Fedallah, and speaks to the fire: " 'I now know thee, thou clear spirit, and I now know that thy right worship is defiance. To neither love nor reverence wilt thou be kind . . . No fearless fool now fronts thee.' " He acknowledges its power, but " 'In the midst of the personified impersonal, a personality stands here.' " He finally reads himself in the mystery of the fire which — and this seems very important — does not itself know whence it comes: " 'Oh, thou found-ling fire . . . defyingly I worship thee!' " (Chapter CXIX.)

The sea, the whale, and the fire all symbolize aspects of the ultimate unknowable reality; the very diversity of the symbols is itself symbolic of the mystery, in that no single symbol will express it. If the antago-nist is a mystery, so too is the protagonist; and the sort of conflict that defines character is not possible between two unknown contestants who do not know exactly what they are fighting about — or whether, from Ahab's side, there is a contestant he can define. He is trying to catch Moby Dick in order to discover what he is. Thus the voyage-quest of an idea subordinates characterization drastically. The greatness of *Moby-Dick* depends upon this quality; it moves in another world from the novel of manners; the search into ideas dissolves the very certain-ties upon which characterization flourishes. The problem in the novel of manners is a social problem that is woven of personal relations; the problem of the quest is a cosmic problem made of uncertainties and outside the ambit where certainty is possible.

Two further areas of the book provide materials for the sharper characterization of Ahab: in the nine gams of the *Pequod* he is permitted to react personally to nine different men's ideas about Moby Dick; in the climactic chase he is compelled to translate his conviction into final, ultimate action. The conclusion he seems to have reached when he invokes the St. Elmo's fire cannot satisfy the reader's demand to know Ahab, for it leaves at least two very different courses of action open. He could live on with the wisdom of his insight, cherishing the glow of reason in his own breast and feeling a tragic exhilaration over the grandeur of man's defiance. In this way he could know what one learns from witnessing *Oedipus Rex, Lear,* and *Othello,* for he is not swept on by events as those tragic heroes are; he has had time to think, and he is the captain of the ship. On the other hand, Ahab can continue his doomed quest for vengeance until, fleeing all reason, he immolates himself against the Whale. One course discredits his will, the other his reason.

The nine meetings with other whalers, called gams, bring Ahab into specific, small-scale confrontations with other whaling captains. The first three gams have to do with matters of information and communication.* First is the *Goney* (Albatross) whose lookouts "said not one word to our own look-outs," but "mildly eyed us" as they passed. Its captain raised his megaphone to his mouth, but the wind snatched it away before he could speak, and the ships drew apart, the *Pequod* bound "around the world . . . in tormented chase of that demon phantom that, some time or other, swims before all human hearts . . ." (Chapter LII.) "It was not very long after speaking the *Goney,* that another homeward-bound whaleman, the *Town-Ho,* was encountered." She gave "strong news" of Moby Dick, a wondrous story in which he seemed to act "one of those so called judgments of God which at times are said to overtake some men," but this "secret part" of the story "never reached the ears of Captain Ahab or his mates." (Chapter LIV.) The third gam was with the *Jeroboam*; there was an epidemic aboard, and so the captain spoke to Ahab from a small boat sailing alongside the *Pequod.* There was, furthermore, a mad Shaker named Gabriel

* I am indebted here to James Dean Young, "The Nine Gams of the *Pequod,*" *American Literature,* January 1954, pp. 449–63.

aboard who had got the crew under his control. While the captain talked to Ahab, the boat would now rush ahead, now fall astern, so that the tale was confused and obscured; but they had seen Moby Dick, whom the mad fanatic claimed to be the Shaker god incarnated. Gabriel had killed the mate, Macey, who had insisted on chasing him, without injuring the other men in the whaleboat. The *Pequod* had a letter for Macey, which was passed to the group in the small boat, but Gabriel hurled it back, telling Ahab, " 'Nay, keep it thyself . . . thou art soon going that way.' " (Chapter LXXI.) In these three meetings, the prophetic communications are withheld or confused.

The next three gams have to do with attitudes toward Moby Dick that are impossible to Ahab. First, the *Jungfrau* (Virgin), innocent and incompetent, has to beg oil for its lamps, so totally unsuccessful has been its hunt; her captain is completely ignorant of Moby Dick. A wild chase takes place in competition with her, but Ahab is in no way involved. Second, the *Rose-Bud*, which has never heard of Moby Dick, has fastened to two stinking whales that are so rotten as to be useless for oil. Stubb persuades its French captain to cast them off, for fear of plague, and then digs a valuable harvest of ambergris from one of them. To ignorance of Moby Dick is added inexperience in whaling. With the *Samuel Enderby* there is vital news, for its captain has lost his arm in his first encounter with Moby Dick. He has seen him twice since, too, but has not given chase: " 'He's welcome to the arm he has, since I can't help it, and didn't know him then; but not to another one.' " (Chapter C.)

The last three gams are with ships that may be said to represent plans of action. The *Bachelor*, first, is filled to the teacups with oil and heads home under a fair breeze, with Polynesian girls aboard, fabulously successful. Her captain replies to Ahab's shouted question — " 'Hast seen the White Whale?' " — with " 'No; only heard of him; but don't believe in him at all.' " (Chapter CXV.) After this jolly atheistic "fool" has been left, and Ahab has increasingly moved into the foreground with the corposants scene, which takes place soon after, come two more dramatic and meaningful encounters. The *Rachel*, out of Nantucket, has lost a whaleboat containing the captain's twelve-year-old son. It disappeared, only the day before, fastened to Moby Dick. The captain piteously begs Ahab, " 'For eight-and-forty hours let me charter your ship — I will gladly pay for it, and roundly pay for it —

if there be no other way,' " to help him cruise over the surrounding seas after the missing boat. But Ahab stonily refuses. " 'Even now I lose time. Good-bye, good-bye. God bless ye, man, and may I forgive myself, but I must go.' " (Chapter CXXVIII.) Ahab has thrown away his pipe and his quadrant in earlier chapters, but no act makes his terrible purpose live in the man so vividly as this one does. As if to soften the inhumanity of Ahab's conduct, on the next page Melville has him speak tenderly to Pip, who offers him love: " 'Lad, lad, I tell thee thou must not follow Ahab now. The hour is coming when Ahab would not scare thee from him, yet would not have thee by him. There is that in thee, poor lad, which I feel too curing to my malady.' " And when Pip vows not to desert him, but offers himself in place of Ahab's lost leg, " 'If thou speakest thus to me much more, Ahab's purpose keels up in him.' "(Chapter CXXIX.)

The last gam is with the "most miserably misnamed" *Delight,* which Ahab hails when her captain is in the act of burying at sea one sailor killed by Moby Dick. A shattered whaleboat is the only remnant of four other stout men lost to the White Whale's fury the day before. The *Pequod* presses on, but not quickly enough to miss the words of the burial service and the sound of the corpse striking the sea. Here Ahab says nothing, but on the following day so beautiful is the soft sea and the transparent air, so gentle that beauty, that Ahab "dropped a tear into the sea; nor did all the Pacific contain such wealth as that one wee drop." (Chapter CXXXII.)

By this time he has knowledge, omens, love, and the pitiful eloquence of Starbuck, who begs him to give over the mad chase and return to Nantucket where his wife and child wait. Ahab wonders " 'what a forty years' fool — fool — old fool, has old Ahab been! Why this strife of the chase? why weary, and palsy the arm at the oar.' " He does not know why he goes on: " 'What is it, what nameless, inscrutable, unearthly thing is it; what cozening hidden lord and master, and cruel, remorseless emperor commands me; that against all natural lovings and longings, I so keep pushing, and crowding, and jamming myself on all the time . . . By heaven, man, we are turned round and round in this world, like yonder windlass, and Fate is the handspike.' " (Chapter CXXXII.) This is no answer, and if the hero speaks in puzzlement of himself in the third person, the sense of uncertainty is thereby deepened. It seems that Ahab *has* to go on, in spite of all knowledge and inclination; but this "motive" is not enough to take us farther into his character. Rather it pushes us away. For the idea is in command here; the quest must be carried on to the fatal combat in which Ahab hurls a final spear, cries, " 'Oh, lonely death on lonely life! Oh, now I feel my topmost greatness lies in my topmost grief,' " and goes to his death a few moments before the White Whale turns and sinks the *Pequod* itself. The idea is in command and must have its fullest expression, for that is what the whole book has been leading toward: tragic greatness reaching its apotheosis in defiance. It is not enough as knowledge; the idea must be enacted in order to *live* in the event; this is the way of art. In *Moby-Dick* the idea is so magnificent, so compelling in the realization that one hardly notices these limits of characterization. They are aspects of the book's greatness.

Ishmael is a special example of the dependence of character upon action. He has been the subject of a good deal of discussion by critics, who have sought to determine what happens to him, what he means in the total plan of the novel, to what extent the action is interpreted through his vision, and whether he does not, at the end, assume a meaning and an understanding of events that make him more significant than Ahab. Reviewing the criticism of *Moby-Dick*, one is impressed not by debates or sharply contested issues in the definition of Ishmael, but rather by the opulent variety of characteristics and functions that have been attributed to him.* Howard Vincent, for example, says he "is the chorus character whose commentary elucidates and whose person enfolds the entire work. No less than Horatio in *Hamlet*, Ishmael is the author's surrogate among the *Pequod* crew." Later he is declared to be more central: "For most profoundly, *Moby-Dick* is Ishmael's book as much as it is Ahab's." Indeed he is called the center from which the other characters are illustratively split: "If we see *Moby-Dick* as an account of Ishmael's attempt to find himself, his inner harmony, and if we regard Ahab, Starbuck, Pip, and the others as various of Ishmael's selves, real or potential, Queequeg becomes no less alive as idea than he does as part of the narrative." And his impor-

* See Howard Vincent, *The Trying-Out of Moby-Dick* (Boston: Houghton Mifflin, 1949), quotations from pp. 56, 389, 76, 205; Richard Chase, *The American Novel and Its Tradition* (Garden City, N.Y.: Doubleday, 1957), p. 109; Werner Berthoff, *The Example of Melville* (Princeton, N.J.: Princeton University Press, 1962), pp. 129–30, 181; Lawrance Thompson, *Melville's Quarrel with God* (Princeton, N.J.: Princeton University Press, 1952), p. 85.

tance is again stated: "Ishmael has attained the inner harmony un-
realized by Ahab, because he has come to terms with his environment
as his great captain never could do. Ishmael has subdued his sense of
outrage in the face of events; Ahab's expands to the point of self-
destruction."

Richard Chase has noticed that the status of Ishmael diminishes
from an initial prominence, until "he is always ostensibly the narrator
but in much of the latter part of the novel he is not *felt* as such."
Werner Berthoff is able to set forth a richer catalogue: "The range of
his qualities is genuinely appealing: gaiety, compassion, a quick pleasure in the odd and the picturesque, a deeper elation of spirit in the
presence of the really strange, a zest for sharing his enthusiasms (and
for defining them), a self-awareness that is reassuringly self-deprecating,
and then gusto, flippancy, gravity, sincerity, or awe, as the occasion
warrants." Berthoff praises Ishmael as "observer," "commentator," and
"chronicler" — and then in the next paragraph abandons the whole
enterprise, in effect, by attributing all these qualities to Melville's
style: "But these personal virtues of Ishmael's are really incidental to
the imagination and voice, the authenticating turn of style, that sustain the whole bulky structure of *Moby-Dick*. For all the variety of the
effects achieved, voice and style are consistent throughout the discur-
sive mass of the book." And then chapters later Berthoff universalizes
Ishmael into another sort of persona: "The mythical role Ishmael is
roughly cast in being that of the free, versatile, curious, observant,
adaptable, irrepressible, democratic everyman at home in all times,
places, and conditions." Lawrance Thompson writes of "a cautious
and timid and self-styled cowardly character, Ishmael."

These varieties of explanation could be multiplied indefinitely.
They suggest that the power and abundance of Melville's style have
so stimulated the imaginations of his readers that they have been impelled to soar off in the same style and create, on their own, ranges of
ideas and explanation that cannot be supported — or entirely refuted.
The key to the puzzle (or should we speak of the path that will take
us out of this rich critical forest?) is to be found in the relation of
Ishmael to the plot of *Moby-Dick*. He has no function in the plot. At
first he carries us into the setting. His ignorance and wonder about
Ahab are our ignorance and wonder — until that dark figure steps
forth onto the quarter-deck. He acts as an illustrative figure on the

masthead, at one end of the monkey rope, at the tiller watching the
ghastly flames of the tryworks, squeezing the lumps out of the sperma-
ceti, feeding the warp into the mat as Queequeg carelessly swings the
wooden sword of chance to give the last shaping blow to the process.
In each of these situations — and in many others — he speculates upon
the ambiguities symbolized in them, ambiguities of good and evil, of
comfort and horror, that are central to the *world* of the novel. When
he is at one end of the monkey rope, his speculations about the unfortunate circumstance of interdependence, which may destroy him
through no fault of his own if Queequeg at the other end falls to the
sharks, are very personal. When he explores the terrors of whiteness
he achieves a shuddering climax in "pondering all this, the palsied
universe lies before us a leper; and like wilful travellers in Lapland,
who refuse to wear colored and coloring glasses upon their eyes, so the
wretched infidel gazes himself blind at the monumental white shroud
that wraps all the prospect around him. And of all these things the
Albino whale was the symbol. Wonder ye then at the fiery hunt?"
(Chapter XLII.) At this point the "adaptable, irrepressible, democratic
everyman" has vanished into the voice of the author, who is none of
these.

But he has no function in the plot. He does not engage in a conflict
that leads him to the point of a choice. He is therefore essentially dis-
embodied, and when he takes a form it may be any form that the moment requires. Consistent characterization he does not have; it is possible to attach the rich speculations evoked by the novel to almost any
image of Ishmael the reader imagines. I do not mean to imply a defect
in *Moby-Dick*; but rather to suggest that if we recognize the fact that
Ishmael's separation from the plot makes it impossible to discover his
character, we may go on to more rewarding discussions of the work.*

* The most elaborate, and perhaps the most persuasive, case for Ishmael as the
hero whose insights finally rise above the narrowing madness of Ahab is to be
found in Leo Marx's *The Machine in the Garden* (New York: Oxford University
Press, 1964), where there is a telling analysis of garden metaphors associated with
Ishmael against machine metaphors associated with Ahab — representing the deepest
conflict in American letters. It is the conflict, as I have noticed earlier, that replaces
the problem of the typical novel of manners in our society where an established
system of manners does not prevail. Good as it is, Marx's case seems to me to rest
upon his own interpretation and, particularly, ordering of Ishmael's spiritual progress. There is no action in the plot that firmly separates Ishmael from the many-
voiced, deliberately ambiguous author. And at the end Marx concedes that "In his
role as ordinary seaman, therefore, Ishmael virtually drops out of sight. The figure
who is saved from the wreck is the narrator and symbol-maker of *Moby-Dick*; he is

Moby-Dick is so rich and complex that no view encompasses it, no one perspective sees all its lines and relations. Its grand theme is twisted, tumbled, juggled, turned upside-down, and laughed at; if its idea dominates its action, it also invades matters of characterization and tone. The tension between idea and characterization appears when characters are used to embody aspects of the former. Here it is profitable to set Ishmael aside, because he represents all points of view, and look at the four leading figures as controlled reactions to the main issue.

To the sinewy mystery of the world's power, Ahab stands as a defiance so intense and determined as to be obsessed — if not mad. No matter how powerfully the reader is convinced of the justice of Ahab's view, he will still recoil from the destructive passion of his assault upon it.

Starbuck, next to Ahab, is thoughtful and strong. His pious Christian view of the world's goodness is constantly under stress, both from the inescapable example of Ahab's wrath and from the evidence of the Whale's fearful (if not malign) power. He is upheld by his faith, but he is caught in the squeeze between his captain's will and the Whale's presence, and here his mild piety does not save him. He reads the doubloon with a cadence that begins in firm faith but sinks into despair: " 'A dark valley between three mighty, heaven-abiding peaks, that almost seem the Trinity, in some faint earthly symbol. So in this vale of Death, God girds us round; and over all our gloom, the sun of Righteousness still shines a beacon and a hope. If we bend down our eyes, the dark vale shows her mouldy soil; but if we lift them, the bright sun meets our glance half way, to cheer.' " So far he seems

Job's messenger," saved to "deliver to us a warning of disasters to come." (P. 313.) Or, as in this case, an account of Ahab's final tragic insight. Thus the narrator becomes too nearly the author of the book — or the persona assumed by the author — to have this character controlled by the very materials that the same author has invented and arranged in telling the story. In other words, the author's voice is a rich and compelling aspect of *Moby-Dick*; readers of novels are so familiar with the voices of a Jane Austen, a Fielding, a Thackeray, or a Trollope that they cannot *naturally* apprehend such a voice as a character in the book; it is too typically an author's voice.

An interesting possible exception to my whole theory is suggested here: How does the author succeed in characterizing himself so thoroughly when he *does* nothing in any action? The answer is that he establishes all the moral values, the tone, and the occasions for important choice that occur in the novel. These commitments unite with his constant implied judgments (and stated judgments) to make him a character whom the reader may know very well and with whom he may identify closely. What happens in the recent novel, where we cannot satisfactorily locate the author, will be discussed in Chapters 13 and 14.

strong and confident in the power of faith, but his own words lead him into further depths: " 'Yet, oh, the great sun is no fixture; and if, at midnight, we would fain snatch some sweet solace from him, we gaze for him in vain! This coin speaks wisely, mildly, truly, but still sadly to me. I will quit it, lest Truth shake me falsely.' " (Chapter XCIX.) It is improbable that a believing man would acknowledge that truth might shake him falsely. The paradox in the statement represents Melville's grand irony rather than revealing Starbuck's character; but insofar as it does represent Starbuck it shows him helplessly drawn into the ambit of Ahab's dark understanding.

Going a step down, we come to Stubb and Flask, the lesser mates. Stubb is brave and competent, and he maintains his aplomb by laughing at everything. Jollity is his key, and he pursues the joke into dark corners. He knows, for example, that Fedallah is the devil, with his tail coiled up inside his trousers and his shoes stuffed at the toes with oakum to make it look as if there were real feet instead of cloven hoofs inside them. Flask, still simpler, reduces the world to violence and business. If he must catch whales in order to live, then he must hate them for resisting him. From his hate springs cruelty, and this is his hallmark. "Cruel Flask!" says Melville when he lances the ulcer on the side of the old blind whale. Stubb and Flask have personalities, the former for his language, the latter for his few simple acts, but neither is given opportunity for significant choice.

The manner in which the three mates are presented, combined with the jocular and evasive philosophizing that spreads through the whole book, produces a dimension of tone that means as much, finally, as the great action does. This tone says that the undertaking and the inquiry of the book are a vast joke. Anybody knows that the world is unpredictable; the smart fellow keeps his nose clean and slips by without asking for trouble. American humor traditionally inflates dangers until they become ridiculous or are seen in ridiculous contexts. Mike Fink, Pecos Bill, Paul Bunyan, and their kind make comedies of natural marvels and horrors. "They called the wind Maria . . ." The comic tone spreads over the ship and the sea. It relieves the reader's anguish, so that it may mount to new heights, as do the comic scenes in Shakespeare's tragedies; it suggests that only laughter can make life bearable amid such terrors; it also serves to conceal some of Melville's ripest blasphemies; but above all these functions it makes the whole vast enterprise partly a joke. This embodies a second answer to Ahab's great question, an answer that I find almost as compelling as the dark answer of defiance. Laugh, it says; laugh at the crazy world, for it does not do to think too hard about it, and great things have been accomplished with the light touch.

The double tone adds to the dominance of idea in the novel; it lets the author's intellect preside over the action and therefore over the characterization. Just as it is not easy to conceive an action between the hero and an incomprehensible antagonist, so the characters are dimmed when they are seen now through a tragic and now through a comic lens.

7 *The Idle Inquiry*

AFTER looking into "Heart of Darkness" and *Moby-Dick*, we may expect to find a short tale — really little more than a sketch at first glance — by Hawthorne something of a relief from the profundities of Conrad and Melville. But the relief is illusory: Hawthorne is as ambiguous as Melville, far more so than Conrad. Few journeys into evil have inspired more commentary than "Young Goodman Brown" (1835). It is constructed to be ambiguous. The hero starts off into the dark forest for a meeting that he does not want to acknowledge even to himself. At every step he expresses his doubts with a rhythmic beat, and each beat is counterpointed by something that carries him on to the next step. So he moves along in a sort of dance of movement and counter-movement. Facing and reaching south, he moves steadily north.

Brown has an itch to know evil, and he is going to indulge this itch; but he is also a moralist and a pious believer who knows that his itch comes straight from the devil and can be the instrument of his damnation. Only a moralist, after all, would be so earnestly concerned with such problems! And because he is a pious moralist, who has thought perhaps too much about the matter, Brown has come to wonder whether the devil exists and has the powers commonly attributed to him. Taken from the supernatural to the social, this question translates itself into a doubt about his fellow men. Are they contaminated with the evil that Brown himself has entertained in his thoughts and suspected in others' — or are people generally good (though weak!) and the defect a defect in his own faith?

Faith, indeed, is the name of his pretty young wife, whom he bids good-bye despite her anxious demur one evening and sets off on his journey into the dark forest. He goes deep into the forest, attends a witches' sabbath at the lurid climax of which he confronts his dear young wife, and wakes in the morning under a drippy bush, wondering whether it was all a dream or a real experience.

Hawthorne carefully evades this question. If it was a dream, he says, "it was a dream of evil omen for young Goodman Brown. A stern, a sad, a darkly meditative, a distrustful, if not a desperate man did he become from the night of that fearful dream. . . . they carved no hopeful verse upon his tombstone, for his dying hour was gloom." Brown's journey into the heart of darkness has brought him to the point where he loses faith in his fellow men. Was it a dream or a real experience? Was it a journey into his own heart or into the dark heart of Man?

If the climax occurred in a dream, then the story is realistic and portrays the psychological mechanism by which young Goodman Brown expresses his growing doubt about the goodness of his pious fellow townspeople and of his pretty young wife. The doubt must have been growing just under the surface of consciousness, repressed by the superego of social conformity. The doubts find expression in a dream of such force that Brown awakes convinced and woefully disillusioned. Crucial in this dream sequence is the moment when he finds the ribbon from Faith's hair, falling through the dark night of the forest, which prepares for the climax of the witches' sabbath itself, where he comes face to face with Faith under the ceremonial authority of the devil himself. Again and again he has expressed both his hope and his doubt by invoking Faith as he moved toward the final discovery. On the way to it he has met such a goodly number of the pious citizens of his town that the final vision of evil in Faith is little more than confirmation of what he has expected. By his dream, then, the subconscious becomes conscious, bringing out what Austin Warren has aptly described as "the devastating effect of moral scepticism."* Brown's faith in man was gone, and his dying hour was gloom.

The other reading of the story is less superficially credible, but it

*Austin Warren, editor, *Nathaniel Hawthorne: Representative Selections* (New York: American Book, 1934), p. 362.

comes to us backed by centuries of tradition. The use of the supernatural, whether in religion or superstition, whether indeed in *Hamlet* or *Macbeth*, represents man's belief in realities that do not lend themselves to simple objective verification. Just as the deepest secrets of religion are called "mysteries," so the deepest fears of ordinary men have been embodied in ghosts, goblins, demons, and all the unnumbered host of the invisible world. So strong is the tradition of the supernatural that, so far as literary probability goes, the fantastic reading of "Young Goodman Brown" is more acceptable than the realistic psychological one! Hawthorne, furthermore, has interwoven these two possibilities so tightly that it is impossible to show that either one represents the accurate reading of the story.

If we could establish the moment when Brown sat down on his journey and fell asleep, we could prove the realistic reading. Or could we? The dream quality represents the unconscious for Hawthorne, in many stories; but it also represents the dark terrors of the supernatural. So its presence tells us nothing. In "My Kinsman, Major Molineux," Hawthorne uses the dream quality to suggest the subconscious. Critics have agreed that it is one of Hawthorne's finest stories, as well as that it deals with the expression of the young hero's Oedipal death-wish against his father, who is represented in the story by his uncle, Major Molineux. To achieve the dream quality, however, Hawthorne fills his story with intimations of the supernatural, which are ostensibly explained as the errors of a "shrewd" but gullible young man who finds himself in the middle of a Colonial citizens' uprising against the British governor, the signals and preparations of which he misinterprets. Thus dream, supernatural, and mystery story are interwoven with great skill, suggesting ironic densities of vision that confound any attempt to nail down a single simple truth. It is, rather, more instructive to look at our story closely and see how the author manages the transition from the real journey upon which Goodman Brown certainly starts to the nightmare of self or Man into which he journeys.

Hawthorne delights in quiet hints. The opening paragraphs tell us that Brown's wife was "aptly" named Faith, that she was "young," "pretty," and "but three months married." She begs Brown to tarry with her " 'this night, dear husband, of all nights in the year.' " When he persists in his intention she innocently hopes, not that he will fare well, but " 'may you find all well when you come back.' " The passage grows richer under the scrutiny of hindsight: Is Faith trying to protect her husband or herself? Is she inspired by some divine prescience to protect her husband from the devil — or is she inspired by the devilish certainty that she herself will attend the sabbath and does not want her husband to know what she is? Brown is distressed; he thinks "there was trouble in her face, as if a dream had warned her what work is to be done to-night." Already the ambiguities of the dream motif have been foreshadowed, for later development. As Brown proceeds, there are many intimations that we are moving into the subsconscious. On his road, the trees "closed immediately behind" him, putting him in a solitude that has this special quality: "the traveller knows not who may be concealed by the innumerable trunks and the thick boughs overhead; so that with lonely footsteps he may yet be passing through an unseen multitude." The passage suggests the isolation of the dream but at the same time restates the central problem of the story: are we journeying into the heart of Brown or of mankind?

The first character he meets, who is slowly revealed to be the devil, first is described as "bearing a considerable resemblance" to Brown, "though perhaps more in expression than features." This suggests that it is not family but human nature that is involved in the resemblance. He offers Brown his staff, to help quicken his pace; but Brown rejects it, saying that he now intends to return home, having scruples " 'touching the matter thou wot'st of.' " Here it is most interesting that the devil neither threatens nor exhorts nor uses force. He significantly suggests that they " 'walk on, nevertheless, reasoning as we go,' " and Brown "*unconsciously*" resumes his walk in order to discuss the question. In the discussion, Brown appeals to the reputation of New England for piety, while the devil replies from solid experience of his transactions with "the Great and General Court." A moment later Goody Cloyse, " a very pious and exemplary dame," appears in the distance, and Brown turns aside so as not to meet her. Actually, he withdraws to contemplate, and the events that follow take place, it is hinted, in his mind. In a breath of time, Goody Cloyse cries, " 'The devil!' "; mentions Brown's father as his familiar; and calls Brown himself a silly fellow. The devil now speaks to her in "the shape of old Goodman Brown," offering not his arm but his staff to help her. His refusal of his arm to the old woman reinforces the suggestion that the devil uses no force or even physical assistance, only freedom and doubt.

At this point Brown casts up his eyes, not in faith, but "in astonish-ment," and when he looks down again Goody Cloyse and the devil's staff have both disappeared — back into the subconscious from which they came.

Now he talks with the devil, who discoursed "so aptly that his argu-ments seemed rather to spring up in the bosom of his auditor than to be suggested by himself." Brown suddenly sits down and refuses to go another step; whereupon the devil appropriately vanishes, leaving him to his thoughts with these last words: " 'and when you feel like moving again, there is my staff to help you along.' " Now come the tramp of hoofs and the voices of the riders, passing within a few yards of the young man's hiding place but — and here Hawthorne underlines the intention of his ambiguity by saying, "owing doubtless to the depth of the gloom at that particular spot" — "neither the travellers nor their steeds were visible." The "particular" spot is the darkness of Brown's heart, so to speak, and it is from these invisible voices that he hears word of "a goodly young woman to be taken into communion" that night. The speakers are the two stalwarts of the town whom Brown had invoked earlier against the devil's general talk about his transac-tions with "the Great and General Court." It is most significant that these voices come "talking so strangely in the empty air." There fol-lows a turmoil of cloud and sound ("though no wind was stirring"), of noises and voices, in which the spirit of dream or vision is powerful as the young man thinks he hears the voice of Faith.

Now he is "maddened with despair," laughs loud and desperately, and rushes forward through the forest "with the instinct that guides mortal man to evil." Freely he gives vent to "horrid blasphemy" and demonic laughter, appearing more hideous than the fiend himself. After this climax of self-induced evil, Brown sees the great multitude gathered for the ceremony, the good and the bad alike of his town, including "all whom [he had] reverenced from youth."

From the climax of evil, in which the devil explains that all men are united in a bond of horrid sin and Brown is confronted with his dear young wife, the dream quality fades back. The sabbath vanishes, Hawthorne speaks as if Brown were awaking in the dark, cold, damp forest, and the horror with which he shrinks from his fellows as he re-enters the town sets him apart in a darkness that seems to be only his own. The ambiguity remains in that Brown's dark heart is a human heart, like others; but there is no doubt that the symbolism of the central experience represents a penetration of the subconscious. The insights all come from invisible voices. Yet the final meaning of the story draws upon both aspects of the ambiguity: moral skepticism is blighting, yes, but there is reason to doubt the purity of everybody, and the total purity of the saints. One man's mind must be a key to other minds. What the dark heart feels touches the dark heart of the reader in some part. If evil is everywhere, only faith can combat it; that is, one must *will* to believe in one's fellows, for the evidence will not prevail over the cold reason of the unloving observer. This dark counsel has been fittingly described as producing "an all-pervading atmosphere of uneasiness and anguished doubt,"* and the more carefully one reads the story, the more richly ironic becomes the interplay between the dark heart within and the dark world without. The complex truth is to be relished, not reduced.

Journey motifs, as we have seen, tend to dramatize ideas rather than characters because the crises are spots of intellectual fire rather than the choices by which character realizes itself. This story is built around the intellectual puzzle of dream-against-reality, the subtle modulation of the journey from a physical fact to a moral symbol of deepening fascination with evil, and the allied notion that the penetration of the dark forest is a penetration of the universal unconscious. There is also, at the end, a powerful realization of evil-as-enchantment, as a wild force whose energy carries all before it. All these ideas relate to the general experience of sinfulness in the Christian tradition; they do not serve to particularize a character. What one remembers about this story is the situation — the dark impulse that impels Brown to leave his young wife and journey into the forest. The story is a pattern of idea, situation, and action, in which character does not emerge.

Randall Stewart has identified certain "recurrent themes" in the writings of Hawthorne.† These are ideas which appear repeatedly when the situation suggests them, without reference to their validity for the particular character who is present at the moment. In this story they pop out almost automatically: the community of sinners; the sympathy of the human heart for sin, which enables the sinner to

*Richard Fogle, "Ambiguity and Clarity in 'Young Goodman Brown,'" *New England Quarterly*, December 1943, p. 454.

†Randall Stewart, editor, *The American Notebooks of Nathaniel Hawthorne* (New Haven: Yale University Press, 1932), Introduction.

"scent out" sin under whatever bright disguise its bearer lives; the special power of secret sin; the obsessive, consuming quality of sin; and the heavy influence of the past on the present. His favorite recurrent theme appears in a sentence of the devil's speech: " 'It shall be yours to penetrate, in every bosom, the deep mystery of sin, the fountain of all wicked arts . . .' " Whether one sees them as defects because they come almost automatically from Hawthorne's pen or merely the bright sparks by which his dark genius evokes the shock of recognition, they obscure the particular choice that begins to define a particular character.

The theme of the story is the general *nature* of man as deduced from the artist's experience. He uses a symbolic journey to represent the *typical* human relation to evil, and he transmutes the problem and choice that would identify a particular character into the supernatural ambience and the unconscious motivation that make the "hero" fade into uncertainties, even vanish into the reader's gentle, speculative disquiet of self-doubt. Here is a curious foreshadowing of the modern dissolution of character by the generalizing categories of psychology.

8 *Freedom Afloat—and Adrift*

MELVILLE in *Moby-Dick* is not concerned with the void between the individual and the state; he leaves social problems to assail the Ultimate. The story carries the little world of the *Pequod* in a quest for the demonic secret of the universe, a quest that begins and continues away from the patterned manners of a class-bound society. The voyage explores a mystery, and the action moves by stages deeper and deeper into the idea of evil that has taken possession of Ahab. The story involves certain constants of human relations, like courtesy, authority, and friendship, as well as certain universal conditions like prudence and respect for the law of gravity; but these do not come with the flavor and tone of a particular society and so do not serve to define character very concretely. Nor does the action use these elements centrally; instead of a social problem there is a working out of Ahab's Question about the Whale. Ahab hunts. The Whale hides, until finally the forces are ready to reveal themselves in the catastrophe. Ahab proves his own lack of prudence, while the Whale proves that nature is sometimes horribly destructive. As we have seen, the character of Ahab emerges in a confusion of insight and defiance because although he must comprehend the ultimate mystery of good-and-evil-joined he must also carry into final action the defiance that makes him at once great and, doubtless, mad. This confusion is a small defect in the magnificence of the tale, but it shows how the demands of an action contrived to elucidate an idea may produce confusions of choice or motive that conceal rather than reveal character. We may agree that there is no simple answer to the mystery of evil, that it would be silly to present one, and that for this problem greatness of treatment is dependent upon a degree of ambiguity; but the hero who embodies and sustains this ambiguity through the tale is therefore bound to be himself a mystery rather than a rounded and realized character.

Huckleberry Finn (1884) turns Ahab's quest upside down to have a "natural" man explore the jungle of society. Huck's voyage down the river is a journey into the heart of social evil, into a body that is rotten and repulsive where it is not merely ridiculous. Huck is untutored and independent of most social influences. He has, however, absorbed the darkest social teachings on the inferiority of the Negro and the sanctity of property. These teachings constitute his conscience, and the most obvious conflict-and-choice in the story has to do with it. We shall see presently how the problem characterizes Huck. *Whether* it does has raised some surprising questions about the book in the minds of our best critics.

There is something strange, for example, when so astute a scholar as Lionel Trilling (a scholar, moreover, who has given valuable insights into the form of the novel of manners) can write that, "as Pascal says, 'rivers are roads that move,' and the movement of the road in its own mysterious life transmutes the primitive simplicity of the form: the road itself is the greatest character in this novel of the road, and the hero's departures from the river and his returns to it compose a subtle and significant pattern." He is echoing T. S. Eliot, from whose *Four Quartets* he quotes:

> I do not know much about gods; but I think that the river
> Is a strong brown god . . .
> > almost forgotten
> By the dwellers in cities — ever, however, implacable,
> Keeping his seasons and rages, destroyer, reminder
> Of what men choose to forget. Unhonoured, unpropitiated
> By worshippers of the machine, but waiting, watching and waiting.

"*Huckleberry Finn,*" he continues, "is a great book because it is about a god — about, that is, a power which seems to have a mind and will of its own, and which to men of moral imagination appears to embody a great moral idea. Huck himself is the servant of the river-god, and he comes very close to being aware of the divine nature of the being he serves."*

*Lionel Trilling, *The Liberal Imagination* (New York: Viking, 1950; quotations from Garden City, N.Y.: Doubleday, 1953 edition), pp. 117, 109.

Mr. Trilling explains that Huck's intense moral life derives almost wholly from his love of the river, which is a symbol of power, charm, and, we must suppose, goodness. The search for Huck's character leads between the boy and the river, certainly, but the discovery of it is not easily made. Huck tells the whole story and maintains a fairly consistent point of view throughout, but whether the form of the book allows a credible character to emerge is a question whose challenge to dozens of thoughtful critics has been met by an extraordinary variety of explanations. There are a good many forces and ideas in the book that do not permit Huck to define himself by participating in a plot that moves through the central morals and beliefs of a stable society.

Huck introduces himself as the humorless narrator who occupies one of Mark Twain's comic poses — that of the Simpleton.* The pose comes out on the first page, when Huck explains, "When you got to the table you couldn't go right to eating, but you had to wait for the widow to tuck down her head and grumble a little over the victuals, though there warn't really anything the matter with them." Here the pose allows the exaggeration of American humor. It gains sympathy for the ignorant innocent. It also projects a dual vision into the story: both the naive boy and the sardonic author are always present. In the author's eyes the Widow Douglas's grace is an unintelligible farce, it is a soulless imposition on an innocent boy; it is a gross caricature of religion. This duality is not all of *Huckleberry Finn*, to be sure, but it is always present, overlaying the boy's tale with a mantle of humor and satire that exists in a very different dimension from the boy's mind. Huck is also superstitious; he knows a thousand signs, omens, and auspices; between his fears of bad luck and his store-boughten conscience he is never quite comfortable. He lives in a dark world.

At times the comic pose of the Simpleton merges with the sardonic accent of Mark Twain. On prayer: "I judged I could see that there was two Providences, and a poor chap would stand considerable show with the widow's Providence, but if Miss Watson's got him there warn't no help for him any more. I thought it all out, and reckoned I would belong to the widow's, if he wanted me, though I couldn't make out how he was agoing to be any better off then than what he was before, seeing I was so ignorant and so kind of low-down and ornery." (Chap-

---

* These have been effectively described and classified by John C. Gerber in "Mark Twain's Use of the Comic Pose," *PMLA*, June 1962, pp. 297–304.

ter III.) At other times it represents the ultimate in naiveté, as when Huck believes Tom's account of "a whole parcel of Spanish merchants and rich A-rabs was going to camp in Cave Hollow with two hundred elephants, and six hundred camels, and over a thousand 'sumter' mules, all loaded down with di'monds, and they didn't have only a guard of four hundred soldiers, and so we would lay in ambuscade, as he called it, and kill the lot." (*Idem.*) Here Mark Twain is obtrusively present, grinning and clowning with Huck's fantastical credulity.

When Huck's vicious, drunken Pap appears, all poses vanish while Huck matter-of-factly tells about the meeting. For a while Pap takes Huck's dollars, gets drunk, and winds up in jail. When the "new" judge undertakes to reform Pap with a nice mixture of faith, sympathy, and exhortation, the dual vision reappears. The judge talks to Pap about temperance till "the old man cried, and said he'd been a fool, and fooled away his life; but now he was agoing to turn over a new leaf and be a man nobody wouldn't be ashamed of, and he hoped the judge would help him and not look down on him. The judge said he could hug him for them words; so *he* cried, and his wife she cried again; Pap said he'd been a man that had always been misunderstood before, and the judge said he believed it. The old man said that what a man wanted that was down, was sympathy; and the judge said it was so; so they cried again." (Chapter V.) Presently the judge is so moved that he "said it was the holiest time on record, or something like that." And that night Pap climbs out the window, gets roaring drunk, breaks his arm in two places, "and was most froze to death when somebody found him after sun-up. And when they come to look at that spare room, they had to take soundings before they could navigate it." (*Idem.*) Here behind Huck's deadpan recital appears Mark Twain's scathing exposure of the cheap sentimentalism which he found whenever he looked at the multitude of fools and do-gooders. But Huck is never aware of such attitudes, although he is identified with them because of the emotions they arouse in the breast of the reader. These emotions mount as Pap takes Huck off into the woods, beats and abuses him, and rants about the evils of a "govment" that lets niggers wear white shirts and won't "sell a free nigger till he's been in the State six months." (Chapter VI.)

Huck leaves in a canoe that floats by on the rising river, first contriving Tom-Sawyer-like evidence that he has been murdered and laying a false trail of the murderers. He puts in at Jackson's Island, meets up with his old friend Jim, who is now a runaway slave, finds the famous raft — and the idyll begins.

Characterization by the display of intellect is nowhere more richly and delightfully fulfilled than in the conversations between Jim and Huck. Jim's superstitiousness and credulity charm, touch, and fascinate. Here is a spirit with no shame, no reticence, and perfect trust, living on hope in a world that promises nothing. Huck is neither so gullible nor so trusting, and he likes to play tricks on Jim. One of them gets Jim bitten by a rattlesnake, with four days of agony. Huck is ashamed of himself, and does not tell what he has done. Linked to the flair for tricks is Huck's gift of lying. He does not, as a matter of principle, tell the truth when a lie will serve; and he lies with a somber felicity that casts a veil over him. This lying plays a dual role in the intellectual plan of the story: on one hand it is, like his evil conscience, something he has learned from society; but on the other it is a defiance that establishes his goodness against the corrupted propriety and respectability of society. It does this because it makes Huck a bad antisocial boy flaunting the official hypocrisies by which society imposes its shabby will on its ignorant and intimidated members. So lying and stealing become signs of "natural" innocence. These paradoxes engage the reader's sympathies and, I believe, mislead his judgment — so that his empathy with Huck is stronger than his sense of Huck as a character. A triumph of style, of irony and impudence, keeps the reader engaged. It is, of course, a version of pastoral, by which the commentator assumes a pose of rustic impudence and makes either devastating or impertinent comments upon social practices that he innocently oversimplifies for the purpose of making his thrusts more telling. Insofar as the sardonic Twain is speaking, one's intellect is aroused and one's knowledge of Huck as a character is obscured or by-passed.

From time to time Mark Twain is carried away by enthusiasm and does a pure virtuoso piece. An example is what happens when Huck and Jim discover the wrecked steamboat. Inside are a murderer and two other men who plan to murder him for his money. Huck and Jim steal the skiff of these men, because their own raft has pulled loose, and escape. Presently Huck begins to feel sorry for the abandoned rascals; he pulls up beside a moored steamboat and tells the most fantastic tale, calculated to get the captain and various people in the nearby town confused to the point where it will take them weeks to get their bearings again. Huck's pity for the murderers brings about cruel confusion for the innocent. The suggestion is that moral anarchy prevails; that Huck's innocent good intentions are essentially impotent; that the whole business is very funny.

This sort of virtuoso foolishness prevails when Huck suffers through his great moral crisis over helping Jim to escape. On the one hand his conscience dictates extravaganzas of inhumanity: "Jim talked out loud all the time . . . He was saying how the first thing he would do when he got to a free State he would go to saving up money and never spend a single cent, and when he got enough he would buy his wife, which was owned on a farm close to where Miss Watson lived; and then they would both work to buy the two children, and if their master wouldn't sell them, they'd get an Ab'litionist to go and steal them. It most froze me to hear such talk. . . . Thinks I, this is what comes of my not thinking. Here was this nigger which I had as good as helped to run away, coming right out flat-footed and saying he would steal his children — children that belonged to a man I didn't even know; a man that hadn't ever done me no harm." (Chapter XVI.) But finally Huck, who can't make himself give Jim up, decides "what's the use you learning to do right, when it's troublesome to do right and ain't no trouble to do wrong, and the wages [of feeling bad] is just the same?" He might as well do "whichever come handiest at the time," and that is what he does.

Later, when Huck comes back to the problem and defies his conscience, flaunting every respectable value he has learned, declaring his willingness to go to hell, he is embracing damnation for love. He is not by any means rejecting the code of his society; rather he is looking damnation squarely in the eye and accepting it. He is electing to go to the devil because this is the way to keep his friend beside him. The reader is enraged at Huck's feeling of guilt. He wants him to see that he is acting from love and loyalty and to denounce the society that has imposed evil values on his natural goodness. Impelled by his rage at Huck's very real distress, the reader is likely to swallow the assumptions that underly this sequence, for emotional identification is a stronger power over the mind than reason.

And some swallowing is required, for the assumptions will not bear rational scrutiny. They are the assumptions of primitivism: that society is evil and natural man is good. They are very old assumptions, and they are close to the heart of the American Dream of Adamic rebirth, but they move counter to the simple facts of history, which are that man has generated his "best self" through the refining processes of civilization. Compassion, humanity, trust, sensibility, imagination, objectivity, and responsibility are refined into man through social conditioning of the raw, greedy, impulsive, cruel natural child. The mind of man has conceived and developed these civilized qualities, but they do not appear in the child or "come naturally" to him.

At the same time, civilization can become so corrupt and sophistication so debased and crafty that we reach for a purer model, a pristine image behind (or under) the tarnish. Something in the language we use here — finding the "unsullied" or "pure" behind or beneath or before the corrupted actual — conjures us into seeing an *earlier* purity, which we easily transmute into an earlier man, a noble savage. If we used different words, if we spoke of an *ideal* that had been formulated by centuries of patient thought, an ideal rarely achieved, occasionally touched, but often betrayed because its elements were used by pretense and greed and vanity for their despicable ends, we should be using terms that would not trap us into seeing good as earlier and therefore more primitive than the corrupt present. Even here I have slipped in using the word "betrayed," which assumes some pristine entity to be betrayed. I should have said forestalled or prevented. The slip is instructive.

But the pattern of primitivism has been solidly established over the centuries, so that when our emotions are aroused by Huck's injustice to himself, we thoughtlessly use it to make Huck good because he is uncivilized and Nigger Jim even better, as he certainly is in the story, because he is even less tutored than Huck. The tradition of primitivism has been bred into the American Dream by innumerable repetitions. The New World promised a new start, a second Eden, and the image of Adam of course was evoked by the other theological images. This great tradition adds its force to our anger and makes the picture of untutored goodness acceptable and, moreover, credible. With these delusions firmly clinched, we sally straight into another dream — everyman's dream of idyllic escape and freedom. It makes boys run away from home. It makes men hunters and fishers. It accounts for the fascination of mountain, stream, and sea for us all. Escape.

> The woods are lovely, dark and deep.
> But I have promises to keep,
> And miles to go before I sleep . . .
>
> [Robert Frost, "Stopping by Woods on
> a Snowy Evening"]

The poet handles the problem more wisely than most men, who re-enact and ritualize their dreams of escape year after year; as Thoreau said, "From the desperate city you go into the desperate country, and have to console yourself with the bravery of minks and muskrats." Nursing the dream of escape that goes all the way back to the pioneers' westering and continues today in popular literature, entertainment, and advertising, the American yearns for faster automobiles and remoter wildernesses.

And there is much more than this. The journey-as-archetype carries us back through Western literature — Odysseus, Aeneas, Beowulf, Parsifal, and a host of other mythic figures go on quests from which they achieve maturity for themselves and at the same time express the spirit and the history of a people in epics and bibles that define as they embody the people's profoundest dreams of themselves. The westering is a tradition, and the impulse to escape and adventure haunts the American imagination.

These myths and traditions produce so powerful an emotional identification that it is very difficult to stand back coldly and ask who Huck *is*, because he enacts our own dreams of escape. But what does it mean to say that the river is the greatest character in the novel? As a bit of rhetoric it should perhaps not be taken too seriously, but one cannot banish the thought that the experience of fabled escape has given the novel its force and warmth, whereas the character of Huck will not bear close scrutiny. He is so wrapped in style and in intellectual shenanigans by Twain that our own laughter drowns out the patient, serious analysis that would take him apart and look at him coldly.

When Mr. Trilling writes that the river is the greatest character and that it embodies a "great moral idea," he is, I believe, reaching for a better objective correlative to his feeling than Huck, because he balks at describing Huck as a great moral agent. He senses the presence of Mark Twain playing casuistical tricks with right and wrong. He knows there is something basically the matter with making Huck and Jim a pair of saints in a world of scoundrels. What is wrong, of course, is that all the patient civilized goodness — the idealism, order, courage, and fidelity, the art and the law — which is a product only of civilization, has been left out of Mark Twain's romantic and simplistic dialectic. Mr. Trilling senses this fraud, but the power of Twain's archetypal symbols on top of his appeal to American idealism is too much for him (as indeed it always has been for all of us!) and he acknowledges its force by declaring the river a god embodying a great moral idea.

The first conflict wears itself out at Chapter XVI, when Huck and Jim pass Cairo in the fog and the raft is apparently destroyed. Huck had decided not to turn Jim over to the law — and Twain did not know how to go on. He laid the manuscript aside for three or four years (1876 to 1879 or 1880*); and when he took it up again he explored a darker recess of social evil. The feud between the Grangerfords and the Shepherdsons shows people of courage and manners who have been killing each other for thirty years over a forgotten incident. Huck's friend, Buck Grangerford, does not even know which family first killed or was killed. The mad feud goes on between people who have great courage, kindness, and courtesy. One is forced to admire them as people and feel impotent fury against the custom that is consuming them all. One's sense of impotence comes just from this fact that the people are good, for such people do not seem to evince enough evil to account for their terrible conduct.

Mark Twain's language takes the reader so compellingly into the middle of this folly that he has to believe in it. Huck's ignorant goodness makes him the ideal medium to experience and wonder at it — and by his bafflement to enlist the reader's indignation, for Huck does not have confidence in his moral intuitions to denounce the feud; and he does not have strength or opportunity to act against the generous people who have taken him into their home. His choices therefore are not choices but tensions of fear, doubt, and bewilderment. He loves Buck and idolizes the beautiful Sophia, whose elopement with Harney Shepherdson brings on the final series of killings, which include young Buck. As usual, Mark Twain moves in and out of Huck's story, sharing our tenderness for Huck and our indignation at what this incomprehensible vision of evil will do to his innocent heart.

* See Walter Blair's article, "When Was *Huckleberry Finn* Written?" *American Literature*, March 1958, pp. 1–25.

At the end of this episode Huck comes back to Jim, who has found and restored the raft. The action carries into a scene that powerfully continues and enriches the motif of river-against-land, which Mark Twain seems to have seized upon with renewed feeling when he came back to his manuscript. Having discovered the bodies of Buck and his cousin Joe and "covered up their faces" and "cried a little" for Buck who was "mighty good" to him, Huck finds the raft afloat in the dark — and Jim on it waiting. "I never felt easy till the raft was two miles below there and out in the middle of the Mississippi. Then we hung up our signal lantern, and judged that we was free and safe once more. I hadn't had a bite to eat since yesterday; so Jim he got out some corn-dodgers and buttermilk, and pork and cabbage, and greens — there ain't nothing in the world so good, when it's cooked right — and whilst I eat my supper we talked, and had a good time. I was powerful glad to get away from the feuds, and so was Jim to get away from the swamp. We said there warn't no home like a raft, after all. Other places do seem so cramped up and smothery, but a raft don't. You feel mighty free and easy and comfortable on a raft." (Chapter XVIII.)

Coming back to the river takes Mark Twain on into several more pages of sensuous, ecstatic realization. His fluid prose uses concrete detail to evoke the scene and its tone with uncanny perfection. Huck and Jim speculate on whether the stars were "laid" or just happened, and the stars remind Huck of sparks: "Once or twice of a night we would see a steamboat slipping along in the dark, and now and then she would belch a whole world of sparks up out of her chimbleys, and they would rain down in the river and look awful pretty; then she would turn a corner and her lights would wink out and her pow-wow shut off and leave the river still again; and by-and-by her waves would get to us, a long time after she was gone, and joggle the raft a bit, and after that you wouldn't hear nothing for you couldn't tell how long, except maybe frogs or something." (Chapter XIX.) Such passages make the river a gentle paradise for a new Adam.

But in this new peace there is hardly time to draw a great breath of the river air before the land comes to them again with its evil. This time it is that infamous pair, the Dauphin and the Duke, who compound evil by invading the sanctuary. They take over the raft, victimizing Huck who does not dare defy them lest they turn Jim over to the law. Huck enlists our sympathy through a repetition of the earlier moral dialogue in which he decided to protect Jim. He recounts the fraud and rascality of the usurpers without denouncing them earnestly enough. So the reader becomes indignant at Huck's moderation.

Put together, all these sets of incidents suggest that Huck as character is a function of the reader's empathic identification with his field of vision. As we proceed toward the contemporary novel, we shall witness a shrinking of the self, partly because the bundle of gestures and eccentricities that form a Dickens character are not regarded as exactly "normal" today. As I noted earlier, eccentricities that are neuroses have been classified and tabulated by psychology so that they have become universal menaces to the well-being of the harried modern self. Stripped, then, of its grotesque mannerisms, its identifying eccentricities, and its alien neuroses, the modern self moves toward what I call the naked eyeball that is a Hemingway character. It is a pure or abstract vision that stands in a focus of violence and looks out at the conduct in the world that terrifies or appalls it. The reader, as I have said, identifies himself with the naked eyeball and feels by empathy the being who lives behind the eyes. This identification — or empathy — is intuitive rather than based on concrete knowledge, but if it makes the reader stand directly at the lens of that naked eyeball it produces a powerful sense of a character. The compelling force of such identification is a prime reason for the impact of Hemingway on his readers. His simplest word moves like an act because it tells what is *happening* in the hero's field of vision. Here also is where Huck Finn gets his strength. His reader looks into his field of vision, experiences what he presumably feels, and adds the further irrational element of indignation to cement his identification with what he senses to be Huck Finn. Hemingway warmly acknowledged his debt to *Huckleberry Finn*, saying that "all modern American literature comes from one book by Mark Twain called *Huckleberry Finn*."

Can it be that Mark Twain's hero prefigures the modern man in search of a self? In the dual vision of Huck and Mark Twain, modern society is totally rejected; the trip down the river is, in one sense, a journey into the heart of darkness, for each contact with the land or invasion from it reveals a darker facet of man's depravity. So horrifying is the progression that some critics have been impelled to write feelingly of the growing tragic vision of Huck, although in fact he does not change a bit because we don't ever know him to the point where we could mark a definite change. We know his field of vision, mixed with Mark Twain's sardonic glare and the language of pastoral defamation. The picaresque action sustains the uncertainty and fragmentation of the moral agent that *might* form at the focus of serious choices in significant social situations. After the guilty rebellion against his conscience, which is certainly a sophistical tour de force, Huck is more acted upon than acting. He remains watching and careful. And having no significant plot, Mark Twain (after many delays) wound up his story with an ending that does great violence to what has gone before. The Tom Sawyer tomfoolery of freeing Jim from his cell takes the dignity away from both Jim and Huck. Jim is no longer the same man, and Huck has relapsed into comedy.

Mark Twain's problem was to devise an action that would use the meaning of the journey down the river. To do so he would have had to know what the meaning of the journey was, and here he seemed to be uncertain. Another way to formulate the problem is to consider that a significant plot would contain and develop its meaning as it worked itself out. Aristotle, to whom we cannot return too often, said that tragedy or happiness existed as actions rather than as states of being. Meaning too resides in the action which embodies it; if we can see clearly what happens we have the substance about which to think as well as the events that will constitute our experience. The meaning of *King Lear* is right there in the action: it consists of what happens, and there can be no mistaking the events of that overpowering play. Mark Twain, on the other hand, never did clearly know what was happening or what was going to happen. That is why he delayed writing the story so many times, and that is why he was so hard pressed for incident at the end.

I have said that the journey down the river is a journey into the heart of darkness, but other reasonable explanations of it have been proposed. Leo Marx has said that it is, in various perspectives, a boy's idyll, an epic sweep past the life of the Mississippi Valley, a joyous flood of pure laughter, and — most of all — a quest for freedom.* The last idea provides a thematic crisis when the raft floats by Cairo in a fog and presumably cuts off Jim's escape into free territory. Thereafter it gives motive and force to Huck's own thinking and to his movement

---

* Leo Marx, "Mr. Eliot, Mr. Trilling, and *Huckleberry Finn*," *American Scholar*, Autumn 1953, pp. 423–40.

between the raft and the land. He remarks that one feels "free" on a raft. It is twisted and outraged when the Dauphin and Duke invade the sanctuary of the raft and, later, treacherously sell Jim again. A further climax of the theme appears when Huck finally says, "All right, I'll *go* to hell," and commits himself to helping Jim escape under Tom Sawyer's romantic leadership. Jim has fled from the tyranny of slavery, Huck from the tyranny of respectability, and both specifically from the pious hypocritical greed of Miss Watson. But an idyllic, dreamy, wistful, passive floating downstream on a raft is not, finally, a purposeful quest for freedom. What it has in romantic escapist appeal it lacks in energy and purpose. Huck and Jim don't much care where they are going, so long as the raft is floating free; and this essential lack of direction is powerfully demonstrated by the way Mark Twain and Tom Sawyer have to take over and manage the action once the heroes have left their passively floating Eden of innocence.

As long as we can keep Huck and Jim as our eyeballs the journey is, if not a quest for freedom, at least a romantic dream of escape; but when Mark Twain intrudes, the journey is a sickening penetration into the heart of social evil, which reaches a climax in the long tirade of Colonel Sherburn, in whose acrid denunciation of mass man the vision of Huck has quite disappeared and the jaundiced eye of Mark Twain has taken its place. Mark Twain was in fact so totally disgusted with society (because of his own secret identification with its gilded stupidity) that he could not contrive a plot that moved seriously through its central values, manners, and beliefs. He could not look at it without throwing up his hands and uttering a scream of furious repudiation. He simply could not seriously accept the problems and the accompanying conduct of typical adults. Mockery, scorn, denunciation, ridicule, and hate poured forth when he addressed himself directly to the consideration of the society of his time. Thus he could not devise a serious plot, and by the same token he could not develop serious mature characters with what we might call sophisticated problems. The aimless floating of the raft is therefore a perfect vehicle for Twain's charming but aimless vacillations among romantic primitivism, tender nostalgia, withering fury, and magnificent relish of frontier eccentricity and excess. His magic ear for language makes every line a delight, but his vision of man and fate makes substantial characterization impossible.

In the course of a few pages there are many Hucks, negotiating among the author's comic poses; from one chapter to the next Jim turns from a beloved figure of Adamic purity to a minstrel comic. These observations may give us new insight into a condition described by one of the great critics of the novel, E. M. Forster. "In the losing battle that the plot fights with the characters," he wrote, "it often takes a cowardly revenge. Nearly all novels are feeble at the end. This is because the plot requires to be wound up. Why is this necessary? Why is there not a convention which allows a novelist to stop as soon as he feels muddled or bored? Alas, he has to round things off, and usually the characters go dead while he is at work, and our final impression of them is thorough deadness."*

These are the words, I suspect, not of the critic but of a tired novelist whose subtle insights into the ways of the mind were frustrated by his inability to devise actions that would grandly body forth those insights. The trouble with *Huckleberry Finn* is not that the plot fights a losing battle with the characters but that there is no firm theme to be *realized* in the plot; hence the action must turn into melodrama and the characters, having no firm beginnings, do not develop in great problems and decisions but recede into deeper obscurity as the melodramatic conclusion takes over. Henry James had a very complex version of exactly the same problem, as we shall see. He explored his characters at times with such relish and sophistication that he identified more capacities for action than could possibly be expressed; not being able to commit himself to meaningful development through significant crisis and decision, he too sometimes wound up with melodrama, sometimes with obscurity.

* E. M. Forster, *Aspects of the Novel* (New York: Harcourt, Brace, 1927; quotation from 1954 edition), p. 95.

9   A Sargasso of the Sinister

SOME three decades a-borning, Katherine Anne Porter's long novel, *Ship of Fools* (1962) was awaited devotedly by the admirers of her subtle symbolism and polished sentences. What would this great short-story writer do with the full scope and sweep of a novel?

Ship of Fools is a new journey into the heart of darkness, as the author explicitly states in a preliminary note. ". . . this simple almost universal image of the ship of this world on its voyage to eternity . . . suits my purpose exactly. I am a passenger on that ship." We can assume that the passengers on the ship will be selected and organized to embody some significant classification of twentieth-century man, and that the voyage itself will carry a theme and somehow penetrate deeper and deeper into an idea.

The book starts brilliantly. In Veracruz, Mexico, a collection of travelers embarks on the German steamer *Vera* bound for Bremer-haven. The sailing day is August 22, 1931. The cast includes types and nationalities almost too numerous to summarize, and in fact the reader will be halfway through the book before he has got the cast sorted out. Germans, Swiss, Spanish, Cubans, Mexicans, Jews, Swedes, four Americans, and a steerageful of 876 poor Spanish souls, workers in the sugar fields, being deported from Cuba because of the failure of the sugar market, are introduced in little groups that represent their connections before the voyage started or just as it began. About forty characters are introduced in this manner before — and as — they begin to interact and develop larger patterns of relation, intrigue, and conflict.

The tone is established in the first pages by the description of Veracruz, "cynical by nature, shameless by experience, hardened to showing its seamiest side to strangers," and of a beggar, "shambling and crawling, the stumps of his four limbs bound in leather and twine. He had been in early life so intricately maimed and deformed by a master of the art, in preparation for his calling, he had little resemblance to any human being. Dumb, half blind, he approached with nose almost to sidewalk as if he followed the trail of a smell, stopping now and then to rest, wagging his hideous shock head from side to side slowly in unbearable suffering." (Page 4.) This is what man has purposefully done to man, an index of what is to come, and the following dense, detail-packed pages carry out the intention: "So the travelers fretted, meeting up with each other again and again in all the uncomfortable places where they were all fated to be, sharing the same miseries: almost unbearable heat, a stony white rage of vengeful sunlight; vile food, vile beyond belief, slapped down before their sunken faces by insolent waiters. All of them at least once had pushed back a plate of some greasy substance with a fly or a cockroach in it, and had paid for it without complaint and tipped the waiter besides because the very smell of violence was in the air, at once crazed and stupefied. . . . All had taken to a diet of black coffee, lukewarm beer, bottled synthetic lemonade, damp salted biscuits in tin boxes, coconut milk drunk directly from the shell. . . . The steady trivial drain upon their purses and spirits went on like a nightmare, with no visible advance in their pressing affairs. Women gave way to fits of weeping, men to fits of temper, which got them nowhere; and they all had reddened eyelids and badly swollen feet." (Page 11.)

The qualities of tone that sustain the whole book emerge more clearly in the sardonic hostility of the treatment of two Germans, Lizzi Spöckenkieker and Siegfried Rieber: " 'Ah, you men,' she screamed joyously, 'you are all alike!' She leaned over and whacked him three times on the skull with a folded paper fan. Herr Rieber was all ready for a good frolic. How he admired and followed the tall thin girls with long scissor-legs like storks striding under their fluttering skirts, with long narrow feet on the ends of them. He tapped her gently on the back of her hand with his forefinger, invitingly and with such insinuation she whacked him harder and faster, her teeth gleaming with pleasure, until the top of his head went florid." (Page 23.) Her laugh is later described as "a long cascade of falling tinware." (Page 287.)

In similar vein appear David Scott and Jenny Brown, American painters living together, grimly, viciously destroying each other as they fight their way from scene to scene; William Denny, a rich, contemptuous, lecherous Texan, a flower of Southern bigotry; Herr Glocken, a repulsive German hunchback whose mixture of arrogance and servility epitomize one aspect of the nation; Frau Baumgartner, keeping her son in a leather suit in the stifling heat, is another aspect; Frau Rittersdorf, who writes in her journal about the "all-guiding Will of my race," and Frau and Professor Hutten, who devote themselves to a puking bulldog, are others. They brood over their shabby lives, bully their children, and slide into grudging relations with the other passengers. The gamut takes us from the lice and maggots of the rotting German soul down to pure concentrated polished evil in the shape of a troupe of Spanish zarzuela dancers — four bitches and their pimps who prey upon the other passengers like vultures tearing carrion away from jackals. Part I, of sixty-eight pages, displays most of the characters and lets four or five of them reveal the first layer of their dismal selves.

Part II continues the undertaking, starting with a morning of deviltry by the six-year-old twins of one of the Spanish dancers, Ric and Rac, and proceeding to introduce new people and let others reveal themselves in a second and third vignette. There are scenes exploring the drunken Baumgartner; David's Quaker parentage; Dr. Schumann's precarious heart; La Condesa, who is beautiful, damned, crazy, and being deported from Cuba; the handsome German, Freytag, beginning to discover to himself his intention to cast off his Jewish wife. As he remarks of ship life, "people on voyage mostly went on behaving as if they were on dry land, and there is simply not room for it on a ship. Every smallest act shows up more clearly and looks worse, because it has lost its background. The train of events leading up to and explaining it is not there; you can't refer it back and set it in its proper size and place." (Page 132.)

Miss Porter is obviously setting out to supply the train of events leading up to and explaining the present characters. She simplifies the task by giving in detail the thoughts of perhaps a dozen of her people, who become by this means somewhat more humanized, whereas those who are seen only from the outside are more strange, freakish, and alien. But if the zarzuela dancers, for example, are presented as if they were too wicked and frightening to be internally knowable, the characters whose thoughts are revealed in detail do not seem any better as a result. It is not exactly true that on ship, "Every smallest act shows up more clearly and looks worse, because it has lost its background," because when we know more and more about Jenny and David, or Freytag, we find them *worse* than they appeared superficially. While one set of characters thinks nakedly for the reader, a strange person like La Condesa develops mystery. She has attracted a band of six Cuban medical students who are going to France. These wild lads make a cult of the Condesa, but whether she delights them with her obscenities or interests them because she is crazy remains a mystery. A certain nobility grows up about her, via this mystery — and indeed she gathers grandeur because she remains unknown! Literary technique, of which point of view is a prime example, is generally considered to impose its discipline on the artist and by this discipline to become the instrument of discovery. Just as the limiting lines on the tennis court make all the skills of the game possible, so the techniques of the poet or novelist constitute the forms within which expression is made possible. The form, in short, is not only the medium of expression but the substance of it. Viewed in these serious perspectives, Miss Porter's trifling with point of view seems whimsical, if not frivolous.

Once the characters are known, endless pages are filled as they speculate petulantly or vainly or fearfully or lecherously about each other. It is a veritable flood of gossip in the spirit of a concierge. When the Germans gossip about the enormity of having — if indeed they are having — a Jew at the captain's table with them, their disgusting arrogance is balanced by equal arrogance from the Jew on board, Herr Löwenthal. Presently a minor storm breaks as the Germans discover that Freytag though not Jewish has a Jewish wife and banish him to Löwenthal's table. These people have such miserable, stupid, vapid souls that to explore them is degrading. One rotten apple from the stinking barrel is more than enough. But we have to eat one after another. The stinking barrel, to be sure, is an image of a larger one. It is the fat German soul that Miss Porter hates — hates with such passion that she never tires of scraping and flaying away at it. Her pen is an instrument of vengeance. The Germans at the captain's table turn presently from their fatuous Jew-hating nationalism to intricate, vicious bickering among themselves, becoming if possible more petty and despicable with each exchange. They fawn upon the captain and stick little barbs into each other. Rieber and Lizzi Spöckenkieker appear in scene after scene, flirting, pawing, wrestling vainly on the deck behind a funnel, shrieking with artful lechery but never getting into bed together. When it suits her purpose, to make them more contemptible, Miss Porter reveals their thoughts; when she wants to expose them as caricatures, limned with bold strokes of her glittering prose, she stays outside their minds and makes them dance like lewd puppets.

We learn a good deal more about Jenny, who has let herself become involved with an utterly destructive man. David has set himself to destroy her confidence in her painting and so in herself. She is superior one moment, with a fine zest for life and exquisite taste, but she is also totally lost and despairing. One does not know what is the matter, really, for the author's tone seems too cruelly sharp for her to be saying that life is always tragic for the brave. This statement must be made with compassion, and there is no compassion in *Ship of Fools*. Jenny's floods of tenderness for David are never pure; if she can soften his resentment she will turn on him while he is soft and cut him to the bone. At one moment she tells herself that he is a bad fellow, a profound mistake in her life; and at the next she throws herself upon him in a rapture of contrition. The many conversations between Jenny and David have no *issue* except the question of whether they will go to France or to Spain, and it is quite plain that even this is not an issue but a vehicle for their quarreling. So their conversations are repetitious and circular, exposing frustration, hostility, and discontent in ways that vary only as the steps in a dance vary from one moment to the next. The quality of their dance of mutual exacerbation is revealed in the first passage or two, and thereafter it merely weaves more of itself, over and over. It is not edifying because it does not develop, and it is anything but pleasant or beautiful as an object of aesthetic contemplation. At the end of the voyage, whether they part or whether they go together to France or Spain does not make an iota of difference to the "meaning" of the book.

Another couple, Professor Hutten and his frau, play a variation on the theme of Jenny and David. The professor is the ultimate bore.

When he can trap an audience, he lectures, and what he says is so flimsy, so theoretical, so totally apart from experience and reality that it seems the ultimate in fatuity. We are taken into Frau Hutten's mind while the professor lectures, at the captain's table. She tells herself that he is a saint. She recalls that she has always saved him "for the higher things of life . . . No one had ever seen the professor carry even the smallest parcel in his hand — not even a book to and from the school. . . . She had done it with pride and love . . ." (Page 291.) And more, she had disciplined his rebellious students, wearing them down into "eager submission." But now her thoughts take us on into the depths, as we discover the cost of her pride in being the perfect German wife: "He even, and this was so sweet the tears almost came to her eyes, seemed honestly to believe they had never had a quarrel. She encouraged him in this. If he had forgotten their first five years, well and good, let him. For herself, she could never forget, for the many lessons taught her then had gone into her blood and bones, and changed her almost beyond her own recognition. By now she remembered these hard lessons dimly and without that secret fury against her bridegroom which even at its hottest she had known for what it was — treachery to her marriage vow" (page 292) of perfect subjection. Thus has she sustained his saintly confidence in the goodness of man, suppressing her knowledge of evil gained by her daily experience and observation of it — and making herself the pattern of total identification with his smallest thought or whim.

Then suddenly, at the captain's table, when there is a pause in his lecture about the goodness of man and the benevolence of God, she blurts out her smothered convictions: " 'I do know well there are many evil people in this world, many more evil than good ones . . . we encourage these monsters by being charitable to them, by making excuses for them, or just by being slack . . . And we do not punish them as they deserve, because we have lost our sense of justice, and we say, "If we put a thief in jail, or a murderer to death, we are as criminal as they!" Oh what injustice to innocent people and what sentimental dishonesty and we should be ashamed of it. Or we go on blindly saying, "If we behave well to them, they will end by behaving well to us!" That is one of the great lies of life. I have found that this makes them bolder, because they despise us instead of fearing us as they should — and it is all our own weakness, and yes, we do evil in letting them do evil without punishment. They think we are cowards and they are right. At least we are dupes and we deserve what we get from them. . . .' " (Pages 294–95.)

Coming unprepared and unexpected, leading nowhere and making no change in any human life, this speech seems nevertheless to express the author's last word on the human condition. This is what she believes about the ship of fools, upon which she acknowledges herself a passenger. This is the situation. People are either evil or spineless. The hardy evil prey upon the spineless mass, who by their weakness and tolerance and compliance contribute to the power and scope of evil. The generalization applies to virtually every character in the book. Frau Hutten ends her speech by trailing off in the middle of a sentence; in her thoughts she agonizes over her guilt in having uttered an idea contrary to her husband's: "Now, I have ruined his life . . . She had offended . . . against her husband's main conviction on which everything else in their marriage was based soundly: that a wife's first duty was to be in complete agreement with her husband at all times . . . more especially, the faintest shade of public dissent was a most disloyal act." (Page 295.)

In the following scene he turns upon her, his saintly pose dissolving into vicious tyranny; but their cabin door is open, Bébé the bulldog is gone, and the quarrel must wait as they hurry off to seek him. From this point the frail theme — if it is the theme — of evil abetted by spineless indifference presides over a slight thickening and cohesion of events that have till now been without direction or unity. Concha tries to seduce Johann into murdering his dying uncle. The twins throw Bébé the bulldog into the sea; he is rescued by one of the poor wretches in the steerage, who drowns while saving him; and the Huttens discover their love again in obscene copulation while Bébé pukes salt water on the cabin floor.

A few pages later the professor is lecturing about the prevalence of evil, completely reversing himself and echoing his wife's disturbing little speech. This detail illustrates the quicksilver verbal changes that prevent any character from defining himself so that one can take him seriously or even believe in him.

The evil twins snatch the Condesa's pearls and throw them overboard, for which they are savagely beaten by their parents, who had planned to steal the same pearls. The zarzuela company are persecuting the passengers who refuse to buy tickets to a lottery, by pinning impertinent notices about them to the bulletin board, and nobody dares react to this effrontery. Part II ends on page 360. With tempers frayed, evil flagrantly parading itself, and only a bit more than a hundred pages remaining, we expect the action to take hold and translate these elaborated elements into a meaning. But nothing different happens. The mass of characters flows on past like a muddy stream going into the ocean, coloring it for a distance, and fading out. The big party looms as a *Walpurgisnacht* that will witness a worthy climax. What happens is an evening of nasty, sordid, drunken violence. Denny, the despicable Texan, is too drunk to punish the Spanish bitch who has been teasing and taking his money all voyage; he gets his face beaten bloody with the sharp heel of Mrs. Treadwell's slipper, though why that calm woman should act so is a puzzle. Lizzi Spöckenkieker is screaming drunk. The big Swede, Hansen, breaks a bottle over Rieber's head. The boy Johann finally goes ecstatically to bed with Concha, another Spanish bitch, in a ghastly parody of fulfillment that the author seems to find romantic. Jenny is about to be seduced by Freytag but passes out cold — and so on. It is a night of small eruptions — rather of bursting pimples on souls that heal over without marks. Afterwards, the people gather themselves together and disembark, at various ports, pretty much the same as they embarked at Veracruz.

The Condesa provides a good case study of the relation of character to action. She is fifty, still beautiful, elegant, and yet, if we are to judge from her libidinous gestures and the shocked expressions of young sailors when she backs them into corners and talks to them, thoroughly depraved. (But we never learn what she says.) She also sniffs ether and confesses to Dr. Schumann that she began her sexual adventures at the age of four or five. It is hinted that she is entertaining the Cuban medical students, singly and in pairs, in her cabin, and they certainly think she is crazy. Yet she says she has fallen in love with Dr. Schumann, and in her several conversations with him makes what seem to be the wisest if the most disillusioned comments that anybody makes in the course of the novel. At one point "her eyes were wild and inhuman as a monkey's"; at another she "gave him a melting glance of confidence." (Pages 203, 205.) Before she leaves ship at the Canary Islands the good doctor has — we are told — fallen desperately, carnally in love with her, corrupting his pious soul, shaking his precarious heart, and sullying the image of his devoted wife. The emotion is not believable because it takes a great deal more to make probable a good, pious doctor's falling in love with a depraved and crazy addict. It seems contrived out of an animus toward all men, even toward mankind. The outlook is so cold, so cruel, so cynical that one comes out of it into the sunshine as from a nightmare, chilled to the bone. There is no point in the book where the reader identifies with a character, which is to say that at no point does a character face a choice that the reader can take seriously enough to care about. The writer has stepped out of life and now looks at it with the hostile rancor of one who hates the people who are still a part of the living world.

The author's malice is plain enough, but what of the Condesa? She too remains a mystery because she does not *do* anything; she is not involved in any significant action related to any serious social or moral issue. It is grotesque and inconceivable that the doctor should fall in love with her, the while he pumps her full of drugs against his better judgment. More grotesque is his sudden insight, after he has seen her put ashore almost penniless at Tenerife, that he had been guilty of "criminal sentimental cruelty" in tormenting her with his guilty love and yet refusing "her — and himself — any human joy in it." (Page 373.) This inspiration lasts while he writes her a letter, and then "his perverse infatuation began to fade, and with it his distrust and hatred of his love — it had been only a long daydream." (Page 374.) Such wild jumps from black to white cheat any act of its possible meaning, making it only a momentary figment of the writer's irresponsible whim. It is the sort of eccentric invention that we expect in a short story, not the large significant outcome that justifies a long novel. It almost sounds — as described here — as if the author were satirizing the rotten German soul of the doctor, but no — he is the character for whom she has the most respect.

The zarzuela company goes ashore at Tenerife and robs one little shop after another, while the other passengers watch but do nothing — and the theme of evil and spinelessness recoils upon them when they are cheated of the money they have all allowed themselves to be cajoled or bullied into spending on the lottery tickets. This theme of evil abetted by the spineless mass of mankind takes on allegorical trimmings, simply by repetition, because it is always the Germans who pompously rationalize their failure to do anything about the crimes they witness. Shades of Dachau! The Lutzes, who saw the twins throw the Condesa's pearls overboard, later try to qualify and back away from the simple facts, proud of their ability to stay legally apart. Others who have watched the Spaniards robbing the shops later buy more lottery tickets hoping to win a share of the loot. The Huttens quickly forget even the name of the poor soul who was drowned while saving their fat bulldog. Whenever the Germans talk they build walls of words between themselves and reality — and between themselves and the reader, for they become so grotesque in their fatuity that no one can take them seriously, let alone identify with them. They are not capable of becoming involved in an issue that could lead them to a change in their lives. The moral apathy of the Germans was apparent in their first scenes. Four hundred pages later they are the same unpeople, expressed by their static wallowing in grotesque vanity, pompous discourse, and sick cruelty. A nation may be indicted, but there is no plot — as if the author, having herself stepped out of life, were determined to give no one of her own creations a chance to live.

It is tempting to dwell a moment longer on this special relation between character and action. To identify with a character, one has to identify with his problems, which is to say with his choices. Thus one can identify with the hero of the simplest western melodrama if he is faced with a crucial decision. In order to represent such a problem, the author has to see the world, alive, from the eyes of his character and face the implications of the situation and the choice that is possible. As we shall see when we examine more closely the naked eyeball of a Hemingway character, it is possible to identify and sense a character when nothing is provided by the author except a point of view from which danger and violence are seen. In that position, the reader empathizes the character whose field of vision he is sharing. If, on the other hand, the writer does not believe in his characters, that is, cannot identify with them, he will not be able (or will not want) to put them in situations where they are faced with significant decisions. Unless he believes in his characters he cannot believe in their problems. This seems to be exactly Miss Porter's problem with *Ship of Fools*: she does not value any of her characters; she does not take them seriously; she does not see them as having significant problems that might be resolved by significant choices. They are, instead, a collection of grotesques whom she impales on the point of her pen and holds up to ridicule. She does not grant them any free life, any power to make a vital decision and so affect their destinies. They are held up naked and wriggling while she strips their petty souls bare. This gives her occasions for scintillating prose, but it prevents the characters from defining themselves in a serious plot.

The closing pages of the story do not resolve anything; they merely relax and dissipate the mild tensions that have existed. Nothing is resolved because no issues existed as vital problems. There were no avenues open to any of the characters, who were all locked in a prison of isolated, ridiculous self.

In the journey pattern, the form has been dictated by the theme rather than by character or action; instead of a problem made of and in a social context, the author has a more abstract or universal problem, such as the nature of evil, which dictates a form of movement through space as an analogue to exploration of the idea. With this form, the development of character must be somewhat confused or neglected, although other values may emerge of the highest order. Miss Porter's journey, however, does not take us into an idea, for she has no idea of importance; and since she has no plot she does not have characters whose problems make them live. Her ship is only a platform upon which a crowd of puppets are paraded.*

* After completing this chapter I was gratified to see the same assessment of Miss Porter's work — and particularly of this novel — made more fully and more severely in William L. Nance's *Katherine Anne Porter and the Art of Rejection* (Chapel Hill: University of North Carolina Press, 1964). Mr. Nance finds a pattern of rejection everywhere in her writings, expressed in critical withdrawal by the intellectual characters and destructive attachments by the less gifted or fortunate. He notices that "She is not capable of leaving her characters free to act and to change. Her scorn for the majority of them, usually tiresome, occasionally takes the form of skillful parody," and "One characteristic of the rejection pattern which was sometimes partially concealed in the short fiction but appears with painful clarity in *Ship of Fools* is its utter lovelessness." (Pp. 164, 166.)

PART IV

The Great
Transition

WHAT I am trying to indicate by the somewhat portentous title of
this part is that here we shall observe the primacy of the action reduced
and diluted by ideas. The journey patterns of the previous part were
obviously chosen because the author elected to use an expository rather
than a strictly dramatic form. He knew that he was embodying an
idea, and his form was the shape of his idea translated into a movement that represented it.

The novels discussed in this part have rich, full, and even elaborate
plots. But at the same time they have so powerful an element of idea
that it prevents the plot from prevailing. To put it simply, the meaning is not contained in the action. The author is doing things independently of the story he tells. He is manipulating themes and ideas in
and around it. This does not make for a specific new kind of novel but
rather for a widening stream of variations — all of which affect characterization. They affect the concept of man, the process of characteriza-

tion, and the result. It is impossible to keep abreast of this great flow. To try to account for it all would be to reach generalizations that might not be adequately shored up with specific referents. I have therefore chosen to go in detail into a very few interesting samples in order to suggest the kinds of variations that close scrutiny discovers.

Thomas Hardy has been accused of managing coincidences, in defiance of probability, to indict the gods for wanton torture of man. Study of the action in *The Return of the Native* shows that the characters are fully discovered and expressed through their own choices — and that the troubles they bring upon themselves are so entirely probable that their author had to devise coincidences in order to make them seem more tragic and less self-destructive. Henry James always generates more ideas than he can dramatize, and his novels come out as contests between what the action can show and what James brings in through speculation and discussion. He generally cannot let his characters be fully accounted for by his action, and sometimes he finds it necessary to obscure events while he and his characters speculate ambiguously about the meaning of what they have, somewhat elusively, done. The gestures of aristocracy, as explored by Calder Willingham and Nancy Mitford, reveal characters who pose and perform one sort of self but are thrown into modern worlds where their problems cannot be handled within the traditional patterns of gentle conduct. The results can be amusing, tragic, or horrifying. In this part, then, I examine novels where the story does not exclusively generate the characters, because, to repeat, the author is doing things independently of the story he tells.

10   *Character and Coincidence*

IN THE opening pages of *The Return of the Native* (1878), Thomas Hardy elaborates a theme with a series of symbolic images which he modulates so that, by the time he has got to the end of his first chapter, the theme has been considerably enriched and qualified. At first the bright sky and the dark heath seem to be bold images of two sharply distinguished principles: ". . . their meeting line at the horizon was clearly marked. . . . the heath wore the appearance of an instalment of night which had taken up its place before its astronomical hour was come . . . while day stood distinct in the sky. . . . The distant rims of the world and of the firmament [at the horizon] seemed to be a division in time no less than a division in matter." (Book I, Chapter 1.)

The bright sky and the dark heath seem to be two aspects of life — aspiration contrasted with ability, freedom or will against fate, or intelligence against the dark compulsions of instinct. The glowing sky stands for the potential, the hope, the release; the dark heath for the forces of character and fate that oppress and defeat them. Thus the first statement; but Hardy presently introduces a suggestion of dark power and *life* in the heath which reach up in concord and sympathy toward the darkening sky: "And so the obscurity in the air and the obscurity in the land closed together in a black fraternization towards which each advanced half-way." Here are mystery and conspiracy in the unfolding of which the lucid candors of the sky have been endowed with a demonic intent. The sharp line of the horizon, between aspiration and defeat, has vanished. And with such words as "prison," "dignity," and "sublimity" Hardy goes on to suggest that the nighttime

of the heath is indeed the most fitting symbol of the condition of man,
". . . a place perfectly accordant with man's nature — neither ghastly,
hateful, nor ugly . . . but, like man, slighted and enduring; and withal singularly colossal and mysterious in its swarthy monotony." It is
beautiful, because "Men have oftener suffered from the mockery of a
place too smiling for their reason than from the oppression of surroundings oversadly tinged." (I, 1.)

At this point the duality or balance between good and evil has been
veiled by "the obscurity in the land," which represents man and rises
up to fuse with the growing darkness of the sky. This symbolic setting
in preparation for the action suggests a union of human and fatal
darknesses that should guide us in understanding the relation between
character and coincidence in the story.*

As soon as these patterns of light and dark have been established, a
further change is wrought upon them. The natives appear with their
burdens of furze and light a huge bonfire on top of the Rainbarrow,
against the skyline. A dozen other fires are in sight, at various places
on the heath, each with its particular color and shape. Thus when the
light of the bright sky, which I have identified with reason, freedom,
and hope, fades, it is replaced by a darker light from human hands.
The darker light has the wild character that the author has already
attributed to the heath, and it is tempting to see in it a further symbol
of the groping dark purposes by which humanity makes its way toward
its puzzling ends. They might be the purposes declared by the passions, which certainly make constant use of the intelligence although
they use it to irrational and frequently destructive ends. Eustacia Vye,
first seen silhouetted against the darkening sky, then by her fire, described as "Queen of Night," with hair that "closed over her forehead
like nightfall extinguishing the western glow" (I, 7), is literally and
figuratively associated with darkness. It is tempting to notice the similarities between these dark fires and the fire of the tryworks in *Moby-*

* This novel has the *densest* plot texture I know. It absolutely teems with incident, and every detail contributes to the total action. Thus it would take many
tedious pages to tell the story — that is, to retell the story — in full, and I have
chosen instead to talk about it in a way that is different from my approach to the
other novels under discussion. The fact that every incident, almost, in the book involves physical activity like meetings and walking from place to place — and mum-
ming, dancing, fire-building, and dice-casting, to name only a few — contributes a
sense of external forces working on the characters, which in turn enriches the
apparent power of coincidence.

Dick, of which Ishmael exclaims, "Look not too long in the face of the fire, O man! . . . believe not the artificial fire, when its redness makes all things look ghastly" — but presently reverses himself to acknowledge a "wisdom that is woe." (Chapter XCVI.)

Further attention to human passion — perhaps a suggestion of its isolating, euphoric effect — appears in the strange, illuminated elevation of the natives with their bonfire on the top of the dusky barrow: "It seemed as if the bonfire-makers were standing in some radiant upper storey of the world, detached from and independent of the dark stretches below. The heath down there was now a vast abyss, and no longer a continuation of what they stood on; for their eyes, adapted to the blaze, could see nothing of the deeps beyond its influence." (I, 3.) Is it reading too much into this passage to see an extension of the light and dark imagery to express the illusions by which men temporarily blind themselves to sterner realities — whether the childish exuberance of the natives or the flame of passion lighted and fed by Eustacia?

In the following scene on the barrow, the points of interest are indicated by lights — Eustacia's fire above and the tiny light in the window of the Quiet Woman Inn below — and by the sudden frightening appearance of the reddleman asking the way to Mrs. Yeobright's house. Flames, human flames, in the gathering dusk.

A final passage in Chapter 1 dwells on the permanence of Egdon Heath. It is more stable than the sea; it is unchanged since Roman, since prehistoric times, since the last geological change, abiding with a steadfastness that is equated with its permanence as a symbol of the nature and condition of man. Now, with these dark symbolic intentions so firmly established in the opening pages, we are led to wonder anew about the status of coincidence in Hardy's cosmos. Is he indeed going to present a tale in which the bright and reasonable visions of men are thwarted by the incompetent, frivolous, or diabolical god described in his poem?

> "Has some Vast Imbecility
> Mighty to build and blend
> But Impotent to tend
> Framed us in jest and left us now to hazardry?

> "Or come we of an Automaton
> Unconscious of our pains? . . .
> Or are we live remains

Of Godhead dying downward, brain and eye now gone?"
["Nature's Questioning"]

These possibilities are suggested by the popular opinion of Hardy, but they are not indicated by the symbolism which appears to be so carefully developed in these opening pages of the novel. It would seem that it is time to take a fresh look at the role of coincidence in *The Return of the Native*. Accident will move an action that depends upon malign cosmic powers or upon pure nothing. In either event the characters will not control their fates and will therefore shrink as characters.

The first coincidence is the fact that the marriage license procured by Damon Wildeve for himself and Thomasin Yeobright was made out for Budmouth instead of for Anglebury. This error causes Thomasin to flee in shame both from the town and from Wildeve (and we recall that she has cause for anxiety in the fact that her aunt had already forbidden the banns, inflicting a mortal insult on Wildeve). She meets Diggory Venn; the event is also the occasion for Wildeve's returning to Eustacia when she lights her signal fire that evening. Very much depends upon this accident. Yet it is not really an accident; it is the purest example of that expression of an unconscious motive that we now call a Freudian error — and at least two characters recognize it as such: " 'Such things don't happen for nothing,' " said the aunt. " 'It is a great slight to me and my family.' " (I, 5.) Diggory Venn has the same reaction: "After what had happened it was impossible that he should not doubt the honesty of Wildeve's intentions" toward Thomasin. (I, 9.) Eustacia goes even further, trying to make Wildeve admit that he intentionally delayed the marriage because of his passion for her. Wildeve's attachment to Eustacia and his desire for revenge on Mrs. Yeobright are abundant motivation for his "mistake," and the skillful manner in which he exploits both interpretations of his conduct is further evidence that such use was not entirely unforeseen by him. Although he later rather neutralizes these insights into his subconscious motivation by telling Eustacia plainly that the error with the marriage license was an accident, he does not radically alter the reader's impression of him. Mrs. Yeobright's contribution to the "coincidence," likewise, is a substantial expression of her pride, her inflexibility, and her determination to keep Thomasin from Wildeve. She inflicted the original insult; she now carries Thomasin away from the

Quiet Woman by the back window while Wildeve is serving mead to the singing natives in the front room.

The character of Eustacia Vye is something of a puzzle because we expect Victorian reticence in a Victorian novel — and Hardy is so unreticent that many readers are unable to believe what is written on the page. Eustacia is not presented in the very act of love, but she is described in quite unequivocal terms as a sophisticated, promiscuous sensualist who is willing to take almost any risk to attain new intensities of passion. Yet she is also beautiful, dignified, intelligent, and noble. Vulgarity, Hardy writes, would be impossible for her. "It would have been as easy for the heath-ponies, bats, and snakes to be vulgar as for her." (I, 7.) Her dignity and taste are partly natural, partly absorbed by her from the austerity of the heath country, where the remembered glitter of Budmouth is transformed by her romantic imagination into a fairyland instead of transforming her into something tawdry, as it might have done if she had stayed on there.

Her dignity survives her liaison with Wildeve — and even the ignobility of being jilted by him. She can still be imperious in saying, " 'you may tempt me, but I won't give myself to you any more' " and thus rekindle his desire. When she has spurned his caress and sent him away, "Eustacia sighed; it was no fragile maiden sigh, but a sigh which shook her like a shiver." (I, 6.) Physical desire impels her: "she seemed to long for the abstraction called passionate love more than for any particular lover." Her sense of the flight of passion "tended to breed actions of reckless unconventionality, framed to snatch a year's, a week's, even an hour's passion from anywhere while it could be won. . . . Her loneliness deepened her desire." (I, 7.)

Eustacia is innocent and pagan in her sensuality. Hardy seems to attach no moral stigma whatsoever to the simple fact of her eager quest for sexual sensation. We are led to pity her isolation, admire her intelligence and spirit, deprecate her fierce pride, and perhaps contemn her snobbish sense of class (although we cannot be sure that an Englishman would completely agree on this last point). If she is to become implicated in a tragic web, it will be through no simple moral retribution for her physical sins — but perhaps because her life has confused her endowments into a strange mixture of innocence and sophistication: "As far as social ethics were concerned Eustacia approached the savage state, though in emotion she was all the while an epicure. She had advanced to the secret recesses of sensuousness, yet had hardly crossed the threshold of conventionality." (I, 7.)

The qualities noted above have been established through conduct — a word that may be taken here to designate purposeful, committed actions that *cost* something and presumably have consequences. Wildeve has defied Mrs. Yeobright, he has proposed to Thomasin, he has made his fateful error with the marriage license, and he has been deeply involved with Eustacia. She in turn has taken Wildeve, rejected him, and then on this critical evening lighted her passionate little fire to draw him back again. The plot that is launched by these early actions does not seem to express a deterministic view of causation. Here are not people swayed by chemistry or social forces but by their own strong natures. They think, choose, and act. The wild setting that surrounds the Victorian proprieties suggests these personal elements that brood or explode around them. The plot moves among circumstance, ignorance, folly, and the characters' powerful dispositions of mind and temperament in a tragic pattern — to which pity and terror rather than blind indignation against fatal coincidence are the proper aesthetic reactions. If the indignation nevertheless appears, is it perhaps because modern man expects more in the way of justice and order from life than the Greeks did? We must return to this question.

Eustacia is offered by Diggory Venn the opportunity to escape to Budmouth, with employment that would not demean her. This she instantly rejects; and with this rejection — carefully placed before the return of the native, Clym Yeobright — she has freely chosen to stay in the lonely country that she detests.

"Accidents" continue to thicken the plot: Mrs. Yeobright in attempting to fan the dying embers of Wildeve's passion for Thomasin sends him straight back to Eustacia. Yet there is more than accident; there is complex irony in the sequence that shows Mrs. Yeobright pridefully rejecting Diggory Venn's renewed suit for Thomasin's hand, thanking "God for the weapon which the reddleman had put into her hands," straightway lying to Wildeve to make him fear that Thomasin will accept Diggory Venn — in order to provoke his jealousy — and withal turning the subsequent events in a direction utterly counter to her intentions: "By far the greatest effect of her simple strategy on that day was, as often happens, in a quarter quite outside her view when arranging it. In the first place, her visit sent Wildeve the same evening after dark to Eustacia's house at Mistover." (I, 11.) This is not the piti-less meddling of a cruel Fate in human affairs, but the quite probable outcome of human pride, mixed with folly and ignorance, attempting after the most superficial analysis to control a complicated pattern of people, situations, and motives. The inadequacy of Mrs. Yeobright's understanding is at this point abundantly obvious.

There are two plain reasons why Mrs. Yeobright's plan to manipulate Wildeve into marrying Thomasin misfires. She is ignorant of the fact that what Wildeve wants most is to marry Eustacia and leave Egdon Heath. And, obviously because she is engaged in the symbolic action of enacting the situation which she wishes were the fact, she overplays her hand and gives Wildeve the impression that he is being triumphantly rejected in favor of a new suitor: " 'The woman, now she no longer needs me, actually shows off!' Wildeve's vexation had escaped him in spite of himself." (I, 11.) This result of the interview is pre-cisely what Mrs. Yeobright did *not* want. Headstrong pride and mis-calculation have achieved it, not malign or blind Fate. Human motives are seldom so expertly laid bare in the novel. If the ensuing interview, in which Eustacia rejects Wildeve because she believes Thomasin has rejected him, is based on an utterly false premise, that is, after all, life. Nor should we forget that Eustacia and Wildeve have been quarreling and at cross-purposes for some time, and that her "supersubtle, epicu-rean heart" is never titillated by certainties. Passion flares brightest when she is uncertain or frustrated. Novelty is her goal, fidelity her abhorrence. The stage is set.

Thus we come to the end of Book I, with all except one of the major characters introduced and their lives tangled by passions and errors that have been fully accounted for. It is not an indifferent or incompetent God who is responsible but human qualities that are almost as old as Egdon Heath. I see the superstitious stupidity of the natives — which Hardy pushes past the grotesque almost to the absurd — as his grim background reminder of the frailty of human reason.

As we move into Book II, what looks in the accumulation like coin-cidence appears in the detail to be something else — personal frustra-tion or the reversal of expectations. It strikes Eustacia with painful force that she has set the stage for an attachment between Clym and Thomasin by her part in preventing the latter's marriage to Wildeve. This reversal horrifies her selfish heart: " 'Oh that she had been married to Damon [Wildeve] before this!' she said. 'And she would if it hadn't been for me. If I had only known — if I had only known!' " (II, 7.) The reader doubtless stands by this time on Thomasin's side, but whatever his reaction to Eustacia's consternation it cannot fail to add a mite to his sense of human purposes gone awry: once again a character has brewed a plot only to discover that there were elements in the mixture that produced a result quite contrary to his taste. Yet the headstrong and selfish plans of Eustacia could hardly be expected to work out along the simple axis of her yearnings, not when her sight is so blinded by passion.

Almost every meeting in the novel seems to involve an element of unexpectedness if not chance. Hardy dwells on the lonely emptiness of the heath, developing an atmosphere of desolation in which the appearance of any person is a surprise and the meeting of two an event. Diggory Venn, who has set up camp and posted himself every night by Rainbarrow to assist at any meetings of Eustacia and Wildeve, knows just where to find the latter with Eustacia's note of rejection and the presents he is to return for her. Yet when they meet, Wildeve jumps as if nipped by the devil himself, and when they part, after their ironic interview, it would seem as if they had conferred on the outer fringes of Chaos: "When the reddleman's figure could no longer be seen, Wildeve himself descended and plunged into the rayless hollow of the vale." (II, 7.)

A most moving and tender scene builds on these impressions when Thomasin takes her solitary departure for her marriage to Wildeve. She goes like a lamb to the slaughter on an altar built by Folly, Error, and only a little of Chance. Mrs. Yeobright's pride of family, which has motivated her various insults to Wildeve, is the prime cause; her failure to inform Clym of the facts is another. Diggory Venn's passion is still another; he has carried notes and spied on Wildeve; he has given Mrs. Yeobright the idea for her lie to Wildeve which presently caused the cooling of Eustacia's ardor; he has carried the news that finally caused Wildeve to marry Thomasin in spiteful haste; and he has directly contributed to the growth of these unlovely motives in that worthy's heart. Wildeve likewise has acted in ignorance, rushing into marriage to spite a Eustacia who has virtually forgotten him. In this confusion of ignorance poor Thomasin is victimized by her goodness and strength of character!

Yet something more than convincing details of accident piled on miscalculation must make this event morally and psychologically probable. What is it? It is Thomasin's frailty, which expresses itself in stubbornness, making a virtue of suffering where she has not strength to impose her will on a situation. She is the person made to abase herself and be a victim. We recognize the nobility of such people, yet we feel that their goodness is too willingly bared to the scourge of misfortune. Their very nakedness makes one shrink from them, while they take on the outrages which in this imperfect world one should evade:

> Does he survive whose tongue was slit,
> To slake some envy of a king's?
> Sportive silver cried from it
> Before the savage cut the strings.
>
> The rack has crumpled up the limb
> Stretched immediate to fly;
> Never ask the end of him
> Stubborn to outstare the sky. . . .
>
> It is no virtue, but a fault
> Thus to breathe ignoble air,
> Suffering unclean assault
> And insult dubious to bear.
>   [Elinor Wylie, "Heroics"]

Perhaps the fastidiousness of the poet who makes this comment is excessive, but it expresses a feeling that is very common, although often repressed. It is indeed too much that Thomasin should suffer the unclean assault of a Wildeve; and she does consent to it, finally, herself, just as Eustacia has elected to stay on the heath and Clym has elected to return to it.

The character of Clym Yeobright, withheld for 150 pages, destined to be central to the story, demands careful scrutiny. The unhappy force of coincidence seems to mount as we draw into the main action. Could he not have worked out a satisfactory life with Eustacia if it had not been for these misfortunes and accidents he could not control? Hardy writes that Clym is "unfortunate" in being intellectually advanced beyond the readiness of the rural world to respond to his visions: "To argue upon the possibility of culture before luxury to the bucolic world may be to argue truly, but it is an attempt to disturb a sequence to which humanity has been long accustomed. Yeobright preaching to the Egdon eremites that they might rise to a serene comprehensiveness without going through the process of enriching themselves, was not unlike arguing to ancient Chaldeans that in ascending from earth to the pure empyrean it was not necessary to pass first into the intervening heaven of ether." (III, 2.) To announce that Clym lives by a high order of idealism and then introduce these considerations in this language would seem to display an ironic attitude toward him; to label the stupid natives "Egdon eremites" passes the ironic, even borders on the derisive; the notion of preaching a "serene comprehensiveness" to such yokels is ridiculed in the telling. Hardy proceeds, somewhat more gently, to explain that Clym's mind is not well proportioned, that well-proportioned minds do not make heroes and prophets. But he does not say that Clym is the stuff of greatness: here he leaves the reader to look at the facts and judge for himself.

What the facts show is a deep vein of self-destructiveness that runs right through the Yeobright family. We have glanced at it in Thomasin. Repeatedly we see Mrs. Yeobright making things hard for herself. Clym is not to be outdone by his womenfolk. Reading stubbornly on until he has ruined his vision is the act of a man who is subconsciously bent on self-destruction. One may argue against judging too harshly his original venture of making eremites of the yokels, but here the evidence cannot be gainsaid. He is challenged, of course, by the nagging reproach of his disappointed mother, but alas he has inherited a broad stripe of her character. Like Eustacia, he has also a generous share of the endowments that enable mortals to cope with their frailties, namely, intelligence and cultivation, and like her he will not use these unique aids.

An extraordinary bit of evidence to this effect slips in so quietly that one is tempted to see in it a glimpse of Hardy's unconscious mind as he develops the more obvious motives of his hero. Although arguments do not prevail with his mother, Clym finds that feelings do — that Mrs. Yeobright shares his contempt for mere physical comforts and will, in spite of her ambitions for him to rise through the world of business, intuitively participate in his contempt for the great world. Then comes a strange sentence: "From every provident point of view his mother was so undoubtedly right, that he was not without a sickness of heart in finding he could shake her." (III, 3.) It seems to reveal that Clym *wants* his mother to disapprove of what he is doing. Could there be a more expressive demonstration of his rebellious and self-destructive motives? His silver cord must vibrate when, finding that he has given an exhumed urn full of bones to Eustacia, his mother only comments, " 'The urn you had meant for me you gave away.' " Her disapproval of Eustacia is so fierce, and her expression of it so ominous, that Clym's growing passion is almost matched by the emotional force of his conflict with his mother. After his evening on the heath with Eustacia's kisses, mother and son glare at each other over tea. This doubles his emotional involvement in the wooing.

It might almost be argued that the glowering contest over Eustacia has allowed Clym to modify the original plan of opening a simple school for the natives. That is, his destructive attachment to his mother is satisfied by the new issue, so that now he can please Eustacia by planning a much more impressive operation which will ultimately put him "at the head of one of the best schools in the county!" Thus easily are his ideals accommodated while the basic destructive drives are kept strong and tense. The images of light and dark, introduced early in the book, are fused in a complex of symbolism by Mrs. Yeobright's flashing reply: " 'You are blinded, Clym,' she said warmly. 'It was a bad day for you when you first set eyes on her. And your scheme is merely a castle in the air built on purpose to justify this folly which has seized you, and to salve your conscience on the irrational situation you are in.' " (III, 3.) Seldom has reason been so expertly used in the cause of emotion. In the following scene, when Clym becomes engaged to Eustacia, he sets up a second version — like the subplot in *Lear* — of his destructive relation with his mother. Now he will have two women raging, for Eustacia cannot remain content on Egdon Heath, and Mrs. Yeobright's blazing antipathy for Eustacia is almost completely without basis in observed fact. The fact that she is entirely correct in her estimation of both Eustacia and Wildeve should not be pressed too severely: people respond to others' expectations of them; Mrs. Yeobright gives them no sign of the affection or trust that people commonly repay with good conduct. She expects the worst; they oblige.

The ensuing quarrel between Eustacia and Mrs. Yeobright, in which she says words about Eustacia that can never be unsaid, guarantees a permanent hostility between her and the girl. This hostility, which is perhaps the major cause in the tragic action, has grown from deep psychological roots carefully traced by the author. Here is no coincidence, no accident at all. And it will appear that the passions thus generated are strong enough to create all the "accidents" that follow.

Mrs. Yeobright first offends Wildeve by not entrusting Thomasin's inheritance of golden guineas to him — and then makes the error of choosing a dolt like Christian Cantle to deliver them. Thus she has incited Wildeve and played into his hands. Why should he not take revenge by winning the money from Christian? And in the confusion that follows it is not surprising that Diggory Venn, having won the money back, should give it all to Thomasin. The sequence is melodramatic and theatrical in the extreme, but not the result of accident. Hardy says that Venn's error "afterwards helped to cause more misfortune than treble the loss in money value could have done." (III, 8.)

Well, perhaps, but here Hardy is not letting the facts speak for themselves. The estrangement between Eustacia and Mrs. Yeobright has already been effected, as we have seen. It feeds on incidents that could be explained in a moment between people who did not question each other's good will. But Mrs. Yeobright's tone and phrasing in asking Eustacia whether she has received a gift of money from Wildeve are mortally insulting. They fully account for Eustacia's tearful recriminations. Mrs. Yeobright's question, moreover, is based on pure hostile suspicion which leads her to imagine events that have not occurred — as she has done before. If Hardy had not interpreted this action with the discourse on ill-chance that I have just quoted, the reader might well believe that the quarrel he has witnessed was provoked by Mrs. Yeobright's ungovernable temper and animus. With such a woman, no accident is required. She makes the trouble, prevents the "accident" from being explained away, is determined to quarrel with all of her young kinsfolk, and does.

In this interview, a boiling masterpiece of charges and countercharges, the two women pour out their accumulated grievances. In view of their explosive hostility, it is hard to imagine their maintaining a friendly conversation under any auspices. The guineas are the flimsiest pretext for Mrs. Yeobright to search out Eustacia and blame her for everything. Without that pretext, she would plainly have soon found another. Near the end of the interview the truth is stated:

"Don't rage at me, madam! . . . I am only a poor old woman who has lost a son."

"If you had treated me honourably you would have had him still,"

Eustacia said, while scalding tears trickled from her eyes. "You have brought yourself to folly; you have caused a division which can never be healed!" [IV, 1.]

When Clym's eyes fail, he deserts Eustacia for sixteen hours of furze-cutting a day. He abases himself to the ranks of the meanest, returning home to fall exhausted on his bed. This is not philosophy; it is — however unconscious — a cruel assault on Eustacia and doubtless on his mother too. It is an extravagant neglect, a virtuoso piece of folly by a man with so luscious and moody a wife. He is tempting her to quarrel with him, so that he can suffer more, and of course she does. And how ironic that while pursuing this course he should add outrage to injury by being aggressively cheerful:

Eustacia's manner had become of late almost apathetic. There was a forlorn look about her beautiful eyes which . . . would have excited pity in the breast of any one who had known her during the full flush of her love for Clym. . . . Clym, the afflicted man, was cheerful . . .

"Come, brighten up, dearest; we shall be all right again. Some day perhaps I shall see as well as ever. And I solemnly promise that I'll leave off cutting furze as soon as I have the power to do anything better. You cannot seriously wish me to stay idling at home all day?" [IV, 3.]

Idling at home, no, but he could be a companion to her and she could read to him. There is willful neglect in his sixteen hours of exhausting labor. Yet he does not want her to go to a village dance. The speech in which he bids her go is a model of sick martyrdom and self-pity: " 'Go and do whatever you like. Who can forbid your indulgence in any whim? You have all my heart yet, I believe; and because you bear with me, who am in truth a drag upon you, I owe you thanks. Yes, go alone and shine. As for me, I will stick to my doom. At that kind of meeting people would shun me. My hook and gloves are like the St. Lazarus rattle of the leper, warning the world to get out of the way of a sight that would sadden them.' " (IV, 3.) This is touching, but every word of it is false.

Hardy humanizes his heath with a number of similes drawing on more or less unpleasant human physical details. The road crossing it is likened to the part in a Negro's hair. The barrow on the side of the valley appeared "as a wart on an Atlantean brow." The pool by Eustacia's house is "like the white of an eye without its pupil." In a storm, "each stem was wrenched at the root, where it moved like a bone in its socket." And there is "a knot of stunted hollies, which in the general darkness of the scene stood as the pupil in a black eye."

These grotesque images draw human and physical nature together. They give a slightly disagreeable smell of mortality to the heath. They also effect a certain interpenetration, a psychic symbiosis through which each absorbs the qualities of the other. If the heath is a shaggy monster, man is the living image it portrays. His conduct will reflect the icy winds, bleak skies, and tangles of twisted vegetation on harsh soil. The human being to whom these scenes are beautiful must have strong sympathies with them. Stubborn emotion and endurance of mien are qualities that dominate Mrs. Yeobright and Clym — and lead them to tragedy. The heath is thus not a moving force but a symbol of these human qualities; it makes a comment on man's nature rather than giving its qualities to man (as happens in *Wuthering Heights*), and so it seems to detract from the tragic stature that might have been suggested if man had been associated with the setting through nobler images.

The self-destructive impulses, which seem to account for the tragedy far more significantly than coincidence can, make *The Return of the Native* a novel of the greatest insight into character and motivation. The lacerations of the Yeobrights are set forth with such penetration and perspicacity that they reward careful study and repeated perusal. But the question nevertheless reasserts itself: is this a tragedy or a despairing indictment of Fate?

Coming late into the tragic arena, Hardy has penetrated further into the subconscious than Shakespeare, for example, generally had to do. Hamlet moves on a great stage. The Yeobrights move, really, among their psychological complexities, which Hardy fully accepts as inseparable from the nature and plight of man. They are not "abnormal"; they are not to be eliminated by manipulation of the patient's environment; they are the condition of man. Among them grow aspiration, fortitude, loyalty, and devotion, which Hardy also accepts as realities. Revealing so many destructive flaws among the nobilities of his characters, he makes their contests against error and mischance seem more inevitably doomed to failure than those, say, of Othello. Hardy's tragedy is brought on, perforce, by more ignoble mischances, more petty failings, than those of past heroes. Feelings of bafflement and indignation therefore constantly threaten to divert, replace, or obscure the tragic emotions of pity and fear. Hardy, it appears, participated in such a division of feelings toward his subject — and the confusion may have been nourished by a projection into the novel of insights and experiences with which he was too personally involved to achieve for them the aesthetic distance essential to high tragedy. This is one's judgment as the novel sags, occasionally, among the dreary quarreling or morbid self-pity of the characters. It moves back to a far nobler plane when Eustacia makes her fatal attempt to be a magnificent woman.

A bold reinterpretation is suggested: perhaps the coincidences are introduced and stressed to make the tragedy seem *less* due to human frailty! Without them, the defects of the Yeobrights and Eustacia would seem to make their defeats inevitable. The coincidences make them appear less due to the qualities inherent in the characters and therefore more due to tragic flaws in the universe. Hardy, in short, is not blaming coincidence but rather using it to take some of the "blame" from his characters. But the trouble is that the flaws in the universe do not remove the flaws in the characters, and so the tension in the novel is sometimes painful rather than tragic.

This shifting of "blame" appears signally in the extraordinary circumstances by which Mrs. Yeobright is left standing before her son's door because he is fast asleep on the floor and Eustacia is talking to Wildeve at the back. The mother has built so strong a case against herself that some such device is essential to reclaim the reader's pity for her. Yet it would not be completely reclaimed — Eustacia's uneasiness and fear of meeting Mrs. Yeobright are too thoroughly justified — if it were not for the older woman's anguish and death. The coincidences and her suffering go a long way toward recalling the tragic emotions; yet they do not, finally. There is too much indignation, too cruel a sense of man's inadequacies, too complete an absence of the tragic recognition and insight by which a suffering character is ennobled. Hardy's universe is ignoble, flawed, almost repulsive — "like the white of an eye without its pupil."

Few novels, however, so grandly demonstrate the force of the plot in determining character. In a lesser action, these people could seem to be a set of stupid fools. In Hardy's plot they have great occasions for the making of their perverse decisions. What they do affects fatal destinies and shattering passions. Their various decisions do not admit of reconsiderations or corrections. Each step taken moves the entire person, with a stately and fearful tread. The movement toward doom is grand. And so the characters are constantly raised, by the action, above the pettiness to which the same motives in a sordid urban setting might reduce them. Protected from triviality, they are often grand in the simplicity of their fatal drives.

The balance in the novel is between the tragic grandeur of the action and the self-destructiveness of the characters. The former is of a Grecian majesty, the latter expresses itself sometimes with Aeschylean nobility, sometimes with neurotic perversity.

11 *The Illusion of Action in Henry James*

WHAT happens in a story by Henry James and what the event does by way of defining character are questions that take on veils of obscurity because his style generates a sustained uncertainty as to what he is saying. The mystery of what he is saying becomes confused with the mystery of what has happened, why the character has done what he has done, and what the act has meant to him. Except for rare bits of dialogue — and even in most of them — the style is James talking subtle circles about his subject. And whereas in Hardy every event is translated into dramatic incident, James discusses far more questions of sensibility and motivation than he can even begin to translate into action. The reader very often does not know what has happened, while he tries to infer what it meant, nevertheless, to the character. And all the while action, character, and theme are bathed in the rich heady flow of James's own sensibility. For all the famous control of point of view, which looks from just over Strether's shoulder in *The Ambassadors* (1903), seeing only his field of vision, recording only his direct response in word or thought, still James is there continually commenting on his "poor man" and sharing with the reader his tender concern for Strether's innocence.

James hints at so many overtones of attitude and motive, suggests so many intricate possible reasons for an action by one of his characters, that endless varieties of interpretation are opened up. The delicacy of his sensibility, the range of his speculations, the lush flow of his style, all put layer upon layer of diffusion and refraction between the plot and the reader. These involve exquisite, enchanting complexities of ethical sensibility, but since they cannot all have been enacted by the characters, it is virtually impossible to say where the characters *are* in the Jamesian kaleidoscope or which side of them is up at any moment.

James's intelligence was staggering. His Prefaces seem to touch upon every insight that has occurred to his critics, although he conceals a good deal more than he tells. He understood the problems created by the irrepressible play of his intellect over any situation, just as he knew that many of his insights into the female temperament and the battle of the sexes could not be fully enacted for a genteel audience. He did try to control his intellectual exuberance by writing not only plays but also novels that were like plays in that everything said was said by the characters. Such a novel is *The Europeans* (1878), which is simply a play in novel form. It makes a striking contrast to *Washington Square* (1881) and *The Bostonians* (1886), where the plots almost disappear under the profusion of Jamesian speculation. But even the dramatic novel could not contain the Jamesian flood. *The Sacred Fount* (1901), which is a short novel almost entirely in dialogue, is the most totally mystifying of all his works. Nobody is sure what is happening in it; nobody knows whether the characters are saints, monsters, or maniacs; the many explanations of it have nothing in common except acknowledgment of the fact that the novel is obscure. James hinted that there was a clue, a guiding idea that would set all the parts in proper relation, but nobody has been able to put his finger on it.

And now a final general point that I believe is of utmost importance in foreshadowing what happens to characterization in the twentieth century: James initiates the aesthetic notion of objectivity. Acknowledging his debt to such European writers as Flaubert and Turgenev, he continually returns to the notion that the writer must let the facts speak for themselves. His ideal comes in the word "render," which he uses instead of "describe." A situation is rendered if scene and dialogue are so vividly represented that they speak for themselves, without auctorial commentary or explanation. It is amusing that the James who formulated this ideal so well and so often was also the James who loaded his stories with personal discussion, whose impulse to discuss was indeed so overpowering that he often dictated a discussion of what he was going to write that was longer than the story turned out to be when completed. It is amusing, but it is also significant; for I believe that the confusion between the ideal and the practice has been of great consequence in the development of the novel since James. It is because of James's example that what was offered as objectivity was in fact ambiguity — and has been accepted humbly as if it were only objectivity. Twentieth-century critics have, again and again, raved and glowed over James's "luminous" rendering of incredible subtleties, while they have groped in some confusion for a clue to what those subtleties were. The fact that two generations of professors teaching *The Ambassadors* failed to notice that one fat chapter had been printed out of the proper order (Chapters 28 and 29 were reversed in the only edition available as a text) is itself a glowing illustration of the point.

But the effect of James's confusion might have eventually faded away if it were not for the reinforcing example of Joyce, who seized upon it and straightway raised it to the 10th power. In his *A Portrait of the Artist as a Young Man* (1916) we shall find Joyce performing an extraordinary reduplication — a sort of amplifying electronic feedback — of the Jamesian doctrine. For it is there that he presents, through his hero, the aesthetic of objectivity with such terms as "clarity" and "brilliance" and the notion of the epiphany at which the reader has a moment of total identification with the situation being presented. And with this doctrine of luminous objectivity comes a book that is not clear at all but on the contrary tremendously ambiguous. Two generations of critics have humbly worked on it always with the assumption that it was utterly clear if they could just read it correctly, but alas the differing interpretations proliferate with every critic. When *Ulysses* appeared under the counter six years later it was the ultimately ambiguous book. Superbly clear and objective — and totally ambiguous! From it has grown the notion of a great author's moral detachment from his subject: he describes (or renders) a world so dense and complex that nobody can see it all at once and no two readers can see the same things in it.

This, as I try to show more fully in my last chapter, is humbug. But what potent humbug! Objectivity in fact has made ambiguity, which has in turn inspired the concept of moral detachment of author from subject; and this rapidly produces a tidal wave of irresponsibility — of books in which the author just puts down words and sentences to see whether they will say anything to himself or to any reader. James stands at the beginning of a trend, then, which has produced some superb fiction and a good deal of nonsense, along with a lot that is in between these extremes. Its implications for characterization are basic, tremendous.

THE PROBLEM IN CAPSULE

"The Real Thing" (1892) is a little story of James's that displays an interesting dominance of theme over event and character. The focal character is a painter who has a special commission to make woodcuts for an *édition de luxe* of a long-neglected novelist who has recently come into the public favor. The painter is on trial for the first volume and will be commissioned to do the rest if his work is satisfactory. He needs a pair of gentlefolk among his subjects — not necessarily for his models, however — and lo they appear in the shape of the Monarchs, who are almost too good to be true. From the polished boot to the lifted teacup, they are the perfection of dress and punctilio. The husband has left the army at fifty, they have lost their money, and in sum they are desperately poor. Having lived by their manners and style among the aristocracy (for they are real gentlefolk), serving to swell a progress or augment a scene, full of high manners and a bit obtuse, they have no way in the world of earning a living except, perhaps, this distaste-ful expedient of modeling. They are not professionals; they are, for this job, the real thing.

The painter is touched by their predicament, drawn to their simple goodness, eager to make use of them. He sets to work, but it's no go. His pictures come out stiff and cold; they just will not do. He has to get professional models, who turn out to be a couple of definitely low-class individuals. Somewhere between their artificial but effective posing, their contrivance and flair, and the painter's imagination a spark is struck and the illustrations come out exactly as the latter wants them to be.

The thesis of this story seems to be that the *idea* of gentility is the real thing, whereas its embodiment in actual people weights it with a millstone of human inadequacy. The idea is shining and pure while it exists in the mind; when it is seriously lived it becomes stiff and crass. The professional model, like the artist himself, treats the idea as an idea, as an inspiration for creative expression.

This is a tricky point, which is enriched (or confused?) by various complications and overtones. The Monarchs seem to be good but pitifully empty under their glossy surfaces. All aristocrats are not hollow shells. Granting that the gesture of aristocracy tends to be a parody of the idea, still it is an idea conceived and enacted by man — who else? — through centuries of civilization. If the Monarchs have acquired the manners and trappings of aristocracy, have they not themselves achieved artistic creations? If their polished surfaces are so much shining fraud, then the artist should never have seen them originally as the real thing. On a second level, the plight of the Monarchs intrudes. They are actually hungry. Mrs. Monarch tries to make herself useful with the tea things and even, in a masterly irony, with the costuming and makeup of the Cockney model. The artist is very sorry for them, but the fact that he must face the realities of his task and get models with whom he can work, or starve himself, involves him in a choice that is a foregone conclusion. If he doesn't sell his illustrations, he will not be able to buy tea even for himself, let alone the Monarchs. The artist, then, has an experience and learns something about the poor Monarchs, but he does not really confront a serious decision. Finally, the story does not make it clear that it is any harder to see an image of aristocracy in a couple of stiff, decorous old people, who do indeed have the manners and the clothes and the style, than in a gay pair of models who can strike a clever pose. Either set of models would seem to demand a reincarnation as they passed from life through the mind of the artist and onto his canvas. Some readers see the issue as life versus art: truth is stranger than fiction, and less real. In a cinema on, say, Pasteur, an actor could play the leading part better than the man himself. Diderot's "paradoxe sur le comédien" affirms that one must *not* experience the emotions if he is to act them effectively. But a model does not stand in the same relation to the painter that the actor stands in relation to the audience at a play or cinema. The important creative act comes after the model, who is only a convenience of colors and shape. These, and doubtless several more ideas about the relation between the artist and the reality *and* the idea that he seeks to represent, are suggested by James's treatment of his little situation.

In "The Beast in the Jungle" (1903) James tells an extraordinary mystery story in which the crucial fact is withheld until the very end. But this is a fact of character. The hero, Marcher, lives with the belief that some great event is destined to happen in his life, more likely a catastrophe of some sort than a stroke of fortune. It is a strange thing for a man's thoughts to be dominated by such an idea. Stranger, perhaps, is the fact that the second character, a lady named May Bartram, is attracted to him in his reserved and quiet life and elects to wait with him and see what the great event is when it comes. So they share a continuing unknown presence, which they discuss and explore for years and from every angle; the hero comes increasingly to think of himself only in relation to it. His character, then, takes shape as a withholding, watching, wondering, speculating on the presumed but unknown event. When, if, and how will it happen?

Well along in their lives and deep in the long story, the lady reveals that she knows the event but cannot tell him. He is willing to keep matters this way. Finally she dies, taking his secret to the grave. Later, at the cemetery, the truth bursts over him. She loved him and he never realized it, never spoke. His whole life was suspended, unfulfilled because he could not reach out from himself and recognize the total, unwavering love that was there beside him year after year.

The suspense that goes with the telling of this long tale — really a novella — is considerable. James manages so cleverly that the secret is not revealed although the facts are all present. Marcher's great choice is not to choose, not to see, not to respond. In this pattern he becomes increasingly self-centered, fatuously so. After the secret has been revealed, Marcher takes shape in the completed picture as disgustingly, loathsomely self-centered. He is a monster of selfishness — and a stupid fool.

May Bartram is more difficult to think about in retrospect. James does not explain why she would dedicate her whole life to such a clod — and not merely dedicate it but also abandon all other possible avenues to fulfillment while she waits with Marcher for the momentous event. More than this, however, she feeds and pampers Marcher's gluttonous infatuation with himself. She talks and talks with him about it, so that nothing else can come into his mind; she is as responsible as he for the paralysis of self-absorption that makes it increasingly impossible for him to look at her and see what he is missing. The moment of discovery, at her grave, brings a conviction, charged with feeling, that Marcher has failed to respond to a magnificent love, but the lady's conduct, reconsidered after the facts are all in, could be interpreted as either totally stupid self-destruction or a cowardly (pitiful?) refusal of life by her. The latter is of course a perception of psychology-in-depth that was not beyond James.

It is not beyond him, but it does not satisfy as a specific explanation. It is not rendered (to use James's favorite verb) by the quality of the story as it is told, for that is one of deep, "high" mystery, breathless wonder, and exquisite readiness of perception. The two characters live in a rapture of expectation. It is, rather, an offshoot of James's dominant preoccupation, everywhere in his work, with *renunciation*. His people are everywhere missing the boat, failing to speak or act, retreating into a hundred protective corners where the self huddles in a posture of refusal, refining its perceptions and sensibilities precisely because it is not strenuously living.

The masterly narrative of "The Beast in the Jungle," the long-withheld disclosure, the deep texture of James's fabric of mystery — these make an unforgettable story. But suspense takes the place of motive and decision. The explanation of the lady's conduct cannot be known until after the end of the story, and at that point her motives are not alive and dramatic but strictly objects of abstract speculation. This speculation is not *in* the story but in the later analysis by the reader. It involves the reader in estimating and judging rather than in aesthetically experiencing the event — how it luminously *was*, as James might express it. Whatever was "rendered" of the lady during the story is reinterpreted by the final disclosure, and the reinterpretation discovers elements that cannot be accounted for. If she was merely stupid, the tone of the story is outraged in retrospect. If she was enacting a death wish, a rejection of life, that too could not easily be reconciled with the tone of her sensibility during the story.

The story, then, does not create characters but rather renders a profoundly disturbing experience of renunciation. Two characters seem to move through the tale, but they vanish in the emotion that is achieved at the end. In many later stories and novels James used renunciation as a door to self-knowledge and the refinement of his characters' sensibilities. In this story, as in *Washington Square* and other early works, the theme of renunciation has a dominating life of its own. Most interesting, however, is the way James's speculative intelligence plays fast and loose with the action and robs it of the ability to carry the meaning of the story.

DISCOURSE ON FEMINISM

The Bostonians (1886) and *The Portrait of a Lady* (1881) are the two most elaborately written and, to use Irving Howe's phrase, "lavishly composed" books of James's middle period. The fact that *The Bostonians* comes five years later than *The Portrait of a Lady* shows that James did not always move forward — or at least he did not move forward with his special problem of getting his ideas into a working plot so that they became organically related to characterization. But perhaps what seems to be a lapse in the later novel is to be explained by the fact that its ideas were so interesting to James that he digressively luxuriated in them and forgot the characters that would, in a more integrated book, have worked them out in terms of themselves. In any event, James's variety is one of his special distinctions. *The Bostonians* is like no other book that he wrote, and it becomes an extreme case of his special quality: whereas with respect to character many of his plots disappear into involutions of theme where more ideas and more possibilities of motive and reaction are suggested than could possibly be enacted by the characters, so that what the character *is* becomes increasingly mysterious, his plots nevertheless have, virtually without exception, powerful elements of melodrama and suspense. *The Bostonians* is particularly lavish in commentary, in psychological insight, in vignettes of character, in Gothic sensationalism, and in melodrama.

The subject of this special book is New England's reforming tradition, which comes out under the sharp point of James's pen as complacent and ridiculous. Its complacency mirrors the American image of itself as the new world of virtue and quality, a world that is self-consciously better than anything else that has existed in history. It becomes ridiculous as it plunges into hysterical feminism, with all the excesses of spooky ignorance, visionary clairvoyance, and mesmerism disguising power drives and lesbianism. James turns this world over and over again, prodding and probing, mimicking with brilliant wit, until he turns it inside out and reveals a nasty thing under the ridiculous surface. The ambience of this world of feminist folly is brilliantly evoked; by its very nature, what happens in it is ludicrous and pretentious; hence the author will be hard pressed to make its activities furnish a serious plot.

Verena Tarrant is the central character. She is poor, beautiful, uneducated, and gifted in some way that makes her the cynosure of feminists, quacks, and all the shabby fringe of misfits who band together with any program that gives them a sense of union and power. Her gift is inspirational speech, and when she first appears she is a mysteriously automated creature of her father, who is a "mesmeric healer." He works upon her with a hypnotic massage (*not* a message) until she goes into her trance and speaks like an ethereal angel. Her subject is woman's rights, in a vague way — but not so vague that those who have made this their cause do not pounce upon her to worship and exploit.

Basil Ransom is an intelligent and humorous Southern gentleman, a lawyer, who believes that women should and do fulfill themselves most splendidly as wives and mothers. If the feminists accuse him of wanting to suppress and enslave women, he insists with great charm and fervor that he adores women and wants them to be truly happy. His healthy, generous, candid masculinity is as persuasive to the reader as it is villainous and stupid to the feminists. When James is exposing their follies with his finest wit and relish, he lets Ransom delight in the wonderful absurdity of it. When Verena at their first *tête-à-tête* delivers a short oration on the status of women in European and American culture, Basil Ransom "listened to this considerable statement with a feeling which, as the current of Miss Tarrant's facile utterance flowed on, took the form of an hilarity charmed into stillness by the fear of losing something. There was indeed a sweet comicality in seeing this pretty girl sit there and, in answer to a casual, civil inquiry, drop into oratory as a natural thing." (Chapter 24.) But for all his wit and masculine balance, Ransom is enchanted by Verena's beauty and freshness and candor.

The other major character, Olive Chancellor, is a New England Puritan, educated, well connected, and rich. She is severe, intellectual, and so militant that she eats, drinks, and breathes woman's rights. She has discovered Verena and is promoting her with a total "dedication" that hides even from herself the lesbian nature of her attraction.

A fourth character, Mrs. Luna, is strictly a tool. She is Olive's widowed sister, lives in New York, tries hard to ensnare Ransom, who is a distant family connection, and serves the plot with confidences and intrigue. She is a vulgar, dishonest chatterbox whose lies are of no interest to the reader but who assists the author as a useful means to connect the main characters — the Jamesian *ficelle*.

A novel of 464 dense, full pages cannot be summarized. The relation of character and action will appear well enough if we examine the conduct of the Jamesian narrative through the central hundred pages of the story. The plot is very slight. James presides over it, draws it out, by standing right in the middle of it and talking about it. Starting with Chapter 23, at page 214 (of the Modern Library edition), he takes about 5000 words to tell how Ransom, with a free day while in Boston on business, goes to Cambridge on the chance of finding Verena at her parents'. He lurks near Olive Chancellor's house, meets a comical, dowdy feminist departing therefrom, and gets Verena's address from her. In the next chapter, he finds Verena at home and talks with her; but little passes because James takes up so much space talking *about* what is happening. Rather than exploit the dramatic possibilities in a dialogue about why Ransom came to her parents' instead of stopping at Olive's house, James plunges into Ransom's thought. When Verena says it is a pity she wasn't at Olive's today, "Ransom made no answer to this; he was incapable of telling Miss Tarrant that if she had been he would not have called upon her. It was not, indeed, that he was not incapable of hypocrisy, for when she had asked him if he had seen his cousin the night before, and he had replied that he hadn't seen her at all, and she had exclaimed with a candor which the next minute made her blush, 'Ah, you don't mean to say you haven't forgiven her!' — after this he put on a look of innocence sufficient to carry off the inquiry, 'Forgiven her for what?' " (Chapter 24.) And after Ransom has made it clear that he came to see only her, James steps into her mind with "It may be communicated to the reader that it was very agreeable to Verena to learn that her visitor had made this arduous pilgrimage . . . with only half the prospect of a reward; but her pleasure was mixed with other feelings, or at least with the consciousness that the whole situation was rather less simple than the elements of her life had been hitherto." (*Idem.*)

Again a few pages later, instead of letting Ransom and Verena talk James tells the reader in a most patronizing manner what she is thinking: "Verena thought this very graceful, but she was not sure it was not rather sophistical; she would have liked to have Olive's judgment upon it." (Chapter 24.) This mockery of her character prevents her from expressing herself in relation to Ransom, prevents her from living and growing in relation to him. Thus handled, characters cannot interrelate and will not develop. Bemused in their thoughts, they must be presumed to sit and stare at each other, till Verena speaks of Harvard and offers to show Ransom around the "enclosure," as James calls the Yard. She looked at him "with an eye that seemed to brighten"; this is all that Ransom — since the "seemed" represents his understanding — can see; but then James goes behind the scenes again to tell us about her feelings: "Her offer had a frankness and friendliness which gave him a new sensation, and he could not know that as soon as she had made it (though she had hesitated too, with a moment of intense reflection), she seemed to herself strangely reckless. An impulse pushed her; she obeyed it with her eyes open. She felt as a girl feels when she commits her first conscious indiscretion. She had done many things before which many people would have called indiscreet, but that quality had not even faintly belonged to them in her own mind; she had done them in perfect good faith and with a remarkable absence of palpitation. This superficially ingenuous proposal to walk around the colleges with Mr. Ransom had really another color; it deepened the ambiguity of her position, by reason of a prevision which I shall presently mention." (Chapter 24.) Here Verena is endowed with an inwardness that is not visible to Ransom, and the interplay that discovers and develops character is prevented because the author steps in and talks about what might be *happening* between the characters. The involutions and subtlety of James's style, furthermore, confuse the picture given by the bareness of what has actually been said.

This is illustrated when, a few pages later, Verena makes a statement that is naively mechanical and objective — quite out of keeping with the intense private feeling revealed in the passage quoted: " 'See here, Mr. Ransom, do you know what strikes me?' she exclaimed. 'The interest you take in me isn't really controversial — a bit. It's quite personal!' She was the most extraordinary girl; she could speak such words as those without the smallest look of added consciousness coming into her face . . ." (Chapter 25.) So the gap between what Ransom sees and what James lets the reader see in her mind completely conceals any living relation between the two people. As the conversation goes on for several pages, nothing but nonsense passes between them. Verena makes some stupid remarks. She "struck Basil Ransom as constantly simple, but there were moments when her candor seemed to him preternatural." (*Idem.*) The candor continues when she speaks, but it cannot be reconciled to the complexity of thought that James has privately disclosed. With one hand he explores thoughts, with the other he scatters a few inane remarks, and one cannot think coherently about the character.

After the superficial and inconclusive meeting at her home, Ransom sees Verena again a few weeks later when he is invited by card to hear "An Address from Miss Verena Tarrant" at what turns out to be a home "of the fashionable world" in New York. At the beginning of this meeting Ransom is permitted to evaluate Verena; rather, James steps in and does it for him, explaining with perhaps a touch of fond, patronizing irony (one cannot be sure: what is said represents James well enough, but its finality stands in amusing contrast to the fact that Ransom is falling in love) that "He understood her now very well (since his visit to Cambridge); he saw she was honest and natural; she had queer, bad lecture-blood in her veins, and a comically false idea of the aptitude of little girls for conducting movements; but her enthusiasm was of the purest, her illusions had a fragrance, and so far as the mania for producing herself personally was concerned, it had been distilled into her by people who worked her for ends which to Basil Ransom could only appear insane. She was a touching, ingenuous victim, unconscious of the pernicious forces which were hurrying her to her ruin." (Chapter 26.)

Now where there is opportunity to advance the acquaintance with a long personal conversation, James interposes a crusty interview with Olive Chancellor and a gushy entrapment by Mrs. Luna in a second room, which prevents Ransom from hearing all of Verena's talk. The talk itself, for Ransom, "had about the value of a pretty essay, committed to memory and delivered by a bright girl at an 'academy'; it was vague, thin, rambling, a tissue of generalities that glittered agreeably enough in Mrs. Burrage's veiled lamplight. From any serious point of view it was neither worth answering nor worth considering, and Basil Ransom made his reflections on the crazy character of the age in which such a performance as that was treated as an intellectual effort, a contribution to a question." (Chapter 28.) With Verena trapped among her incredible follies and Ransom sharing James's subtle and penetrating malice yet being at the same time a no-nonsense chivalric sort of fellow, the two are held light-years apart; they are joined by the tenuous and purely melodramatic filament of romantic love. It is melodramatic because it is not allowed to develop over mutual interests and exchanges; it is pure attraction, which certainly happens (as everybody knows) but is not edifying unless it marks the beginning of a meaningful relation through which people change.

These incidents have occupied some 85 full pages, and precious little has happened between the characters. While James's profuse and meandering discourse has taken all the space, the characters have been kept apart by the devices of melodrama. Mrs. Luna is pure malicious gush. Olive is so totally at cross-purposes with Ransom that conversation merely hardens their animosity.

On top of the romantic ties between Ransom and Verena, James has two other complex relationships to deal with. Ransom is in a contest with Olive for control over Verena. And Olive's relation to Verena must be explained in detail if the forces against Ransom are to be known. Olive simply loathes Ransom. She gets deathly pale and rigid when she sees him. After she overcomes this typical paralysis, she accuses him of all the crimes man has historically committed against woman, revealing that it is not equal rights but REVENGE that she wants. Ransom and she have no mode for accommodation, because they do not want in any way to come closer. She is Svengali to him; he is a wolf to her, after her Trilby. If she attacks him, he laughs at her, and this is unbearable.

As for Olive and Verena, the tie is powerfully lesbian on Olive's side. She thinks her motive is to share a noble crusade on a high intellectual level, but it is clear enough that she lives in a state of unwholesome passion for Verena that is the more frantic because it is completely inhibited. Verena is trapped by her own gift of tongue and her simplicity. With inadequate — because uneducated — judgment, she nevertheless takes herself very seriously. She has a sense of destiny. James identified this as a fatal characteristic of American women. They have been trained to see themselves as Chosen People destined to save the world. When they are sexually attractive, so that men are disposed to humor their whims, they can be swept on to euphoric fatuities of self-assertion that make them less and less womanly. James saw the type as spinster and lesbian, but they flourish just as sharkishly within the marriage bond. Indeed they often find marriage the perfect field for man-killing. James as author and Ransom as his hero see these fierce, overbearing, unwomanly women as latter-day inheritors of Puritan drives and Puritan inhibitions unleavened by learning. However much they know, they don't know enough, for their book-learning is always the instrument of their thrashing assertive ferocity. The books they have read are so many chips on their shoulders which do not add to their judgment. As they age they become pathetic or ridiculous — Miss Birdseye in this book is a prize specimen — and this will be Verena's state unless she is "saved."

Olive is of special interest because she has reached this condition while still a girl. Family, wealth, and breeding have made her very strong; she is sure of herself and she has social power to wield. Her cold hatred of men has been translated into a feminist crusade before the book opens. When she finds Verena, then a tool of her father's mesmeric quackery, she immediately sets about taking her away from him. She easily persuades Verena away from the shabby home in Cambridge, to live with her in high dedication — and luxury — with opportunities to meet distinguished people and speak to select gatherings. But with growing acquaintance and the inevitable improvements of poise and dress, Verena's beauty is bound to attract desirable men. Olive lives in an anguish of jealousy, for as Verena's world expands it becomes increasingly difficult for Olive to know her every thought and action — and no less than this will satisfy her lesbian passion. After Verena has been attracted to Ransom, she deceives Olive for the first time by concealing a letter and a meeting with him. This small incident is the substance of several chapters as Olive learns about it, suffers over it, and finally brings it out in the open with Verena and talks about it. But still the two girls hardly touch: Olive is icily determined to keep Verena for herself, but she certainly sees nothing amiss in her interest. Verena on the other hand can be utterly candid because she believes herself unalterably dedicated, yet she enjoys fame, praise, and the attentions of men. Two people who do not understand their own motivations — and who are also inhibited by a high Jamesian formality of manners — can hardly come to grips with moral choices that are defined and evaluated. The closest they come is when Verena finally reacts to Olive's cross-examination about Ransom: " 'Why have you a manner as if I had to be watched, as if I wanted to run away with every man that speaks to me? I should think I had proved how little I care. . . . you don't do me justice.' " (Chapter 31.) Olive responds with a long embrace and a kiss.

As the narrative sweeps toward the end, it gathers some momentum and there are scenes in the finest Jamesian manner, where the magnificent language speaks for the character present, without auctorial intrusion. Olive, for example, is summoned by wealthy Mrs. Burrage who wants Verena for her charming son. "People like Mrs. Burrage lived and fattened on abuses, prejudices, privileges, on the petrified, cruel fashions of the past. It must be added, however, that if her hostess was a humbug, Olive had never met one who provoked her less; she was such a brilliant, genial, artistic one, with such a recklessness of perfidy, such a willingness to bribe you if she couldn't deceive you." (Chapter 32.) Mrs. Burrage has the aplomb to remark that her poor boy "will never again care for any girl as he cares for that one. . . . I am not at all good at resigning myself, but I am excellent at taking up a craze," revealing the frankness and boldness that only the vigorous rich can enjoy. To get her way, she will put her fortune at the disposal of the Cause — or promise to. Here is characterization at its best. Olive is flattered, suspicious, penetrated. The reader can infer a full character for Mrs. Burrage: she is firmly based as a type; she has been confronted with a basic problem of her son's future; and she has decided that Miss Tarrant's individual qualities more than make up for her shabby background. When Olive asks the inevitable questions — Have you met the parents? Why do you insist that I control Verena? How do I know you would continue with the Cause once you had Verena married to your son? — Mrs. Burrage is able to keep her handily on the defensive.

The scene is especially delightful because Olive is secretly in mortal combat with her conscience. She knows that this is a magnificent opportunity both for Verena and for the Cause, and she is beside herself with anxiety as she tries to think of justifiable ways to resist the marriage. She fences disdainfully and not very successfully. But instead of making the most of it, James steps across his stage and into Mrs. Burrage's mind: "If we were this moment to take, in a single glance, an inside view of Mrs. Burrage (a liberty we have not yet ventured on), I suspect we should find that she was considerably exasperated at her visitor's superior tone, at seeing herself regarded by this dry, shy, obstinate, provincial young woman as superficial. If she liked Verena very nearly as much as she tried to convince Miss Chancellor, she was conscious of disliking Miss Chancellor more than she should probably ever be able to reveal to Verena." (Chapter 32.) This is very good, but

it would be so much better if it were permitted to develop in the conversation, in dramatic exchange. But the scene is not lost by this intrusion; it continues to mount as Mrs. Burrage puts her finger firmly on
the sorest spot and tells Olive that her son would, after all, be a safer
refuge than some unknown danger that might fall upon Verena if
Olive persisted in her attempts to keep her entirely to herself. Olive
immediately thinks of Ransom; she leaves the interview in a turmoil
of conscience and self-deception, wondering "whether she might trust
the Burrages or not. By 'trust' them, she meant trust them to fail in
winning Verena over, while at the same time they put Basil Ransom
on a false scent." (*Idem.*) Olive has been superbly characterized here.

The portrait of Olive deepens as she is driven from one device to
another in trying to keep Verena. Uncontrollable passion sweeps over
her prim intellectual calm, flattens her authority, swamps the sturdy
logic by which she had so often proved to Verena that she must *hate*
Ransom. She becomes desperate and abject, unable to control her violent animosity to Ransom or to conceal her passion for Verena. By the
middle of the book Olive's cause has been ridiculed and discredited,
and very soon thereafter the Cause has become irrelevant, the issue
being Olive's personal aberrations. The social problem, then, has vanished into the bold disclosure of lesbian conduct. In the modulation
from the first problem to the second one, it is possible to see first
the social sources of the aberration and then the close study of the
"disease" itself. The ponderous, deliberate opening, which makes the
essay element in the first 200 pages of the novel very heavy, does serve
this purpose. Once Olive has become a "case" the Cause is embodied
in the octogenarian figure of Miss Birdseye, a monument of devotion,
who has dedicated her whole life to good works among the poor, the
mistreated, the benighted. She is neither lesbian nor avid for power.
James bathes her last hours in a mellow sentimental light, and her
death scene reduces the three major combatants to spasms of tenderness and tears. By this means he moves his story from the tone of contest and satire to that of romance, in preparation for the melodramatic
ending.

Ransom meantime is making all these velleities academic by persuading Verena to spend, not an hour, but the whole afternoon with
him — and here a good deal of solid talk takes place. Ransom finally
attacks in full seriousness, delivering himself of ideas that seem rather

too insightful for a buoyant Southern gentleman, in sentences that improve upon the best of Philip Wylie and Simone de Beauvoir multiplied by each other. To Verena's narrow personal reference (" 'There you are — you women — all over; always meaning yourselves, something personal, and always thinking it is meant by others!' "), he responds that he is trying to save his sex " 'From the most damnable feminization! I am so far from thinking, as you set forth the other night, that there is not enough woman in our general life, that it has long been pressed home to me that there is a great deal too much. The whole generation is womanized; the masculine tone is passing out of the world; it's a feminine, a nervous, hysterical, chattering, canting age, an age of hollow phrases and false delicacy and exaggerated solicitudes and coddled sensibilities, which, if we don't soon look out, will usher in the reign of mediocrity, of the feeblest and flattest and the most pretentious that has ever been. The masculine character, the ability to dare and endure, to know and yet not fear reality, to look the world in the face and take it for what it is — a very queer and partly very base mixture — that is what I want to preserve, or rather, as I may say, to recover.' " (Chapter 34.) These ringing words make Verena "slightly sick"; she could not "imagine anything more crudely profane," although she surely is not (as we have known her so far) capable of grasping what he has said. So far as the issues are concerned, Ransom and Verena are in different universes — his insights, admirable in 1886, are still impressive in 1966 — yet he continues to bait her.

The fourteen pages of Chapter 34, which record this conversation, are absolutely superb dramatic writing. Here Verena discovers rich feminine responses to Ransom's eloquence and expertness. She replies with the wit and ingenuity of a fine woman at bay before an almost irresistible masculine appeal. Her reactions are so powerful, so dignified, so fine that she actually *grows* under our eyes during these fourteen pages more than she has in the 335 pages before. At this rate, if James could and would sustain it, the interplay between these two people would quickly raise them to a richness and subtlety of character from which Verena would never give a further thought to the sick miserable sophistries of Olive Chancellor and her mean tribe. The Verena of these wonderful pages is simply not the Verena of the rest of the book. She has pushed the patronizing, sententious author right off his own stage. But unfortunately the author is in charge, and as

soon as he gets hold of himself he puts her back in her place and proceeds with the story he is determined to write. That story has got to
protract the dominance of Olive Chancellor's lesbian passion and her
silly theories.

Some critics, operating by deduction, conclude that Ransom's extreme male assertiveness *must* be as eccentric as Olive's feminism; they
ridicule his pride in having sold a simple article to a review. But Ransom must be judged by what he *says*, and when he speaks he is always
lucid, eloquent, witty, judicious. He must be judged by his part in the
plot — not by deductions with respect to the status of chivalry in an
industrial society.

The last hundred pages of the novel are, nevertheless, exciting. The
contest between Olive and Ransom mounts in intensity, but now in
terms of sheerest melodrama. At the end, about to commit herself irrevocably to a platform career by speaking to an enormous audience,
Verena at the last possible *second* runs through the stage door and off
with Ransom. Tremendously exciting it is, but it is quite obvious that
the intellectual issue, which is the presumed subject and focus of the
book, does not function in the characters' motives. These issues are
not joined or clarified between Ransom and Verena. Romantic love
simply takes over finally and she blindly chooses love. It is true that
James on several occasions declares that Ransom's brilliant and penetrating sentences go straight to Verena's heart and make it beat with
pain, but these reactions are distilled, discussed, interpreted, filtered
through James's intelligence — for though he has to tell us that Verena
is grasping some of these startling truths he has also to keep her under
Olive's sick but powerful will, ruled on both sides of the contest by
emotion rather than intelligence. Verena's penultimate decision to
give up Ransom is brought about by the introduction of a new and
very sentimental emotional force — the resigned and blameless passing
away of dear old Miss Birdseye; yet even so the actual decision is not
portrayed. At this point the narrative is recounted in long explanatory
paragraphs by James, speaking in his own voice. The heroine he needs
for this resolution must be predominantly emotional. The magnificent
woman that slipped through his fingers for a chapter and was a breath
away from becoming a great woman has to be suppressed, reduced,
fitted back into a situation that is dominated by suspense as the moment of her fateful choice draws inexorably close.

A first reading will find *The Bostonians* exasperatingly slow. When the characters meet and clash, as in Chapter 34, the drama is magnificent, with an unparalleled balance of personality and intellect. But James keeps his characters apart about ninety per cent of the time while he discourses in his own voice about what they felt or believed during the somewhat indefinite stretches of time between confrontations. Most of the confrontations, furthermore, are related in rather summary fashion by James, as events in the past, not presented for the reader to witness directly. Several are not even related but are kept mysteries to build suspense concerning where the characters are now and what they will do next. There is a striking range in point of view from Verena so enveloped in mystery that the reader does not know where she is or what she is thinking to Verena in full view dramatically reacting to Ransom to Verena having her inmost thoughts revealed and discussed by James, yet in summary fashion after the event, which is also reported rather than presented. A good master's essay might describe and analyze these shifts of method and find more Jamesian purpose behind them than has been so far discovered. We can say, however, that among these methods and points of view James gives us a great deal of Jamesian insight and a certain lack of characterization. The social world he creates is wonderfully real, and its people seem to be there, very much alive, but the action is not built out of their problems and choices *essentially*. Most of the book is James's discussion of these matters, the characters appearing and disappearing according to their creator's whim. The most agonizing scene, near the end, where Verena decides to reject Ransom and become a public figure, is neither presented nor even described. We know Olive and Mrs. Burrage better than Verena.

The action — a man wooing and winning a girl — is not significant enough to sustain the whole book. The clash of theories about woman's rights, on the other hand, is only slightly dramatized and mostly filtered through the screen of James's discussion. The melodrama at the end is exciting, but it so greatly reduces the depth of the characterization that it probably leaves a weaker impression of the intellectual merit of the book than appears on a second, less bewildered reading. In any event, there are enormous gaps between James's intellectual subject and the subject of his action. The characters emerge in the little scenes where they are allowed to interact, and then they tumble into these enormous gaps and vanish.

LAUNCHING THE AMERICAN GIRL

The Portrait of a Lady is a great puzzle of a book on first reading, its 850 pages piling up equivocal evidence as to why Isabel Archer does what she does. There is no real question about what she does, but why she does it is a question from one end of the book to the other. Yet it is one of James's most popular and most widely read novels. The broken type in the Modern Library college edition suggests how many thousands of sophomores have made their way through it.

The story can be briefly summarized. Isabel Archer, whose name carefully suggests a beautiful huntress, a Diana, is an American orphan, innocent and charming, fired with a typical American conviction of her value and her destiny. She rejects a young American of fine character, named Casper Goodwood, travels abroad, and there refuses the hand of an English lord (Warburton) who offers her a marriage of fabulous dignity, position, wealth, and love. She is willed a large fortune by a very rich old American uncle who wants to see what such a charming girl can do with the freedom that wealth can bring. She travels to Italy and in Florence meets and marries Gilbert Osmond, a cold devil who comes to loathe and despise her and discovers frightful capacities for making her miserable. Her good American suitor, still deeply in love with her, her cousin Ralph, the English lord, and others beg her not to marry Osmond. Later, when they realize her plight, they beg her to leave him; but even though she has learned that he married her in bad faith, for her money, and that he is not at all the man he appeared to be, she chooses to stand by her terrible mistake.

A large part of the book — like the typical best of James — is taken up with his great, glowing, beautiful panoramas of people in the rich settings of private estates and public monuments. The scenery comes to life miraculously shining, glamorous, soaked in tradition, bathed in culture. From her sparse New England beginnings Isabel moves through such riches of international sophistication that the reader will identify her spirit with these settings in which he sees her.

Against this background, the novel makes its first, powerful impression as a story of innocence flowering — and beguiled, of romantic idealism pathetically entrapped but then rising to tragic heights as it chooses to accept the destiny that has overtaken it. The idealism seems to be taken seriously, for Isabel is allowed to enact her problem and her decisions in high seriousness if indeed also in some obscurity (and through some surprisingly dark openings, as we shall see). The richness of texture in the international setting, the splendor that attaches to Isabel by virtue of the sort of people she attracts, the Gothic enormity of the predicament in which she entangles herself by her own free choice — these make high drama and romance. The story is interesting, exciting, and deeply moving.

The motivation that accounts for this high romantic drama is plain enough: Isabel's vitality, which expresses itself in her constant and powerful belief that she was born to *do* something important, speaks more precisely in her abiding notion that she will guide and inspire some human destiny. This aspiration impels her to reject Casper Goodwood because he is already strong — if any reason is needed beyond the fact that she does not love him enough or simply isn't ready to settle down at the age of twenty — and to reject Lord Warburton because he has so much to offer that it seems there is nothing significant that she can do for him. With him, indeed, everything would be done for her. Gilbert Osmond then makes the perfect appeal. He offers no fierce pursuit to the huntress. He shows immense taste, talent, intelligence, and poise. Most of all he appears somehow immobilized so that he is not doing anything with his capacities — and perhaps Isabel's money will open the necessary doors. This is the perfect appeal to Diana. How could she know that he is a monster with an iron will, no scruples, no pity — or that Madame Merle, the most charming and sophisticated person she has ever known, is Osmond's mistress, mother of his child, and has dedicated herself to steering the huntress into his waiting jaws so that there will be money to educate and launch her daughter and greater comforts for the man she still, despite her better judgment, loves? Noble innocence is beguiled by a combination of intelligent wickedness and extreme bad luck. This is pathetic; it is heartrending. But what of her final decision, when she has a second chance, when Casper Goodwood and Ralph Touchett both beg her to leave the monster for a new life? The answer is a heroic idealism: she will abide by her error, no matter how it came about. She becomes a tragic figure by this decision, because a union of fortune with her special qualities has conspired to destroy her.

Beneath this romantic Isabel there is a very different character, in whom the sexual aberrations that were to be treated with explicit and withering satire in *The Bostonians* are present although they are veiled under layer upon layer of glamour, romance, and indirection. James loved to turn Polonius's phrase — "And thus do we of wisdom and of reach/ By windlasses and by assays of bias/ By indirection find directions out . . ." (II, i, 64–66) — to his own uses; he boasted of his own indirections, teasing his audience with the thought that they might never wholly catch up to him and certainly could never be sure that they had. Perhaps some of the dark thickets in Diana's quest may be penetrated if we search for the clues that mark the trail.

Isabel's deeper, hidden character is a product of three forces:

First, she is not educated enough to know how to judge people. She lacks social insight; she has not seen enough of the world; she has not lived in a social milieu that would guide and develop discrimination because there were rules to control conduct. She has read some books, to be sure, which have given her a feeling of emancipation, of having touched great minds, but she has not enjoyed the benefits of a social environment that would wisely control both her opportunities and her reactions to them. She is profoundly unsophisticated. Little Pansy, the daughter of Madame Merle and Osmond, who has been raised in a convent and who is totally obedient to her father in the manner of an old-style European child of gentle birth, is still displayed as better equipped to choose a husband than Isabel. Perfectly obedient, Pansy is clear-eyed; even if she cannot have her way, she can refuse a marriage that would not make her happy.

Second, Isabel has been fired with a sense of power, freedom, and destiny. This is a quality that has become increasingly characteristic of American women, whose energy and beauty give them early maturity (of a most rudimentary sort, but nevertheless it is maturity) and an eagerness to press forward and make their mark on the world. Their beauty and vitality have been praised until they are convinced that they are superwomen, and they are impelled to be aggressive and dominating. The problem has been explored and discussed by many writers in the 1950's and 1960's; it is astonishing how astutely James identified it in the 1880's. Isabel is determined to make a distinguished career for herself, but James never endows her with a specific talent or shows her working toward a specific creative goal. The vision glitters before her — but without a definite form. It is therefore not surprising that her energy should in time come to be directed toward guiding and inspiring *someone else's* career.*

Third — and most important — she is sexually frigid. Here we have to snoop among James's indirections; he has recorded the evidence, but he has only hinted his interpretations of it. She is frigid partly because she has not been educated to a proper notion of the relation of man and woman. The idea that a woman is happiest and most fulfilled when she identifies herself with a man and dedicates herself to pleasing him — the knowledge that this can bring self-respect, freedom, and the utmost respect and deference from the male — is a product of education that is definitely non-American. The idea is most eloquently stated by Basil Ransom in *The Bostonians*, five years later, where James creates a frigid lesbian to evoke the assault. Isabel's sense of emancipation and personal destiny does not basically involve a man, and so man seems a threat to her. Her frigidity is therefore also partly a product of her drive to express herself in some notable way. The energy released in aggressive feminism seems to generate hostility to sex because, obviously, men have already created greatly in every field and a woman must surpass them to achieve distinction. Career women do not have to be unwomanly, and sexual fulfillment does not have to suppress a woman's creative talents, but the absence of a proper social education in marriage and the fact that men have got ahead of women in emancipation and creation work together to make man seem the enemy who must be avoided, punished, surpassed. These attitudes are embodied in frigidity. The other side of this coin is a sense of martyrdom, a self-mortifying abjectness, which is strong and obvious in the character of Olive Chancellor of *The Bostonians* but which can come veiled in heroic postures of renunciation — as it does in the character of Isabel Archer.

As Mark Twain proved with his celebrated passage about the solitary esophagus floating on motionless pinion, people do not like to read long descriptive passages when they interrupt exciting action. Thomas Hardy knew this so well that he used the same passages over and over again in different novels — and nobody noticed until many years later. The last chapter of *The Portrait of a Lady* is remarkably exciting — one does not know until the very end whether Isabel will

* Has it been pointed out that this is exactly what is the matter with Hedda Gabler?

respond to Casper Goodwood's last passionate appeal — and therefore it is very easy to skip some long passages full of metaphors telling how she feels when he kisses her; but James's explanations are right there, and they are quite clear if one reads them patiently.

Before doing so, however, let us look at the more obvious motive, the one that operates among the various characters who wish Isabel well. It is pride, of course. The two sets of motivations are not completely separate. Aggressiveness, frigidity, and pride are all of a piece, all facets of the same hard crystal. If it is self-centered aggressiveness that makes Isabel fix upon Osmond as the man she can inspire (and direct!), it is pride that makes her refuse to admit how bad a choice she has made, pride that impels her to keep an impenetrable front to the world, and pride that causes her agonies at the thought of reversing herself. When she finally confesses her plight to the eccentric Henrietta Stackpole — who is emancipated, frigid, and lovable herself — this dialogue ensues:

"What does he do to you?" Henrietta asked, frowning as if she were enquiring into the operations of a quack doctor.

"He does nothing. But he doesn't like me."

"He's very hard to please!" cried Miss Stackpole. "Why don't you leave him?"

"I can't change that way," Isabel said. . . . "I don't know whether I'm too proud. But I can't publish my mistake. I don't think that's decent. I'd much rather die."

"You won't think so always," said Henrietta.

"I don't know what great unhappiness might bring me to; but it seems to me I shall always be ashamed. One must accept one's deeds. I married him before all the world; I was perfectly free; it was impossible to do anything more deliberate. One can't change that way," Isabel repeated. [Chapter 47.]

This is the firmest summation; it comes after a series of humiliations at the hands of Osmond that are the more exquisite for being administered with the rapier cuts of a man who never raises his voice, never abandons the posture of gentility, and never fails to convey his disdain, disappointment, and dislike. Isabel meanwhile is in touch with the other men who love her — Lord Warburton, Ralph Touchett, Casper Goodwood — before whom she must act the consummate lady that she now is.

In the final scene of the novel, which occurs some five years after her marriage, when she has lost a child and suffered outrages from the venomous dislike of her husband — outrages that are balanced by the maturing dignity of her bearing — and when she has heaped up the certainty of even greater outrages in the future by virtue of the fact that she has defied his authority and made a private visit to England at the dying wish of Ralph Touchett, she is confronted by Casper Goodwood, whose dedication and goodness are beyond question. He has followed her from Rome, having in the meantime discerned her plight. " 'You can't deceive me any more,' " he says; " 'you're the most unhappy of women, and your husband's the deadliest of fiends.' " Now he continues, " 'I understand all about it: you're afraid to go back. You're perfectly alone; you don't know where to turn. You can't turn anywhere; you know that perfectly. Now it is therefore that I want you to think of *me*.' " She puts him off with a phrase, but what she feels is extraordinary. She feels "that she had never been loved before. . . . this was different; this was the hot wind of the desert, at the approach of which the others dropped dead, like mere sweet airs of the garden. It wrapped her about; it lifted her off her feet, while the very taste of it, as of something potent, acrid and strange, forced open her set teeth." Those set teeth, in the context, represent her life-long resistance to sex. He easily, convincingly sweeps aside every argument of pride or propriety: " 'a woman deliberately made to suffer is justified in anything . . . We can do absolutely as we please; to whom under the sun do we owe anything?' " (Chapter 55.)

And she is giving way, for speaking at random, "she had an immense desire to *appear* to resist. . . . The world . . . seemed to open out . . . to take the form of a mighty sea, where she floated in fathomless waters. . . . here was help; it had come in a rushing torrent. . . . she believed just then that to let him take her in his arms would be the next best thing to her dying. This belief, for a moment, was a kind of rapture, in which she felt herself sink and sink." In this flood of sexual symbols, she struggles: " 'Do me the greatest kindness of all,' she panted. 'I beseech you to go away!' " (Chapter 55, italics added.)

He kisses her, and the kiss moves her like fire but turns her to stone: "His kiss was like white lightning, a flash that spread, and spread again, and stayed; and it was extraordinarily as if, while she took it, she felt each thing in his hard manhood that had least pleased her, each aggressive fact of his face, his figure, his presence, justified of its intense identity and made one with this act of possession. . . . But when darkness returned she was free. . . . She had not known where to turn; but she knew now. There was a very straight path." (Chapter 55.) Obviously it is not a path toward anything; it is a path straight *away* from the terrifying sexual response that Casper has evoked. What else could it be? How could the lightning that has coursed through her veins confirm her in notions of duty or pride that have just been discredited by reason and were already discredited by Osmond's deliberate cruelty? Her straight path is the stiff rigidity of her terror of sex, which has never been so strong because she has never before felt such desire.

This somewhat "hidden" meaning is hidden mainly by two elements: James's ubiquitous indirection, which makes every conversation somewhat mysterious at first reading, every description of Isabel's thoughts puzzling because of the way he mixes his own commentary with a representation of her point of view; and the proportions of the novel, whereby the vast majority of his pages are devoted to scenes in which the splendor of the international setting and the dignity of the people surround Isabel with her riches of discovery and sensibility, while the suppressed neurotic motivation comes out less often and less directly. But the exposition of this meaning is nevertheless to be found from one end of the novel to the other. Only the crucial years of Isabel's marriage to Osmond are skipped, for which the gains in suspense and interest almost justify the concealing of the process of her growth.

The structure of *The Portrait* James thought inferior only to that of his masterpiece, *The Ambassadors*. It is built in three great acts, each with dramatic climaxes and superb long scenes in which the characters talk their way to their conclusions and decisions plainly before the eyes of the reader. The first part, of about 300 pages, contains the extended exposition of Isabel's character, her introduction into Gardencourt, the English estate where she meets her benefactor, Daniel Touchett, and his son, Ralph, destined for an early death, who loves Isabel without speaking and who understands her perhaps best of anyone in the book. Here she attracts Lord Warburton and refuses him, and here at the end of the "act," Daniel Touchett dies. The second part, of about 200 pages, takes Isabel to Italy, where Madame Merle prepares her and she accepts Gilbert Osmond's proposal of marriage, the immediate consequence of which is that she is compelled to defend her choice in revealing scenes with Casper Goodwood and Ralph Touchett. The third act, occupying the last 350 pages, jumps to about four years after the marriage, and contains several fine scenes — Isabel's dedication to Osmond's daughter, Pansy, and her valiant attempt to maintain her dignity while she resists Osmond's attempts to force a marriage betwen Pansy and — of all people! — Lord Warburton. This leads to the scene that James prized most in the whole book, where Isabel sits up through the night in a long reverie in which she thinks through and faces the full deadly error of her marriage. Her discovery that Pansy is Madame Merle's daughter follows; then the news comes from England that Ralph is dying and would like to see her; Osmond forbids her to go, with cruel and callous sophistry, and in defying him she confirms his hatred and assures herself of his active, undying rancor. After Ralph's death, in England, comes the concluding scene, already described, in which she flees in terror from Casper Goodwood's final proposal and kiss.

The structure is almost perfect, the great revealing decisions are dramatized, and the subject of the novel is serious and significant. The puzzle that James creates by his richness and indirection offers a continuing reward for the devoted reader. A source of annoyance to some is the fact that Isabel is so uneducated, so passionately determined to think the best of herself, so headstrong at the most crucial moments in her life in rejecting the advice of people who know the world better than she and who are concerned for her well-being to a degree that is quite beyond her appreciation or her desert. But in representing her beauty, her candor, her overabundance of ideas and idealism, and the enormous power of her beauty and charm over the men who know her well, James is not saying that she is perfect. If she is a goddess, she is Diana the Huntress, with all the tragic implications of the part. The greatness of the portrait comes in James's profound awareness of the fact that people must grow through and away from their psychic disturbances. The elements, which would be called neurotic today, that make Isabel a case are for James the elements of life, from which a person works out his destiny. Between the given psychological limitations and the elaborate and unpredictable forces of the world, he sees a free self that grows as it struggles among these fatal elements. The growth is never free, but Isabel's plight has a grandeur of elements through which she lives deeply. She evolves from a foolish, smug, self-centered girl to a woman who has faced life and acquired poise and dignity — at a terrible cost, to be sure, for she is trapped like a plant that has grown in a tunnel. So long as she is contained by her pride and her fear of sex, she cannot escape. This understanding is so poignant that the reader does not lay down the book with calm of mind, all passion spent; he is rather tempted to take comfort from the fact that Isabel is only twenty-eight years old and will (he hopes) not be able to endure Osmond indefinitely.

It would take many pages and quotations to show how carefully James has presented the evidence of Isabel's headstrong determination to impose her untutored will on the world. She has all sorts of answers, for example, none of which really makes sense, to the objections of her friends and suitors to her marriage to Osmond. Henrietta Stackpole, Mrs. Touchett, Ralph Touchett, and Casper Goodwood present their doubts in different ways and get different sorts of proud and unreasonable answers. With Casper she is proud, angry, agitated, defiant, and totally unreasonable. "Five minutes after he had gone out she burst into tears." (Chapter 32.) When she is informed of the engagement, Mrs. Touchett explains Madame Merle's deep duplicity in playing for time by assuring Mrs. Touchett that she would prevent the marriage all the while she was using the time thus gained to promote it. Isabel refuses to see. Mrs. Touchett defines Osmond's inadequacy — " 'he was not a man to take trouble. Madame Merle took the trouble *for* him. . . . He has no money; he has no name; he has no importance' " — and Isabel insists that choice of a mate is a personal matter. Ralph Touchett then explains that Osmond is a "sterile dilettante" who will impose his small vain snobbism upon her, and she replies with a flood of rhetoric to the effect that she is marrying him because he is small. (Chapter 33.) She is dramatically shown being trapped by the supreme devilish artistry of Osmond's wooing. He leads her to believe that he is the man of great potential, somehow caught on the shore, whose "boat she can launch" with her fortune. He carefully avoids showing any passion until she has been caught by her headstrong, undisciplined mind. He lets the huntress catch him.

The jump from Act II to Act III of our drama, over about four years of marriage, raises questions that should not be asked if the critic is committed to looking at the completed work and not at what might have been written. If these four years had been covered, James would have had to write another four-hundred-page volume to show how

Isabel's pride compelled her to adjust to the sort of personality that Osmond wanted her to display to the little world he wanted to impress. At the same time he would have had to show how she could live with all the evidence of Osmond's meanness so long without reacting violently to it. And he would have had to invade the marriage bed and be present at the breakfast table in ways that were as offensive to his fastidious spirit as they would have been unacceptable to the editors of the *Atlantic* in which the novel was appearing serially.

By jumping these years, James heightened the mystery. He was able to show a new Isabel in sharp contrast to the girl at the end of Act II. He used the duplicity of Madame Merle, gradually discovered by Isabel, as a substitute for showing what had happened between Isabel and Osmond during the years that were skipped. If that story had been told, the force of the plot by Osmond and Madame Merle would have been almost irrelevant. The procedure also fits in with James's intention (here achieved at its best) of giving his story in great full critical scenes, scenes in which everything is said, alternating with equally rich sequences in which he indulges to the full his unrivaled ability to paint the glow and tone and feeling of a historical moment in a great city like Florence or Rome.

CONVOLUTIONS IN THE MAJOR PHASE

The Golden Bowl (1904) is James's ultimate achievement in richness and ambiguity. He has wrought an enormously complicated action, involving multiple relations among four people. A great deal happens, and with a single exception the reader understands pretty well the actual events that take place; but so delicate are the moral issues upon which the events turn that it is exasperatingly difficult, if not impossible, to determine what the events reveal about the characters who enact them. Between the subtlety of the characters and the indirections, ironies, condescensions, and evasions of the author it is close to impossible to know what is morally happening. One often cannot tell whether James is praising or mocking, for he can identify himself with a point of view that he is presenting with such effusions and ecstasies of sympathy that whether he is praising, mocking, or merely representing remains a mystery. One sensitive critic has been led (or perhaps it would be better to say driven) to the conclusion that James sees the grimness and bitterness of life inseparably fused with its beauty and blessedness, "that neither cancels out the other; and that the ambiguity is intended to express precisely this experience of their permanent, inseparable fusion."* But if this is so it forces us to the disturbing and very modern conclusion that the characters themselves don't know what they are or why they act as they do. James too must be waiting for Godot.

The story is about Charlotte Stant, Prince Amerigo, Adam Verver, and his daughter Maggie. Charlotte is a sophisticated English girl without money who is in love with an Italian prince of impeccable polish and culture — but no money either. Marriage is out of the question, for they are both too firmly attached to the exquisite things that only money can buy. But Charlotte can introduce the prince to her old friend Maggie Verver. Adam Verver is a very very rich American whose wife has died and who has devoted himself utterly to his daughter. Maggie and her father are so close that one does not know whether the attachment is transcendent or unnatural. Apparently it is the former, for Mr. Verver believes that marriage and motherhood are essential to the fullness of his daughter's happiness. He sees the prince as potentially the choicest item in his vast collection of treasures.

Here is the first ambiguity: between Mr. Verver's love for his daughter and his tendency to regard people as if they were valuable objects, the quality of his spirit is not apparent. As a patron of the arts, he has limitations. He can relish the thought that "no Pope, no prince of them all had read a richer meaning . . . into the character of the Patron of Art" than he, and yet James adds the devastating qualification that what he cared most about was that "a work of art of price should 'look like' the master to whom it might perhaps be deceitfully attributed." (Chapter 8.) It must be the real thing, but it is even more important that it look like the real thing. He collects art treasures as treasures, and he sees people in the same scale. The prince is to him, at one point, "a representative precious object of art," and the prince himself notes, even while he is basking in the Ververs' delight, that "they felt remarkably, so often, things he hadn't meant, and missed not less remarkably, and not less often, things he had." (Chapter 7.) From another angle, James explains that the Ververs were not carried

* Dorothea Krook, *The Ordeal of Consciousness in Henry James* (Cambridge: The University Press, 1962), p. 324.

away by the intricate beauties of great works or by the polished brilliance and subtlety of a supremely cultivated person like the prince, "but they liked to think they had given their life this unusual extension and this liberal form, which many families, many couples . . . would not have found workable." (Chapter 25.) Adam Verver, then, is exceedingly proud of *having* the prince as Maggie's husband, of being able as a self-made American millionaire to accommodate a prince into his establishment and to furnish him lavishly, but he is more tolerant than appreciative of the perfection of the prince's cultivation. Adam is not crude, by any means, but he is, as his name indicates, innocent.

The prince, whose name is Amerigo, moves like a prince into the new-found land, the paradise of Adamic opulence which is the Ververs' establishment. How much he loves Maggie is not shown, but his great civility and tact are richly demonstrated in the way he neither resents nor repels Maggie's continuing absorption in her father. A child is born to crown Maggie's happiness. "It was of course an old story and a familiar idea that a beautiful baby could take its place as a new link between a wife and a husband, but Maggie and her father had, with every ingenuity, converted the precious creature into a link between a mamma and a grandpapa." Such is the prince's forbearance that he sees his child only "at such moments as he judged discreet in respect to other claims." (Chapter 9.)

With all these riches, Maggie is troubled by one flaw: she sees her young father's happiness as less complete than her own. James complicates the problem by suggesting that Mr. Verver is both a love and a responsibility to his daughter; he is on her heart and also on her conscience. Living now in two great houses, well separated in London, the Ververs must neglect the prince or neglect each other. Charlotte Stant is available to solve this problem. She is called upon to help widen the circle of experience, to Open Doors for the establishment; and presently Maggie introduces the notion that Mr. Verver should marry Charlotte. Again the motives are very complex. Adam Verver admires Charlotte's exquisite taste and cultivation, and he enjoys her company, but he also looks upon her as a possible addition to his collection. James explains, "Nothing perhaps might affect us as queerer, had we time to look into it, than this application of the same measure of value to such different pieces of property as old Persian carpets,

say, and new human acquisitions . . . it served him at present to satisfy himself about Charlotte Stant and an extraordinary set of oriental
tiles of which he had lately got wind." (Chapter 11.) More than this,
however, Mr. Verver understands that his separateness and possible
loneliness are on Maggie's conscience, and he wants to lift even this
burden from her. So he marries Charlotte for Maggie as well as for
himself. If the Ververs are exquisitely selfish, they are also exquisitely
considerate. Nor, in the opulence of security that goes with their
wealth, do they conceal any more from Charlotte and the prince than
they conceal from each other.

The moral intricacies here are dazzling. How much are the respective *sposi* "paying," what are they buying, and how much are they
giving in these contracts? What obligations do they assume? These
questions are eclipsed (but still there!) by the fact that Charlotte and
the prince, still deeply in love, consummate their passion in one bower
of bliss while Maggie and her father indulge their affections, their
consciences now wholly at rest, in another. Charlotte and the prince
convince each other that they are doing their duty if, above all, they
keep the Ververs in their state of blissful innocence. In view of the
subtlety and complexity of the values that have been set forth, the
reader cannot be confident that adultery is the only crime on the
calendar.

The serpent that makes his way into the Ververs' paradise is, properly, the knowledge that there may be evil as well as good in their
world. Once they have discovered the adulterous relation that has
been going on during their absorption in each other, they seem to
conclude, independently, that they must recapture their respective
sposi without letting anyone know what they have discovered. This
means that Maggie and her father are concerned to keep their discoveries from each other *and* from the prince and Charlotte. While
Maggie undertakes to gain — or regain — the prince's love, she also sets
about separating him and Charlotte, even if this means sending Charlotte off to live in a barren American city somewhere west of cultivation. Each of the four has to make very considerable sacrifices if the
demands of decency and propriety are to be satisfied. Both Adam and
Charlotte pay a great price in renouncing the riches of European society and art — to say nothing of the company of Maggie and the
prince and the principino. Maggie gets her way; she gets the prince

wholly to herself and sees Charlotte transported, with as it were only a silken thread of a halter about her neck, off to the wilderness.

The events of the story are clear enough, with one exception: that is whether the affair between Charlotte and the prince is a single lapse or is continued over a year or more. The facts as dramatized would seem to indicate that there was one single, elaborately planned week-end together; but the human probabilities cannot be satisfied that way. If Charlotte and the prince had their relation constantly in mind — as they certainly did — they could not have undertaken such life-consuming connections for a single meeting. We must take the single deed as James's way of rendering a sustained affair.

The events, then, are clear, but what they mean on a moral scale is very hard to determine. Of course the proprieties have to be respected. Such a design for living could not be allowed to continue. But who is *right* in essence? The Ververs use their great wealth to arrange people's lives according to their fancies, without primary consideration for the people as people. The Europeans, in turn, practice old-world guile on new-world innocence. The innocents learn fast and — using the power that goes with their wealth — bend the old-world evil to their higher uses. These formulations suggest their opposites: The prince and Charlotte give the Ververs something that is more precious than all the wealth in the world, namely sensibility and cultivation. They also give the Ververs as much love as those Edenic predators are capable of receiving, for love is like a fluid that rises to the level of cultivation; and the Ververs are not refined to the point where they can communicate on the highest level. At the end, American ruthless power regains its ascendancy over the poor Europeans. Charlotte is led away by her silken halter, while Maggie remains glittering with abundance, privilege, and social status. In the story, Charlotte is at a moral disadvantage before Maggie: she tries to cover her trail by suggesting that she has to take Adam off to America to protect her marriage from Maggie's interference. The reader, and Maggie too, know that this is false, that Mr. Verver has decided upon the move, but one does not necessarily sympathize with the proprieties at this point. Maggie is too ready, too powerful, to command all sympathy.

One may also be put off a bit by the depth of understanding and confidence suggested by the superlatively ambiguous last conversation between Maggie and her father. Maggie says, in final praise of the departing Charlotte,

"I don't see what you could have done without her!"

"The point was," he returned quietly, "that I didn't see what *you* were to do. Yet it was a risk."

"It was a risk," said Maggie — "but I believed in it. At least for myself!" she smiled.

"Well *now*," he smoked, "we see."

"We see."

"I know her better."

"You know her best."

"Oh, but naturally!" [Chapter 45.]

After these words Maggie feels a thrill "in the vision of all he might mean," and the gentle reader wishes he might penetrate surely into a few of these meanings. But James intends to make it quite plain that Maggie and her father *do* understand each other. We cannot, therefore, say that he is projecting a sense of moral relativism, a world in which good and evil are so tangled and fused that a high intuition of their mysterious interinanimation is the *summum bonum* of human sensibility. No, these people are represented as knowing what they believe in and why they act as they do. The problem is the reader's. He has the fullest social background against which to *see* the characters vividly illuminated insofar as all the details of manners, setting, and social conduct are concerned. He follows them from London tea to theater to private auction to country weekend, and they are endowed with the customs and graces of these activities; but in order to *know* them he must understand the motives and the consequences of their crucial decisions against a background of values, a moral scale by which they can be clearly measured.

The official proprieties do not serve for such a measure because they are too simple, and James's treatment of them wraps them in layer upon layer of irony and reservation. More important, perhaps, is the fact that the action is finally a private action; what goes on among the characters cannot be known, much less evaluated, by any public; and so their relations to society are not affected. The real action of the novel is not the contest between Maggie and Charlotte — which in itself is totally secret from the public eye — because once Maggie understands what has been happening Charlotte does not have a chance. The real action, then, is to be found in the way that Maggie and

Adam manipulate the situation so that everything is worked out to their satisfaction, which means that it is worked out completely under their control, down to the last nuance of expression. This is certainly a managerial tour de force (the commercial adjective is appropriate), but it is almost as soulless as a business transaction: certain ends have been achieved, but there is no way of measuring their moral significance. The fact that the proprieties have been maintained — this is easy and obvious; but from the moment that Maggie and Adam take matters into their own hands all public scales are set aside. Adultery ceases to be an offense against public morality and religion and becomes a figure in the private equation by which the Ververs calculate the forces that they intend to command. Whether their solution is a triumph of goodness or only a triumph of power and cleverness remains a puzzle. Slipping among the characters' points of view, suggesting all the private and public measures of rightness, running up and down a gamut of tones in his treatment of all these matters, James does not give his reader a single solid spot upon which to stand. The characters remain, finally, mysterious because there is no way to verify the secret action by which they could be known.

ACTION AND THE ILLUSION OF ACTION

Ideas, beliefs, manners, and social activities are the substance and medium of a novel; they provide what the characters do, what they compete or conflict over, and what they think about others and themselves. They are the materials through which changes in relations among people and changes within people are brought about. They are, that is, unless the writer fails to build them dramatically into his characters' lives. If the "ideal" — by which I mean normative or classical — novel achieves an organic unity of action, character, and theme, it would seem that Henry James has in his criticism defined this ideal to perfection, but close study of his practice shows a great spread between such triumphs as *The Portrait of a Lady* and the works in which the ideas and the characters are not contained in the action and expressed through it.

As a final turn of the screw, let us just look briefly at *The Ambassadors* (1903), his avowed masterpiece. The novel is certainly a masterpiece of construction: it has a symmetry of parts and a consistency of movement and discovery that set a new standard in these respects. As in the *Portrait*, the characters have the most serious problems of their lives to consider, and their choices are worked out before the reader with a high, rich, wonderful clearness (to use some of James's words again) that renders and develops the characters step by step. Crucial discoveries of character come out in superb scenes of fullest exploration and sensibility. One thinks of Madame de Vionnet's abject admission that she is desperately, hopelessly in love with Chad, even while she knows that he is unworthy of her. Or of Little Bilham's scrupulous ambiguity in explaining to Strether that Madame de Vionnet is "too good for Chad," and that it is "a virtuous attachment" between her and Chad, when in each instance he means literally the opposite and yet is telling the higher Jamesian truth. Or of the superb scene in which Sally Pocock, hard and righteous, insults Madame de Vionnet and by doing so impels Strether to shift his allegiance and get, as he says, "into her boat."

But the frailest characterization is that of Strether, whose name is the first and last word in the book and whose vision provides its point of view. He is the central character but he does not interact with the situation as the other characters do. Much of the "drama" is in his discoveries about Chad and his activities, but he does not discover at a moment of choice and then act; rather, he half understands, while James intrudes and shows the reader how Strether's Puritan reserve is such that he cannot let himself entertain ideas that would let him actually see what he is looking at. In scene after scene, then, he is inquiring, shy yet curious. Little by little he understands that what passes for Parisian immorality is kind and sensitive and scrupulous, whereas what passes for New England morality is hard and self-righteous and hypocritical. As these truths begin to make their first dawnings upon him, he delivers a famous speech to Little Bilham in which he urges Bilham to live life to the fullest while he has it in its prime. At the end, when he has burned his bridges behind him by defying the distant dictator, Mrs. Newsome, he refuses Maria Gostrey's outright offer to marry him.

This final decision should characterize Strether finally by showing what he has become after all the events of the story. Instead, it leaves a puzzle because one cannot be sure why he has made such a choice. There are various possibilities: he loves Madame de Vionnet; he does not love Maria Gostrey; or he thinks — a slippery thought — that if he is to make a great moral decision by renouncing his New England security he must not sully the purity of his choice by gaining a loving wife in France; or, he is still too timid to commit himself to a new life. Whichever reason we choose, we are still left with James's characteristic posture of renunciation in the foreground — not only the posture, but James enacting it with his exquisite, attenuated sensibility and style. The elegant periodic sentence ending the book with the word "Strether" epitomizes the way James keeps his own sensibility between Strether and the reader. From beginning to end, while professedly rendering only what Strether sees and says, he is continually displaying his own excruciatingly delicate awareness of all the tones and overtones of the moment. Hence Strether is reduced to being an instrument or medium for the exploitation of James's awareness, and it is understandable that at the end he would enact James's automatism of renunciation rather than make a decision in which his own will and character would be firmly defined.

Illusion or Maya is one of the avatars of Vishnu. Maya is the phenomenal world conceived as a shifting amorphous veil through which one may catch glimpses of reality. Maya flows and glitters, revealing this reality, being indeed an aspect of it, but always distorting and obscuring it. As a philosophical system this is at once profound and suggestive. When it has come to represent the relations between action and meaning in a novel, as it often has with James, it can be exceedingly puzzling, perhaps irreducibly so, for it negates the primacy of the action. Where the action has become an illusion, the characters must also slip and turn and fail to achieve a solid form.*

---

*Dealing with the problem of the "unreliable narrator," Wayne Booth reviews the major critics on key works and concludes, "When one puts together these and the many other conflicting claims about James's characters, he finds himself with an almost maddening chorus of charges and countercharges" (*The Rhetoric of Fiction*, p. 427).

12 *Aristocracy as Gesture*

THE HEROIC POSTURE

A THIRD element that intrudes upon pure characterization through action is the condition of aristocracy in a modern world that increasingly seems to value its qualities in proportion as it generates social conditions in which the aristocratic qualities cannot dominate, as their very nature says they must do. Between the aristocratic ideal and the exigencies of the hard actual modern world, characters are squeezed into caricatures of the ideal. Observing the process of distortion is a highly intellectual enterprise that thrusts the novelist, again, between action and character.

Where there is an aristocracy, the pattern of manners is a conscious, disciplined, and expressive form of communication. Every element, from posture to precedence, is carried along in the way aristocrats talk, and they talk always before an audience, whether or not it is anybody but themselves. Every detail of heraldry, punctilio, dress, and speech is *performed* before this audience, which is also the cast. Analogies with the drama come irresistibly because of one's sense of the aristocrat as performing, as living with a constant element of artifice, as moving upon a stage that is raised and prominent. The more perfectly and naturally — and naturalness is of the very essence — he moves as if to the manner born, the more grandly and graciously he is acting his part. The dancer or athlete performs complex artificial movements (artificial in the sense that they are learned, that they constitute a style) so gracefully that they seem perfectly natural. So the aristocrat. He aspires to a perfection of spontaneous artifice. The Queen of England herself, cultivated to her fingertips, bred to the bone, lives on a stage, and her every gesture is as conscious as it is gracious.

The mastery of manners, or more precisely of a manner, identifies the aristocrat. He is a gesture that cannot be perfectly imitated and that establishes a little drama of relation and communication whereever he moves. Any discussion of British fiction that neglects the atmosphere of aristocratic manners in which it lives and breathes is bound to miss half of the points. The true aristocrat dominates any company. Beside him the miner, the shopkeeper, the Cockney, the magnate, and the servant define themselves in a comfortable awareness of the standard which they serve while it serves them.

The pretenders to aristocracy divide themselves abruptly into two groups — those who make fools of themselves trying to fool the cast and the audience; and those who share with the audience the pleasure of knowing what to imitate and perhaps coming close to success, along with the pride of acknowledging that of course they do not pretend to fool anybody. In this second group, the scholar takes aristocracy as his inspiration, the gentleman takes it as his model.

How does the novel fare here where the world is a stage? Where the aristocracy is not *in* the novel but nevertheless is the sustaining element in the atmosphere, the novel would be totally incomprehensible to a reader who did not know of its standards and of its influence on everyday manners and language. The Englishman who is not an aristocrat is very likely to be playing at being one, and without access to this key one would find his conduct inscrutable, or amazing, or meaningless. The same is true of that other Englishman whose constant preoccupation is to defy the aristocratic tradition. He too has a focal point that establishes the perspectives in which he must be studied.

The tragedy that is peopled with aristocrats has been written by Shakespeare. It identifies the aristocrat as Man and so avoids pretense and problems. But once the British novel came into being there was interplay between the nobility, the gentry, and — let us say — "the rest." Where the comic mode prevails, one of the main sources of interest is the plots that are generated by pretense. They have especial richness because the interplay of have and have-not appears in every sentence that is spoken. The reader is endowed with knowledge of the levels of pretense in the cast, and he glows with discriminating recognition as each character speaks and bespeaks his fatuity or vulgarity. All readers are scholars of aristocracy, students of the drama that goes on always between its world and the related world that lives on the "inspiration" of its breath. The plot itself is probably concerned with people's attempts to be what they are not and to get what they do not "deserve." The unmasking of fraud, the rewarding of modest virtue (which in fact means acting according to one's true status), and the recognition of merit that carries a person a step or so above the status that his birth conferred — these are the staples of comic plot. To enjoy them, the reader must assume for himself the garb and spirit of aristocracy, which he wholeheartedly does, for although no character in the fiction may pretend without being punished, every reader is endowed with the quintessence of an aristocratic stance. He assumes it without pretense because it is conferred upon him with a wink of auctorial humility and complicity. Thus is the reader educated while he is being entertained, for to judge like an aristocrat is a step in the direction of being one. For the reader, the attitude is an intellectual virtue, abstract and pure. But let him presume to *act* in this garb and spirit and he straightway becomes a comic fraud, a "character."

There may be more grist for our mill here than meets the eye at first glance. Does the gentle reader who laughs over the follies of pretenders to status, assuming thereby the perspective of the aristocracy, realize that if he tried to act what he knows (i.e., translate insight into gesture) he too would appear fatuous or fraudulent? If so, he must assume a gap between what he essentially is and what he could perform. Perhaps this means that moral worth is a condition of being, whereas status is a matter of manners or gesture. The Faustian soul discovers itself in an absolute but has to express itself in action. It follows that we can know others only by what they do, although we assume that they have essences just like ourselves. The value of these considerations is that they guide us to see the essential difference between ourselves and a character in a book. We sense the essence, the *is*-ness, of the former, but we can know the latter only by his acts. The aristocrat, oddly enough, is controlled by the manners of his kind; it would seem that he must act in a characteristic way in order to enact his class. Now, the tennis player with perfect strokes — a classic style — is liberated by them, not in any way limited, and beats his opponents; and so likewise do all craftsmen and artists; but the aristocrat is enacting a *self* with his manners rather than just winning a game or making a statue — except that manners are to the self what technique is to the artist or the athlete. They are the medium and the substance of expression at the same time. Only when the style does not function perfectly does it call attention to itself and seem an encumbrance. But it almost always does call attention to itself in the realm of manners.

Where aristocracy-as-gesture presides over a comic action, we have limitations as well as resources. The chief resources are the easy and happy union of conversation and plot, where the pretender reveals himself with the very words he utters to formulate and to advance his plans. His language is gesture: its tone reveals his character, while the plans he discusses give substance to it and to the actions he takes to make it even more solid and plain. The limitations are of two sorts. First, pretense to status is folly, which leads to ridicule rather than insight; so the action is likely not to attain high seriousness. It will rather be what we might call a melodrama of manners. Second, the division that prevails in the mind of the reader between insight and gesture, between what he knows in essence and what he himself could perform, is translated to the stage or the novel. The ideal of aristocracy is sublime, but the individual aristocrat is almost bound to be, to some degree, a parody of himself. Otherwise he is a plaster saint. In the novel he has problems that pure virtue cannot meet, and as he wrestles with them he finds himself in some of the ludicrous postures of the pretender.

The comic delight in incongruity is evoked by the fact that the gesture must be a parody of the essence, because the aristocrat-in-action must face challenges that require undignified responses. Even the great tragedies of Shakespeare are often ludicrous, frequently offensive when performed. The grandeur of language in *Antony and Cleopatra* seldom prevails over the clank of Roman armor and the hairy calves of the actors. Lear lurches straight out of a third-rate Department of Speech. Macbeth out-Hitchcocks Hitchcock. Shakespeare knew this, and attempted to forestall the audience's laughter by using grotesque scenes — as when Lear kneels before his harsh daughters or pretends that he does not know who he is, to be suffering such indignities — but the modern writer does not often have the language for such effects.

There is, however, a difference between language and gesture. The great tragedy, like the epic, demands a grand style, for it is the language that gives dignity and intensity. What Matthew Arnold called high seriousness is the quality with which noble language invests a situation. When the English stage after the Restoration becomes bombastic and even ludicrous, it is the language that does it. It is the language that prevents us from taking seriously what might be great actions.

What spoils the performance of *Antony and Cleopatra*, on the other hand, is the quality of gesture. The noble characters become, as I have suggested, parodies of themselves. No gestures they can make succeed in rendering the noble essences that their speeches contain. Presentations of *Hamlet* and *Troilus and Cressida* in modern dress have been attempts to permit the language to speak for itself, in natural and thoughtful tones, but they add the greater defect of obscuring the image that the mind's eye would like to create for itself. The perfect medium for Shakespearean tragedy today would be the cinema, in which the poetry could be delivered with all its inwardness and depth. Could be, that is, if the flamboyance of cinematic techniques could be controlled and if the actors were able to lose their public selves in their roles. By suppressing their personalities the actors could become characters of tragic or heroic dimensions.

With Shakespeare the aristocrat is Man. But aristocracy runs down into language, manners, and values that parody the ideal of Man from which they descend. So in the British novel the ambience of aristocratic manners, which is the air it breathes and in which the levels of pretense and folly become apparent, is itself divided into layers of perhaps not pretense and folly but arrogance, stuffiness, and eccentricity — to name only a few — which complicate the already troublesome world in which the challenges that face the aristocrat-in-action require responses that are outside the limits of ideal conduct. Aristocratic language and manners, after all, embody and communicate an ideal society only if they do indeed dominate, inform, constitute that society. Their intention, which is always to do this, has never been perfectly achieved and becomes increasingly remote as the modern world moves out from under the noble aristocratic ideal. Let us examine some samples of the aristocratic gesture in the world it never made. And let us begin with the extreme, in the American South, where some writers find the gesture to be as phony as the real world about it is bleak and degraded — then back to Britain and the comic touch of Nancy Mitford.

ETERNAL FIRE IN THE AMERICAN SOUTH

The void between the individual and the state, which in an aristocratic society is filled by a coherent system of manners, values, and beliefs, accounts for the vitality as well as the problems of the American novel. It leads to the romance of Cooper, the formless drifting of Huck's raft, the flight of James to European settings, and the special problems of the American Southern novel. For the South does have a tradition of aristocracy; but the South has in fact lived through historical agonies which have made its aristocratic tradition-in-action a nightmare of violence and terror, rather than merely the gesture that tends toward caricature of itself. If one generalization about the South will stand unchallenged, it is that the Southern novel deals, in many ways, with a tormented and insecure aristocratic tradition presiding over a society full of violence and injustice. Indeed, presiding over is the wrong phrase; it does not preside, it battles furiously with the forces, the realities, that threaten it. And what really is "it" — this aristocratic tradition? It is not an embodied social reality; rather it is an idea which has never been realized in fact but which has nevertheless been the dominant force in the drama of Southern life.

Thus in the South, between the aristocratic myth and the grisly social realities, there gapes a special void — a void that is not merely a social fact but a psychological problem that frequently becomes a psychosis. The Southern hero is seen trying to hold together a world composed of parts that will not go together. Put together they explode in violence. What occurs as a lynching socially is expressed as a psychosis psychologically. Engaged with what would appear to be the most intractable materials conceivable, the Southern novel has nevertheless generated tremendous power. Its forms are as fascinating as they are various; they defy generalization; they demand individual study and description. Rather than grapple with Faulkner, who could well be the serpent to my Laocoön, I should like to explore the struggle with these wild elements that has been carried through by the enormously talented Calder Willingham in *Eternal Fire* (1962).

As a writer, Calder Willingham is a real professional. He has style, abundance, warmth, and control. He can make his words do exactly what he wants them to do, conveying any shade of an idea or an emotion — or several shades at once. *Eternal Fire* is a delightfully sophisticated book about the South that plunges, style and all, into the abyss between the myth and the actuality. It is so expertly constructed, so richly elaborated, and so subtly complex in tone that it is very hard to describe. At the beginning, the tone is flippant. The book opens with a paragraph on the South that sets the scene at the same time that it mocks the moody approach to nature which is perhaps an aspect of Southern sentiment: "In this peaceful land, pretty birds sing and the woodbine twines. Violets and forget-me-nots bloom in the meadow. The wind is soft as a baby's smile, and as warm and gentle as mother love. Only an occasional random tornado moils the scene and disrupts nature. True, the summer sun is a fiery furnace; it boils the blood, cooks the brain, and spreads a fever in the bones. But the same fearful orb, in collaboration with the sweet rain generated by its power, makes the little flowers grow."

A diagram of the characters would show, in the center, two people who are innocent, loving, modest, kind, generous, tender, and beautiful. Two darlings each with a flaw — not a defect, but an aspect that makes them vulnerable to the world's evil. Randy Shepherdson III, at twenty-three, is heir to a considerable fortune that includes Carthage Hill, a magnificent manor house and estate in Georgia. Laurie Mae Lytle, twenty-two, whom he adores and who adores him, has a sexual drive, always feared and suppressed, which now in her engagement to Randy threatens to drive her out of her pure mind. Both of them have been raised to regard lust in a woman as an evil, disgraceful thing. Laurie can't even speak of it to Randy, but she is under a serious strain. The solution for them is to get married, quick, for they are star-crossed and ideally matched.

Ranged around this Adamic center and pressing in upon it are menacing rings of greed, depravity, vanity, and degeneracy. The wickedness is extravagant, almost exuberant. It is intelligent and resourceful, too, and the degeneracy that is available for its uses is as abundant as maggots on a rotting carcass. The rotting carcass almost invisible under its squirming mantle of maggots is the South as Willingham sees it. The carcass is apparent as a form, but it is almost totally buried under the degeneracy and corruption that feed upon it.

The closest circle around the Paradise of love (a circle which in this cosmos is also the *primum mobile*) is Judge Ball, who is first citizen of the town of Glenville, lives with his wife at Carthage Hill, and is Randy's guardian and trustee. They are remote cousins of Randy, who of course lives at Carthage Hill too, as its rightful owner. The Judge has lost a large part of Randy's fortune in various unlucky ventures. With rigged books and local prestige he has concealed the losses, and his gambler's heart is sure that he can recoup everything in a couple of years; but he must turn over the entire property upon Randy's marriage. By a strange clause in his father's will, if Randy marries before he is thirty, it must be with his guardian's consent, or he may be disinherited. The Judge works from this point, and he tries to leave nothing to chance. If forbidding Randy to marry Laurie Mae does not succeed, he will invite Laurie to tea and have her mortally insulted by a flock of bitchy relatives jealous of Randy's fortune. If Randy still insists, the Judge has laid various traps and snares to discredit Laurie Mae in his eyes.

He has summoned Harry Diadem to come to Glenville and affirm that he is Laurie Mae's cousin and in one or several ways to prey upon her. Legal action for her property, "proof" that she is part Negro, seduction, whatever else the situation may suggest to the Judge's fertile invention are all possibilities. Harry Diadem is a wicked, pitiless man, in the barren wasteland of whose soul nothing brings warmth so much as his avocation of seducing women. They challenge him. Virgins of seventeen, chaste matrons, all difficult "scores" are his meat and drink; he is a true artist at seduction, and he is more vicious and accomplished than anyone can believe until he reads the book. Harry keeps a notebook with a record of his "scores," graded from A to D, so he can remember them, for after success he generally casts them aside.

Another of the Judge's agents is a broken-down drunk ex-policeman named Whit Galladay, who lives in a trailer with his wife, Myrtle, and his beautiful red-headed nineteen-year-old daughter, Poppie. When they get drunk enough, all three make love together. The Judge has the damaging information about Whit's past — how he lost his badge and his home for attempting while drunk to rape a young girl — and with a mixture of threats and promises he has engaged Whit to spy on Laurie Mae and to locate Harry Diadem and bring him back to town.

Whit, for all his irregularities, is a good-hearted fellow who has known Laurie Mae as a neighbor for many years and cannot be convinced that she is anything but a very good and very kind girl.

A bookkeeper named Louis Elvram Parsons has discovered the errors in the Judge's accounts. He has come to the Judge demanding a mere $50,000, which he believes Randy's vast estate, even though depleted by the Judge's extravagances, can easily afford. Parsons has led a quiet workaday life, but he aspires to run off and live it up in Miami with a blowsy slut called Sugar Dolly. The Judge easily persuades his black-mailer that he cannot pay blackmail from the penitentiary; Parsons must sit by and wait or even cooperate with the Judge to prevent Randy's marriage. Sitting around and waiting with Sugar Dolly turns out to be a nerve-racking business: she is convinced that their throats will be cut, while his frail gentility — expressed in sanitary cir-cumlocutions and grotesque elegancies — is increasingly horrified by her vulgarity.

A hearty resource of the Southern novelist, in this connection, is the combination of Ciceronian rhetoric and genteel diction in which the Southern aristocratic myth expresses itself. Everybody knows about this language and in some way reflects it. The lowest bum is touched by its richness if not by its ideal delicacy. The writer therefore has re-sources of characterization at his fingertips that are not available in the North. Elegance, sincerity, pomposity, evil can be revealed in a sentence or two with a subtlety limited only by the writer's craft — and here Willingham is phenomenally skillful; he has no master among Southern writers, for his touch is defter than Faulkner's. Witness Sugar Dolly at breakfast with Louis Elvram Parsons, in the hotel at Glenville. She is jumpy as an old rhino, and not without reason:

The other breakfasters in the sunlit dining room looked all right, but then you never could tell and Sugar Dolly's nature was not over-trusting. That fatty over there by that there funny bush in the pot, him for instance with them little old mean squidgy eyes. Probably just as soon take out a knife and cut on you as look at you. Watch out for little old squidgy eyes or one fine morning you'd wake up with your throat sliced from ear to ear.

"Call yourself cookin' that egg?" asked Sugar Dolly.

"Pardon, Madam?" said the waiter.

A stiff smile creased Mr. Parsons' face. "It's all right," he said.

"It ain't all right a bit," declared Sugar Dolly. She pointed a rigid finger directly down at the two fried eggs nestled in strips of bacon. "Them eggs are *raw*."

"Raw, Madam?" asked the waiter.

"Hell, yes, raw," said Sugar Dolly. The polite black face infuriated her; the smart nigger was acting like she'd never been in a hotel before. "The yallers are all puddly and the whi-ites ain't nothing but so much snot."

"Shall I return them to the kitchen, Madam?"

"You better, if you don't want 'em throwed in your black face," said Sugar Dolly.

"Certainly, Madam," said the waiter.

"And shake your ass," said Sugar Dolly.

The waiter strolled off without bothering to reply, utter cool revulsion on his face, the plate balanced in his fingers and held off to one side as if it contained a decaying toad.

"Uppity black son of a bitch," said Sugar Dolly. "He'll prob'ly take 'em back to the kitchen and spit all over 'em."

"Must you make these distressing scenes?" whispered Mr. Parsons. "Must you constantly make these scenes?" [Page 50.]

The forces of light are slender — only a runty moron named Hawley Battle, who believes that Laurie Mae is literally an angel, and worships her and is dedicated to protecting her. Hawley is not bright, but he is terribly strong — as strong as Harry Diadem is vicious. Two pure hearts and strong characters in Randy and Laurie Mae add something to the forces of light; but the contest would be terribly unequal if the evil ones did not turn upon each other.

In fact, the forces of darkness are an armful of eels for the Judge. Whit Galladay balks at turning the fiendish Harry loose on Laurie Mae. In order to bring him to heel — and frighten the importunate Parsons — the Judge forces Whit to beat up Sugar Dolly. Whit can do it only if he is drunk, and then he loses control of himself and the results are frightful. Meanwhile Harry Diadem sees through the Judge's problem and plans in ten minutes and sets about turning them to his own advantage. The tea party at which Laurie Mae is perhaps to be humiliated by the unannounced arrival of a flock of Randy's nasty female relations takes the bit in its teeth like a wild stallion. The country aunts and cousins, bursting with crude color and loquacity, fall for the girl. The party warms up fast:

More laughter. Randy, who had always found Cousin Mim's marriage routine a bit of a vulgar bore in the past, joined in heartily. It sounded funny to him. Cousin Mim — what a card! He winked at

Laurie Mae across the sun dial. Her eyes were shining with happiness and she was laughing in great amusement at the gesticulating, shouting Cousin Mim.

"It's true, damn it! I spent seventeen months fighting off Henry, and it wore us both to a nub. By the time we got to that dad-blame bed I was screeching like a hoot owl and poor Henry looked like he'd come down with hookworm!" . . .

[T]he old South had been dotted with personalities of the ilk of Cousin Mim, like lopsided daisies hither and yon in the Dixie dew. Every family tribe of any consequence had one or two of them. The Judge was one and Cousin Mim was another. The favorite trick of them all, the common denominator of their craft, was to blurt out the awful truth with a shocking disregard for convention. Since only those in an unchallengeable position could risk such a thing, characters of this variety flowered only amongst the gentry. . . .

Randy felt a nostalgia for the old South. He had forgotten in New York what masters of social intercourse Southerners really were. He felt a renewed respect for the gifts of his people. Any of them here, even the revolting Buggie, could talk. . . .

Was the South in reality "degenerated"? Were there not compensating human factors in the system of caste and class, factors that already had begun to destroy the system itself? Could not Laurie Mae's own rise from ignorance and subjection be regarded as a straw in the wind? . . . The South was *not* a degenerate land and those who called it so were liars and slanderers. In reality, the South was a battleground of the good and evil that burns in contradictions in every human heart. [Pages 186–87.]

But right here the energy of the characters takes off at a gallop. Laurie Mae who has never drunk hard liquor gets herself well plastered on good Bourbon and tries desperately to seduce Randy in his bedroom. We know of her passion, and so her conduct is entirely probable — and touching — and so is Randy's horrified and chivalric reticence. They stagger downstairs to find that Laurie Mae's old, senile, alcoholic grandmother has crashed the party blind drunk and is making an unbelievable spectacle of herself. The South is full of lusty surprises; the worst foot has been put forward on both sides, yet total disaster has been averted; it *looks* as if Laurie Mae and Randy are over the hump.

This bare skeleton of a summary takes us up to about page 200 of the novel's 630 pages. The language is, depending on the reader's palate, appalling or refreshing. It pulls absolutely no punches in presenting the conversation of lower-class toughs, thugs, sluts, slobs, and provincial snobs. There is not even the selective tidying practiced by a Faulkner. This bold truth if it were only faithfully obscene and illiterate would not have much value. Obscenity can be dismal and boring. But Willingham's language is deft, apt, charged, glowing; it will bring roars of delighted laughter from all but the most censorious readers.

Every discussion puts the characters into new situations and relations and confronts them with vital decisions. Every scene carries the plot forward and leads the characters into more complex relations, new vistas of problems and choices, new discoveries and revelations of self. Thus the characters get richer and fuller as the plot moves into more intricate tensions and more dramatic consequences. There is a surprise on every page, a new insight in every confrontation. The story vibrates with life because every decision, every word spoken, is embedded in a plot that *keeps right on moving*. The author has the skill and the abundance of invention to let all these scenes have, as it were, lives of their own. There is a great deal of talk, so that what happens grows directly out of the interactions among the people there. It *happens* dramatically, and the people grow increasingly alive with every word they speak. What happens is character-in-action, character more fully known because it is more fully expressed and involved. The richness and subtlety of the language give life to people as strong as they are varied, who in turn make the plot grow bigger and bigger with the sheer life they put into it.

This is true up to a point, from which the generalization becomes somewhat less valid. If the point cannot be placed exactly, it can nevertheless be sensed and located fairly closely. It is the watershed, let us say, toward which we mount as the plot thickens and the suspense increases. At the top, the tension mounts into the bizarre: it is the overspecialized concentration of sex and villainy that carries the story over the peak into an area where the central manners and values of a society are no longer revealingly explored.

Harry makes his first assault on Laurie Mae when he visits her unexpectedly one evening to tell her that he is her cousin — and it is a near thing. Working expertly on her compassion, striking fast and strong, he has her almost down to her bare skin and overpowered. The Judge and Whit are watching from an empty house next door. Hawley Battle is up in the magnolia tree in front. Laurie Mae bites Harry's thumb clean to the bone, in the nick of time. When Harry leaves, Hawley catches him and nearly kills him. The Judge didn't expect Harry to seduce Laurie Mae. Now he offers him $10,000 for his real plan: to "sell his mother" and let it be proved, in the lawsuit, that she was a whore and his father a pimp. Laurie Mae is persuaded to fight the case. She has bad trouble with Randy over that bitten thumb of Harry's and the round of parties and plans added to the continuing agonies of frustrated desire because the wedding has to be postponed two or three weeks to allow time for the trial makes her frantic, sleepless, and unable to eat. There is a heat wave, too.

Working on his other pawn, Harry, at the trial rehearsals, with contempt and insults, the Judge has him too at fever pitch. Harry controls himself only for the $10,000 and the happy thought that he will be able to blackmail the Judge for the rest of his life. But the Judge is far ahead of him, fraying his nerves for the greatest double cross of the century. At the trial, Laurie Mae is humiliated by extensive cross-examination (indignantly defended by the Judge, in a way that makes it worse) on the matter of the bitten thumb. How in the world, presses Lawyer Underwood, did she ever let Harry get into a situation where he could tear off her clothes? But the heart of the case proves beyond a reasonable doubt that Harry is indeed her cousin, that his mother was a whore and his father a pimp who ran the whorehouse. On top of all this it is brought out that Harry Diadem's father was a quarter Negro! In his summing up, the Judge turns on Harry. Any white woman who lands in a nigger-run whorehouse is blameless, having been victimized by satanic wiles and violence:

"Today, with an increasing vigor, a concerted effort is being made in this country to destroy the South. . . . We hear the whimpers of bleeding hearts who tell us with pious horror that the Negro is underprivileged and abused.

"This, my friends, is not only a dastardly lie, it is a shrewd and cunning attempt to destroy us. . . . Our niggers have a good life down here. But the point of it all is not to tell the truth, the point is to undermine us and destroy us, to grind us down into the dust.

"Where will it lead? . . . Why, the next thing they'll be asking is to sit in the front section of the buses and streetcars. . . . And then they'll ask to be served in white restaurants, and that won't end it either, because then they'll commence to howl and demand they be allowed to go to white schools! Don't think it's incredible, my friends. I have studied the statements of nigger leaders and that is just what they want, and they'll get it, too, unless we stand up on our hind legs and refuse to allow them to have it."

The real culprit, he concludes, rising in his eloquence, is not the fallen flower of Southern womanhood:

"The real culprit is mongrelism. . . . The Negro race is not a bad race, if pure. Niggers are cheerful, hard-working, happy people, with the minds of thoughtless and irresponsible children. The white race, if pure, is the source of all the civilization and progress the world has seen. Not one single solitary colored race has ever produced a worthwhile civilization. They still drown babies in China and burn widows in India. Think about this. What's wrong with Mexico, Cuba, Brazil, and all those run-down dirty little countries in South America? Mongrelization. That's what's wrong with them."

The result is that mongrelism

"is a devil's broth of a creature, a half-human monster endowed with the intelligence of the white race transformed into a diabolic cunning; and at the same time, the simple animal nature of the Negro is transformed into ungovernable lust and a hideous animality."

And now, Harry Diadem, he concludes:

"your days of passing yourself off as a white man, your days of polluting white girls and women with your mongrel seed, your days of wandering through the world like a slimy half-breed cur are finished. . . . Deputy Slade! Arrest that mongrel nigger, and put him behind bars where he belongs!" [Pages 411–14.]

The Judge has the goods on Harry, too, for he is wanted for statutory rape and other crimes in various states. Afterwards, "The sense of having created a masterpiece possessed him with a gentle and delicious euphoria. . . . The triumph was total. Everything, to the last detail, had worked with a precision that was a marvel to behold. The wedding of Miss Lytle to Randolph was shattered. Furthermore, neither of them had the remotest idea how it had been done." (Pages 419–20.)

This tour de force, this cadenza, this virtuoso piece of creative scoundrelism, which puts Harry out of circulation and Laurie Mae in mortified disgrace, might seem to reach a peak of extravagance — but no, we are barely under way into the realms of devilish invention and consequence. The brew that Willingham has mixed continues to bubble and generate its horrors. At this point indeed we seem to have been carried beyond a revealing exploration of the central manners and values of a society, although it can be argued that the rich, lush elaboration of the Judge's contrivance is an expression of Southern rhetoric, of the elements of Ciceronianism and chivalry running free in a society where the myth prevails but does not control. And so it *must* be argued, for sensible Laurie Mae despises "fashionable" Southern society and does not care enough about what it thinks to cancel the marriage. True love does not alter when it alteration finds, or bend with the remover to remove. Oh no, the trouble comes from a different aspect of the contest between myth and reality. Randy cannot get over his righteous indignation at the fact that Laurie Mae kissed Harry. This impels her on to an icy explanation that her aunt Lucy Belle (Harry's mother) was *not* a nymphomaniac and that girls, normal girls, *do* have powerful sexual drives that are *not* merely occasions for having children. Randy is good and gentle, a true aristocrat, but he is hemmed in by convention; contemptuous as he is of the South, he cannot look some facts in the face with the woman he is to marry. Nor can he be reasonable enough to agree that Harry is sick and to be pitied. Chivalry says he is a psychotic monster. Thus just when it might seem that Willingham has cut loose from the social earth, he turns out merely to be a step ahead of his reader. In the midst of his thickening plot, he can present a conversation between Randy and Laurie Mae that allows each one to reveal and discover himself further. One is drawn back to total acceptance of the characters and their problem, and from their discussion one is even taught to understand that there are good and sufficient reasons for Harry's appalling conduct. Being raised in a whorehouse and seeing his mother beaten until she becomes insane and commits suicide is not calculated to produce a model citizen.

The Judge's armful of eels are squirming and snapping furiously, however. No sooner has he got Harry into jail, beaten, bloody, and defeated, than he has to buy him free so that he can make yet another attempt on Laurie Mae's virtue. Contrivance now mounts upon creation until, in a stifling warehouse full of baled cotton and watched over by the devoted Hawley Battle, finally, in a scene that touches a new crest of eroticism, Harry seduces Laurie Mae. We are well into the tornado promised in the first paragraph of the book, which now bursts in a full violence. It is not merely that evil triumphs over innocence, but that nature cannot be contained in the hypocrisies of the Southern myth. Laurie Mae has been pushed too far. The story carries the reader now to the ultimate question of whether reason and love can prevail, in the end, or must the hypocrisies prevail and destroy what might have been an ideal marriage? But enough of the story; the reader should be permitted to enjoy it fresh. Indeed the story itself is so absorbing that one cannot lay the book down once he has got into it, so absorbing that it takes a second reading to free him from the narrow tunnel of suspense so that he can look around and appreciate the psychological insights and, particularly, the way in which every incident in the book is *motivated* by the interplay of character and situation at that point.

Calder Willingham's language and plot take off into the higher levels of burlesque. His extravagant invention, married to his exuberance of language, in the intricate and sinewy plot, leads to fantasies of motivation and deed which although thoroughly absorbing and convincing are carried beyond the limits of human possibility. The evil of Harry Diadem, the cadenzas of craftiness tossed off by the Judge (who is first citizen of the town), the dedication of Hawley Battle, though made probable by the action and psychologically justified, nevertheless go beyond the bounds of human expectation. Such things don't happen. Calder Willingham is coruscating on thin ice in a stratosphere beyond the limits of human possibility.

Why does this happen, when all the criteria of character in action seem to be so superbly fulfilled? It is because there is still another level of theme and intention present. Willingham's wild extravagance of language, character, and plot compose a satire on the South. He is saying — no, not saying but expressing his belief that the South does not, after all, make sense. It has too many extremes and excesses, the abyss that yawns between the chivalric myth and the dreadful reality is too vast to be reasonably bridged. Even a logical, motivated, tightly constructed action generates enormities that do not, in retrospect, seem to express a livable human society of possible people. But what about *King Lear?* Is it any more acceptable as a picture of the human condition? Yes, it is, because it carries on into images of human greatness, through agony and understanding, that enlarge our sense of the human spirit, our notion of human capacity. Without *Lear* there would be less Man for men to conceive.

Willingham's insight is somewhat different in kind, for it is inspired by a critical genius. It pictures a society that is there, all right, but unreal. The smiling surface generates the incredible tornado, and this sort of explosion is everywhere latent in the society and in the individual people. This is the life that *exists* and moves but that is contrived, artificial, unconvincing — in short not *real* in that it does not finally make real people or logical sense. It exists, but it is not probable; we should insist that it was not possible if we did not know that it existed. Perhaps it would be less paradoxical to say that it is phenomenal but unessential. Where the parts should join to make a substantial fabric, just there there is a void, a nothing. The parts are real enough but where they should cohere in an *order*, social or personal, they do not finally join. Just there is the gap, the bottomless abyss, the void showing through the places where the parts do not touch and join. If the South is to be known, it must be in the terms of its essential *un*reality. Essential is the key word: the range and violence of the activities prevent the conception of an essence that lives behind them. The Judge, to put it concretely, is a figment of his own rhetoric; like Conrad's Kurtz, he is a voice speaking from a void.

These insights demand a comic and satiric spirit. They cannot be soberly explained — one must discuss them in paradoxes — but they have been rendered by the wild extravagance of language, energy, and invention glowing and flaming in *Eternal Fire*.

THE REAL THING IN THE WRONG WORLD

Nancy Mitford and Calder Willingham have in common a subject that can be described in the same general terms: it is the adventures of an aristocratic ideal in a world containing many elements that will not adjust themselves to that ideal. Willingham's aristocratic tradition is a mythical force, an idea that has never achieved social reality, in constant tension with the inner personal contradictions and the external explosions that have rumbled from Fort Sumter to Montgomery. But Nancy Mitford writes of an aristocratic world so different from the American South that the contrasts are extraordinarily and delightfully illuminating.

Stanley Vestal used to tell a story about the Indians of the Great Plains to illustrate how they felt about their place in the world. Out in the middle of the unfenced and unbounded prairie he met a plains Indian, alone on his horse.

"How!" he said, by way of salutation, and then asked after the Indian's home, "Where tepee?"

The Indian replied, "How! Brave don't know where tepee."

"Oh, then you're lost?"

"No. Indian *here*; tepee lost."

This is the aristocrat, about whom the world revolves. Nancy Mitford's aristocracy, furthermore, is firmly based in values and manners and a long solid tradition. It is a fact, without question. It sees its values with candor and lucidity. If its members comprise an extraordinary range of eccentricity, prejudice, and dedication, they all nevertheless communicate in terms of values which they profoundly know and accept. Whatever the vagaries of their conduct (which as we shall see are considerable), they know in what respects they can count on each other. Their problems come from a world that has changed at increasing speed since World War I. How do they live in it? How do they serve it? How do they respond to its pressures? Can they, especially, raise their children in it without losing the old values?

The last is the big question. The aristocratic narrator of *Don't Tell Alfred* (1960) — which is a better example for this study than the more famous *Pursuit of Love* (1945) or *Love in a Cold Climate* (1949) because it has more invention, less autobiography than they — obviously believes that the world is moving out from under her very fast, and that the force and effect of the aristocracy is perhaps in its last half century. Her quality, however, is to see the world change with humor and dignity. She will relate to it, live in it, and serve it, but she will not modify her basic values a particle — and if the world rejects them (as it will), so much the worse for it. Poise, humor, dignity, flexibility, and service are qualities that make very admirable people. Nancy Mitford renders these qualities through what her characters do NOT say and through what they do in special situations. Otherwise they convey a "moral certainty of self" which marks the aristocrat and makes him move with a special sort of self-confidence in any situation. It comes out in the fact that he feels no need to explain, to justify, or to apologize. Like the Indian, he makes a center wherever he is, and the wheel of events turns around it. It never occurs to him to question his importance; if he entertains such a question it refers to the value of those outside the pale. Yet his certainty of self does not diminish his profound sense of service. It comes to about the same thing, indeed, whether the aristocrat feels that he exists to serve society or that society exists to serve and locate him. The essential point is that society without the aristocrat is unthinkable — foreseeable, of course, but still unthinkable, for without what the aristocracy represents society is nothing. Caught in this paradox, the narrator's only dignified attitude must be a humorous one.

The aristocracy of *Don't Tell Alfred* is represented by a spectacular range of types and generations. In the distance is old Uncle Matthew, Lord Alconleigh, an opinionated individualist who has presided in one way or another over the lives of the others. Having handed the ancestral estate over to his son, against the advice of the few people in the area with whom he was still on speaking terms, he violently challenged every innovation in its management, took an intense and unjustified dislike to his son's wife, whom he held responsible, and stamped off to take a flat in London. There he befriended a taxi driver whose time and services he pre-empted (money being no problem at all) almost completely and with whom, before the novel is ended, we find him taking a nostalgic pilgrimage, in the taxi of course, to Ypres, to renew their memories of great battles in World War I in which they had participated.

The narrator, Fanny, who is Uncle Matthew's niece, is now Lady Wincham. Her husband, Alfred, is at the opposite extreme from Uncle Matthew. He is Professor of Pastoral Theology at Oxford, a man of great intelligence, wide knowledge, and total dignity. He has secretly advised the government, and as the novel opens he has been made ambassador to France, where his most troublesome diplomatic problem is the disputed ownership of the Minquiers Islands — three miserable rocks in the Channel that are covered at high tide.

Present only by name and repute is Fanny's mother, who is never called anything but the Bolter. At the age of sixty-five she has just married her ninth husband, a lad in his twenties, who has persuaded her to put her money into a travel agency, where it will earn lavishly, instead of leaving it in stodgy bonds. It is a mark of the family's aplomb that the Bolter is not hidden under a bushel of shame. Quite the contrary, everybody knows and talks about her, down to the youngest, without explanation or apology. There is no feeling that she has "betrayed" her class or that her class should feel some guilty responsibility for her. There she is in the firmament, moving in somewhat erratic cycles and epicycles to be sure, but plainly visible and endowed with her own light and mass.

Fanny stands as a mean among these extremes. She is modest but not shy, conservative but not aggressively so. She accepts the task of running the Embassy in Paris calmly enough, confident that her assistants and advisers will show her the way with the details, while she can continue to carry on her prime responsibility of making life comfortable for her distinguished husband. She does not dwell upon her sense of duty. She does not complain about her responsibilities but accepts them naturally and wholeheartedly. Through the whole book she says nothing intimate about herself except that she had loved one of her sons more than the other and wondered whether she was therefore accountable for the latter's problems. For the rest, she tells what happens by recounting events as she saw them and participated in them. Everyone is therefore presented objectively, without prying or speculation into psychological motivations. This reserve accounts for the balance of dignity and humor that is maintained while some extraordinarily funny events take place.

The younger generation provides the activity. First to burst upon the scene is Basil, the favorite son, who has taken a brilliant degree at Oxford and then temporarily disappeared. Since the parents' firm policy is never to ask questions or to interfere with advice, Baz has not gone off in rebellion exactly, or even defiance, but in pursuit of life on his own terms. His return is unheralded. The door of Fanny's room "burst open and a strange figure loomed into the room. Side whiskers, heavy fringe, trousers, apparently moulded to the legs, surmounted by a garment for which I find no word but which covered the torso, performing the function both of coat and of shirt — such was the accoutrement of an enormous boy . . . my long-lost Basil." (Page 91.) The brilliant lad who took a first in history at Oxford in the garb of a Teddy! The Bolter's new husband, whom he now calls Old Grandad, is in fact his own age and an old friend — and they are in business together.

Over breakfast he explains how the racket is run:

"Grandad assembles the cattle and I herd it to and fro. In plain English, Grandad, with many a specious promise and hopeful slogan — 'No hurry, no worry if you travel the Grandad way' and so on — gets together parties of tourists, takes their cash off them and leaves me to conduct them to their doom. Ghastly it is — fifteen to a carriage across France and worse when we change for the peninsula. Then, when they finally disembark, more dead than alive after days without food or sleep, they have to face up to the accommodation. 'Let Grandad rent you a fisherman's cottage' says the prospectus. So he does. The beds are still hot from the honest fisher folk prized out of them by yours truly! That's when the ruminants begin collapsing — disappointment finishes them off. Anyhow the old cows drop like flies when the temperature is over a hundred — Britons always think they are going to love the heat but in fact it kills them — we usually plant one or two in the bone-orchard before we start for home. I keep a top hat over there now, for the funerals, it looks better . . .

"They can't speak any language bar a little basic British and they've got no money because Grandad bags whatever they can afford for the trip before they leave. So they are at my mercy. You should see the letters they write when they get home . . . threatening my life and everything." [Pages 93–94.]

The women are all deluded by their lust for foreigners, whereas the men are exhausted and have concentrated their little remaining emotion and energy on revenge against Baz, who lies face down on the sand, keeping his face pale while his back tans, so that his bloodthirsty charges will not recognize him. He has abandoned his plans for a career in the foreign service, explaining the merits of travel bureaus:

"You see, we hold the national tourist industries in the hollow of our hands. There's nothing they dread more than a lot of unorganized travellers wandering about their countries exhibiting individualism. They'd never force a tourist on his own into those trams and hotels — he'd go home sooner. But you can do anything with a herd and the herd must have its drover. As he keeps the tickets and the money and the passports (no worry) even the most recalcitrant of the cattle are obliged to follow him. No good jibbing when the conditions are ghastly because what is the alternative? To be stranded without hope of succour. So the authorities need us; the tourists need us; we are paramount. Oh, it's a wonderful profession and I'm lucky to have the family backing which got me into it." [Pages 96–97.]

Fanny asks in horror about his career, but he explains that he is not going to waste the best years of his life, like his father, to end his "days in a ghastly great dump like this." Having finished an excellent breakfast while he told this grisly tale, Baz is about to make his way back to the Gare du Nord where his hungry sheep are stranded without food or hope on account of a railway strike, but Fanny insists that he bring them all immediately to the Embassy where she will serve them breakfast in the garden and pay for a bus to take them to the Channel.

We expect a plague-ridden mob, but Fanny says that she "was not at all surprised when Basil's Britons turned out to be entirely delightful, very different indeed from the furious, filthy, haggard, exhausted, sex-starved mob which anybody not knowing Basil and not knowing England might have expected from his description. They were, in fact, sensible, tidy and nicely dressed, covered with smiles and evidently enjoying this adventure in a foreign land. . . . The Britons were full of his [Basil's] praises and when he explained that I was his mother they crowded round to tell me what a wonder boy or miracle child I had produced." [Pages 98–99.] They do not know that they are in the Embassy, having come in through the garden gate, and they assume that Fanny is a hotel-keeper. Nobody explains these matters, and the tourists continue to give enraptured accounts of how Basil has guided and cared for them and by superhuman strength, determination, and ingenuity got them to Paris when thousands of other unhappy travelers are stranded who knows where in the provinces. They are going to subscribe for a memento to Basil when they get home!

Basil drops into the Embassy from time to time during the summer, and Fanny seems to become reconciled to his making a career in the travel business. The line is let fall while more disturbing ones take over. Next is the sudden entry of the older son, David, just as an important dinner party of fifty people is about to be seated. He "came crab-wise into the room, pulling after him a blue plastic cradle and a girl attached to its other handle. He was dressed in corduroy trousers, a duffle coat, a tartan shirt and sandals over thick, dirty, yellow woollen socks. The girl was tiny, very fair with a head like a silk-worm's cocoon, short white skirt (filthy) swinging over a plastic petticoat, a black belt, red stockings and high-heeled, pointed, golden shoes." (Page 114.) Observed by deputies and cabinet ministers, Fanny rushes forward to embrace and kiss her son. There is a Chinese baby in the basket. David introduces the girl as Dawn, without further explanation. Since the great dinner table holds exactly fifty, Fanny sends two assistants off to a restaurant to make space for the newcomers, who are welcomed to the party as naturally as if they were dressed for a Mayfair wedding. Here you have the aristocracy displaying its moral certainty of self with absolute — in the fullest sense of the word — aplomb. The only harsh note is that David complains about being seated next to his wife, an impropriety at formal parties that he might have overlooked in view of the lateness of his arrival and the state of his clothing.

David, also with a brilliant degree at Oxford, has gone Zen. The Chinese baby has been adopted as a token of one-worldliness. Dawn turns out to be the daughter of an English bishop. The pair are stopping on their way — afoot — to the East, but they settle down in the Embassy, freeloading, studying Zen, and talking the most unspeakable Zennish nonsense while the ambassador tries to master his rage. This eruption might seem to be enough for one summer, but the younger generation has more bombs to burst. There are two younger boys at Eton, who defy the master, depart in a rented Rolls Royce, and disappear somewhere into the deeps of London. It transpires that they have jobs packing electric razors, at £9 a week, which gives them enough to live on and spend their evenings listening to the latest frenzies of jive.

Through these calamities Fanny maintains her discretion and firmness, taking proper care of Alfred and doing what is expected of an ambassadress. While sons and relatives swarm in and about, the issue of the Minquiers Islands grows hotter. England sends sharp notes, France's national pride is wounded, and the alliance is shaken. Charges that one or the other nation's custodianship has not built schools or paved roads (on islands that are submerged at high tide) point up the absurdities of modern nationalism. Lord Wincham bringing his tact and wisdom to bear on such a problem represents the plight of the aristocratic ideal of service in the modern world, where it confronts the ignoble and the ludicrous on every side and also in its own imperfect human vessels. Faced with the situations thrust upon him by the modern world, the aristocrat's gestures must often caricature the ideal. Alfred never loses his dignity or dedication, Fanny conducts herself with a quiet firmness, but they cannot escape being involved in absurdities when they relate to this mad world they are serving. The predicament of an ideal put into ludicrous situations cannot be corrected so long as it clings to its notions of service and leadership. Without them it would not be itself, but having them it must relate to a world that it can no longer control.

The action reaches a climax of fun and absurdity when the two young fugitives from Eton arrive with a jive idol named Yanky Fonzy. They are followed by a mob of teenagers that fills the street and garden, stops traffic, and looks as if it is going to invade and sack the Embassy. It is in fact a peaceful mob welcoming its idol, but it is mistaken for a political mob furiously demonstrating against England's stubborn insistence on having the Islands. Under such pressure, the English government retreats from its foolish position, relations are soothed, and Alfred can presumably direct his attention toward more serious matters. The climax does not resolve the personal affairs of the boys, which are dropped more or less as they are: David heads east (his energy restored by hormones, his psychic disturbances as strong as ever), Basil goes on confidently with the travel bureau, and the two younger ones decide to make another stab at their educations, with a tutor.

Here is a classic example of how the plot determines characterization. By humor and dignity the author establishes the tone of the aristocracy — its ideals and its manners: what might be considered its social context — but the farcical plot puts the people into situations where they have no profound or noble choices. Humor is their defense against the world *and* the follies they are forced to engage in, but it comes as a screen between them and the reader. It deflects attention to itself and to the author's gracious wit and objectivity, while it allows the characters to be concealed behind it. Alfred is kept at an aloof remove. Fanny does not follow him into diplomatic sessions, nor does she permit him to reveal personal conflicts. He can be a model aristocrat because he stays at a distance, moving so little that his statuesque ideality does not have opportunity to caricature itself by action. Basil is gaily hiding whatever serious problems he may have. Neither one is permitted to come downstage and speak his heart to show what sort of heart he has. Thus it may be largely Fanny's gracious, relaxed, businesslike tolerance, her sense of duty while not taking herself too seriously, her love for husband and children that still lets them be themselves, and her poise in the most incredible situations that provide the ambience of aristocracy as the stuff of which the other characters are presumably made. I say presumably because their substance is inferred rather than known. They cannot become seriously individualized because they serve in a plot that makes their problems more or less ridiculous.

It is true that if they had less energy they would all get into less trouble. The excess of vitality is what makes them amusing rather than pathetic or desperate: they seem to accept full, even joyous responsibility for whatever predicament they find themselves in — even though the author allows the children on various occasions to assail the values of their elders or the mode of their upbringing. If we work this factor of *élan vital* into the equation, we might conclude that the energy generated by the aristocratic ideal is still a match for the modern world. The aristocracy may be overwhelmed, but it will have had more glory in the struggle than the victor. Uncle Matthew, for example, is a hundred-per-cent self-made eccentric, a bundle of wild prejudices, fierce pride, and heedless willfulness. He would not seem to be in any way creatively or intellectually opposing modernism, yet he has an uncanny nose for its phoniness and its hollowness. Seen from the eyes of the modern organization man he is a hairy monster from the Teutonic jungles; but if we look from his side at the modern world we respect his ferocious rejection of it. Better ferocity than unctuous flabbiness. In other words, what by itself might seem a grotesque caricature, seen against the headless disorder of our times is admirable and lovable — yet still it does not engage in a plot that will allow it to achieve positive definition of character. Uncle Matthew lives in a domain bounded on four sides, as it were, by values, tradition, manners, and surface personal eccentricity. We know he is in there somewhere, but we don't find the man himself. So with the others.

Perhaps, after all, it is only the spirit that lives, caricatured by its avatars from Quixote to Uncle Matthew. Perhaps the caricature is implicit in the gesture, for the gesture was designed to fill out the garment of privilege and make it seem essential to the idea, rather than a covering to shield the bearer from its heat and its brightness.

PART V

Modern
Consequences

It SHOULD be possible at this point to see more clearly how the character-action relation has been evolving from earliest times — and how "moral" has grown into theme and then into idea and then into the state where a new sort of mixture has appeared.

When only the deed mattered, characterization must have happened so naturally that it was almost an unconscious process, like walking. The clause "when only the deed mattered" assumes a theoretical starting point when the action was the essential substance of a fiction. Then the reader or audience considered only what the character did and judged him by that; but even "judged" carries us too far, for such an audience presumably was there to see what would *happen*. When the concept of a motive behind the deed appeared, the character became a bit more elusive, and this elusiveness depended upon a quantity of difference between what the character did and what he may have intended. That is, when the motive was assumed to be fully expressed in the deed, there would have been little thought of motive as a concept because it would have been contained and revealed in the deed. Iago examining his own motives and giving contradictory explanations of them reveals a stage in characterization that may have been surprising to the audience, unless its members had already seen *Hamlet*, where motive and deed are forced apart by the situation.

A third phase appears with the idea of an essential self behind the motives and the actions, which would be imperfectly represented by any set of actions. This is the first step toward the point at which the deed became an outrage imposed upon the self, the point at which any act was too limited to express or liberate the spirit — the infinite spirit that struggled in the cage of its flesh, which in turn was housed in the prison of this world:

> There I walked, and there I raged,
> The spiritual savage caged
> Within my skeleton; raged afresh
> To feel, behind a carnal mesh,
> The clean bones crying in the flesh.
> [Elinor Wylie, "Full Moon"]

Lyric poetry is one very rewarding sort of response to this sense of the human condition. For our investigation, it symbolizes the separation of character and theme from plot — a fascinating irony of which is the fact that as the notion of character becomes more and more intricate it becomes increasingly difficult to reveal through an action. The greatest optative resource of characterization — modern depth psychology — turned out to be its most acrid dissolvent: the psychological approach tends to make all characters one character; and with its focus upon the many-layered traumata of his development, it makes him such a bundle of conflicting tensions that his acts are almost irrelevant to what he complexly *is*. The line from romanticism through realism, naturalism, and modern psychology is, in this respect, a continuum. In the novel, this trend leads to the point where the world is looked at from the internal point of view of consciousness rather than from the external point of view of the observer who sees an action. In character, it produces a hundred versions of the diminished self, a few of which will be examined in the final chapter. What they have in common is that character takes formless form apart from significant action; they are enormously interesting reflections of our time.

Between the novel like *Pride and Prejudice*, where character, plot, and theme are so perfectly integrated that all three appear inseparably in every situation, and the novel where the self seeks meaning in a void of social un-meaning, there is a middle area, fluid and shifting in its forms, of novels in which the idea dominates both the plot and characters who enact it. The novels are good, bad, and indifferent; their characters too may be mere contrivances or round and interesting, the latter particularly when the idea generates a substantial action to embody itself.

The novels discussed in Parts III and IV participate in the trend, but with differences. The symbolic journeys of Part III are contrived for the special purpose of giving form to ideas; and in the novels of Part IV there are still powerful *stories* being told in spite of the intrusion of various disturbing or uncontrollable ideas.

Chapter 13 of this part presents a sequence of novels whose actions seem to spring from ideas and whose characterization grows better and better up through Conrad and Cozzens, on the main line, and Fitzgerald and Mary McCarthy in lesser ways. But in the main the idea threatens to take over and subordinate the action in a way that also subordinates characterization. Chapter 14 deals with the extreme consequences of these tendencies that now appear signally where the ideal interdependence of action, character, and theme has evaporated. The drift toward thinking of character as essence rather than as action carries from the elusive to the ambiguous to the impalpable — and on toward characters with strong feelings, perhaps, but no substance with which to act or no value systems in which to locate themselves so that they *can* act.

13 *The Idea Men*

MUD HUTS OF INTELLECT

NOVELS of idea, even when they are very thin in character and action, may appeal to their contemporary readers by the charms of topicality, wit, or style, for which novels have always been eagerly read, just as they are for the interest of reportage or satire. (We shall look at examples of all these.) Ideas would seem to be more important for most readers than character, and they are indispensable for nearly all. For example, Jack London's tremendous popularity depends not upon substantial plots or profundities of characterization, for he has neither, but upon his ideas. His books dramatize the concepts of atavism, survival of the fittest, struggle for existence, and purity of breed — in short, the popular image of Darwin and Spencer forcibly conglomerated into a structure of rebellious socialism. *White Fang* (1906) is the story of the noble savage becoming a super-dog among the civilized huskies. *The Call of the Wild* (1903) dramatizes atavism: a domestic husky joins the wolf pack. *A Daughter of the Snows* (1902) and *The Sea Wolf* (1904) explore supermen (and women) and survival values on the frontier and the high seas. I have tried to show elsewhere how badly London's ideas are fitted into his actions, how he generally begins with Darwinian forces and winds up with a Victorian moral,* and the appeal of his ideas is emphasized by the fact that they have interested a host of readers even when put into the most naive stories. The

* See Chapter 5 of my *American Literary Naturalism, A Divided Stream* (Minneapolis: University of Minnesota Press, 1957).

example of London shows that popularity does not indicate an integrated excellence of character, action, and theme — far from it. London's characters are romantic extremes, his plots outlandish mixtures of blood and contrivance. His style is shrill, his tone feverish and sophomoric, his heroes an embarrassing series of glorified Londons — yet he is still read by untold thousands.

A short step up from London brings one to the level of Sinclair Lewis's *Babbitt* (1922), another novel of ideas in which character plays an unusual part. *Babbitt* has been incredibly popular all over Europe as the ultimate exploration of the go-getting American businessman of the twenties. It is still on more reading lists for American Studies in Continental universities than one likes to count. Its horrible popularity is Phoenix-like: we may reduce it to ashes, but it will rise to peck at us, renewed, indestructible.

Babbitt burst like the apocalypse on the early twenties. Its hero's name became a byword that is still with us. The book supports my contention that, in the long run, ideas are more important to the success of a novel than character or plot, even though they do not necessarily assure distinction. Proof of the fascination of ideas lies in the fact that the plot of *Babbitt* is quite infantile, the characterization is incredibly poor, and yet the book was and still is read with delight. The influence of *Babbitt* abroad is incalculable. Western Europe has had two images of the United States. One is of a soulless commercial monster controlled by uneducated fools who in turn are frightened by mobsters. It is a land of folly and disorder, a land of incredibly bad taste, bad manners, half-baked ideas, hare-brained get-rich-quick schemes, political corruption, lynchings, hillbillies, poor education, and social chaos. The second image is of a nation with the most stable government in the whole world (a government that has kept its form through uncounted revolutions in the other "civilized" nations), with the most advanced technology, with the readiest imagination to generate new ideas and make use of them, with the highest and most practically active idealism and generosity that any nation has ever evinced, and — *mirabile dictu* — with the best poets, novelists, dramatists, composers, and architects in the world. This latter image is reflected in the influence of American styles and gadgets, the enthusiasm for American movies and American popular music, the spread of American painting, and the extraordinary currency of American books in Europe. But most of all it is by the written word that the mind is made up or changed, and *Babbitt* is the American written word that seems to have been most widely read and to have spread the "bad" image of the United States.

Babbitt is powerful satire. It holds the American Way up to bitter castigation, representing its follies in a sequence of concrete incidents that jump nimbly from item to item of the presumed American scene. In the early 1920's it answered a strange and special American need, which must be traced and explained. This country went into World War I with total dedication and idealism. For centuries our backs had been turned on Europe while we developed the West and wondered about the Great American Novel. The war brought a massive reversal, for unaccustomed as we are to half-measures, we determined not merely to help the Allies against the Hun but to revise the whole calendar of European injustice, oppression, and bigotry. We would free her from the dead hand of the past; we would mark her map anew with reasonable borders; we would, in fine, make the world safe for democracy. It was not a war but a crusade, and America has never been more passionately committed to any cause. Then came the Treaty of Versailles, where American idealism was betrayed by Old World evil and guile, leaving us nothing but empty hands and disenchantment, demonstrated on the political front by our refusal to join the League of Nations. Once more we washed our hands of Europe.

But hand washing was not enough. Our stains, like those of Lady Macbeth, became obsessions that would not give us peace. Anger and frustration changed to guilt — a national guilt that made us turn upon ourselves and abuse everything American. The reaction is psychologically common enough, and in the 1920's it found a warehouse full of emotional fireworks ready to be touched off. The attack on the small town was launched by Anderson's *Winesburg, Ohio* (1919). H. L. Mencken writing in the *American Mercury* made us rejoice to think ourselves a nation of boobs. Lewis joined the pack in full cry with *Main Street* (1920), which spelled out in detail the stifling social bigotry of the small town. F. Scott Fitzgerald in *The Great Gatsby* (1925) anatomized the corruption of the American Dream between the irresponsibility of the well-bred Buchanans and the phony illusions of Gatsby whose dream was tinsel. Hemingway hit the scene very soon to trace the scars on the body of hope, and in 1926 *The Sun Also Rises* began with an epigraph about the Lost Generation of shattered, disillusioned, expatriated heroes.

Babbitt makes a climax of self-abuse. It sets out to ridicule one aspect of American life after another, and we must look at it item by item in order to see how totally impossible it would be for any character to be all the characters that George Babbitt is said to be. He is, in fact, a moving image of American insecurity; the reader's guilts, fears, and shames are exploited, one after another, to make him react to one shameful, sentimental, nostalgic, or exasperated situation after another. He identifies with Babbitt as he experiences these emotions, and so he may be conned at first reading into thinking that Babbitt is a possible person, but the illusion vanishes with a second reading. The numerous Babbitts subsumed under the single name may be itemized by episodes.

Our hero, forty-six, pink, pudgy, balding, wakes to the rasping sounds of suburban morning, which he resists by snuggling down into a few moments of reverie about his "fairy girl" of romance. He is made ridiculous by details; his alarm clock "was the best of nationally advertised and quantitatively produced alarm-clocks, with all modern attachments, including cathedral chime, intermittent alarm, and a phosphorescent dial"; he creeps out from under a blanket that was "forever a suggestion to him of freedom and heroism. He had bought it for a camping trip which had never come off. It symbolized gorgeous loafing, gorgeous cursing, virile flannel shirts." Gritty, petulant, repetitious, he struggles up to consciousness till his "sleep-swollen face was set in harder lines," then bumbles through washing and shaving and assumes the aggressive role of dynamic businessman. (Chapter 1.) The presentation continues to ridicule him by associating him with such objects as B.V.D. underwear, silver cigar-cutter, elk's tooth, and Boosters' Club button; these banal objects match the flow of banalities from his lips: his opinions are canned, superficial, shallow, and ludicrously self-contradicting. Let the following passage of Babbitt's opinion stand for fifty others like it that are scattered through the book. Reading the headlines at breakfast, he proclaims:

"But this, say, this is corking! Beginning of the end for those fellows! New York Assembly has passed some bills that ought to completely outlaw the socialists! And there's an elevator-runners' strike in New York and a lot of college boys are taking their places. That's the stuff! And a mass-meeting in Birmingham's demanded that this Mick agitator, this fellow De Valera, be deported. Dead right, by golly! All these agitators paid with German gold anyway. And we got no business interfering with the Irish or any other foreign government. Keep our hands strictly off. And there's another well-authenticated rumor from Russia that Lenin is dead. That's fine. It's beyond me why we don't just step in there and kick those Bolshevik cusses out." [Chapter 2.]

The catalogue of banalities pronounced by Babbitt is a sparkling tribute to Sinclair Lewis's documentary zeal; if there was a stupid opinion on anything uttered during the period, there it is coming again from the mouth of the hero. One cannot help being delighted by the rich authenticity of what Lewis's ear has caught and his pen recorded:

"How do those front tires look to you?"
"Fine! Fine! Wouldn't be much work for garages if everybody looked after their car the way you do."
"Well, I do try and have some sense about it." [Chapter 3.]

Everybody who dreams of escaping to the north woods, who catches himself uttering obvious remarks about the weather, who wishes from time to time that his life were more significant, or who makes a fool of himself giving up smoking every other week will know lively twinges of guilt as he laughs at the barren but pretentious soul of George F. Babbitt of Zenith in the American Middle West. This guilt is periodically relieved by renewed doses of the hero's socioeconomic opinions, for to these the reader can feel immeasurably superior:

"A good labor union is of value because it keeps out radical unions, which would destroy property. No one ought to be forced to belong to a union, however. All labor agitators who try to force men to join a union should be hanged. In fact, just between ourselves, there oughtn't to be any unions allowed at all; and as it's the best way of fighting the unions, every business man ought to belong to an employers'-association and to the Chamber of Commerce. In union there is strength. So any selfish hog who doesn't join the Chamber of Commerce ought to be forced to." [Chapter 4.]

Babbitt is a hardheaded, enterprising real-estate broker, which means that he knows how to bribe a politician, how to fix up a false front to hide the fact that he is also developing and building, and how to turn the screws down hard when he has a client or renter at his mercy. He is sharp, knowledgeable, energetic, hypocritical, and as crooked as he ever needs to be to get anything he wants. As the evidence of his success mounts along with the evidence of his colossal ignorance of anything but the data of his business, the image of American commerce goes down, down, down. It goes down so fast and so far and so fantastically that one is led to generalize on the fact that satire causes distortions which make chameleons of people.

And not many pages pass before Lewis, making a virtue of necessity, acknowledges that his hero is a quick-change chimera: "He was, just then, neither the sulky child of the sleeping-porch, the domestic tyrant of the breakfast table, the crafty money-changer of the Lyte-Purdy conference, nor the blaring Good Fellow, the Josher and Regular Guy, of the Athletic Club. He was an older brother to Paul Riesling, swift to defend him, admiring him with a proud and credulous love passing the love of women." (Chapter 5.) Acknowledges, yes, but he continues to multiply Babbitt's roles at a dizzy pace. As Babbitt jumps from a position to its opposite, he plays the gamut of pride and guilt, of stupid arrogance and secret shame, of loud-mouthed Josher and the man with a hundred gnawing insecurities.

It seems just possible that this pattern is a symptom of the neurotic self — and thus a reflection of the nation stretched in agony between indignation and guilt, between abusing ungrateful Europe and abusing its own booboisie-dominated self. As an individual or a nation agonizes in such continual incongruity, its sense of self dissolves. It finds itself adopting a series of poses, among which it moves with weakening confidence. It thrashes about in bewilderment, abusing itself and assailing the "others" before whom it fancies itself to be cutting a sorry figure, and it continually reveals that it is harried by uncertainty. The amorphous character of the hero and the acidulous venom of the style in *Babbitt* reveal these frightening doubts which are relieved by explosive laughter rather than by insight.

The episodic ridicule of American life continues. Correspondence courses suffer next, and Babbitt as usual contradicts himself in every sentence. A flashback shows how he was tricked into a loveless marriage, which is not without affection now, and which has brought three typical children into the household.

Babbitt and his wife give a painful dinner party, with too much food and drink, boisterous talk, and table-tapping. After it, Babbitt is bored and disgusted with his life. He plans a trip — wifeless! — to the Maine woods with Paul Riesling, finds the experience boring, then good when it is almost over; returns to more frantic work; participates ridiculously in golfing and movie-going. Then he makes a great, utterly fatuous speech to the State Association of Real Estate Boards and discovers Talent. Local fame comes with a flood of Booster speeches that he delivers. The Babbitts prevail upon a social leader to come to dinner. The party is a fiasco and the invitation is not returned. In the following chapter the situation is reversed: The Babbitts go to dinner at the home of an old friend who is down on his luck. The dinner is a fiasco and the invitation is not returned. Next the church-as-Rotary-Club is lampooned. Getting involved in fund-raising brings Babbitt close to a very rich and pious old man named Eathorne, with whom he is able to work up some shady and profitable deals, the best of which is privately buying options on land that he is acting as broker to buy for the Traction Company's new line. Thus he is able to sell the land to himself and then to the Traction Company at a fat profit.

When Paul Riesling, who is Babbitt's sentimental escape-valve, shoots his nagging wife and is sentenced to three years in prison, Babbitt goes into a prolonged depression and yearns for Adventure and Escape. These come when he takes a manicurist to dinner, talks to a "radical" lawyer named Seneca Doane, whose flattery and name-dropping he gobbles up so avidly that he begins to wonder whether his Boosters aren't too hard on the workingman. Now labor trouble breaks out with several major strikes and demonstrations. The Boosters naturally are 5000 per cent for a firm hand: " 'I don't believe in standing back and wet-nursing these fellows and letting the disturbances drag on,' " says one Clarence Drum. " 'I tell you these strikers are nothing in God's world but a lot of bomb-throwing socialists and thugs, and the only way to handle 'em is with a club!' "(Chapter 27.)

That morning Babbitt had seen Seneca Doane in a tiny workers' parade that was broken up by the militia. For the worst reasons of vanity, discontent, and confusion (and not even really on the strikers' side) he nevertheless takes the liberal view: "Babbitt heard himself saying 'Oh, rats, Clarence, they look just about like you and me, and I certainly didn't notice any bombs.' " (Chapter 27.) The "fellows" begin to look at him as if he is "nutty," and he begins to draw the reader's sympathy because the businessmen are so stupid and brutal against him. They eye him suspiciously, and he feels "vaguely frightened."

Sharing this crumb of right feeling, Babbitt is drawn to a sultry

widow named Tanis Judique, who so flatters his damaged ego that he
defies his Booster pals at the daily lunch, slips into heavy drinking and
wild parties — and balks at joining the Good Citizens' League, recently
organized to combat "red ruin and those lazy dogs plotting for free
beer." Now, Babbitt's leftish swerve has been motivated by pique plus
Seneca Doane's name-dropping; his affair with Tanis Judique is entirely selfish and sensual; his drinking is wildly excessive; yet he becomes sympathetic because the Boosters are such boobs and because
Lewis plays on the reader's insecurities. "Anybody" could be caught in
the toils of his lower nature if the unlucky circumstances conspired.
And poor bewildered stubborn childish Babbitt becomes the prey of a
small-scale witch hunt. He shakes Tanis off, then yearns for her, quarrels with his wife, and is going in frantic circles — when Lewis pulls
the weeping fortissimo stop on his sentimental organ. Babbitt's wife
has acute appendicitis; in the emergency all the old homey loyalties
rush back in, friends rally round, and Babbitt is so overwhelmed by
their forgiveness that he vows never to stray again. He instantly becomes the leading red-baiter of Zenith. It is quite nauseating.

The fact that Lewis can make the reader feel some sympathy for
Babbitt, in his final rosy glow of togetherness, shows again how cleverly
Lewis has worked on him. The novel's plot is held together like
autumn leaves in a gust, which is to say that the incidents are held together by the covers of the book and little else. The hero has no character; he is a complex of banalities, uncertainties, and huffiness. Only
such a meandering and inconclusive action could produce so cipherous
a man, and only the clever concreteness of Lewis's appeals to the
reader's fears could delude him into *feeling* that he had indeed identified with him.

Most significant for our inquiry is the fact that the flimsiness of the
action, the superficiality of the characterization, and the meanness of
the controlling idea are organically balanced and unified. The organ-
ism, however, is a kind of stunted cactus, raised in an agronomy of
venom and guilt.

ACTION AS SPOOF

Peter De Vries contrives a special sort of tour de force in his witty
explorations of exurbanite life in Connecticut. In, for example, *The*

Tents of Wickedness (1959) he works up an impudently outrageous plot with a fantastic set of human relations, to express something of his sense of how modern man has become entangled in so complex a web of customs, social practices, aesthetic oddities, and half-truths that he does not know where his spirit has its home or how all the parts of his multifarious being are related.

The plot concerns Chick Swallow, who goes from Treehouse to Doghouse to Madhouse in three parts. Chick's fluctuating, amorphous self is composed of a wide and subtle knowledge of modern literature, a delusion that he is a masterly psychiatrist, and a good nature that carries him shambling in and out of the various highroads and byways in the small exurbanite town of Decency. Chick is aware that life copies art, and he continually enacts this awareness by thinking of his current situation in the style and language of Marquand, Faulkner, Fitzgerald, Hemingway, Proust, and Joyce — one after the other. The imitations are not always parodies, but the sly use of them is always very funny. With the language of Faulkner he endows a slight incident with an ambience of wild psychotic frenzy so that it becomes much more than it was. Yet he is always aware that he is imitating the emotional tones of characters of these favorite authors, so that his own self takes shape in a frivolous feeling that he really isn't anybody because he has no style of his own in which he seriously lives. His deftness with literary mannerisms can be said to represent (if not to symbolize) modern man's division among the multiplicity of things and occasions in his world. Chick's subtle sense of literary styles and the modes of life that they render indicates perception, observation, and a considerable literary flair, but he does not — perhaps cannot — allow himself to become so engaged that at any point he drops his literary filters and looks directly at a person or situation. Indeed, he suggests that the linguistic medium, which mediates between people and things, is a decisive force molding "reality." When a man becomes conscious of it, he can never be totally spontaneous or innocent again; he can never quite believe in the objective actuality of something. This is a condition of despair, perhaps, but with Chick it appears as a free-wheeling zest, a gay fantasy in a world that flows and shimmers like a kaleidoscope. Chick's facility conjures the reader into sharing the notion that his favorite modern writers have all created worlds that have become superficial fads, that generations of college-educated nitwits have made cults and mannerisms out of the visions of Hemingway and Fitzgerald.

More than this, Chick loves to develop metaphors and similes that manhandle any situation into farce. He speaks of "the stark immaculate pines standing like Breughel trees, the snow falling like grains of Bromo-Seltzer." (Page 113.) Or "Appleyard was picking a flaw in his logic politely, as one picks a bit of cork from a guest's wineglass." (Page 105.) "These waves plashed on a tame Westchester shore, endless little gasps of amazement. . . . From a radio came the strains of *Charmaine*, like scraps of silk fluttered on the spring night," and so on. (Page 137.) He speaks of "an island of coagulated stockings known as a hooked rug" in the boss's office. (Page 73.) These strictly verbal manipulations introduce an element of craziness into any situation.

This glittering linguistic buffoonery sustains a plot that defies the ordinary social verities as extravagantly as it mocks ordinary language. Chick conducts a question-and-answer column on personal problems in the local paper. His secretary calls him Doctor, and he cannot resist inviting his more troubled correspondents into his office for consultations at which he plays the role of sage and mental healer. Although his sister tries to dissuade him from this practice by telling him that people say, "When you think things can't get any worse, see Chick Swallow," he is undaunted. (Page 58.) He moves in on his brother-in-law (her husband), Nickie Sherman, with a hoax calculated to shock him into Facing Reality and Integrating His Personality, which Chick deduces has suppressed inclinations toward duality. Nickie having inherited a small income refuses to work, neglects his family, and tries to be a master sleuth in his spare time. When Chick hears that his sister is ready to divorce Nickie, he arranges a "murder" in which, after Nickie has deduced the height and motive of the killer, the corpse gets to his feet with a yawn and makes Nickie the laughingstock of the community. Nickie responds by becoming a really split personality. As "Johnny Velours," he robs one house after another and even woos his wife, whom he has "met" at a local pub. The jewels he steals are tucked into odd drawers and corners around his house, becoming handsful of hot potatoes for Chick and his sister.

This misfire of his psychiatric troubleshooting is nothing, however, compared to what Chick gets himself into. He is persuaded to father a child for a zany girl who scorns the bourgeois marriage tie. The girl, having become pregnant, reverts to infantilism. Chick's wife learns All, and Chick goes into a mental breakdown in which he believes he has turned into a pig. These absurdities are a small fraction of what happens in the book, whose plot is as tightly organized as a detective story's.

The novel evokes two rather contradictory notions about its characterization. The whimsical schizoid represented by the fantastic plot is obviously not a character who can be taken seriously or believed in. No such person could exist. The ideas about the modern world that he embodies and enacts are symbolic and humorous extravagances. Yet there is sharp insight into its disorder, and the brilliantly witty language in which the subject is handled makes one realize that the writer knows very well what he is doing. Only humor and extravagance can convey his sense of the monstrous absurdities generated in a time when gadgets and psychology are running wild; but the character who enacts the author's wild fantasy cannot be believed in. He is sacrificed to the idea.

On the other hand, there is a verbal subtlety in Chick's language and in his awareness of the absurdity of his world that makes him seem like a kindred soul — a real character — in spite of the literal impossibility of his actions. These contradictions are reconciled, I believe, in the fact that it is not Chick Swallow who is real but the author who reveals his own sensitive personality in the rich linguistic texture that he has woven. One is delighted by the quality of his perception. He manages to live in our mad world because he can detach it from his sophisticated — if helpless — insight by using language to re-form it into an object of momentary delight. There is really no serious attempt at characterization — and none achieved; rather there is a sharing of attitude and insight with the author. Very much of it depends upon the extraordinary deftness with which he puts his finger on current topical items — turns of phrase, passing fads, trifling styles of dress or manner, temporary drifts in the social or political wind. These items are likely to be irrecoverably gone in a decade or so, but while they live De Vries can make us roll on the floor laughing.

The noble and significant action moving through the most important manners, customs, and values of a society, allowing heroic characters to define themselves through profound decisions, is gone indeed. By having only ludicrous situations and crazy decisions, the author avoids taking a moral position: he does not commit himself even to the point of defining a serious moral issue, let alone allowing a character to confront such an issue and declare himself by his action. If there is a moral force present among these gifted shenanigans, it is the author's dedication to his creative task: this is the responsible human element that the reader respects as well as enjoys. In this the novelist creates an order, although he does not see one.*

IDEA MARCHING ON ONE LEG

In the war novel there are special conditions. First, there is a situation in which life is at stake and decisions mean life or death to those involved. There will be a big plot on a heroic scale. But there is the deeper interest that a war brings into association a group of people who would seldom meet and never be deeply involved with each other in civilian life. The farmer, the mechanic, the hard guy, the beatnik, the poseur, and the intellectual are thrown together in mutual dependence. They all have new relations to explore, *at the same time* that they are facing a totally new way of life. Each one has lived in a little isolated pattern; now he is tested among a group of widely different people. There is a contest for leadership at the same time that there is an ordeal of courage and a test of the values and commitments that have been hidden in the individual's little private protected isolated life. The intellectual has generally felt superior to the mechanic and the farmer, but he has also admired these people who work with their hands and achieve a steady competence in a substantial solid world of things. The farmer and the mechanic are likely to be inarticulate — or in any event their language will not greatly honor them — whereas the intellectual will be tongue-tied for fear that his command of language will set him apart from his simpler fellows. Yet the intellectual always writes the novel, and between his attempt to be a man of action and his need to justify the heightened awareness of his own way of life, he will generate all sorts of sophisticated problems and patterns.

*De Vries keeps his story always outrageous to maintain the ascendency of his linguistic amusements, which engage the reader in his auctorial views on the modern scene. By way of contrast, we may glance at *The Wapshot Chronicle* (1957) of John Cheever, where the author sets a decaying New England village against the giant modern state in order to indulge his own assault on a similar modernism in much the same vein. Half the time, however, Cheever wants us to take his characters seriously. The book is very funny, but it includes such a range of nonsense and sentiment that it is, finally, most untidy.

In his novelette *The Long March* (1952), William Styron has gathered all his forces to dramatize an idea about Jewish character. It is as unsympathetic as it is suggestive. It generates a great deal of imaginative power; and it seems to be going deep into the roots of character until its symbolic purpose takes open charge and reduces the action to an expository contrivance. The story is about a forced march of thirty-six miles in fifteen hours imposed upon a battalion of marines by the commanding officer, Colonel Templeton. The time is six years after the end of World War II; the soldiers are young draftees; their officers are partly regular military men and partly marine reserve officers who have been called back into uniform because of the war in Korea. The characters of significance are just three: the dedicated professional soldier, Colonel Templeton, aged forty-four; Lieutenant Culver, about thirty, who has been snatched from a happy marriage and a promising career to a nightmare of forced training; and Captain Mannix, a huge Jewish bear of a man from Brooklyn, scarred from the last war, passionately rebellious, truculent, sardonic, articulate.

About 5000 men start on the march, in bone-chilling cold and blazing sun, over sandy Carolina roads. It is described as an ordeal for which the men are not ready — certainly not soft reserve officers who have been called back from their comfortable homes — and in fact scarcely 200 of the whole battalion can finish it. After the first three or four hours they are dropping like leaves and being carried off, supine, by the truckload.

The Colonel's motives for ordering such a march are obscure, complex. He is presented as a poseur who absolutely delights in his own perfect composure. No question, no emergency can force him to speak in haste. He seems to have an inordinate vanity in his carriage, his authority, his physical sleekness. Whether he orders the march to punish certain complaining officers, notably Mannix, or to set a record, or to show off his own physical fitness, or from pure sadism — this is the question; for if sometimes he looks like a brainless dandy, at others he looks like a priest. One thing is certain: his professional competence and his authority are absolute. He leads the first hour of the march at a killing pace, and he goes the whole distance on foot.

The story is told through Lt. Culver's eyes, but it is about Mannix. Culver has left a loving wife and a good career; he loathes the military service; he is out of shape, falling asleep on his feet even before the march begins; yet he is one of the handful that finish it. If all but a few officers and about 200 young marines, who have just come out of boot camp, are unable to go on to the end, if the Colonel himself is completely exhausted, it is totally incredible that Culver could have done it. Soft, out of condition, reluctant, he could never have done it, yet the author has to have him along for the point of view, and so he provides the explanation that Culver is so much a marine that his training took over and made a will-less automaton of him. He is said to be gripped by "the old atavism that clutched them, the voice that commanded, once again, *you will*. How stupid to think they had ever made their own philosophy; it was as puny as a house of straw, and at this moment — by the noise in their brains of those words, *you will* — it was being blasted to the winds like dust. They were as helpless as children. Another war, and years beyond reckoning, had violated their minds irrevocably. For six years they had slept a cataleptic sleep, dreaming blissfully of peace, awakened in horror to find that, after all, they were only marines, responding anew to the old commands." (Page 69.) There is nothing to show that Culver would respond like a brain-washed automaton to patterns of obedience established six years before, and thus there is no credible motive provided for his doing the impossible. Nor is there any meaning drawn from it later. Indeed, Culver's thoughts after the march *directly contradict* the motives that have been presented to enable him to do the impossible: he cannot hate the Colonel, "because he was a different kind of man, different enough that he was hardly a man at all, but just a quantity of attitudes so remote from Culver's world that to hate him would be like hating a cannibal, merely because he gobbled human flesh." (Page 117.) But in fact the motives quoted above, which account for Culver's marching, are practically the same as the Colonel's — the total identification (or submission) of one's will to the Marine Corps. Culver was exactly this; he was exactly the same kind of man in the same world as the Colonel. The author, a sophisticated intelligence, intoxicated with words, unsure where he stands among the varieties of peace and wartime commitment, is swept one way and another by his ideas, which plainly dominate both character and action.

The idea that dominates the conception of Mannix is just hinted early in the story. He has already established his general tone of humor and bitterness; furthermore, he "despised the Colonel," and he "de-

spised everything about the Marine Corps." When Mannix's faint protest against the length of the march is firmly but fairly rejected by the
Colonel, his face shows "something outraged and agonized," and he
gives "a quick look of both fury and suffering, like the tragic Greek
mask, or a shackled slave." (Pages 29–31.)

As the march gets under way, Mannix discovers a nail in the heel of
one shoe; the Colonel advises him to ride on a truck, but he refuses to
give up. Rather, "with a note of proud and willful submission," he
limps along mercilessly driving his company, "with the accents of a
born bully." As others begin to collapse, Mannix forces his faltering
men on by sheer will and abuse. He *will not* let them lag or fall. Culver is appalled by Mannix's transformation. He will not give up;
though his foot bleeds and swells, he "mutilated himself by this perverse and violent rebellion." The climax comes after many hours,
when the Colonel finally orders Mannix to go back on one of the
trucks. Mannix refuses, the Colonel repeats his order, and Mannix
blows his top: " 'Listen, Colonel,' he rasped, 'you ordered this goddam
hike and I'm going to walk it even if I haven't got one goddam man
left. You can crap out yourself for half the march . . .' " and then he
curses the Colonel. This does it, for the Colonel *has* walked the whole
way. He drops his hand onto his pistol and says, " 'You quiet down
now, hear? You march in, see? I order you confined to your quarters,
and I'm going to see that you get a court-martial. Do you understand? I'm going to have you tried for gross insubordination. I'll have
you sent to Korea. *Keep your mouth shut.*' " (Pages 111, 112–13.)

Tottering the last six miles, Mannix is described in sentences that
evoke images of Jews in ghettos, in concentration camps, on wailing
walls, Jews outraged and degraded; and the implication is very plain
that these humiliations are somehow sought by the Jew, that they
satisfy his arrogant need to suffer horror upon horror in order to
express the enormity of his resentment against the oppressor: "Mannix's perpetual tread on his toe alone gave to his gait a ponderous,
bobbing motion which resembled that of a man wretchedly spastic and
paralyzed. It lent to his face . . . an aspect of deep, almost prayer-
fully passionate concentration — eyes thrown skyward and lips fluttering feverishly in pain — so that if one did not know he was in agony
one might imagine that he was a communicant in rapture . . . it was
the painted, suffering face of a clown, and the heaving gait was a

grotesque and indecent parody of a hopeless cripple, with shoulders gyrating like a seesaw and with flapping, stricken arms." (Pages 113–14.) The author's intention of generalizing, of symbolizing his own harsh notion of the Jewish soul is clearest in the phrase "a grotesque and indecent parody of a hopeless cripple."

That is about all there is to the story. It is made clear that the Colonel is neither a fool nor a sadist but just a man doing his job, "That with him the hike had had nothing to do with courage or sacrifice or suffering, but was only a task to be performed . . . and that he was as far removed from the vulgar battle, the competition, which Mannix had tried to promote as the frozen, remotest stars. He just didn't care." (Page 111.) Mannix has by his sick need to suffer made a ghastly, revolting parody of human dignity, and in doing so he has stripped himself of all real dignity. He has crucified himself to defy a new world of Romans — but for no Cause at all.

The idea is strong. In order to cram it into his novelette the author has to sacrifice characterization and violate probability. He *tells* his reader a number of contradictory things about the Colonel, yet in the end abandons the problem by saying that he is merely a man doing a job. He introduces Lt. Culver as if something interesting were going to happen to him, but at the end he leaves him with aching legs, exhausted, lonely — but not purged, or strengthened, or enlightened. The idea is much too big for the story. Ever so much more would have to happen to dramatize so complex a system of ideas about the alienation and masochism of the Jew in the person of Captain Mannix. He would, of course, have to discover himself to some degree while making decisions which to some degree he understood; whereas he acts like a man possessed, whose bitterness mounts through cruelty to his men, on to self-destruction.

The bare facts here could have been worked up into several different stories. Basically the rebellion against authority suggests a simple story of immaturity revolting against a paternal figure. On a more complex plane, the focus could be on the cruel tyrant and the means by which he elicits the rebellion of a naive subordinate. D. H. Lawrence's "The Prussian Officer" raises the tale to the study of a homosexual officer tormenting the subaltern he desires, while the latter knows an ecstasy of attraction and disgust in which he commits murder. *The Long March* does not let Mannix develop in response to changing situations. He is merely revealed as the story moves along and we are allowed to see different levels of his gaudy lust for immolation. There is no growth or discovery of the sort that we associate with human people; there is no valid conflict with the Colonel, because Mannix misunderstands him. At one point, so far is he from making a person of Mannix, the author attributes his stubborn persistence to the fact that he is still basically a marine — a notion that belies everything else he does in the course of the story!

The dominance of idea in *The Long March* recalls the *Caine Mutiny* (1951) of Herman Wouk. Through that long novel the psychotic incompetence of Captain Queeg is richly and fully established. At the climax, when the ship is in a dangerous storm and the Captain has lost all control of himself and of the situation, the second officer steps in and relieves him of his command. At the court martial, the mutiny is successfully defended. There may have been some vanity, some self-ishness, some eagerness to make a case on the part of the mutineers, but there is no question that Queeg is psychotic and incompetent. Then in a long final chapter the defending lawyer gets drunk with the mutinous officers, turns upon them, and delivers himself of a two-hour (so it seems) tirade in which he defends the regular officer like Queeg who carries on the navy in peacetime while the likes of the mutineers are living off the fat of the land in civilian prosperity. Most of all, he defends the system of rules and authority by which a naval organization is maintained, insisting that it is in the long run more important than the fact that a single officer working under it happens to be psychotic and incompetent. It is an eloquent speech, but it distorts the significant action of the novel and neutralizes its meaning. This statement applies to action, characterization, and theme. In the novel proper, the wartime naval officer demonstrates the initiative and resourcefulness that make a democracy believe in its ability to survive by defeating armies of mercenaries or the armies of totalitarian dictatorships. A democracy does not want its best men in the military, for it knows that a standing army is a threat to its life. It wants the spirit of freedom to breathe over the land and make every civilian a potential hero. It would rather be Athens than Sparta. The ending of the *Caine Mutiny* makes the heroes over into rascals and the psychotic Queeg into the true-blue conservative stuff that keeps the ship of state afloat. Styron and Wouk both show how modern psychological terms subordi-

nate characters to catch-phrases, with the result that the characters
can be turned inside-out with the turn of a phrase.

STEINBECK'S ECONOMIC MEN

The surefire way for a writer to get himself well misunderstood is to
give an honest — and therefore apparently sympathetic — treatment of
a point of view with which he does not in fact sympathize. If he reveals this point of view without any ironic reservation to indicate his
own detachment from it, he soon finds that there is a substantial reading public that will not put up with such monkeyshines. They want
to know exactly where he stands. Henry James goes through hand-
springs of virtuosity trying to show just how the world seems to his
heroes and heroines, but he never lets these dear people be mistaken
for himself. John P. Marquand, on the contrary, had trouble with
Melville Goodwin, USA (1951) when he presented a general of the
army without any reservation, giving his picture of his world and his
place in it. It is one of Marquand's most impressive works — tedious
because the subject is tedious and painfully limited in values and intellect, but a masterpiece of imaginative realization. Many readers
recoiled; they preferred the heavy-handed mockery of *The Late George
Apley* (1937) or *H. M. Pulham, Esq.* (1941).

Norman Mailer attempted the same mode in *The Deer Park* (1955).
This long novel deals with the world of Hollywood movie people,
their grandiose, almost mystical feeling for their destinies as supermen — beings with such special endowments, such wonderful expectations that they do not themselves quite understand what they are to
expect of themselves. This deep corny seriousness about one's mystical
mission could be made to make itself ridiculous in a few sentences. It
is far more difficult to present it in its own bedazzled vision, gazing
raptly at the stars in their courses which symbolize and perhaps even
control its sublunary progression. This latter is what Mailer undertook and achieved — to render the quality of these strange and wonderful geniuses, who take themselves more seriously than could be
imagined. He tells the story through the eyes of a young romantic who
aspires to success by any means that may come to his enchanted impulse; the young hero is swept up by the torrent and carried along
with such a rush that he does not know whether he is swimming or

sinking. Between dreams of financial glory and starlet-crossed affairs, his reason totters and his head swims over the moral horizon, until he does not know whether he is acting or being acted upon. Fathoms out of his depth, he hardly knows what he is floating in, let alone what sustains him. The characters are defined by their language, their fantastic aspirations, and the frantic situations in which they find themselves. Their notions of themselves are so turgid and mystical that they too are over the moral horizon of ordinary people, and it is impossible to imagine any plot that could bring such notions into serious conflict; for beside the self-absorption of the characters is the fact that they are actors who make a business of creating worlds and selves which they passionately act even while they watch themselves doing it. By a union of art and will they attempt to create sublime actions on cosmic stages, and whether they are ridiculous or aware seems to be more than they or the reader can know.

Slipping back and forth between the sublime and the ridiculous, they do not gather firm substance through actions that will be final for them. One feels that, in the middle of the most crucial scene, they could walk out of the room and forget it all. Mailer conveys all this, but he does not comment; he does not permit himself the easy luxury of irony; he stays faithfully with the grandiose illusions in which his people live. The book is baffling precisely because the characters slip back and forth between the common world of society and the mystical worlds they create. It is impossible to pin them down, for they do not themselves really know what they are. Like *Melville Goodwin, USA* — and for the same reason — *The Deer Park* can be tedious as well as baffling, but it is a triumph of sustained realization.

In John Steinbeck's *In Dubious Battle* (1936) the point of view is so carefully and sympathetically restricted to the characters' vision that the author was accused of holding their opinions. In this respect it is like *The Deer Park*; but it differs basically in that its plotted action is rigorously controlled and contrived in order to demonstrate an idea. It thus offers a classic example of the possibilities of characterization under such conditions.

The story begins with Jim Nolan, presumably in the mid-1930's, joining the Communist Party for typical reasons: "My whole family has been ruined by this system. My old man, my father, was slugged so much in labor trouble that he went punch-drunk. . . . Well, he

caught a charge of buckshot in the chest from a riot gun." His sister
vanished one day, presumably abducted into white slavery. Jim himself had a responsible job, stopped on his way home from a movie to
listen for a moment to a guy talking in Lincoln Square. " 'Cop slugged
me from behind, right in the back of the neck. When I came to I was
already booked for vagrancy. . . . I told 'em I wasn't a vagrant and
had a job, and told 'em to call up Mr. Webb, he's manager at Tul-
man's [department store]. So they did. Webb asked where I was picked
up, and the sergeant said "at a radical meeting," and then Webb said
he never heard of me. So I got the rap.' " His mother died in despair,
and he has just come from her funeral. The Party official explains
that " 'Even the people you're trying to help will hate you most of the
time,' " but Jim wants " 'to work toward something' " so he will get to
feel alive again. (Chapter 1.)

When the official hints that Jim is choosing a hard way, he answers,
" 'Did you ever work at a job where, when you got enough skill to get
a raise in pay, you were fired and a new man put in? Did you ever
work in a place where they talked about loyalty to the firm, and loyalty
meant spying on the people around you? Hell, I've got nothing
to lose.' 'Nothing except hatred,' Harry said quietly. 'You're going to
be surprised when you see that you stop hating people. I don't know
why it is, but that's what usually happens.' " (Chapter 1.)

Why and how it happens is the theme of the novel. The class war,
which takes Jim into California fruit farms, where he helps foment
strikes among the mistreated itinerant pickers, provides the substance
of the action. The details of joining the pickers, working along with
them, gaining their confidence, and helping them work themselves up
to a strike that bursts into bloody violence are set down with meticulous realistic detail; and they are also patiently dramatized, so that
they appear as they seem to the people who live them. Jim works his
way into knowledge, responsibility, and authority. He reasons each
step out and does what must be done to advance the cause of the
Party. This means that he must keep the pickers suffering, guide them
into violence, and finally see to it that they lose the strike so that the
general disposition toward revolution will be strengthened. In order
to make them erupt into violence Jim has to weld the individuals into
a group. While they are separate they think, slowly and stubbornly to
be sure, for themselves. It takes time and patience to bring them under

one of their own kind and persuade them to accept his leadership. And after that, it takes outrage and violence to turn them into a mob. This latter step is understood and expertly controlled by the Communists. As Steinbeck dramatizes it, it results from shocking and callous brutality by the owners. Emotions flame, and the pickers turn wild with fury.

In the intellectual context of the thirties, it was easy to assume that Steinbeck was preaching the necessity of revolution, but a detached reading gives quite a different answer. What happens to the pickers under Party leadership is that they turn into animals. They lose their human dignity and freedom. The point is made again and again through the novel. Its particular spokesman is Doc, a mysterious and saintly figure who appears out of nowhere and devotes himself to tending the sick and wounded in the strikers' camp. He says that he does not take political or doctrinal sides but is merely interested in observing the actions of men under pressures. " 'Group-men are always getting some kind of infection. This seems to be a bad one. . . . I want to watch these group-men, for they seem to me to be a new individual, not at all like single men. . . . People have said, "mobs are crazy, you can't tell what they'll do." Why don't people look at mobs not as men, but as mobs? A mob nearly always seems to act reasonably, for a mob. . . . The group doesn't care about the Holy Land, or Democracy, or Communism. Maybe the group simply wants to move, to fight, and uses these words simply to reassure the brains of individual men.' " (Chapter 8.) The discussion moves artfully close to the core of Steinbeck's thesis when Doc says, in response to Mac's insistence that with a "job to do" they have no time for high-falutin ideas, " 'Yes, and so you start your work not knowing your medium. And your ignorance trips you up every time.' " (*Idem.*) Doc later comments on the dubious battle: " '. . . in my little experience the end is never very different in its nature from the means. Damn it, Jim, you can only build a violent thing with violence.' " The end does not justify the means because " 'There aren't any beginnings . . . Nor any ends. It seems to me that man has engaged in a blind and fearful struggle out of a past he can't remember, into a future he can't foresee nor understand. And man has met and defeated every obstacle, every enemy except one. He cannot win over himself. How mankind hates itself.' " (Chapter 13.) These insights are not unimpressive. Bursting into a conversation, as they do, however, they don't represent a discovery by Doc Burton but a long-pondered thought of the author. They are there not to reveal the Doc but to interpret the action.

Whipped into animal frenzy, led into a bloody contest which they are intended to lose (since world revolution is not supported by well-paid workers), the pickers lose their humanity as terribly as do the owners and vigilantes who harass them. The desirable human qualities of love, loyalty, and reason — the qualities particularly cherished by the humanistic liberal tradition from which America has received its greatest strength — are threatened by the animal violence that takes control of men in the mass. The action of the novel shows the light of reason quenched by the fury of mob action. The latter is slow to take over; it requires expert direction from the Party workers; but when it comes it damages the humanity of both sides, for such violence is not easily outlived or forgotten. Mac, the old hand, explains to Jim about the vigilante spirit, which he hates — but which spreads until it infects all who are involved in the conflict: " 'Why, they're the dirtiest guys in any town. They're the same ones that burned the houses of old German people during the war. They're the same ones that lynch Negroes. They like to be cruel. They like to hurt people, and they always give it a nice name, patriotism or protecting the constitution. But they're just the old nigger torturers working. The owners use 'em, tell 'em we have to protect the people against reds. Y'see that lets 'em burn houses and torture and beat people with no danger,' " and so on. (Chapter 9.)

At this point the pickers have been enraged by the vigilante murder of a broken, punch-drunk, witless old revolutionist named Joy, who was working with them. They carry his frail body until the sheriff, who of course is working for the owners, stops them: " 'I want that body,' the sheriff said. . . . 'You men shot a strike-breaker. We'll bring the charge. . . .' " (Chapter 9.)

The workers' leader intervenes: "London's eyes glowed redly. He said simply, 'Mister, you know the guys that killed this little man; you know who did it. You got laws and you don't keep 'em.' " Then the sheriff backs away from the mob behind London, and "The mob growled, so softly that it sounded like a moan." A few moments later when the tension has eased, Mac says, " 'Look at these guys. They're waking up. It's just as though they got a shot of gas for a while. That's the most dangerous kind of men. . . . When a mob don't make a noise, when it just comes on with dead pans, that's the time for a cop to get out of the way.' " (Chapter 9.) Steinbeck uses animal images in most of his books. Here the imagery is of dogs; men are likened to dogs fifty times, in their changes from sleepy content to frantic expressions of love, and on to blind ferocity. The dog imagery is so rich that it becomes mechanical. Once the strikers beat up a handful of scabs and maim them horribly: ". . . they kicked, growling in their throats. Their lips were wet with saliva. . . . The fury departed as quickly as it had come. They stood away from their victims. They panted heavily." (Chapter 10.)

As the owners become more fearful they become more vicious, and their conduct makes the reader despise them; but the pickers are transformed also. Alternating violence and apathy drain them of humanity. Mac and Jim manage them like circus animals, keeping them fed, exercised, ready. Personality, hardly apparent, disappears in the general mass turmoil. It looks as if the possibilities of rational amelioration are steadily reduced by the emotions released in the mass.

If the obvious conflict is between capital and labor, and the secondary one between the individual's humanity and the mass's witless ferocity, there is still a third level of meaning that is played out by Mac and Jim, who reveal the workings of Party discipline on the human spirit. Compelled for the Cause to nourish a strike that brings horror upon horror to those involved and that will, as planned, have to fail if the long-range plan of the Party is to be served, Mac and Jim must either crack under the strain or be dehumanized. They are both strong at first. When Joy is murdered, Mac wants to use his body to excite the workers, one of whom says, " 'Pal of yours, and you won't let him rest now. You want to use him. You're a pair of cold-blooded bastards.' " (Chapter 9.) Later Mac scientifically breaks up the face of a young boy who is spying and shooting for the owners, but the strain tells on him. Doc Burton says, " 'Mac . . . you're the craziest mess of cruelty and hausfrau sentimentality, of clear vision and rose-colored glasses I ever saw. I don't know how you manage to be all of them at once.' " (Chapter 11.)

And he doesn't. Mac loses his nerve, relies increasingly on his pupil, Jim, and has lost his force by the time he is killed, near the end of the book. Jim gets stronger, wiser, and colder, until he is more machine than man. He is exalted by the sort of cold passion that lives in Inquisitors and fanatics, who fasten on to the idea like grim death and in starving their hearts also forget the hearts of their fellows. When Mac is killed, Jim thinks only of using his body to ornament a new burst of eloquence that will excite the unhappy strikers to new onsets of violence.

Here is the answer to the question raised early in the story: why do the Party workers stop hating? It comes in two parts. They stop hating first because they have joined a team, identified with a group, and are no longer alone. They are also playing at war, living off the land and by their wits, defying all the forces of law and order which subconsciously represent the Father. But as the absorption progresses, they do not hate because they do not feel. They have risen to an intensity above emotion, what Allen Tate called "the cold pool left by the mounting flood." They have been dehumanized. The dog imagery grows more frequent toward the end of the novel, indicating that the characters are galvanized into their fits of apathy and violence more by trigger-quick reactions than by realized emotions that pass through the mind. Somewhere unspoken lurks the suggestion of dogs salivating to Pavlov's bell.

Apart from the dog imagery and the expository discourses of Doc Burton, the thesis of *In Dubious Battle* is completely dramatized. The action proceeds through dialogue and event with meticulous realism; the scenes are vividly pictured, with the people living, talking, deciding in them; there is surprisingly little sense of an author arranging, displaying, or commenting. Yet if one draws back a pace or two for a long second look, the story seems utterly "managed." Every detail, every conversation is present for the sole purpose of adding another brick to the wall of the thesis. Now, this is the same integration of character-action-theme that we saw in *Pride and Prejudice*, but here the subject is not the central business of society but a special limited aspect of it. The characters are so rigidly confined to the task assigned them that they have no chance to define themselves intimately as free people. Ultimately, their choices do not take the reader into their growing selves but rather move him along to the next step in the action. The characters are contrived as types, with a necessary range of variety, but they are not really considered seriously as people. They are there to act out the thesis, which they do conscientiously, but their

various reactions to the pressure of events are trigger-automated like
the reactions of dogs. The realism takes one vividly along through the
meaningful plot, but the meaning *uses* the characters rather than reveals them. The fact that the story is largely dialogue, with each situation growing out of the men's talk, disguises in suspense what appears
plainly enough on a second reading.

The way the thesis controls and dominates the characters can be
seen anywhere in the book. Steinbeck has so much to say that, in order
to pack it into dialogue, so that it *appears* to grow out of the interaction of character and situation, he has to slight everything but the
main drift. The simple workers have to express themselves with groping, ungrammatical directness. In this mode, it takes many pages to
elaborate even a moderately complex idea. Doc Burton has to talk to
working stiffs in terms they can understand, and more than a few
sentences of exposition by him at any point makes them uncomfortable. The passage where Mac beats up the boy who has been caught
near the strikers' camp with a rifle is an excellent example of Steinbeck's narrative-expository technique where the ideas have to be
packed in thick. Mac tells Jim that he is not going to lose his head:

"It's O. K. if you're cold," said Jim.
"I'm a sharpshooter," Mac said. "You feeling sorry for the kid, Jim?"
"No, he's not a kid, he's an example."

After the boy's face is broken and bloody, London, the strikers' leader,
says:

"Shall I wash his face?"
"Hell, no! I do a surgeon's job, and you want to spoil it. You think
I liked it?"

London, who has been "watching him with horror," says:

"Jesus, you're a cruel bastard, Mac. I can unda'stand a guy gettin'
mad an' doin' it, but you wasn't mad."
"I know," Mac said wearily. "That's the hardest part." He stood
still, smiling his cold smile, until London went out of the tent; and
then he walked to the mattress and sat down and clutched his knees.
All over his body the muscles shuddered. His face was pale and grey.
Jim put his good hand over and took him by the wrist. Mac said wearily, "I couldn't of done it if you weren't here, Jim. Oh, Jesus, you're
hard-boiled. You just looked. You didn't give a damn."
Jim tightened his grip on Mac's wrist. "Don't worry about it," he
said quietly. "It wasn't a scared kid, it was a danger to the cause. It

had to be done, and you did it right. No hate, no feeling, just a job. Don't worry. . . . That was like a doctor's work. It was an operation, that's all."

Mac says, "I couldn't do it again."

"You'd have to do it again," said Jim.

Mac looked at him with something of fear in his eyes. "You're getting beyond me, Jim. I'm getting scared of you. I've seen men like you before. I'm scared of 'em. Jesus, Jim, I can see you changing every day. I know you're right. Cold thought to fight madness, I know all that. God Almighty, Jim, it's not human. I'm scared of you." [Chapter 13.]

The two men are so busy explaining things for Steinbeck that one cannot believe in them. They expound these ideas so carefully, spacing the details out in primer doses, that the author's intention shines transparently through. Mac's humanity is taking over, while Jim is growing stronger by freezing his feelings away. The stage is set to dramatize the idea, yes, but the characters are puppets, not people; they dance on strings to the author's direction, and this must be felt by an attentive reader. One must admire the way Steinbeck has wrought his thesis into an action. The sacrifice of character to idea is not to be condemned, perhaps, but rather recognized in this striking example.

The paradox of this novel is that its idea is about character. What Party discipline does to the individual could not be more strictly an idea about character than it is. But it is the bare idea that is dramatized, not the problems of individuals seen in the perspectives of their inwardness to the person who faces them.

THE TESTING OF AXEL HEYST'S PHILOSOPHY

Joseph Conrad stands perhaps most precisely midway between the novelist of manners, whose characters move through the center of a known and ordered world, and the modern novelist in a world that he does not accept, a world that does not provide the order and values among which characters might define themselves.

The snug old world of a Jane Austen novel exists no more, and Conrad is not interested in the conduct of modern people who are protected by the presence of the policeman, the comfort of routine, the general desire to rub along cozily with one's fellow men. Such influences in such settings do not release heroic occasions; rather they limit individuality and prevent self-discovery, for the vitality and excitement have departed from the round of ordinary affairs. Conrad wants his hero to be thrown back upon his ultimate moral self, free to act as he will act when the temptations may be as strong within as the dangers or threats are strong without. But although Conrad abandons the immediate restraints by which society subdues its members, he does *not* reject the values and traditions that it represents. It is in this respect that he is midway between the older novelist who works within the ordered society, accepting its values and its problems, and the contemporary novelist who moves outside of this world because he thinks it has lost its vitality. Conrad's heroes have generally absorbed the great tradition of Western culture, but he puts them in an isolated arena in which it can be tested, purely and deeply, under conditions of the greatest freedom and the greatest stress.

Society is not only stifling; it is also illusory to Conrad, and the activities it sustains are illusory. Nothing seems what it is. The stuffy storekeeper turns out to be a bomb-throwing anarchist. The pious are devils. The ordinary forms conceal nightmares. The student of life finds a mystery at every turn, which forces him back on his own basic moral strength: he must both judge and act on his own because what the world presents is treacherous. Representatives of society met on the outposts of civilization are generally hiding something or pretending to be more than they are. They constitute a parade, as it were, of social grotesques further confusing the hero's perspectives.

There is a third element that is essential in the Conradian nexus. It provides the occasion for the test and decision upon which a novel may turn. This is the assumption that the hero has an *idea* about himself that he seeks to realize. It is an idea of his nature, of his destiny, or of the proper relation of man to society. It is an idea that in some way reflects his judgment of man and life. The question is, how will this idea work in practice? Will it serve or will it betray its hero? Having such an idea makes the hero a man of some force and intellect; trying to realize it makes him even more significant of human aspiration and struggle. The trial of such an idea brings the Western tradition into the action, for it is that tradition which inevitably furnishes the values of which it is made. Thus the action involves the roots of Western society and the imagination of a compelling hero. It is far freer than the action of *Pride and Prejudice,* but it has not by any means cut loose from tradition and value as have the novels of our contemporaries. Conrad's idea enables him to test his hero in an action free of the slipperiness and disillusion that surround problems in the center of our social decay.

The idea takes a great many forms. We saw it plainly operative in "Heart of Darkness," where Kurtz goes out with the highest version of Western humanism to enlighten the savages — and turns into the veriest devil when the temptation to be worshiped proves irresistible to his hollow soul. In *Lord Jim* (1900) the protagonist simply believes he is a hero whereas in every crisis he turns out to be an instinctive physical coward. But he will not give up and accept the evidence of his actions; he must try again on new ground. His struggle and flight touch many people and hurt some of them. Charles Gould in *Nostromo* (1904) believes that society can be controlled (and the men in it bettered) by the control of the material wealth it produces. He sets conscientiously to work on this theory — and discovers the human elements that do not respond to either the attraction or the fear of money.

Most complex and interesting is one of his later novels, *Victory* (1915), to which he brought the resources of narrative skill and human insight earned through the long years of his growth. The hero of this story is Axel Heyst, who has an idea of tremendous power. His father was a philosopher who had soaked Heyst in the evidence of man's evil at the same time that he convinced him of the necessity of avoiding it. Heyst is serious, committed, moral, dedicated. He has accepted man's evil as unalterable. Indeed it is a central and decisive tenet of his philosophy that the idealism which moves one to action in the cause of right is the devil's craftiest snare. Not that he believes in the devil. His idealism is rational and humanistic. It is not from thoughts of an afterlife that he determines to eschew the dangers inherent in action. It is rather from a personal fastidiousness of ethical feeling, an almost aesthetic regard for the clean line of a life unsullied by gross error. His father taught him to believe in man's "right to absolute moral and intellectual liberty," and Heyst proposed to fulfill it by drifting. This would be, as he put it, his defense against life. "He became a waif and stray, austerely, from conviction." (Part II, Chapter 3.) For fifteen years he wandered, "invariably courteous and unapproachable," until the act that launches our story.

The novel demonstrates that Heyst's idea is a bad idea for several reasons: it inspires a plan that defies the actualities of human impulse, whether of generosity, compassion, or love; it evokes fear, suspicion, hatred, and rage in other people; and it brings a spiritual blight upon the man who lives by it, for it dries up in him the very humanity he seeks to protect from contamination. Yet the asceticism of the idea calls up images of religious commitment: Heyst is profoundly kind, gentle, cultivated, intellectual. With almost inexhaustible ambiguities and indirections he is identified with Christ, as we shall see — not directly but obliquely. He is perhaps a Christ of the modern world, the world in which the folly of action has been so powerfully demonstrated by both secular and religious atrocities that this thinking Christ would never undertake to save mankind by action or preachment. An ironic version of Christ, then — ironic and tangential, and of course partial — in his total commitment to the ideal of doing no wrong, Heyst stays detached, apart, unapproachable, and courteous. Heyst's role is, as I have said, not only bad for the human spirit but also a violation of human nature. It is unplayable, and only a remarkable man would attempt it. One day "out there" in the Malay Archipelago, on the Portuguese island of Timor, he meets a fellow named Morrison who is in desperate need of a little money. Morrison was a trader who sailed from one out-of-the-way place to another, giving rice on credit to improvident native villages and harming no one. Now he had been fined by the Portuguese authorities on some flimsy pretext for which they proposed, in default of the money, to auction his brig so that one of them could buy it for a song. Walking the street of the miserable village of Delli, almost out of his wits with despair, Morrison meets Heyst, who has appeared there like an answer to his prayer and offers to furnish the necessary sum of money. Morrison is overwhelmed with gratitude and the sudden anguished realization that, never having been able to save a shilling, he will never be able to repay Heyst. The latter "was as much distressed as Morrison; for he understood the other's feelings perfectly. No decent feeling was ever scorned by Heyst. But he was incapable of outward cordiality of manner, and he felt acutely his defect. Consummate politeness is not the right tonic for an emotional collapse." (II, 2.)

Because he cannot pay, Heyst agrees to let Morrison carry him on his travels as a sort of payment; and because the transaction is embarrassing to them both he agrees eagerly to keep the whole matter secret.

Morrison does not want to be laughed at for letting the Portuguese trap him; Heyst shrinks from the role of heavenly messenger. But their secrecy inspires wonder and gossip, and the word gets about that Heyst is a spider sucking the life out of poor Morrison. Here is the first reward of Heyst's detached compassion: he is misunderstood. But worse follows; the relation develops into a business venture. Morrison insists that Heyst become his partner in the exploitation of tropical coal. He goes home to England to raise funds — and there he suddenly dies. The Tropical Belt Coal Company takes life at this point, makes Heyst its manager on the island of Samburan, and pours men and money into the establishment. Shattered by remorse for poor Morrison, Heyst throws himself into the venture for the course of its short life, and when it is abandoned he remains on Samburan, alone but for a Chinese servant named Wang — a coolie from the coal mine who elected to stay behind with a native woman when the others left.

Quite unconsciously Heyst has meanwhile become the object of the vehement hatred of a German named Schomberg who runs a hotel at Sourabaya. Heyst is not even aware of Schomberg, and the gross animal hates him for this very reason. It is he who spreads the gossip about Heyst's somehow exploiting poor Morrison. But now an extraordinary incident occurs. A female orchestra touring the islands under an infamous German manager stops at Schomberg's hotel (he has a "concert hall" there). The players are virtually slaves in that distant place, prey to the whims and lusts of the German and the brutality of his wife. Heyst appears at the hotel, after eighteen months of solitude on his island, and gives way to a second impulse of idle compassion. As the narrator explains, "this reappearance shows that his detachment from the world was not complete. And incompleteness of any sort leads to trouble. Axel Heyst ought not to have cared for his letters — or whatever it was that brought him out after something more than a year and a half in Samburan. But it was of no use. He had not the hermit's vocation! That was the trouble, it seems." (I, 4.)

An English girl in the orchestra attracts his attention, and when he learns that she is being pursued by the horrible Schomberg as well as tormented by the manager, he carries her off to his island in a masterly coup of impromptu abduction. Some months later Heyst signals to a passing steamer (he knows the captain) and unburdens himself of some richly thematic sentences: " 'I don't care what people may say, and of course no one can hurt me. I suppose I have done a certain amount of harm, since I allowed myself to be tempted into action. It seemed innocent enough, but all action is bound to be harmful. It is devilish. That is why this world is evil upon the whole. But I have done with it! I shall never lift a little finger again. At one time I thought that intelligent observation of facts was the best way of cheating the time which is allotted to us whether we want it or not, but now I have done with observation, too. . . . The world is a bad dog. It will bite you if you give it a chance; but I think that here we can safely defy the fates.' " (I, 6.)

There on his island, deeply in love with a girl who adores him, surrounded by relics of the Tropical Belt Coal Company, and served by the disappearing Wang, Heyst ought to have his peace. But Schomberg, back in his hotel at Sourabaya, nurses his hatred until it becomes his life. He talks about Heyst until he has become a joke and a bore. He talks himself into a private world of fantastic lies about Heyst. Then three deadly murderous devils — Mr. Jones, his "secretary" Ricardo, and a brute named Pedro — descend upon him; they are adventurers, gamblers, looking for anything to do that might turn a profit. Schomberg is so afraid of the lethal Ricardo that he is almost paralyzed. Ricardo (second in command) carries a knife strapped to his calf and would disembowel Schomberg with one thrust almost as soon as look at him. Terrified, burbling with panic, Schomberg tells Ricardo of Heyst — that he has a beautiful girl and a treasure in gold at Samburan, that he is defenseless and ripe for the picking.

When these three devils appear at Heyst's island, the stage is set for the catastrophe. They have weapons and craft, and they are pitiless. Heyst is more than defenseless; he is innocent; he proposes to act with his accustomed gentlemanly politeness; and though he has fallen deeply in love with the girl his playful detachment of manner remains and he is unable to free himself from it and respond fully and openly to her adoration. He does not fight the invaders because his habit of urbane and jocular detachment has become too strong to change. He acts like a gentleman when he should act like a tiger among wild boars. It is left to the girl to match her wits and her knowledge of evil against them. She could have prevailed, too, for the feral Ricardo is as lecherous as he is deadly, and he would even betray his master to satisfy his lust. She works cleverly and bravely to divide the enemy; but

Heyst's attenuated spirit is capable of doubt. Her lower-class origins, her sordid homeless past make it seem just possible that she is attracted to Ricardo. While she burns with "a blinding, hot glow of passionate purpose" to trick Ricardo and to save her love, he wavers. She signals to him to leave her with Ricardo. "What reason could she have?" he wonders. "Was it the prompting of some obscure instinct? Or was it simply a delusion of his own senses? But in this strange complication invading the quietude of his life, in his state of doubt and disdain and almost of despair with which he looked at himself, he would let a delusive appearance guide him through a darkness so dense that it made for indifference." (IV, 9.) He does not feel deeply enough to meet the situation. Thus at the crucial moment he stands motionless while she is shot, just when a move on his part could have saved the day. Her victory is in finally making him realize her love though he cannot acknowledge his own. She dies with the knife that she had tricked away from Ricardo clasped to her bosom. Her victory of love is her sacrifice. It is also her message to Heyst by which her pure spirit speaks to him through the barriers of his fastidious and doubting heart. Yet:

Heyst bent low over her, cursing his fastidious soul, which even at that moment kept the true cry of love from his lips in its infernal mistrust of all life. He dared not touch her, and she had no longer the strength to throw her arms about his neck.

"Who else could have done this for you?" she whispered gloriously.

"No one in the world," he answered her in a murmur of unconcealed despair. [IV, 13.]

After such knowledge, what forgiveness? Heyst kills himself after uttering his last recorded words: " 'Ah, Davidson, woe to the man whose heart has not learned while young to hope, to love — and to put its trust in life!' " (IV, 14.)

So much for the story, which is a tale to keep old men from the fireside and children from play, it is so exciting and so moving. Its subjects of love, passion, courage, and loyalty are profoundly united in the problem that it dramatizes. Heyst brings his whole civilized background to the action, and he discovers and reveals his character as he responds to the issues, the desperately final issues, that rise up to face him. The idea controls the action, certainly, but Conrad is able to make his characters live roundly and fully in working it out. One can ask for no more.

But there is a great deal more, nevertheless, in the way of symbolism, by which Conrad brings extraordinary further riches to his idea. If we think of the action as constituting one major mode or perspective by which character is revealed, we can consider the two patterns of symbolism as two further avenues into the same problem. There is Christian symbolism, and there is psychological symbolism: the first sets Heyst's problem of action versus withdrawal up against the backdrop of Western tradition; the second lays it out through an inquiry into the nature of man. The two patterns of symbolism are never allowed to interfere with the characters in the story. The relations between the people — and their thinking about people and problems — are presented in terms that grow directly out of situation and plot. The symbolic meanings are separate and do not appear at all in the basic line of the story; they are on a different plane until one has read and re-read the book and moved up from action and character into the larger system of ideas and values in which the symbols move. Without invading the story, they connect it to the modern Western tradition. This is unusual. In, for example, *Moby-Dick*, the Whale is at the center of the story, functioning as a real creature in a way that proliferates symbolic meanings. There is a continuum from the concrete leviathan to the symbol of nature, to the symbol of cosmic power, to the symbol of man. Moby Dick is whale, nature, macrocosm, and microcosm simultaneously, and in his presentation there must be a neglect of individual human characterization. In *Victory*, on the other hand, the story is first and separate, particularly for Heyst and the girl. We shall see some slight thinning out of characterization where the idea just begins to compete with the plot for control of some of the other characters.

The Christian symbolism is boldly announced with the name of Heyst. However it might be pronounced in Swedish, it is certainly rhymed with Christ by an English-speaking reader. The girl whom Heyst rescues from her soiled plight with the orchestra is named Magdalen, called Alma, and this makes the suggestion inescapable. A writer like Conrad does not use such a name accidentally. When he has carried her off to his island, furthermore, Heyst gives her a new name — Lena, as if to deny her a soul. Her love for him goes beyond passion; it becomes an enraptured dedication. She tells him that she is nothing except what he thinks her to be, which is another way of saying that he has given her a soul. It may be a profoundly ironic commentary on

not merely Christianity but religion itself that the passion, the goodness, and the selfless sacrifice are in the worshiper, while she imagines
that they come to her from the soulless object of her worship. Yeats
might have been thinking of Lena when he wrote:

> Both nuns and mothers worship images,
> But those the candles light are not as those
> That animate a mother's reveries,
> But keep a marble or a bronze repose.
> And yet they too break hearts — O Presences
> That passion, piety or affection knows,
> And that all heavenly glory symbolise —
> O self-born mockers of man's enterprise
> ["Among School Children"]

— though in fact he was surely thinking of his own enraptured dedication to his image of Maud Gonne. Heyst also resembles Christ in his
various declarations that he is "not of this world," although the many
mansions of his father's house do not seem to include one in another
world. For the modern world does not allow for the luxury of escape
into the supernatural; Heyst has thought his way through all such
possibilities, under the tutelage of his father, and concluded that he
must wander in the orbits of this terrene earth for his allotted time.
Heyst is also Christlike in his charity, which struggles with his impulse
to withdraw and stay free of action. Yet he differs in that his pity is the
next-best emotion to the contempt that his father recommended. He is
several times connected with images of fish and fishing. "Action . . .
The barbed hook, baited with the illusion of progress . . . 'And I, the
son of my father, have been caught too, like the silliest fish of them
all,'" Heyst says to himself, even in the first days of his passion with
Lena. Looking at the "relics" of his father (books, furniture), which
he had had sent out to his island, he felt "like a remorseful apostate"
because he had accepted the managership of the Tropical Belt Coal
Company, and he considered its failure "the failure of his apostasy";
he decided to remain on the island, expiating his transgression where
it occurred. (III, 1.)

Christ in the modern world, having witnessed the excesses committed in the name of righteous indignation, might seek to remain
charitable and detached, doing the most possible good by doing no
evil, shunning on his second sojourn the temptation to drive the
money-changers from the temple and thus inspire millennia of cru-

sades, tortures, and extirpations. Being charitable and shunning evil is a much more modest enterprise, but even this attracts and titillates the latent violence in man. Heyst drives Schomberg into frenzies of antagonism, and he infuriates both Ricardo and Mr. Jones. Indeed, Heyst has no weapon against the rarefied essence of evil he finds in Mr. Jones. Like Hamlet, he sees that the world that has produced a Jones will not be cleansed by his violent elimination. The very conscientiousness of his motive makes for paralysis. If he is, like Christ, "tempted into action," while knowing its evil consequences, he will not be surprised by what follows. But how despairing for the son of God to find his impulses tainted by the circumstances in which he must act!

Looking further into the Christian symbolism, we find an unholy Trinity in Mr. Jones, Ricardo, and Pedro. The last is sheer stupid beady-eyed strength ready to serve its masters. Jones and Ricardo are more devilishly charged. Jones hates women. Ricardo hates drink. They are ascetics of evil, dedicated against the spirit. Jones hates the loving, life-giving principle. Ricardo hates drink because it slows down his lethal reactions. Both are devilishly free from any trace of *caritas*. Jones is repeatedly identified as the devil: Schomberg saw "Mr. Jones's devilish eyebrows" and the gleams beneath them directed upon him, and "he shuddered as if horrors worse than murder had been lurking there." Again, the "spectral intensity" of Jones's glance petrifies Schomberg, for his "lifeless manner . . . seemed to imply some sort of menace from beyond the grave." When Schomberg presently capitulates to their demand (accompanied by frightful threats of fire and death) that they be allowed to conduct a regular game of cards on his premises, he says, " 'I've been already living in hell for weeks, so you don't make much difference.' " (II, 5.)

It is even possible in the following passage to see Conrad with tongue in cheek hinting that Jones is offended at being mistaken for someone less than the devil himself:

"I wish you would carry her [Schomberg's wife] off with you somewhere to the devil! I wouldn't run after you."

The unexpected outburst affected Mr. Jones strangely. He had a horrified recoil, chair and all, as if Schomberg had thrust a wriggling viper in his face.

"What's this infernal nonsense?" he muttered thickly. "What do you mean? How dare you?" [II, 5.]

On the story level, the reaction shows Jones's abhorrence of women; on the symbolic level, it is the devil offended by lack of respect — and also perhaps recalling that the present forms of his angelic followers are the hissing vipers in hell. No wonder he chooses to walk the earth. Again, the fear he inspires is a "superstitious shrinking awe, something like an invincible repugnance to seek speech with a wicked ghost." (II, 6.)

Ricardo is clearly one of Jones's devil servants, an automaton of evil. He is generally likened to a cat, with green eyes. At one point, after a description of Ricardo stretching exactly as a cat does, Conrad writes in a tone of surprise that he leaned back "in a completely human attitude"! Conrad hints that he is a sort of imp out of hell, a simplified contrivance of the devil: He "was not used to prolonged effort of self-control. His craft, his artfulness, felt themselves always at the mercy of his nature, which was truly feral and only held in subjection by the influence of the 'governor,'" his Satanic master; and a moment later, "Though his movements were deliberate, his feral instincts had such sway that if he had met Heyst walking towards him, he would have had to satisfy his need of violence." From this frightful prospect, Conrad turns to the picture of Heyst talking with Jones: "the conversation of an evil spectre with a disarmed man, watched by an ape [Pedro]." (IV, 1.) "His will having little to do with" his conduct, Ricardo threatens from the nightmare Otherworld. Yet for all this freight of symbolism, Ricardo talks with so much individuality, with so definite a style, that he appears as a rounded person in the story.

Heyst's servant, Wang, is something of a puzzle in the Christian pattern. He comes, of course, from the Celestial Empire, and he is a sort of spirit — a practical spirit — who attends to Heyst's physical needs without more than a word or two of orders a day. He has a spirit's quality of appearing and vanishing in perfect silence, as Conrad repeatedly reminds us, like an Oriental Ariel; but he has exclusively (good) material motives: he serves Heyst, takes care of his wife, whom he conceals behind a protective wall, and clears a bit of the jungle in order to plant a garden. If there is a Christian ideal of service here, it is not readily apparent and does not seem to enrich the theme.

An elaborate psychological symbolism is established by the suggestion that all of the characters on the island, except Heyst, are somehow unreal. Their unreality consists of their being dependent upon Heyst's awareness of them. This makes them aspects of his thought and hence aspects of himself. Not only does Lena say, " 'Do you know, it seems to me, somehow, that if you were to stop thinking of me I shouldn't be in the world at all!' " but later, when he tells her about his life, "For a long time the girl's grey eyes had been watching his face. She discovered that, addressing her, he was really talking to himself. Heyst looked up, caught sight of her as it were, and caught himself up, with a low laugh and a change of tone." (III, 3.) As the principle of life and love, she is appalled and terrified at the evidence of Heyst's remoteness. She cleaves to him, but he seems *essentially* apart. In the story, he is much less apart than he conveys to her. He speaks of poor Morrison and the boredom that came when he in gratitude insisted that Heyst travel with him: " 'One gets attached in a way to people one has done something for. But is that friendship? I am not sure what it was. I only know that he who forms a tie is lost. The germ of corruption has entered into his soul.' Heyst's tone was light, with the flavour of playfulness which seasoned all his speeches and seemed to be of the very essence of his thoughts. The girl he had come across, of whom he had possessed himself, to whose presence he was not yet accustomed, with whom he did not yet know how to live; that human being so near and still so strange, gave him a greater sense of his own reality than he had ever known in all his life." (III, 3.) Here while terrifying the "story" Lena with the fear that he will leave her, he reveals that she is, psychologically, the missing part of himself.

The symbolic intention of the psychological pattern is explicitly indicated (but not spelled out) shortly after the murderous trio appear at the island. After helping with their luggage, Wang, who grasps their deadly menace in an instant, runs off to his compound. Coming to the bungalow, Heyst finds Lena sitting in the dark, the lower part of her dress glimmering faintly in the light of the lantern that Wang has left on the step. "The gloom of the low eaves descended upon her head and shoulders. She didn't stir." Her unreality is suggested. Then Heyst makes a comment that stresses Wang's unreality: " 'Ran, did he? H'm! Well, it's considerably later than his usual time to go home to his Alfuro wife; but to be seen running is a sort of degradation for Wang, who has mastered the art of vanishing. Do you think he was startled out of his perfection by something?' " And just a sentence later Heyst extends the impression to the unholy trio: " 'Upon my word . . . now that I don't see them, I can hardly believe that those fellows exist!' " " 'And what about me?' she asked, so swiftly that he made a movement like somebody pounced upon from an ambush. 'When you don't see me, do you believe that I exist?' " (III, 8.)

Thus all the other characters are pronounced unreal, ghostly, or in some way dependent upon Heyst's thought — and this in a single passage. In the symbolic context, this means that they are all *aspects of Heyst*. They constitute a schematic laying-out of his nature into five parts, played by five "ghostly" actors. With Heyst, this makes six actors, three good and three bad. Heyst is the intellectual principle of his trio. Wang is his practical, serviceable agent: he cooks, cleans, gardens, and flees with Heyst's pistol to protect himself and his wife. Heyst is then left defenseless because his intellect is not united to his practical capacities. He could, that is, defend himself, but he does not. Lena is his loving, life-giving capacity. She is rapturously affectionate, protective, adoring. But she too is rejected. When she has charmed Ricardo's knife away from him and he is lying on the floor kissing her foot, Heyst, appearing in the doorway, believes that she has betrayed him for "one of her kind." Her glorious power is rejected, at the moment of its triumph, by Heyst.

In the evil trio, plain devilish Mr. Jones stands in the middle as the distilled evil intellectual essence of Heyst. He is the evil realization and fulfillment of Heyst's detachment from people. Jones hates the world. Physically he is a skeleton — frail, detached, languid, poisonous, and positively loathing the life-giving female principle. In their long discussion that takes place while Lena is charming the knife away from Ricardo, Jones dwells on the unworthiness of women until he has prepared Heyst to misinterpret the scene as he — and Jones — come in to discover Ricardo at Lena's feet. At this instant Jones, in the rear, asks Heyst to "just stoop a trifle" and shoots over his shoulder grazing Ricardo with the bullet that plunges fatally into Lena's breast. Jones is clearly the dark shadow of Heyst, his evil essence, speaking his darkest throughts, acting the ugly impulses they release.*

* Since writing this I have seen a discerning comment by Gerard Pilecki ("Conrad's *Victory*," *Explicator*, January 1965, item 36), showing that Mr. Jones suggests Heyst's father. He is twice described as wearing the same sort of blue dressing-gown as the elder Heyst; and when Heyst comes upon the scene of Ricardo at the feet of Lena, "He moved automatically, his head low, like a prisoner captured by the evil power

Jones's two attendants match Lena and Wang. Ricardo, his active extension, is cruel and destructive. He is also treacherous, which is to say that Ricardo does not even work for Mr. Jones any more. He is eager to betray him for the girl. When Jones turns and shoots Ricardo (having on his first try just grazed him and killed Lena), he enacts on a brutal plane exactly what Heyst has done (through him) to Lena! Jones abhors women, has translated his feelings into homosexuality or the asceticism of murder and pillage. Ricardo as servant translates Jones's cold withdrawal into active onslaughts against what he calls the "tame" ones. If Lena draws Heyst back toward love by her passionate determination, Ricardo impels Jones deeper into his icy retreat. Heyst, then, could be a Jones; he has the elements of a Jones still fortunately impure; in the dynamics of his developing character it is still Lena that expresses this side of his nature rather than Ricardo.

Pedro, a strong, wild, almost speechless, filthy savage, also cooks for Jones and Ricardo. He is brute strength ready to act for his masters — a mindless servant who shows that evil does not value the physical world, does not see the beauty in practical and efficient things. Pedro cooks in the dark, over a flickering fire — a witch's brew, not the clean food served by Wang.

These meanings may now be discovered somewhat earlier in the story. The key scene comes when Heyst and Lena, still new in their love and unknown to each other, climb up to the top of the hill and sit down for a long talk. When Heyst tells her about Morrison, finally using his name, she is aghast, for back at the hotel she had listened day after day to Schomberg's mad ravings about how "that Swede" had fastened upon Morrison like a leech, sucked him dry, and then sent him home to die in the miserable English cold. Now Heyst is a shaken man because he has broken the mold of his life — and for a second time; he is forced to doubt his convictions and his consistency. So he is outraged to discover the calumny of Schomberg. Having taken the step from his detachment, he is horrified and furious to see that Lena had believed the story, and that she now takes a moment to reject it. How

of a masquerading skeleton out of a grave." (IV, 11.) The skeleton out of the grave, controlling Heyst, can very well represent the devastating power of his father's philosophy. The qualifying addition of "masquerading" brings in the richer suggestion that Jones, as I have been affirming, is a mask of Heyst. One idea leads to the other: the son is not only dominated by the father; he is the father, whom he contains.

could she have felt otherwise, not having met Heyst, not having known who the "Swede" was until the end of Heyst's story of Morrison — a story that was so completely different from Schomberg's that she did not make the connection at all until Heyst uttered the name of his dead friend? Yet he is irked to the roots at this unknown invasion of his purity, and unreasonably enraged that the girl should have doubted him even for an instant. His conduct shows that his poise has been profoundly disturbed. He now resents the world. Even more, he resents having to defend himself against it, but he must "stoop" to explain himself to Lena, for he is no longer free from ties.

While Lena is coming to terms with the strange new facts, Heyst's bitterness turns to disgust — and then to tenderness and desire. Lena, badly shaken, "signed imperiously to him to leave her alone — a command which Heyst did not obey." (III, 5.) His considerateness fails, he forces his desire upon her — and immediately thereafter the evil trio appear, for they are incarnations of the impulses in Heyst that have just been released. They represent the consequences of his turning away from humanity. Ironically, they appear when he turns back to humanity with half a heart. The next step is that Wang flees to the hills, and the filthy Pedro takes over the cooking, bringing Ricardo along to the bungalow to eat with Heyst and Lena. Heyst is surrounded by his shadowy ignoble avatars. Spectral selves, mocking him.

The symbolic pattern is almost literally explained by Heyst, with the interesting difference that he does not realize that what he calls " 'the envoys of the outer world . . . evil intelligence, instinctive savagery, arm in arm,' " are in fact projections of his inner world: " 'Think what it was to me to see them land in the dusk, fantasms from the sea — apparitions, chimaeras! And they persist. That's the worst of it — they persist. They have no right to be — but they are. They ought to have aroused my fury. But I have refined [ironic verb!] everything away by this time — anger, indignation, scorn itself. Nothing's left but disgust. Since you have told me of that abominable calumny [Schomberg's], it has become immense — it extends even to myself.' " (IV, 5.)

In discussing motivation, modern psychology has the abominable effect of destroying personality by making everything abstract and classified. It is hence painful to use even the term "psychological" to label this pattern of symbolism so richly developed by Conrad. The whole effect of this symbolism is to give concrete forms for aspects of character that cannot, perhaps, be demonstrated so concretely in action. Disgust, paralysis, scorn, withdrawal, evasion — these do not act. The character can talk about them, or the author can explain them. Conrad has found a way to give them form and let them concretely display themselves in action.

The great masters unite convention and innovation into unexpected and unpredictable triumphs. Conrad goes outside of the formal bounds of society and yet draws upon its essential values, so that his removal is a gain rather than a loss. He has his very special idea about significant men — that they have special ideas about themselves which they attempt to enact and realize — and this serves for him to make every situation, every conversation, every conflict doubly meaningful. The Christian and psychological patterns of symbolism profoundly enrich the suggestiveness and range of his thought. If on the one hand the psychological pattern forces a considerable artificiality upon the characterization of Wang, Mr. Jones, and the latter's two evil servants, the enrichment of motivation that is brought through them to Heyst at the crisis of the story is phenomenal. It enables Conrad to represent two Heysts acting in counterpoint, each one reflecting and defining the other.

The key to the impressive success of this novel lies in the fact that the whole complex of idea and symbol is subordinated to — and therefore presented through — the immediate dramatic exchanges of the characters. Specifically, Heyst's reactions to the girl, to the enormity of Schomberg's calumny, and to the menace of the devilish trio are brought out in vivid and exciting sequences between him and Lena. His reactions grow directly out of the situation and the dialogue that it evokes. They are intensely personal and characterizing; there is never the sense that they are contrived under the dominance of the idea.

ACTIONS WELL INSPIRED BY IDEAS

Conrad's *Victory* represents so unusual and triumphant a success as an idea novel that it does not seem to support any generalizations. In this section I shall therefore try to show, with novels by Cozzens, Fitzgerald, and Maugham, how ideas may inspire very successful characterizations when they are expressed through significant actions. These books have the same qualities as *Victory* although they may not rise quite to its eminence.

James Gould Cozzens's *By Love Possessed* (1957) is an idea novel of heroic and impressive dimensions. It boldly establishes a whole town as its setting and the town's leading lawyer as its hero. The town is traditional, established, unified. It is in eastern Pennsylvania, where American tradition flourishes, not in the raw West, not too close to the polyglot cities, not overrun by industry or poverty or exurbanites. It is a town that has old families, a town where people know each other, a town where Leading Citizens are known and respected.

Arthur Winner, the hero and leading citizen of the town, has a master idea that is suggestive of one of Conrad's. He admires his father, the Man of Reason, who got through a good life dedicated to honor, industry, and intelligence. For Arthur Winner, the law represents man's attempt to formulate a code of reason that will be strong enough, comprehensive enough, and flexible enough to cope with the emotion and disorder of the human condition. The title of the book describes the human condition, in that people seem all to be controlled by forces which are in some way expressive of "love." Vanity, greed, lust, ambition, pride, belief, arrogance — all such dominating or obsessive forces are emotional, and to the extent that they are emotional they *may* lead men into dangers or follies. Insofar as a man is "possessed" by some such delusion, he is not a rational agent and he may become involved in who knows what antisocial conduct.

Assuming the prevalence of such obsessions, which keep most men from being predominantly reasonable and all men from being entirely so, including Arthur Winner himself, the latter nevertheless intends by virtue of reason and self-restraint and the guiding system of the law to do what he can to serve his town, his friends, his family, and himself. This is not exactly a prefabricated plan; his intentions grow along with the problems he meets and the responsibility he gathers because of his general admirable performance. Every problem impels his lively and subtle mind over the landscape of his responsibilities.

Like Conrad, Cozzens is an accomplished writer who knows how to make his people live their problems and work them out dramatically. Arthur Winner, furthermore, is sophisticated and aware. He sees a great deal that goes on under the surface of daily life because people come to him with problems that have got out of control. He becomes involved in these matters, too, because in a small town it is quite impossible to keep all the human troubles in separate compartments. They get mixed up with each other, and they draw Arthur Winner into patterns of self-interest, self-doubt, and conflicting loyalties. He clings nevertheless to the belief that total enlightened honesty, guided by the law, is the only way that will not lead to catastrophe. Wit, knowledge, persuasiveness, patience, reputation — all these are inspired and sustained by the notion of absolute integrity. Following his father, the Man of Reason, Winner knows that he must always be *right* in order to make his way clearly and safely through his network of problems.

The action follows Arthur Winner from problem to problem, showing how he reacts to each one and how the pattern of his problems becomes almost incredibly complex as one after another is added. The pace and intensity increase, and Winner's performance becomes more and more dexterous as it moves into increasingly precarious areas, until finally he comes to the point where he discovers a malfeasance so great in a person so close to him, so respected by the town, and sustaining the security of so many families, that it looks as if he must assist at the ruin not only of the man but also of the town. Here is one of the classic situations for tragedy: the hero by virtue of his strong qualities meets a situation that he cannot handle. Othello's great spirit inspires the jealousy of a man who is too clever for him. Hamlet's idealism makes it impossible for him to play the role of bloody avenger. In the interior monologue that accompanies Arthur Winner through the action, he quotes a great deal of Shakespeare. *Othello* appeals to him particularly, and when he is heartsick at a fellow citizen's downfall because, as Melville wrote, "That immaculate manliness we feel within ourselves . . . bleeds with keenest anguish at the undraped spectacle of a valor-ruined man" *(Moby-Dick,* Chapter XXVI), he recites to himself bits of Othello's cry of anguish:

> O, now, for ever
> Farewell the tranquil mind! farewell content!
> Farewell the plumed troop, and the big wars,
> That make ambition virtue! O, farewell!
> Farewell the neighing steed, and the shrill trump,
> The spirit-stirring drum, the ear-piercing fife,
> The royal banner, and all quality,
> Pride, pomp and circumstance of glorious war!

And, O you mortal engines, whose rude throats
The immortal Jove's dread clamours counterfeit,
Farewell! Othello's occupation's gone!
[III, iii, 347–57]

War is Othello's life, his occupation, the activity in which he finds
and knows his greatness. When he accepts the suspicion that Desdemona is false, his anguish makes him say that his "occupation" has lost
its meaning for him. Arthur Winner quotes bits of this passage as he
reflects on the fact that a man's self-respect is tied up with his *function*;
he sees himself as a successful tailor or banker or mechanic, performing the craft in which he takes form and knows himself. Take away
the craft, and the man is left a ruined shell. When Othello is betrayed
(as he thinks), he leaps ahead to this stunning image of a man bereft
of his craft, his mode of expression gone.

Seeing various people in painful troubles, Arthur Winner comments
on how their lives depend upon the trade or profession in which they
take shape both for themselves and for the world. These speculations
are prophetic, because his own image as the man of absolute integrity,
performing successfully among a welter of problems just because of
this absolute integrity, is very important to him. He is too busy for
heroics or poses of magnificence, but nevertheless what sustains him
is his constant awareness of his own "form." And now his dedication
and honor bring him to a point where he must expose Noah Tuttle.
The other leading citizen, his partner, his relative, the keystone of
local trust, who is also old and sick — integrity demands his exposure;
a hundred acts and statements of Arthur Winner have established the
patterns of honor that must be followed. And now Othello's occupation's gone, for the Man of Reason is going to bring the walls of Broc-
ton, Pennsylvania, tumbling down in catastrophe and chaos. Faced
with such a crisis, Arthur Winner decides that expediency must prevail over honor. Intelligent compromise does better in this imperfect
world than rigid honesty. Thus the tragic situation is not allowed to
fulfill itself, and the Man of Reason moves up to a new level of perception and conduct. It is a level that requires even greater responsibility than rigid truth, and Winner is able to make the tremendous
effort required to overcome a lifetime of principle and take this final
step. This is the crowning idea toward which every incident, every
detail in the novel is pointed.

The situation at the end appears to have been woven by a classical Fate. The chain of cause and effect links back to events that occurred long before the action of the novel. Arthur Winner discovers his partner's malfeasance because of the suicide of one Helen Detweiler. This in turn happened directly because her errant brother, Ralph, had stolen money, jumped his bail, and run off. The charges against him had been dropped, but Arthur Winner did not tell Helen because he could not have told her without also telling her that Ralph had run away. On principle, he would not tell her half the truth; so he told nothing. The suicide, weighing terribly on him, seems to vindicate the principle that only the whole truth will suffice. He has presumed to keep some back in order to spare Helen in her torment and shame and anxiety, and now he has had a part in her death. Thus the chain of incident — it is really a network, for its strands are connected in every direction — includes many of Arthur's past choices that were made with his best will and judgment, as well as scores of events for which he could not be held accountable in any way. Caught in the fatal web, faced with a catastrophe not of his own making, Arthur Winner takes the initiative not merely to remain silent but actively to cover up the crime. The ironic epigraph over his father's rococco eighteenth-century china clock, *"omnia vincit amor,"* embellishing the instrument of inexorable time, commenting wryly on the destructive possessions of all the characters, finally comes full circle to describe the hero with a new irony, namely, the fact that after all it requires love to enable Arthur Winner to rise above his cherished principles and do what is best. For Arthur's possession is pride. It is admirable, certainly, but it is also stubborn. Something more than reason, then, enables him to rise above reason. At the climax, he understands that living in the real world means practicing "the art of the possible," which is another way of saying that "freedom is the recognition of necessity." In the situation given, only limited choices are possible, but among them the choice is indeed free, as free as the hero is able and willing to make it, as free as love is strong to overcome pride.

Arthur Winner develops substantially through the novel. At the beginning he is a tiny bit priggish — very sure of his competence and rectitude — and this in spite of the fact that he has suppressed for over six years the memory of an extraordinary lapse. He has had a violent love affair with the rather unworthy wife of his best friend and partner, Julius Penrose. Julius is badly crippled, and Arthur rightly feels that it would be cruel indeed to let him know that his wife had sought passion elsewhere. Yet the discreditable secret is there, and thoughts of it come out as the web of events tightens around the hero. When Helen Detweiler commits suicide and the knowledge of Noah Tuttle's fraud bursts upon him, he feels terribly isolated, stunned. He says, "I am a man alone"; his occupation is gone; but at that moment Julius Penrose enters and a long conversation follows in which Julius reveals that he has always known of the love affair, that he has loved Arthur Winner with all his faults (not in spite of them), and that he is ready now with advice and comfort. The strength and loyalty and insight of Julius give Arthur a wonderful sense of renewal and joy. They enable him to go forward into the grim task of straightening out, in secret, the chaos of Noah's finances. Thus a richer love, a higher probity than his own appear at the end to bring Arthur Winner help. Such great good luck cannot be predicted, probably is not deserved; its appearance shows that Cozzens finds the world, for all its imperfections, "the right place for love."*

The work of Cozzens suggests certain generalizations on the relation of characterization to such elements as description, interior mono-logue, and auctorial commentary. As I have intimated, and as we shall see more fully in relation to the recent novel, conversation and specu-lation that do not take us anywhere, that do not confront immediate and significant decisions, may generate great varieties of idea without defining a character; instead, they may communicate a sense that the character does not know what he is or where he is going, so that the more he talks (either to himself or to others) the less he is known. But on the other hand a bare and sinewy plot may well dominate its char-acters to the point where they can be known only through simple de-cisions made in moments of extreme pressure or fear. At the extreme this is melodrama, which reduces character to mere outline.

Where the plot is, as Aristotle said, "of a certain magnitude," a dif-ference appears. The speculations of the characters, being tied to the plot, bring richness and fullness to the situations in which they make their crucial decisions. The reason for this fact is that everything de-pends upon what the character's thoughts are *about*. If he thinks in

---

* I am indebted to Frederick Bracher, *The Novels of James Gould Cozzens* (New York: Harcourt, Brace, 1959), for insights into the thematic function of Julius Pen-rose in this scene.

circles about everything — about the plight of the world and his disbelief, for example — he comes out a shadow; the ideas are there, but they are not meaningfully *his*. He could talk forever in this vein without taking on personal form and meaning. But if what the character thinks about is always related to the decisions he will face, if it fills out the body of ideas and intentions that he will bring to the decision, then it will continually enrich the characterization.

This latter is what happens through *By Love Possessed* and the other fine novels by Cozzens. Arthur Winner has a very elaborate mind; it is full of ideas, opinions, information, poems, passages of Shakespeare. As he moves through his eventful weekend he is turning these ideas over and over, and they are comments on the situations, on his part in them, and on the values and the goals that he will bring to his decisions. Thus they constitute a rich body of *self*; they make a rounded, integrated man who is known in far greater detail than one might know his own illustrious uncle. The rhythms of his thought reflect the rhythms of his town, the flow of the life all around him, the give and take of his intercourse with a score of people. The whole complex of what he thinks, how he thinks, and how he acts makes for an extraordinarily rich characterization. The "rhythms of his thought," which come out in a style that has been strenuously condemned as needlessly involuted and difficult, embody the intercourse between the hero and the whole life of the town; they make his relation a felt, an almost physical sensation to the receptive reader.

Rhythm of thought, action, speculation, and final decision, then, conspire to bring out the idea that bursts at the end of this remarkable novel. The action is tremendously exciting, the style is compelling, the theme is profoundly rooted in the study of man in society. Woven into this rich and beautiful texture, characterization is as full and satisfying as one might think possible.

F. Scott Fitzgerald's *The Great Gatsby* (1925) puzzles while it impresses, for its readers often do not think it worthy of the impression it makes. Many of the people in it seem to be cheap and flashy; there is a good deal of melodramatic violence; there is mystery developed by the long delayed throwback into Gatsby's past, which comes very near the end; but there is an impressive *action* in which all the characters are totally engaged, and it is this that accounts for its lasting hold on its readers. This and the subtle union of the action with an idea.

Surrounding, containing *The Great Gatsby* is an ideal of democratic aristocracy, the dramatic exploitation of which gives the novel
its force. The achieved ideal would be embodied in a class to which
anyone could have access, but its standards would be higher than those
that identify a European aristocrat, where inheritance and manners
would be of primary importance. It would require not only manners,
but also cultivation and refinement, elegance of taste and opulence of
setting, candor and courage, and openness to ideas. These qualities
would, in the democratic aristocrat, be *responsible*. They would grace
and dignify the nation, and they would serve it both by examples of
excellence and by active participation in leadership. Open access to
this class is a very important aspect of the American ideal, which assumes that excellence can be attained in this Land of Opportunity by
anyone with the energy, the dedication, and the aspiration.

The novel is about the shapes this ideal assumed in the twenties,
when the country teemed with opportunity and energy — and the controlling essential of responsibility did not effectively operate. Tom and
Daisy Buchanan have all the outward evidences of class; they have elegant manners, dress, physical comfort; they have proper educations;
they live in a fine house on Long Island, where there is a tradition of
American aristocracy. They come, furthermore, from the West, and in
so doing they might seem to have availed themselves of the opportunities of the open society. Theirs is not merely inherited class but
something more dynamic. Gatsby embodies the other part of the
Dream. He is the self-made man who is driving on to achieve the life
to which his material success, in the American tradition, should open
all doors. The lines cross on Daisy Buchanan, who is Gatsby's dream-
girl. He sees in her everything toward which an aspiring American
could aspire. She is beauty, dignity, desire; she is perfection itself.
Gatsby thought he had her once, before the war, after a glorious
month of love, but he came back to discover that she had slipped
through his fingers and into the arms of Tom Buchanan, whom she
has married. Fired as he is by the American Dream, Gatsby believes
that anything is possible to a determined man. He can even turn time
back in its course and take Daisy out of its flow at an earlier stage,
before she knew Tom — and this is what he sets out to do.

So here the two parts of the democratic dream meet in action. Daisy is a trifling, irresponsible woman. Beautiful and elegant, yes, but bored with herself, her world, and her husband. Tom is a racist, a bully, and a philanderer who is currently having an affair with Myrtle Wilson, the coarse wife of his automobile mechanic whose place of business is conveniently located between East Egg (Great Neck, N.Y.?) and Manhattan.

Thus the action moves with its two elements: the Buchanans who are superficially well-bred leisure class but who lack the responsibility that would give ethical weight to their status; and Gatsby who embodies self-made aspiration but whose past is gangster-tainted and whose ideal — Daisy — is flimsy tinsel. Lacking the discipline of morality, he thrusts his great American drive toward an ignoble and foolish object. Not only is Daisy trifling and selfish, but Gatsby's dream of turning back time by sheer exercise of will is an extravagant folly.

Presiding over this action as narrator is Nick Carraway, whose role is a triumph of concealment and ambiguity. We customarily allow a narrator a certain omniscience, since he functions as a device to get the story told; we do not worry about his being fortunately on the spot when crucial incidents take place; we allow him to overhear vital conversations or to be the object of confidences that the character would probably not make (any more than the Shakespearean soliloquy would be delivered in blank verse); in short, he has the special status of a literary device, and he is not expected to enter the problem as the other characters do. But Fitzgerald's Nick Carraway violates these conventions. He opens the story in the moral stance of a man who has always received unsolicited confidences and who now has witnessed events that have deeply shocked him. He has customarily reserved judgment, he tells us, because "the intimate revelations of young men, or at least the terms in which they express them, are usually plagiaristic and marred by obvious suppressions." He reserves judgment in the hope that typical young men are not as bad as they make themselves (plagiaristically) out to be. But now, "after boasting this way of my tolerance, I come to the admission that it has a limit. . . . When I came back from the East last autumn I felt that I wanted the world to be in uniform and at a sort of moral attention forever." It was "only Gatsby . . . who represented everything for which I have an unaffected scorn . . . [who] turned out all right at the end; it is what preyed on Gatsby, what foul dust floated in the wake of his dreams that temporarily closed out my interest in the abortive sorrows and short-winded elations of men." (Chapter I.)

This introduction seems to establish the narrator as a typical author's eye who is directing the reader to take the proper view of the events to be related. Any reader expects and welcomes such guidance, for he does not like obscurity for itself. So this passage acts to interpret everything that follows. It is perhaps only on a second reading that other facts come to the surface — such as that Nick Carraway is deeply involved himself in what has happened.

He has come East in the first place to get out of a relation with a girl that was becoming sticky; he threads a slippery course between at least two girls during the story; he attends Gatsby's great parties, allows Gatsby's gardener to cut his lawn, acts as the go-between to bring Daisy across from East Egg to West Egg to meet Gatsby and renew the affair with him, and continues to carry messages and provide a meeting place.

Finally there is a boozy party at which Tom faces Gatsby down, making him act like a fool — "he began to talk excitedly to Daisy, denying everything, defending his name against accusations that had not been made. But with every word," Daisy draws further away, till Gatsby sees his Dream fade into nothing before his eyes, "struggling unhappily, undespairingly, toward that lost voice across the room." (Chapter VII.) Whatever his shortcomings, and they are formidable, Tom Buchanan has made Gatsby babble like a shifty thief exposed, and Daisy on the spot gives up all thought of going to him.

Coming back from the city, Daisy at the wheel of Gatsby's car kills Tom's girl friend. Myrtle's distracted husband thinks it was Gatsby and shoots him dead, then kills himself. Nick Carraway knows the facts, and his contribution to justice consists of going loyally to Gatsby's deserted funeral. This is remarkable conduct for a man who has declared that his "tolerance . . . has a limit," that he wants "no more riotous excursions with privileged glimpses into the human heart"!

Nick has participated in the action, crucially, by bringing Gatsby and Daisy together. He conceals the facts of Myrtle's violent death. He is so careless in his own relations that one of the girls, Jordan Baker, accuses him of being morally "a bad driver," just as Daisy turns out to be — both morally and actually. After the fatal accident he spends the night talking to Gatsby, who still clings to his Dream, refusing to believe that Daisy will not telephone him. But though sorry for Gatsby, Nick goes off to the city without notifying the police; thus he is responsible for Wilson's mistake, which impels him to shoot Gatsby. This would not have happened if the police had been informed that Daisy was driving.

Out of his deep compromise, Nick broods over the funeral, deplores the desertion of Gatsby in death by the rats who fed off him in life, goes back to the West, and begins his account of his "riotous excursion" by explaining that Gatsby had a "heightened sensitivity to the promises of life . . . an extraordinary gift for hope, a romantic readiness such as I have never found in any other person." (Chapter I.) Thus is the Dream corrupted (it is interesting that Nick speaks of Gatsby as "corrupted" but having "an incorruptible dream") by all of the major actors in the story. Dishonored responsibility, wealth from crime, yearnings so intense that they are transmuted into ideals, yet nonetheless false — and all this twisted and tainted in the telling by an immoral narrator. The idea, rich and subtle, grows through the action, the characters working it out scene by scene and growing impressively themselves as they do so. There has always been a bit of a mystery about *The Great Gatsby*, revealed by the way its readers seem to disapprove of its moral tone yet find its characters unforgettable. This reaction occurs because the plot is so richly dramatic that the reader experiences more than he can analyze.

W. Somerset Maugham's *Of Human Bondage* (1915) is an idea novel of ordeal, experience, and discovery; its action is superficially social, essentially psychological, dramatically human. A young man of good family, with a clubfoot, studying to become a doctor, suddenly finds himself possessed by an irresistible passion for a cheap, vulgar, selfish waitress. Although he observes Mildred's ignorance and dishonesty and his friends tell him that she is a whore in spirit and conduct, he is infatuated with her. He offers her marriage and she flouts him; when he takes her in, pregnant, and provides for her baby by another man, she attracts and seduces his closest friend. Later he discovers her actually streetwalking and again brings her home to stay with him; now he is revolted by her but still locked in a bondage that is more than compassion, duty, or habit — and yet contains all these in addition to the sour dregs of a passion that prevents him from loving any other woman.

The action spreads over a few years — the time of Philip's medical training and early practice — but is told in such meticulous detail that it seems like the lifetime that such an experience is to a young man who is literally fighting for his life against the ultimate Protean adversary of his own unconscious.

As Mildred sinks lower into prostitution and disease, Philip moves into the independence of a busy career; but it is independence rather than freedom, for he feels like a dead man moving among the living, crushed under a heavy weight of shame and despair. Perhaps it is lucky for Philip that Mildred is as cruel, stupid, and heedless as she is, that she contributes greatly to his final liberation by degenerating so rapidly into a syphilitic slattern; but perhaps his abject bondage and his social superiority have brought out the worst in her by giving her unexpected opportunities to wallow in the noisome fleshpots of London while mistreating a man of patience, honor, and compassion. In any event, layer upon layer of character is revealed in the author's faithful and dedicated presentation of the details of Philip's long ordeal.

So complete is the reader's identification with Philip's experience and final exhausted liberation from his bondage that he would not typically — or at first reading — see it as a contest with the ultimate Protean adversary of his own unconscious. Philip's bondage is a self-destructive (call it masochistic) act of resentment against the world that has inflicted him with a clubfoot. He is punishing it by punishing himself; the ordeal must go on until he has earned for himself the measure of accomplishment as a practicing doctor that finally overbalances the weight of self-pity with which he has always lived. But the struggle is so vividly, so concretely realized by the author that it lives in the growing character which it produces and *not* as the abstract psychological idea that ultimately emerges.

Readers of this novel at the time of its publication did not breathe the glib formulations of popular Freud all day long and therefore probably did not — most of them — ever see in the book the sort of case study that is buried in its powerful story. We can speculate with interest on how far we have moved since then by considering that Faulkner's tormented characters like Joanna Burden, Hightower, Joe Christmas, Sutpen, Quentin, and Caddy were *first* read as psychotic aberrations perhaps too extreme to be properly subjects of fiction — and only later understood as Faulkner understood them, which is as typical suffering people. From Maugham to Faulkner the novel has described a tremendous circle, in this respect, and is now going in the opposite direction — yet around the same circle.

IN AND OUT OF COLLEGE WITH
MARY McCARTHY

Mary McCarthy has written a pair of idea novels that range at opposite ends of her strident small gamut. *The Groves of Academe* (1952) is one of the cleverest college novels of our time. Its virtue is a plot that enables it to penetrate the essence of the academic situation as few novels have done — precisely because so very few novelists have been able to devise satisfactory actions for the college scene. This fact depends upon the special nature of the academic community. A university has on its faculty, on the axis of ability, poles of genius and stupidity that are absolutely worlds apart. On the moral axis, likewise, it has poles of pure saintliness and nasty scheming that are also improbable worlds apart. On both of these axes the range is much greater than one might find in a business or any institution that is not so intense, so closed, so varied. There is, furthermore, in a typical university such a gross disparity between the professed ideals of intellectual dedication and the actual varieties of paranoia and chicanery that it is exceedingly difficult for the novelist to find a tone that will do justice to them all. If he clings to the noble dedication, he produces sticky sentiment that convinces no one. Theodore Morrison's *The Stones of the House* (1953) is an honest endeavor of this sort, which comes out dripping. If he lets the comic elements that abound among such incongruities take charge, he will pile buffoonery upon grotesquerie more to our amusement than to our edification.

Some college novels have been wonderfully funny. R. G. Kelly's *A Lament for Barney Stone* (1961) winds up with two infuriated teachers in physical combat made utterly ludicrous by the fact that neither one knows how to hurt the other; they throw books inaccurately, their wild swings miss, they even try to butt with their heads, reducing themselves to total frustrated exhaustion which stands as an image of their academic lives. Geoffrey Wagner's *The Asphalt Campus* (1962) soars into wild extravagances of academic intrigue. And then there is the administrator who is driven to fiction to vent his wrath upon the whole mad stubborn intractable pack of professors. Former President String-fellow Barr has written such a novel in *Purely Academic* (1958), which is very funny and thoroughly insignificant. There have been many more. Kingsley Amis's *Lucky Jim* (1954) and Bernard Malamud's *A New Life* (1961) explore the absurdities with more relish than restraint. John Aldridge's *The Party at Cranton* (1960) is a wickedly clever lampoon of — apparently — Princeton, in which one dimly perceives figures that *might* possibly resemble, now and then, distinguished professors, but in which the plot is too delightfully crazy to let substantial characters develop. Vivienne Koch's *Change of Love* (1960) tries to freshen up the personal relations of her professors by taking them to the American Seminar at Salzburg, Austria; but so far removed from their roots her people do not play for keeps: the changes of love are too easy.

But supposing that the author suppresses his humor, what is going to *happen* in the academic novel? What sorts of actions are possible? In general, they must turn upon struggles for power that are almost bound to be ignoble and that touch only the edges of the real academic world that is concerned with the search for truth and the art of teaching. The search for truth does not lend itself to good plotted action unless someone is trying to steal someone else's idea. The noble art of teaching can be made dramatic only if the professor becomes involved with a girl student. So what is left are the struggle for promotion, the struggle for the presidency between liberal and conservative factions, and the struggle for academic freedom and tenure when some professor speaks his mind about a sacred cow and is fired by a stupid irate board of trustees. These actions inevitably generate wickedness and chicanery; but at the same time the academic mind observes what is happening with a cynical detachment and wit that take the significance from the events. The long academic perspective reduces people and incidents to trends, statistics, and philosophical patterns. It has happened too often before to make any great difference; the spectacle of earnestness repeating itself is amusing. Villainy too becomes traditional while the academic casts his cold eye upon it. In short, the actions available are not, in general, substantial enough to control the comic and satiric impulses that are generated by the ingredients of the academic situation.

Mary McCarthy has surmounted all these difficulties, in *The Groves of Academe*, by taking her satire seriously and concentrating her fire

on a problem that is more interesting than any of those I have indicated above. It is the dilemma of the liberal intellectual who is committed to the principle of academic freedom even though it is practiced by people of dubious integrity. When a popular professor is dismissed *perhaps* because he is not quite good enough for a permanent
appointment but perhaps because he has been a bit free with radical
ideas in a conservative community, his principled colleagues are on the
spot. If he has been punished for his ideas, then everybody's academic
freedom is threatened, even though he may not have been entirely
sincere or even halfway profound. Issues, after all, always come to a
head on borderline cases: when someone is absolutely right or absolutely wrong he does not become "controversial." So the liberals have
to support on principle a man about whom they have deep and complicated reservations. He is a fairly deep and complicated person, and
on a small campus his colleagues are involved with him on social, personal, intellectual, and political levels. They are also insecure, both
personally and intellectually, and so they are loath to judge lest they
set a pattern in which they might at some time be treated with less
than the total understanding they require. With this limited issue,
Mary McCarthy is able to get her characters involved in an action
through which they all confront serious crises. And these crises are the
very substance of their lives. The upshot is that the "wronged" professor discovers unexpected opportunities — and therefore unexpected
capacities — for rascality. He gets the upper hand over the people who
have stuck their necks out to support him, and he is not above using
it to advance his academic situation at their expense. Which he does.

Everything in this elegantly wrought novel is woven around the
central idea, which makes possible a very rich texture of personal exploration and interaction. When the people talk, they are talking on
a fairly high level about the ideas and issues of which their lives are
made. Their relations involve their closely related academic and personal selves, for it is impossible to say where one ends and the other
begins. Cerebral people, after all, usually fall in love because they are
intellectually compatible, and they hate each other, finally, over ideas.
Thus the action moves right through the central manners, customs,
and values of the academic community, and the characters are totally
involved in it and expressed through it. Their characters are refined
and subtilized by the complexities of self — which are largely complex-

ities of thought — that evolve as they deal with the nuances of their relations to the professor, the college, the community, and the *principles* by which all these elements are related in meaning.

If *The Groves of Academe* is a professional construction by a skilled operative, *The Group* (1963) is a nostalgic tribute to old friends. The pen that is usually dipped in acid was dipped in honey to write this book, which has many pages but no significant action. The half-dozen or so girls who graduated from Vassar in the twenties are thrown upon New York, for the most part, to try to live and love in a confusing world. Some go up; some go down; some go both up and down. One becomes involved with a despicable radical; another marries a benign millionaire and moves to Texas. The author only partly conceals the fact that she adores one, envies another, and dislikes a third. There are rich tangles of sex, politics, art, intellectual aspiration, and the dreariness of moving among bums and eccentrics; but there is no plotted action that carries through some serious problem and conflict. The reason for this is that the girls of "the group" were real girls with strong personalities who came out of Vassar intent upon making something notable of themselves and, thereby, of the world. But the gears don't mesh: the world of love, art, and politics is too complex; the girls are likewise so attached to their own different backgrounds that they cannot be seen as reflections of the society in which they move. They come from different worlds, and they pile Vassar on top of family and hometown, and so they are in New York but not of it. They are sojourners in Manhattan whose past is contained in their personalities; so their problems are not firmly related to the society through which they move. Indeed, they don't move through it in any firm sense; they float through it on a different wave length, which is another way of saying that their gears don't mesh with those of New York.

The book has hundreds of ideas but no central idea that is rendered through an action. It is not really a novel, but a yeasty collection of memoirs, vignettes, and observations.

OTHER NOVELS, OTHER IDEAS

All the arts seem to become increasingly specialized as their traditions grow from age to age. What is profound in one period may be obvious in the next just because it has been treated so well already. It has been said that Shakespeare cast a blight over English drama for centuries because poets of his stature could not manage themes like his. The novel has moved from subject to subject, and from form to form, using its materials up as it has explored them; and it seems inevitable that the modern novel should generate — as it has done — a bewildering variety of forms dominated by a still greater variety of ideas.

We have seen in this long chapter that many of the modern ideas that control novels have the effect of limiting the characterization because they use a limited aspect of man to enact them. Steinbeck uses men in an economic struggle, dominated by fear and violence. Sinclair Lewis's Babbitt is caricatured by the satire on American boobs, boosters, and businessmen. William Styron's long march rolls out a very narrow thesis. It would be possible to pursue the inquiry into an almost endless range of ideas about man, revealing corresponding limits, fads, and fashions of characterization, but brief comments on a few more novels must suffice. Joseph Heller's wonderful *Catch-22* (1961) deals with soldiers in a mad world; wild humor slips into frenzy, thence into nightmare, and finally into the extravagantly impossible as Milo, who starts as an "operator" using air force transport to conduct a business in supplies and contraband over the whole Western Theater of Operations, dealing with friend and foe alike, finally bombs his own headquarters with a squadron of its own planes, in order to meet a contract. This crazy extravaganza makes the whole business unreal, and one cannot of course believe in the characters involved. Nor does the author expect us to do so. That's the point.

Lawrence Durrell's Alexandrian Quartet (1957–60) is the perfect example of the dependence of character on action-idea. The idea underlying the tetralogy is that objective reality is not to be determined, that what people "know" is the field of vision (and he means something comparable to a magnetic field) in which the viewer surrounds the presumed object with his own conceptions. The observer selects, imagines, orders, and therefore *makes* a world known only to himself. The "person" called Justine, whose name is the title of the first volume, moves through different events in the eyes of different people. In the first book she is presented by Darley, who seems to render the author's controlling vision. But not at all: we later "see" Justine in such different situations and incidents — which are said to be the "same" incidents that Darley observed! — that she becomes a different person. Then questions arise about whether she is an objective person at all. Incidents all through the books form people so effectively that it is shocking to discover in a subsequent scene that they were not "really" so, and then to find that one doesn't really know what really is.

Virginia Woolf experimented with time and point of view in *Mrs. Dalloway* (1925) and *To the Lighthouse* (1927) so intricately that her action was profoundly obscured. Reputable critics have insisted that Mrs. Ramsey in the latter book is a goddess of goodness and perception, sacrificing herself to her family. Other reputable critics have said that she is a possessive, destructive mother who makes her children neurotic because of her animosity to the father. Mrs. Ramsey's perceptions are presented through a delicate and feeling prose, but what she actually *does* is not made clear; hence the continuing confusion about what she is. The novel flows out in streams of consciousness that still do not relate closely to a plotted action. The events, indeed, *happen*, but there is no clear conflict to present the people with clear choices. Thus a highly subtle and intellectual woman, who was also very sensitive, just failed to convey what her people were. Like Mary McCarthy of *The Group*, she was writing about real people who came to her as full personalities revealing bits and pieces of themselves from time to time, rather than being created by a sustained action. *Mrs. Dalloway* exhibits an idea about the nature of consciousness and the flux of being. The story stops in time and takes up a series of people's simultaneous thoughts and actions that are happening in or near a single spot in London; then a bell chimes and a single consciousness becomes the scene, and the story moves back and forth among its memories; then a bell chimes again and the place where the person is becomes the static site where a number of minds are explored; then another shift and we are ranging again back and forth in a single mind.* Something happens in this book, I believe, but I did not know what it was until the author explained in her introduction to the Modern Library edition: "Of *Mrs. Dalloway* then one can only bring to light at the moment a few scraps, of little importance or none perhaps; as that in the first version Septimus, who later is intended to be her double, had no existence; and that Mrs. Dalloway was originally to kill herself, or perhaps merely to die at the end of the party." A certain

---

* David Daiches in *The Novel and the Modern World* (Chicago: University of Chicago Press, 1939) has an excellent exposition of the form of this novel.

quality of consciousness is projected by the flowing observation and reverie of the character, but she is revealed only in a stylized, fanciful, puzzling series of glimpses.

In *Eyeless in Gaza* (1936) Aldous Huxley grappled with the idea that one's past is the substance of one's present. That is, what one seems to "be" in the present instant is not merely the result or product of everything he has done but the accumulation of his past acts in his memory. His mind is filled with the images, feelings, and thoughts that represent his past experiences. These constitute his consciousness and continually interact with the situation in which he finds himself. In order to give form to this idea, Huxley abandoned chronology and jumped back and forth among incidents in his hero's past, trying in this way to show that one's past is present in self rather than stretching out in an orderly diminishing perspective to where it meets the vanishing point in early childhood. Huxley's novel renders the fact that some events distant in time are close to the center of the present self. The method makes the items of past experience, rather than the passing items of a sustained action, assume an order of importance rather than an order in time. Finally Huxley had to catch up with the character and release him into an action, but since he was preaching non-violence and non-action at that time, the book at that point became more obviously an essay than it had been, although like all of Huxley's novels it was primarily an essay.

Robert Penn Warren has given a sort of mirror image of Huxley in *All the King's Men* (1946). Its action is contrived to demonstrate that people are absolutely what they are before they reveal and discover themselves in action. The structure of the book tells that Willie Stark contained his history in himself from the beginning. His youthful drive to stir up the grass roots and gather a following so that he could head a reform government was a drive to power that was using the only means available. The novel begins with Willie Stark near the top of his power, accompanied by the men who have served him and fed on him and, in various ways, been corrupted by him. Then when the action jumps back to his political beginnings, the reader looks for what made Willie the frightening dictator he became; and seen thus in the author's perspective of hindsight the early events must appear as *explanations* of what Willie later became rather than as events in an action to which Willie freely responded and through which he genuinely grew into the man he became. The jumping back and forth in time continues until it becomes obvious that what Willie essentially is is not a product of the action, but rather that the action is a projection of his absolute and timeless self — it is the print of his form. This, I take it, is the theory expressed by the structure of the novel.

It might be possible to argue that Warren's management of time makes for more effective characterization precisely because it stresses the ever-present and essential self of Willie Stark, but I should prefer to say that the character of Willie Stark emerges in spite of the thesis and the fractured chronology — and because the context of southern society and politics is so rich and the sequences where we see Willie in action are so vividly dramatized. Willie grows and defines himself in action, even though Warren's thesis abstractly tells us that he does not change, for *All the King's Men* is as rich and complex a story as our time has produced. It moves through the heart of the South, through politics, society, through the agonizing problems of the intense and dedicated Southerner who finds himself entoiled in a tradition that he fiercely hates and loves and *is*. It is the same South that Calder Willingham ridicules; but Warren deals with more responsible, more serious people. They are as torn and tortured as Willingham's, but they are people of more scope and intensity. They do not parody the Julipocracy of white goatees and broad-brimmed hats, suh; they are charged with the South, and they seize it by the throat in ferocious combat with it and themselves. Their problems, in short, are immeasurably more intense.

It may not be accident that this novel tells a version of the story of Huey Long — that Warren's fine intelligence worked on the rich historical materials to evolve something richer than either his own mind or history alone could have produced. We are reminded of the Greek dramatists' continual reworking of the great stories of the house of Atreus, where invention piled upon invention, enriching the old tales with layer upon layer of depth and meaning. Warren is a Euripides, late and sophisticated, of the Huey Long saga, and this rich story lives in his book no matter what tricks he plays with simple chronology. And they are not tricks but rather expressions of the plenitude generated by a great story. The novel is full of ideas about people, society, government; it sustains an elaborate symbolism in the story of Jack Burden, Willie Stark's closest friend and adviser, whose growth toward freedom and wisdom constitutes an enactment of the meaning of Willie's agon. *All the King's Men* has a tremendous subject in a magnificent story.

Warren's other novels would reward a detailed study of character and action dominated by idea. Every one grows out of a complex and subtle idea, and Warren has frequently — as in *At Heaven's Gate* (1943), *Night Rider* (1939), and *World Enough and Time* (1950) — elaborated an action rich enough to carry the idea effectively without being too obviously dominated by it. In other novels the idea dominates completely and both characters and action are obviously contrived. Parts of *World Enough and Time* come closest to the quality of *All the King's Men* because it too uses historical materials, but it deteriorates toward the end into particulars that become grotesque. Unmanaged history can be as unsatisfactory as an invented story that hasn't enough flesh on its bones.

14   *The Diminished Self*

I HAVE noted in the previous chapters so many foreshadowings of the diminished self that the present chapter must come as something of an anticlimax. At least, I hope so. What we have been tracing is a double convergence toward a vanishing point — a long perspective of which one side is the action and the other the notion of man. The figure of a perspective will not stand too much weight, because we began with the assumption of a time "when only the deed mattered," when people saw a play or heard a story in order to see what *happened*, and the character was identified in the deed. What he *did* mattered, thus, with the primacy of the action; there would have been little thought about what he *was*, and it was possible for Aristotle to say that a tragedy could exist with an action and no characters — but not the opposite.

When the notion of motive apart from the deed appeared, the unity of story separated into the two aspects, or lines, of action and character. Down through the centuries of story the great overpowering actions have perforce been used and reused until they have become less inspiring for the later writer. *Antigone* and *Hamlet* and *Lear* are as great as ever, but they cannot be written again in the twentieth century because our problems have grown so much more various and special. On the other hand, the concept of character that I assumed to have emerged when the motive was separated from the deed moved on to the notion that no deed could fully and truly represent a deep character, and then went on into the romantic belief that any deed, any setting was inadequate to the spirit and therefore an outrage to it. Through this evolution it is plain that character came to seem a mixture or interplay among essence, motive, and deed; then perhaps more essence than act; and then so complex that no act could reveal it. So as we move into the twentieth century character often becomes a repository of a vast amount of knowledge and feeling that has a life of its tormented own apart from any serious action in which the author might engage it. Add to this the fact that what it knows and feels rests upon a quagmire of unconscious horrors that smear and confuse and distort it, so that its conduct may reflect the opposite of its conscious intentions, and we have come to a point where the well-made, dramatic action no longer can perform the function that it has generally performed in the past.

Thus, to return to our figure, down the perspective of time the lines of character and action have moved toward a vanishing point at which they merge into not unity but chaos, chaos in the literal sense of the unformed elements of being, chaos as the thrashing welter of nothing:

> At length a universal hubbub wild
> Of stunning sounds and voices all confus'd
> Borne through the hollow dark assaults his ear
> With loudest vehemence
> *[Paradise Lost, II]*

— his ear who would look for form in the newest modes of the novel. All the materials are there — and in utmost abundance — but they will not take form without an action "of some magnitude." These generalizations obviously do not apply to all fiction of our times. I am speaking of tendencies, which take various forms.

With Hemingway, for example, we have a very special treatment of the self, for his actions are often disguises for meanings that are only implied among the movements of his characters. Hemingway seems to reduce the self to a terrified will moving in a focus of menace or violence. Salinger and Updike contrive actions to demonstrate the pettiness of life as it presents itself to their diminished men. A step further finds actions that are nightmares of unwilled drifting or trances of blind groping search for the unknown self. And at the end we come to Bellow and Beckett, perhaps, where action has vanished into a void of despair, all-knowingness, or frenzied absurdity — and definable character with it.

The special paradox of our time is that psychology in all its tremendous resources, which promised to open up depths and complexities of character for which there had been neither adequate concepts nor adequate modes of analysis in earlier times, has in fact witnessed (if not presided over) a steady diminution of the self. Witnessed is perhaps the more accurate word, because although psychology has greatly affected our notions of what constitute the self, the *actions* of modern fiction have diminished the self about as much as the insights of psychology do. The two influences together make our problem.

When psychology strips away the eccentricities that gave body and individuality to a character of, say, Dickens, labeling these eccentricities as kinds of neuroses, and puts them in pigeonholes where they stand as aspects of the environment that the struggling self must fight through or dispose of in order to gain freedom, what is left is the "naked eyeball" of a character that is nothing but an embattled consciousness surrounded by fearful and threatening menaces. The self has shrunk to a point of frightened view, surrounded by neuroses that it does not see as aspects of its essential self, just as it does not assume moral responsibility for the social evils among which it fearfully moves. Having cut these ties, it is isolated and desperately aware of its isolation. It lives with the questions "What am I?" and "What shall I do?"

This naked eyeball finds itself in plots of vastly diminished importance. The great moral issues that confronted Antigone or Hamlet and gave them tremendous choices by which to discover and define themselves have shrunk down to small problems which often evade moral evaluation, so that the diminished character slips from uncertainty into action by accident or impulse rather than moving deliberately through a personal crisis that gives him importance and form.

Our problem may be understood in one sense as a change in the relation between the *self* and the *will* in modern man.

Where the self includes a great bundle of mannerisms, habits, attitudes, eccentricities, or personal excesses, it appears to be as it were covered with several layers of protective armor through which one must penetrate to get to a central, more simple and typical — therefore understandable — self. Yet as I write this I realize that it is a modern rather than a Victorian way of viewing character, and the error underlines my point: the Victorian self of a Dickens character is a complicated thing with many aspects, capable of acting in unpredictable ways, possessed of responses which it may call upon in a new situation, capable also of baffling one's expectations while not violating probability. There is no simple central self that sits in the middle of these complexities, for the self is the whole complex. Such complexity and richness of character provide what I should call a sort of moral inertia or momentum that reduces the emphasis on will. The character acts by just being. His personal qualities are forces from which action flows naturally and without effort of will. Being and acting, in short, go so closely linked that will and judgment are not called upon and hence tend to be minimized. The character does not think before he acts; he acts what he is, just as a steamroller moving down the street does not stop to think before it crushes an object thrown under its roller. I have commented upon these qualities in the characters of *Pride and Prejudice*, in Chapter 4.

Such characters tend to be seen from the outside. Why? Perhaps it is not possible to imagine what they are to themselves. Perhaps, just because they act without thinking, like steamrollers, it would be misleading to explore their privacies of spirit. (Mr. Collins tells all about himself.) This is of course another way of saying that they appear in novels that have substantial and significant actions. Perhaps their exteriors, their eccentric and unpredictable actions, so inspire and challenge the writer to employ his descriptive talents that he would not willingly forgo the occasion.

Dickens, Trollope, Thackeray — all professional *writers* — present their people in full dress, from the outside, clothing, features, mannerisms, speech, in rich full stories. The heroes and heroines enjoy fullest treatment. Thackeray's Becky Sharp, for example, is presented from the outside in scene after scene in which the reader observes her speech, her reactions to a variety of new situations, her clothing, her tastes, her scheming, her flattery, her overwhelming ambition to be a great lady at whatever cost. The 900-page novel never ceases to discover new facets of her very full self. Calculation does not always guide her. She has her own instincts and her ignorances to deal with. She often acts herself into situations where her will is not happy to find her. She embraces the complexities of her society and she is their playground and their host. With her, situation and decision seem to be linked, for the inertia of her considerable self brings action almost automatically in response to a situation. What a modern character might see as a problem, she instantly responds to as an occasion.

Beside such abundance, the hero of the modern novel (and it is significant that I speak only of the hero: what modern novel explores and displays its minor characters the way Dickens or Trollope did?) is of a leaner breed. He is usually involved in a psychological conflict: fears, neuroses, complexes, inhibitions are almost the air he breathes; but they are *not part of the self*. They have been so thoroughly explored and defined and catalogued by the psychoanalysts that they cannot be seen any more as individual eccentricities. They are now parts of the environment, the intimate milieu in which the hero moves. But his problem is to win through these obstacles to — what? So far as I can see it is to the memory of the struggle. When the fears and ghosts have been laid there may not be much left. Like the hero who has made his way through a tempest of bullets, he sits — the excitement gone — in a vacuum of praise and beatitude. These comments apply even to such an extraordinary novel as Dostoevski's *Crime and Punishment* (1866). During the main action, Raskolnikov's psychotic complexities are certainly *not* seen as part of the environment; they are part of the self, but only very precariously so, for the self is struggling to master them. And at the end, when the conversion, which is tacked on, aesthetically, like an afterthought, has indeed taken them away from the self, we no longer have the Raskolnikov of the story but a new and shrunken man.

HEMINGWAY'S NAKED EYEBALLS

In the writings of Ernest Hemingway the eccentric Victorian self has shrunk down, losing its variety and therefore its weight and momentum, until it is almost nothing but will. The difference between him and Thackeray or Trollope is simply enormous. Consider a story like "The Killers" (1927). One has to read it two or three times before he realizes that Nick Adams is the central figure. The story begins in a lunchroom in a small town; it is entered by two American gangsters who tie up the cook, frighten the waiters into submission, and stand with their shotguns ready to kill Ole Andreson when he comes in for dinner at six o'clock. Ole has apparently "got in wrong" with a mob of gunmen or racketeers. He is to be shot by these paid executioners. Or if they fail, another squad will be assigned to the task. Sooner or later, Ole will be killed, but tonight Ole does not come in for his dinner, the gangsters leave, and Nick Adams, who has watched all this nightmare with a sort of paralyzed horror, goes down to Ole's roominghouse to warn him.

He finds Ole in bed, his face actually and symbolically turned to the wall, saying that he knows they will get him in time, but he just can't bring himself to get up and go out. Nick Adams returns to the lunchroom and says that he is going to leave town because he " 'can't stand to think about him waiting in the room and knowing he's going to get it. It's too damned awful.' 'Well,' said George, 'you better not think about it.' "

The impact of the two gangsters, dressed like dolls, with tight coats, gloves, and derby hats, the amusing reactions of the cook and the manager of the lunchroom, the pathos of Ole Andreson — these occupy the reader's attention so that, as I have said, he does not see until a second reading that this story is about the discovery of evil by Nick Adams. Nick's self is his will. He observes, and with the greatest possible effort he decides to do one thing: warn Ole Andreson. That done, he shrinks back into his absorption in his will, wondering how he will come to terms with a world in which pure evil exists apparently unchecked by law or reason. Nothing is known of Nick Adams but the frightening discovery and the ensuing fixation of his thoughts on the evil he has discovered. The reader gets only the slightest sense of Nick's appearance or personality, indeed virtually none, and it is not until well into the story that the point of view shifts from the strictly objective reporting of what is done and said to the slightly more personal identification with Nick as he goes alone to the roominghouse to speak to Ole. Even here the reader does not share his thoughts, but the identification with Nick's cautious and sensitive awareness is powerful by the end of the story. This cautious and sensitive awareness is a naked will. Nick is completely exposed to the experience. He has no attitudes, convictions, or mannerisms that act for him in this situation; so he watches, and there is no glass between his psychic eyeballs and the cold wind of evil that blows into his face. There is almost no personality revealed — just the tense willed reactions of a man fearfully, surprisingly involved.

It is well to remark that the method and structure of this story are appropriate to the particular effect achieved. It is a story of discovery, in which the anonymity of the observer serves to compel the reader's attention to the bare facts as they add up, one by one, to a pattern of demonstrated yet unaccountable evil. Hemingway's imitators have too frequently taken the manner over without thought for the particular sort of effects it serves. I would just suggest here that such imitators were attracted by the bare style without quite knowing what it meant. This is an extraordinary tribute to the style.

Be this as it may, Hemingway returns again and again to the protagonist who is a naked eyeball. The story "Big Two-Hearted River" (1925) is an outstanding illustration of the theme. It is the story of a man who goes fishing in the country. The hike to the familiar river, the selection of campsite and pitching of tent, then the dinner of canned beans, ketchup, and bread, are described with meticulous factual accuracy and thoroughness — and with such persuasive absorption in detail that, to its first fascinated readers, the writing seemed to achieve a new dimension of realism. Part II of this story describes the next day's fishing. The protagonist catches some fine trout. When he loses a "big one" he has hooked the excitement is so intense that he has to rest and smoke a cigarette: "The thrill had been too much. He felt, vaguely, a little sick, as though it would be better to sit down. . . . He went over and sat on the logs. He did not want to rush his sensations any." Nick cleans the fish and looks down the river where it goes under low cedar branches into a swamp: "In the swamp fishing was a tragic adventure. Nick did not want it. . . . There were plenty of days coming when he could fish the swamp."

Well, this does not sound like much, in synopsis, yet it has been as widely read as any piece of good modern American writing. On the third or fourth reading of this story one may, with luck (as Hemingway would have said) discover its meaning and the reason for its power. The fishing trip is the complex ritualistic enterprise of a soldier returning from World War I, trying to re-create an idyl of his youth in order to strengthen his feeble grip on sanity. His meticulous attention to detail is his effort to keep his thoughts away from the war and his head wound. He walks past several good campsites in order to tire himself so he will sleep. The fishing itself is a release but also an intense nervous strain; Nick requires the intensity for its power to control his thoughts, yet "He did not want to rush his sensations any."

Here, then, is a story that is important for what it does not say. Its meaning is all the incidents that the ex-soldier does not allow himself to recall. It is like the negative of a photograph, where everything is the opposite of what it appears; and the reader of this Hemingway story probably has to be given this key if he is to understand it at all. One or two clues in the story, such as the fact that the whole country-side has been burned over and the grasshoppers have turned black from eating the cinders, make the meaning unmistakable once you have the correct perspective.

What has become of the self here? It has dissolved into pure will. Nothing remains of it but the desperate will of the protagonist to hold on to his nervous stability. The reader knows him only by sharing the tension of this precarious and agonized act. It would seem that the reduction of the individual could not be carried further, yet Hemingway makes the story glow with life and interest. In a context where the individual is losing his idiosyncrasy — his individuality — Hemingway packs every word and phrase with felt life. The hero (who is, of course, Nick Adams) powerfully engages the reader's attention and has ironically become the model for a whole generation of authors who felt the energy of this writing without quite grasping its meaning. John O'Hara, James Cain, and a host of others grading down even to Mickey Spillane have copied Hemingway's style, made it the hard-boiled fashion of our times, without the intensity of meaning that gives life to the fact. In an inferior way, nevertheless, these writers participate in the enterprise of making the individual a shrinking, naked eyeball of bare will — and even where the eyeball is not vividly alive, the concentration on detail has added to the vitality of modern American prose. The more or less anonymous heroes who move through the works of these lesser writers tend to become caught up in violence; the violence makes for suspense, and in its focus the hero suffers danger, anguish, perhaps outrage. Presumably he does, for he does not choose; he merely responds. He is known only insofar as the reader infers what it would be like to be in his situation. Here is a new kind of melodrama, and it has inspired western cinemas like *High Noon*, which perfectly copies the style.

The Hemingway hero is a lens moving around a great circle into which he looks — but the *he* is rather assumed than known. We know what he sees, which is a world of violence, terror, despair, and rebellion. All the violence of that world impinges upon the lens, the naked eyeball, which sees while the assumed self behind it suffers, flinches, endures, and hardens. The transaction between this world and the wary, shrunken, damaged self cannot be labeled by the word plot. The hero does not move through the central manners and values of his society. As Philip Young says, he peers through a crack at the violence to which he reduces experience. "It is a world seen through a crack in the wall by a man who is pinned down by gunfire. The vision is obsessed by violence, and insists that we honor a stubborn preoccupation with the profound significance of violence in our time."*

The real action of these short stories is concealed and symbolic. It is a ceremony of exorcism practiced by a kind of magic, for the writer is subduing his demons by a strategy of ambiguous projection; he is pushing his own private horrors into incidents that partly reveal them while at the same time they charm them psychologically off to a distance. They express how the personal horror came, or how it felt, or what it was like at some point in the process of recovery. And thus they aid the recovery by taking the emotion from the writer and setting it apart, and at a safer distance, in the story. The sense of this great strategic enterprise comes with the reading of a whole series of Hemingway's stories, although it was not generally understood until Philip Young explained it.†

Hemingway's early novel, *The Sun Also Rises* (1926), presents a cabinet of people working more openly in this area. They are in a world of too much and too cheap. It is the world of the twenties, when every value and ideal has seemingly been debauched by and after the war,

---

* Philip Young, *Ernest Hemingway* (Minneapolis: University of Minnesota Press, 1959), p. 40.

What becomes so striking in Hemingway's stories is indeed the culmination of a long trend. With the vision of a great genius, William Butler Yeats traced it all the way back to the Renaissance, and he found it very strong in the mid-nineteenth century, as Edward Engleberg has shown in his penetrating volume, *The Vast Design: Patterns in W. B. Yeats's Aesthetic* (Toronto: University of Toronto Press, 1964). He writes, "In Yeats's analysis of the structure and meaning of the *Comedie Humaine*, one glimpses at its best the orientation that fed and sustained his beliefs about art. He saw the entire epic as a vast design of society dominated by a Darwinian struggle in which 'each character [is] an expression of will.' And will is 'passion which is but blind will . . . always at crisis, or approaching crisis; everything else seems eliminated, or is made fantastic or violent [so] that the will, without seeming to do so, may exceed nature.' Thus the vast epic design reduces itself ultimately to the intense passion of a single, powerful image of will." (P. 32; the quotation from Yeats is from *Essays and Introductions*, London: Macmillan, 1961, p. 444, and was written early in this century.)

† See Philip Young, *Ernest Hemingway* (New York: Rinehart, 1952).

and the admirable characters try to scour their lives of its stains while they struggle to live in their own private hells. They eschew abstractions, fashion, enthusiasm, and any sort of fine language. They speak instead in a sort of spiritual shorthand while they reduce their lives (as far as possible) to the acts of loving, eating, drinking, and fighting which cannot be corrupted by the world's pretense and cant. The hero, Jake Barnes, who has been injured and rendered sexually impotent in the war, stands as a symbol of the Lost Generation, trying to ride out life's hurricane under bare masts. Around Jake and his frustrated love, Lady Brett, the characters group themselves in contrasting extremes. Robert Cohn imitates without understanding the needs of Jake and Brett, who drink, for example, in a ritualistic effort to keep their taut nerves from snapping. Cohn imitates these people because he has no will and therefore (in Hemingway's world) no self. He is always wondering whether his postures are correct and how he impresses other people; whereas Jake and Brett, bright naked eyeballs, are possessed by their efforts to live decently in the corrupt world.

Jake and Brett are not triflers, not idle spendthrifts, not empty ciphers seeking identity. They are strong people seeking integrity, trying to achieve decency and morality by paying for it with clean money: "The bill always came. That was one of the swell things you could count on. . . . You gave up something and got something else. Or you worked for something. You paid some way for everything that was any good. I paid my way into enough things that I liked, so that I had a good time. Either you paid by learning about them, or by experience, or by taking chances, or by money. Enjoying living was learning to get your money's worth, and knowing when you had it. You could get your money's worth. The world was a good place to buy in." (Chapter 14.) From a man in Jake's situation, these are words of great intelligence and courage: they are the words of a man who is making a highly disciplined effort, against heavy odds, to achieve integrity, decency, and pleasure in life. The extraordinary thing about Jake Barnes is his conviction that the world is a good place to live in and that he has paid no greater price than it exacts of anybody who wants to live seriously. This is the more remarkable in that Jake's goals must be held to the minimum. He cannot have Brett. He must adjust to living with his sexual impotence.

At the other end of the scale from Robert Cohn is a Greek Count

Mippipopolous who has achieved stability with money, sex, drink, and friendship — all earned by rigorous self-denial and self-discipline. The casual reader may think him a comic figure when he tells Lady Brett, "You got class all over you. . . . I'm not joking you . . . You got the most class of anybody I ever seen" (Chapter 7), but she twice says that "he is one of us" (Chapters 4, 7), and he explains that he has lived a great deal, got to know "the values" (Chapter 7), and is now very happy. He is rich, too. In an action that is highly symbolic in the context, he shows Jake and Brett his arrow wounds healed with heavy scars in front and behind, where the arrows went into the side and came out his back.

"Where did you get those?" I asked.
"In Abyssinia. When I was twenty-one years old."
"What were you doing?" asked Brett. "Were you in the army?"
"I was on a business trip, my dear."   [Chapter 7.]

No further explanation, but the Count's answer is basic to the system of values in which wise and careful payment buys decency and peace — with luck, of course.

For Hemingway the bullfight has become both an actual and a symbolic ritual — a dance of life because it touches death. Technique and peril unite to evoke moments of perfection, moments where the will is the act and the self in exquisite harmony. (It can be argued that the bullfight is an immature, if not an unwholesome ritual. Hemingway's general interest in sport and bloodshed was in constant danger of deteriorating into bathos; and whereas Hemingway's life was disciplined by his writing, his imitators, lacking that resource, are likely to remain boys after they are fifty.) As a consequence of the absorption of the self into will we have a concept of man that does not provide a role playable through the five acts of life. It cannot live always in danger or love, and when these external resources of intensity have been used up, what remains?

Wilson Follett, in his Introduction to the Modern Library edition of Meredith's *The Egoist*, writes that an enormous gulf has opened between 1877 and today. He says: "The central fact, the change behind all changes, is the modern annihilation of the Will, both as a valid concept and as a working tool. Up to our own generation man had embraced the belief . . . that he was at least partly the master of his own fate; and, acting on that belief, he had often made his conviction actually work. It had the important pragmatic sanction that it made him feel at home in his world, a world of moral choice. It is among the ruins of that world that we now grope. We see ourselves as lost and rootless in a universe without meaning — victims of malevolently blind forces, in and outside ourselves, that predetermine our actions and reduce our will and our vaunted reason to mere delusive reflexes." Meredith's world of will is light-years away, he says. This common view seems so absolutely contrary to mine that it demands some comment. I should say that the vision of a blind, purposeless cosmos grinding itself down into gray entropy was popular around 1900, and for a decade or so thereafter, having come to the public through such popular philosophies as Ernst Haeckel's *The Riddle of the Universe* (1899), Herbert Spencer's *First Principles* (1862), and popularizations of Nietzsche's thought. It was invoked ostensibly to deny the will, but if one looks behind this verbal stratagem he will see that it is really denying the existence of a certain moral order to which it did not wish to be bound. The success of this strategy isolates the will but does not destroy it. The rejection of the traditional Victorian moral order actually adds a tremendous burden of moral responsibility to the modern will, which must define and achieve its own moral order without the aid of social or supernatural sanctions.

I read *The Sun Also Rises* as primarily a book about individuals seeking such a moral order. In a key scene Lady Brett explains why she has given up the young Spanish bullfighter: " 'You know it makes one feel rather good deciding not to be a bitch. . . . It's sort of what we have instead of God.' " (Chapter 19.) Jake, too, wants to live so that he can feel good. But with our desperate contemporaries of the forties and fifties I think the isolated will has ceased to struggle for morality. It seems often only to watch the world happening to it. It is too busy discovering to define and achieve a moral stance. It wants to adjust, to succeed, perhaps, but it really doesn't want anything violently enough to constitute a moral passion. The dissolution of the self seems to have left the will without anything to push against.

The action in *The Sun Also Rises* is fundamentally different from the sort of story we are accustomed to, where what happens is watched at some distance by an observer. Much of this story is watched through the naked eyeball of the hero. It is contrived to conceal his damaged nerves and his efforts to come to terms with the world, while it demonstrates various more and less decent ways of operating in a damaged world with damaged human instruments. Activities abound, but the actions that involve each character are slight. The Count has already achieved his lucky adjustment; he has no plot. Mike and Bill display their qualities; starting as similar adventurers they move in opposite directions: Mike becomes drunk and abusive, while Bill shows humor and restraint. Mike drifts away from Brett; Bill faces no very serious choice. Brett moves desperately and erratically; she yearns in anguish for Jake; she sinks to run off for a turn with Robert Cohn, rises to break off from the young bullfighter. Cohn acts always without understanding his models. He illustrates the sort of un-person that emerges by imitation of what seems to him glamorous and rebellious in the conduct of Brett and Jake. This leaves Jake who observes a good deal, feels love and compassion for Brett, moderated contempt for Cohn, affection for Bill, enthusiasm for bullfighting, and a sense that his values and judgment are absolutely right even if his luck has been bad and his nerves are shot. He helps Brett somewhat with understanding and assistance, he goes fishing with Bill, and he engages toward the end in a long swim, which is so carefully described as to become a ritual ablution following his somewhat sordid excursion into the wasteland of human relations. They have all been living in a dry month, waiting for rain, like Eliot's old man; they are all more or less Fisher Kings in the modern wasteland, and it may not be too much to suppose that Hemingway meant us to see Jake, impotent like the Fisher King in Eliot's poem, who although he sees London Bridge falling down falling down falling down undertakes at least to set his own lands in order. Jake, that is, at least knows where he stands; and during the story he makes some progress in mastering his nerves. He stays even with his plight, and for him staying even means getting ahead.

The contemporary world always has topics, attitudes, and activities which, discussed in current phrases, constitute its flavor or tone. They convey what it feels like to be living at such a time, but they convey it only to someone who is living then. With these elements a novel communicates like a personality with its contemporary readers. It exudes the flavor of its attitude in every sentence, putting the reader in a living cell of his own world. Without much of an action, *The Sun Also Rises* has a wonderfully rich atmosphere, which the reader breathes with every sentence. But even between 1926 and 1966 the world's atmosphere has changed, and young people have reactions to the book that Hemingway would not have expected. They see it as presenting a world of way-out swinging people having a ball. It is not easy to convince them that this is for real, man, and there is no solid action by which one can prove the point to them.

JOHN O'HARA'S NOTION OF HOW IT WAS

John O'Hara is a special example of the creator of naked eyeballs. His characters are frequently speaking ciphers who make strong impressions upon the people with whom they communicate but who never seem to develop palpable lives of their own. One might almost describe them as magnetic fields, which exert force or attraction without being visible. The crucial conversations in *Appointment in Samarra* (1934) are particularly of this sort; the central characters are moving voids, obviously visible to the other characters but invisible to the reader. One sees a hand holding a drink and hears a voice, but there is no person.

In *From the Terrace* (1958) there are minor characters of some density, or at least of a surface effectiveness, but they are announced and characterized by superficial appearances and mannerisms: wealth, an addiction to court tennis, or membership in exclusive clubs. The hero, Alfred Eaton, has all the materials to be a real person except a self. He has been neglected for many years by a father who loved his older brother and who could not forgive Alfred for the death of the beloved son. So Alfred plays it cool and close. He is a watcher because he does not know where he belongs or whom he loves. He broods over his guilts, which seem to be expressions of his feelings of being unloved, although they live in his mind as his failure to speak or act at times when he might have saved the lives of two girls who loved him. We are told that he is respected at prep school and at Princeton, that he behaves satisfactorily in World War I, that he dresses well, attracts women, and is not afraid of a fight. He married a cold-blooded sensualist who does not believe in love and engages in wholesale and perverse experimentation. But mostly we see him moving through events in a watching void. His reactions are nostalgic or trivial. The author steps onto the page frequently to tell us that Alfred has learned something; but we seldom see Alfred entertaining a significant thought, and so we do not know him. We know him only as a guy who feels unloved and in consequence is tough, with a drive to get way ahead in the world and a hair-trigger temper — or perhaps it should be called a willingness that is almost eagerness to resent a slight or any sort of imposition. He loves laying it straight on the line with somebody who is about to overstep that line. He tells home truths. He is touchy about every degree of form and punctilio in business, social, and personal relations. These severities are his defense against a world in which from his earliest childhood he has felt unloved and rejected, specifically by his father.

Interesting is Alfred's quality of seeming always to watch, to see what the other fellow will do next, with a wary readiness to spring like a tiger when the other takes a false step. Many of the scenes in the book are quarrels, where Alfred tells somebody off in terms so strong that physical violence is half-expected.

On the one hand he seems to have hundreds of friends; on the other, he is disliked by his closest associates. He makes a fortune on "brains and luck," but after ruining his health working for the navy during the war he returns to New York to find that he has been maneuvered out of the Wall Street financial house of which he expected to become president. In the meantime he has married a second time — into a profound and perfect love that belies his supposed inability to make intimate friends.

At the end he refuses, in a typical quirk of pride, to join the fabulous oil business — as a high executive — of a lifetime friend and admirer. Why? Because he wants to be in business for himself. But he goes into no business; instead he becomes an idle, drinking, trifling club-sitter, close to a comic figure.

The drive, responsibility, intelligence, and integrity evinced by Alfred Eaton do not prepare or account for his stupid end. But it is not Alfred Eaton alone. Nobody in the book can be counted on. If there is a scoundrel, Alfred will at some time find that he has underestimated a man of character. If there is a rock-loyal old friend, Alfred tires of him when he becomes a fatuous playboy or a heedless wolf. The love of his first wife turns to hate and back again to love — until we are told that she is only sensual and cannot love.

O'Hara must have total recall. He pours out a flood of precise detail and of conversation so explicit and so idiomatic that it seems to come straight out of life. His realism says, "This is the way it was," with a sharpness that evokes the memory of Hemingway's goal, expressed with such dedication and humility. But when Hemingway sought to show "the way it was" the detail was disciplined to serve pattern and meaning, whereas O'Hara has neither a clear theme nor a coherent action. The dense life he records flows past for page after page, but it does not go anywhere. A comparable effect might be achieved by a motion picture equipped with telescopic lens and sound track. The sound and appearance of reality would be there, absolutely authentic in physical likeness but still meaningless because no order would be discovered or imposed by such a record. This is merely an illustrative analogy: we do not have examples of totally nonorganized fact in the cinema; we have rather selection and ordering. But a camera could be set just to record, without selection or perspective, and the effect would be like that of O'Hara's novel.

Properly speaking, there is no action in *From the Terrace* but only 900-plus pages of picture-with-sound. No central conflict is developed. There can be no crucial choices because no central issues are there to make the flood of detail cohere into a pattern. With no action there can be no theme — and hence the people in the book although vividly seen and heard are not characters. O'Hara does not know what he thinks about the mass of detail he has remembered and recorded. He does not think about it. This judgment applies to virtually the whole great bulk of his work. There always seems to be an idea at the beginning of a novel, as he patiently sets about filling in the family background and early life of his hero; but the details flood up over the containing banks that might give form and direction — and the landscape of his story is finally covered as far as the eye can see in any direction with the great spread of fact. O'Hara's intense preoccupation with his Irish roots in Pennsylvania, his sense of being from the wrong side of the tracks, certainly gives brilliance and energy to his prose, but after twenty books he still has not made any sense of it all.

In the short story, where in the modern fashion a little fragment of a contest, an overtone of a personal relation, or a sudden flavor of sensibility can integrate the details, O'Hara is a master. He can render any detail of personal style or quality, but the meaning of it all escapes him.

Hemingway is objective but his stories are rigidly organized to make a point. O'Hara is at the opposite extreme: enormous accumulation of fact into no order at all. In the sections that follow I shall be concerned with novels that fall between these extremes, where to some degree the writer's objectivity leads to a detachment from his subject, which in turn causes ambiguity because we cannot tell what he thinks about his characters or how he judges them. This means that the reader will not have the signposts needed to guide his own judgment, and this in turn means that the character will be living by obscure or unknown values — or by no values at all.

ANATOMY OF ALIENATION

J. D. Salinger's *The Catcher in the Rye* (1951) would be my candidate for the book of our time that has been misunderstood by the most people. It is surely the most variously interpreted.* It has been a seminal book in the richest sense of the word, for it has fathered the Beat Generation, creating a role that has been played by increasing numbers since it appeared. Salinger's most fervent idolaters, whose number is a foreign legion in our midst, admiring him for everything he earnestly did *not* intend, have made a hero of his anti-hero and a carnival of what he wrote as almost a case study.

The most obvious way to account for the tone and flavor of *The Catcher in the Rye* is to assume that the hero is telling his story to an analyst or a doctor. It is familiar, even intimate, defensive, bragging, and yet also expostulatory, if not apologetic. It is the bragging note throughout that shows he is talking to a doctor or analyst in the sanitarium where he is recovering from a breakdown that began with pneumonia and shock. He wants to startle, interest, and impress his audience; his comments show that he is talking earnestly to a particular patient listener, who does not interrupt; he also reveals at the end that his story has been told several times, to the point where its heroic lays have been worked up into an Odyssey of which its author is rather proud.

---

*Warren French in *J. D. Salinger* (New York: Twayne, 1963) reviews the literature, summarizes the leading interpretations, and presents his own view — that Holden is physically sick to begin with, that "everybody" fails to give him the "understanding" he needs, that he is not really a rebel, that during the novel he is searching for a " 'nice' refuge from the 'phony' world that threatens to engulf him," and that he is on the way to becoming an artist — probably an actor. Although I do not see the *Catcher* this way, I find Mr. French's whole explanation of Salinger extraordinarily balanced, informed, and perceptive.

At sixteen, Holden Caulfield has just been kicked out of prep school. In fact this is the fourth prep school from which he has been ejected for not working. He is depressed, lonesome, resentful. He knows he has erred, but he also believes that the world is pretty far wrong. It is full of elderly hypocrites and not-so-elderly phonies. Holden loves to horse around, teasing phonies, but his resentments and contempt come matched with a guilt which he is always at work to conceal. When he is packing to leave the school late one evening on a typical sudden impulse, the combination of moods flows in his reverie till it comes to his mother: "One thing about packing depressed me a little. I had to pack these brand-new ice skates my mother had practically just sent me a couple of days before. That depressed me. I could see my mother going in Spaulding's and asking the salesman a million dopy questions — and here I was getting the ax again. It made me feel pretty sad. She bought me the wrong kind of skates — I wanted racing skates and she bought hockey — but it made me sad anyway. Almost every time somebody gives me a present, it ends up making me sad." (Page 67.) Here is the outlook and spirit in a nutshell, captured by Salinger's incomparable ear. The defiance and superiority only half conceal the loneliness; everything, we might say, frustrates Holden somehow.

He wakes a friend and sells him a ninety-dollar typewriter for twenty dollars, with typical disregard for his parents' money. Then, "When I was all set to go, when I had my bags and all, I stood for a while next to the stairs and took a last look down the goddam corridor. I was sort of crying. I don't know why. I put my red hunting hat on, and turned the peak around to the back, the way I liked it, and then I yelled at the top of my goddam voice, '*Sleep tight, ya morons!*' I'll bet I woke up every bastard on the whole floor. Then I got the hell out. Some stupid guy had thrown peanut shells all over the stairs, and I damn near broke my crazy neck." (Page 68.)

Holden expresses his humor, defiance, and disdain by lying. As he says, he loves to lie. His lies make the world absurd, in the richest existential sense. On the train he meets a pleasant lady who is the mother of one of his classmates. "Her son was doubtless the biggest bastard that ever went to Pencey, in the whole crumby history of the school" (page 71), and so Holden feeds her a line that would make any mother go daffy with relief and gratification. He tells her that the boys wanted her son, Old Ernie, to be president of the class. "I mean he was the unanimous choice," but he was too modest and so a less worthy individual had to be given the honor. He gets the mother into such a state of appreciation that he feels proud of his kindness. "Mothers aren't too sharp about that stuff." (Page 74.)

There are qualities besides his humor that make Holden attractive. He broke his hand knocking all the windows out of the garage when his younger brother died of leukemia. He adores his little sister, Phoebe, who is ten, and he has taken her to movies and on Sunday excursions frequently. He can be good to her without having to look inside himself; he can even give her lectures about good behavior, which she is already practicing.

Arriving in New York, Holden talks to taxi drivers, checks into a hotel since it is still two or three days before Christmas vacation and he doesn't dare go home, goes to a night spot in the Village, returns to his hotel. There he allows the elevator operator to send him a girl, whom he sends away, untouched, with five dollars — and gets beaten up presently by the elevator operator, who returns with the girl demanding five dollars more than the price originally agreed upon. He makes a date with a girl friend whom he professes to dislike, seeks his sister Phoebe in Central Park — and continues to digress on childhood memories and current opinions. He bristles with affluent prejudices, even while he rejects work because money would only force him to buy a lot of phony stuff like Cadillacs: "It isn't important, I know, but I hate it when somebody has cheap suitcases. It sounds terrible to say it, but I can even get to hate somebody, just *looking* at them, if they have cheap suitcases with them." (Page 141.) Holden practices every phoniness, at one time or another, for which he denounces the world.

The more he talks, the more items "depress" him. He walks all the way through the Park in the cold, to the Natural History Museum, but then he decides he isn't in the mood to go in. Finally, with his date, Sally Hayes, he gets to the point: " 'It's everything. I hate living in New York and all. Taxicabs, and Madison Avenue buses, with the drivers and all always yelling at you to get out at the rear door, and being introduced to phony guys that call the Lunts angels, and going up and down in elevators when you just want to go outside, and guys fitting your pants all the time at Brooks . . . I'm in *lousy* shape.' " (Pages 169, 171.) At odd moments he becomes so acute about the follies of the affluent society that he is virtually a Huck Finn, complete

with a phony conscience.* He remembers a previous date at Radio
City with Sally, when he had been disgusted by the stage show — "Big
deal. It's supposed to be religious as hell, I know, and very pretty and
all, but I can't see anything religious or pretty, for God's sake, about
a bunch of actors carrying crucifixes all over the stage. . . . I said
old Jesus probably would've puked if He could see it — all those fancy
costumes and all. Sally said I was a sacrilegious atheist. I probably am."
(Page 178.) Here he is sound enough, but on the whole he is infinitely
more aggressive and heedless than Huck. He goes to a bar that he hates;
indeed, he says, "If you sat around there long enough and heard all the
phonies applauding and all, you got to hate everybody in the world, I
swear you did." (Pages 184–85.)

The flow of tenderness, desperation, and defiance continues as he
gets very drunk, wanders through the Park, and broods over his grievances. He hates schools, phonies, bores, movies, ugliness, and any sort
of responsibility. He continually loses money and possessions, changes
his mind at the point of action because he "is not in the mood" for
something he knows might be good, and like as not goes to another
movie that he hates. He intimates that he prefers a legitimate play.
Yet it is clear that at *any* play he would find cause for an exasperation
that would insulate him from the aesthetic experience. Most actors are
frauds and phonies, he explains. He has taken Sally that afternoon to
see the Lunts, who are *too* good. They are so good, he says, that "When
one of them got finished making a speech, the other one said something
very fast right after it. It was supposed to be like people really talking
and interrupting each other and all. The trouble was, it was *too* much
like people talking and interrupting each other." (Page 164.) Holden's
ignorance here shines through his unending effort to depreciate everything. He can't value the Lunts' quality, and in seeking to find a defect
in it he merely shuts himself away from the play and becomes bored
and fretful. If he likes something, it has to be so offbeat that nobody
else would think of liking it. Jane, for a prime example, when playing

---

*Many critics have worked on parallels with Huck Finn. John Aldridge, *In Search
of Heresy* (New York: McGraw-Hill, 1956), says that whereas Huck's innocence is
"a compound of frontier ignorance, juvenile delinquency, and penny-dreadful heroism," Holden's is "a compound of urban intelligence, juvenile contempt, and *New
Yorker* sentimentalism." (Pp. 129–30.) To this Warren French replies somewhat
irrelevantly that Aldridge "apparently has no concept of the moral complexity of
urban life." (P. 104.) Aldridge also believes that Holden does not learn anything
from his experience.

checkers keeps her kings on the back row and will not move them. Holden refers admiringly to this whim several times. It seems to make Jane special, but in fact he doesn't really know Jane or know whether there is something special in her to know. Since Jane is the girl he likes, he calls up Sally whom he dislikes. He never does get around to calling Jane — but then matters get out of control pretty rapidly.

He steals into his home because he wants to see Phoebe, whom he does seem to love more than anybody else. She quickly guesses that he has flunked out of school again, and he "explains" why: "A million reasons why. It was one of the worst schools I ever went to. It was full of phonies. And mean guys. You never saw so many mean guys in your life." (Page 217.) Yet at the school we have seen him making fun of the misfits. He is on all sides of every moral issue; unable to choose any right way, he explodes in violence. Pencey Prep is just a typical slice of the privileged world that offers a privileged boy whatever he will make of it. Phoebe puts her finger exactly on it: "You don't like anything that's happening. . . . You don't like any schools. You don't like a million things. You don't." (Page 220.)

Holden replies that he likes what he is doing right now — "just chewing the fat and horsing" around with Phoebe, but she wisely rejoins that that "isn't anything really!" (Page 223.) The ultimate evasion for evasion's sake comes in his explanation of why he would not be a lawyer: "And besides. Even if you did go around saving guys' lives and all, how would you know if you did it because you really wanted to save guys' lives, or because you did it because what you really wanted to do was be a terrific lawyer, with everybody slapping you on the back and congratulating you in court when the goddam trial was over, the reporters and everybody, the way it is in the dirty movies? How would you know you weren't being a phony? The trouble is, you wouldn't." (Pages 223–24.) With this infantile mechanism one could reject anything anybody had ever done for himself or the world.

These truths are re-enacted and heightened in the following sequence. Holden steals out of the apartment, telephones, and goes to spend the night with a former English teacher. This man, who has followed his career as he flunked out of one school after another, now gives him some very sound and prophetic advice. He says Holden is riding for a serious fall. " 'It may be the kind where, at the age of thirty, you sit in some bar hating everybody who comes in looking as if he might have played football in college. Then again, you may pick up just enough education to hate people who say, "It's a secret between he and I" [which Holden now says]. Or you may end up in some business office, throwing paper clips at the nearest stenographer. . . . This fall I think you're riding for — it's a special kind of fall, a horrible kind. The man falling isn't permitted to feel or hear himself hit bottom. He just keeps falling and falling. The whole arrangement's designed for men who, at some time or other in their lives, were looking for something their own environment couldn't supply them with. Or they thought their own environment couldn't supply them with. So they gave up looking. They gave it up before they ever really even got started.' " (Pages 243–44.) He winds the lecture up with a quotation from Wilhelm Stekel that nails down the moral and psychological point as clearly as it could be done: "The mark of the immature man is that he wants to die nobly for a cause, while the mark of the mature man is that he wants to live humbly for one." (Page 244.) He goes on to tell Holden that if he ever does take hold and equip himself for productive work, with an education, he will find that he's " 'not the first person who was ever confused and frightened and even sickened by human behavior,' " that many many great men have been just as troubled and have left records of their troubles if he wants to learn from them.

All this advice is so good, so clear, and so unquestionably friendly that Holden might be hard pressed to ignore it, but he has unsuspected resources of evasion. He wakes in the night to find his old teacher sitting by him, in the dark, with his hand on Holden's head. The boy is already very sick, and the man (whose wife is there in the apartment) is undoubtedly keeping track of his fever, but Holden instantly takes him for a "pervert" and rushes off again into the night, adding exposure to exhaustion and bringing himself down to the breaking point. The author does not explain this incident, and the rebellious legions of his young readers can accept Holden's explanation of his flight from wisdom. Indeed, they can reject the wisdom, since it comes from a "pervert."

The fever increases rapidly, and Holden staggers around the city with, probably, pneumonia and, certainly, delirium. He meets Phoebe later and sits in the rain while she rides the carrousel in the Park. He is almost ecstatically excited by his admiration for her.

Now at the end he is somewhere in California recovering, and it appears that he is telling his story (for the severalth time) to a doctor, analyst, or possibly a fellow patient, for he has already told it to an analyst, and it has become something of a heroic saga for him. The high point for him, ironically, is his delirious experience of communion with Phoebe, at the end. He has not learned much — if anything — from his ordeal. He doesn't know what he'll do next or whether he'll study in his next school. "I mean how do you know what you're going to do till you *do* it?" (Page 276.)

Salinger's portrait is witty, tender, and clear. He does not tell us that the English teacher's direct predictions will probably come true, but he does not give much reason to expect that Holden will make a heroic about-face to responsibility and self-knowledge. He leaves him in a smug glow over his delirious, illusory communion with his little sister. Foreshades of Kerouac!

Holden Caulfield's long weekend is an Odyssey, a Bloomsday of negation, emptiness, despair, loneliness, withdrawal. He admits several times that he is a madman, but he says so with pride, for he is really saying that the world is mad. He enacts an obscene and ridiculous parody of Melville's shattering insight: "So man's insanity is heaven's sense; and wandering from all mortal reason, man comes at last to that celestial thought, which, to reason, is absurd and frantic; and weal or woe, feels then uncompromised, indifferent as his God." (*Moby-Dick*, Chapter XCIII.) More obscene than the parody is the fact that two generations of young people have been allowed to take Holden's negation seriously and find such merits as courage and insight in it.

How long can the Odyssey of self-flagellation be sustained? one asks, and What ridiculous thing will happen next? There is even a certain delight in observing so willfully meaningless a rebellion attacking the cornerstones of our society. Anyone knows that our world offers a great deal of sham and glitter, of half-truth and pretense, of injustice and callousness; but the world always has been this way. Our world also offers more opportunity for personal fulfillment to more people, proportionately, than has ever been offered before by any society. It offers so much that it permits a Holden Caulfield to roam at large assaulting practically everything. Permissiveness has moved through moral relativism to moral apathy and on around to the point where the young have been allowed, even persuaded, to see courage and insight in what a disciplined perspective would properly identify as criminal folly. Salinger demonstrates all this from a vantage point so secret that he has become a recluse. He has brought it about that Holden, sick as he is, is a cult into which he himself and anyone else can retreat.

Holden moves right through the central manners and customs of our society — right through its richest affluence and privilege — making a virtue of rejection. His choices are to turn away from choice, to hang up the phone before someone answers because he suddenly "is not in the mood." His most powerful and valuable weapon is simply that he is a madman, as he tells us constantly. Being nutty, he can do anything and be responsible for nothing. The psychiatrists have to listen to him, the doctors must be patient. His parents must pay the bills, worry, and not interfere. And not only can he be held accountable for nothing — his nuttiness is interesting to others, exhilarating to himself. He makes of the outrageous a fashion for others, a resource for himself. And he is proof against reproof. Everybody must handle him with kid gloves, as he knows. He is isolated in his moral void, because he cannot risk serious involvement with anybody. He has to be as nuttily oblivious of others as he is heedless of their advice. For this freedom he pays the terrible price of his loneliness and alienation. Nothing matters because he has broken all his ties. Only Phoebe can get to him now and then, without whose link to the world he would be insane.

I have not fully described the extent to which Holden has made a career of the outrageous. He is extraordinary both in the virulence of his assault upon society and in the energy that he puts into destroying himself. After getting drunk in the Wicker Bar (the bar full of phonies that he shuns), he puts his head in a basin of cold water and without drying himself staggers out into the December night. The next day he sits in a downpour of rain watching Phoebe on the carrousel in Central Park. In reciting his saga he gives these details careful attention, so that no reader can miss the fact that he is sweating, shivering, drenched, and feverish; he also tells about the splitting headache and dizziness that followed. Yet while he stresses these details he largely refrains from explaining or interpreting them. He does mention pneumonia once (so the listener will get the point), but on the whole he conveys the impression that he was unaware of his condition and that he was therefore not responsible for what he was doing to himself. Yet this vivid recollection of his symptoms and of each occasion when he fell or fainted shows that he was continually aware of his condition. While he avoids responsibility by his manner of telling, he also evokes pity, which is what he wants, with his image of a young adventurer, romantic and sensitive, beset by horrors through which he blindly, stoically gropes. Many details contribute to this impression. He provokes his roommate at Pencey Prep to give him a cut lip and bloody nose, and then refrains from washing his face till he rubs some snow on it. The blood is still there when he gets on the New York train and talks to the friendly lady. He adds a further touch by telling her that he is going home for an operation: " 'It isn't very serious. I have this tiny little tumor on the brain.' " (Page 75.)

Holden, as Phoebe so wisely says, doesn't like *every*thing, which naturally includes all the phonies. So if his grapeshot diatribe does knock off an occasional phony he deserves no credit for perceptiveness or insight into the evils of our time. He has established a cult of juvenile impatience with the works and days of all the grownups who rule and run the world. Young men have always rebelled against their elders but have seldom if ever been praised and imitated like Holden for doing so.

Holden's saga is certainly an action, and it produces the sort of character that such an action must produce: a boy who has been spoiled by affluence and permissiveness to the point where he is wild for *order*, upon which communication, self-respect, accomplishment, and even love would depend. But order he cannot have; so he expresses himself in desolating negation. He forms a tentative self out of wit, lying, contemptuousness, and cute maggots like wearing his red hunting cap with the peak sticking out behind and admiring Jane because in checkers she keeps her kings on the back row without moving them at all. He fancies himself a man of exotic insights and imaginings, with his dream of standing by some crazy cliff, in a rye field, and catching the kids who might run over the edge. It's fantastic, all right, but it does not make a life for Holden. Whether he can become an integrated character (a question that is theoretically none of our business) is doubtful; the English teacher, Mr. Antolini, defines the probabilities accurately in the passage quoted earlier.

There is, finally, the interesting fact that countless thousands of young Holdens, frustrated by permissiveness and disorder, have read their plights into his and received the book as a true heroic saga of courage, defiance, and insight. For them Holden becomes a model as well as a hero. Salinger himself seems to have withdrawn into his cult, so that one may finally have to concede that the Beat reading of the book is encouraged by his tone.

THE CENTRIPETAL ACTION

John Updike uses texture and a new sort of pattern in place of linear action. His work might be considered under the category of Idea Men, since *The Centaur* (1963) is rather elaborately patterned upon the myth of Chiron, there is an Index of more than fifty characters from Greek myth to help the reader identify references in the story, and the dust jacket explains that "the author alternates objective chapters with chapters told in retrospect by Chiron's son, and translates the agonized centaur's search for relief into the incidents" of three winter days spent in Pennsylvania in 1947. Thus the dominance of an idea over the management of the story seems obvious. But in fact there is a great difference between this book and, say, Steinbeck's *In Dubious Battle*. There the idea was strictly embodied in the action and characterization emerged in terms of the political-economic struggle, whereas in *The Centaur* the myth (and the densely metaphorical language, of which more presently) serves as poetic enrichment to render the author's intense feeling for a hero (his father) who does not take part in the sort of "action" that we have derived from Aristotle, Shakespeare, and the classic novel.

The story of Chiron, who is immortal, whose man-horse body suggests the incongruity of a great spirit caught in an ignoble job in a small town, and who is suffering agonies from a wound that cannot heal, is a rich symbol to express the author's feeling about George Caldwell. George is adored by his son, who tells much of the story, yet is also the epitome of the adolescent's embarrassing father. He talks too much, apologizes too much, complains about his stupidity, ignorance, and failure in everything he has tried; he is broke, mistreated, and intimidated; yet he is clearly a generous, loving, compassionate, and in many ways very competent man. His agonizing, unhealing wound is his life: it is the anguish of failure and inadequacy that torments him incessantly. Grotesque yet beautiful, awkward among men yet bodied like Pegasus himself, the centaur represents the caged spirit of George Caldwell wonderfully; and in the situations of the novel George acts himself into a compelling image of Chiron. His torment, his energy, his quaint, unlikely capacities evoke the love and compassion that enfold the story.

To the resources of myth Updike adds the resources of poetic language to bring another rich flow of sensibility and emotion to every scene. But it is my constant impression as I read this book that the dense pattern of metaphor is not organically functional: there seems to be no theme or principle in the story that is developed or enriched by the figurative language. It is, on the contrary, a continual playing with the resources of language available to an agile, sensitive, and sophisticated writer — as if a superb juggler were moving back and forth and from side to side on the stage during a performance of *Othello*. These qualities may be observed in the following characteristic passage. George Caldwell teaches science, coaches the high-school swimming team, is in charge of the basketball tickets. He has just had a tooth pulled and an X-ray for some deep, frightening pain in his stomach; he aches all over; he is exhausted; his car has broken down; a student has shot a steel arrow through his leg; the principal of the high school has it in for him; he is stone broke; and he has recently moved with his family to a farm ten miles out that does not even have an outhouse, let alone an indoor toilet. After the JV basketball game,

Those who step outside discover that it is snowing. This discovery is ever surprising, that Heaven can so prettily condescend. Snow puts us with Jupiter Pluvius among the clouds. What a crowd! What a crowd of tiny flakes sputters downward in the sallow realm of the light above the entrance door! Atoms and atoms and atoms and atoms. A furry inch already carpets the steps. The cars on the pike travel slower, windshield wipers flapping, headlight beams nipped and spangled in the ceaseless flurry. The snow seems only to exist where light strikes it. A trolley car gliding toward Alton appears to trail behind it a following of slowly falling fireflies. What an eloquent silence reigns! Olinger under the vast violet dome of the stormstruck night sky becomes yet one more Bethlehem. Behind a glowing window the infant God squalls. Out of zero all has come to birth. The panes, tinted by the straw of the crib within, hush its cries. The world goes on unhearing. The town of white roofs seems a colony of deserted temples; they feather together with distance and go gray, melt. Shale Hill is invisible. A yellowness broods low in the sky; above Alton in the west a ruby glow seeps upward. From the zenith a lavender luminosity hangs pulseless, as if the particular brilliance of the moon and stars had been dissolved and the solution shot through with a low electric voltage. The effect, of tenuous weight, of menace, is exhilarating. The air presses downward with an unstressed sibilance, a pedal note, the base [sic] C of the universal storm. The streetlights strung along the pike make a forestage of brightness where the snowfall, compressed and expanded by the faintest of winds, like an actor postures — pausing, plunging. Upward countercurrents suspend snow which then with the haste of love flies downward to gravity's embrace; the alternations of density conjure an impression of striding legs stretching upward into infinity. The storm walks. The storm walks but does not move on. [Pages 238–39.]

In this vivid writing the images range through myth, atoms, fur, spangles, the Nativity, electricity, music, the stage, a phrase from Shakespeare, and a giant striding figure. There does not seem to be an organic principle to this pouring cornucopia of imagery; it interrupts the story without thematically enriching it. This texture appears throughout the novel. Yet all the emotion produced by the imagery and the detail brings a density to the setting in which Caldwell struggles. His problems achieve immediacy and dimension because the images make the setting sensuous and full of felt life. Caldwell becomes a character partly by virtue of this language in spite of the absence of a significant action because it enriches the setting through which he moves.

The X-ray proves to be negative, father and son finally get home the day after the storm (the son with a high fever), and the next morning as he goes out once more to cope, slogging through the deep snow to the automobile stalled a half mile away, Caldwell dies presumably from a heart attack, barely fifty years old.

His son finds him "the essence of everything obsequious and absurd, careless and stubborn." He is also humorous, desperate, conscientious, ashamed, humble, and totally unselfish. The tone of his dialogue comes through to project an authentic personality. His loving, resentful, tearful wife and his loving, exasperated, and humiliated son bear witness to how tumultuously their lives are sucked into his tornado of loving, striving, and suffering. The fact that George Caldwell is caught in a maze, living an anguish rather than a life, probably accounts for the fact that the novel is partly the son's story. It seems autobiographical, detailing the growth of sensibility, the distillation of early memories, the coming to terms with situation and self that mark the critical stages through which an emerging writer will generally pass. The ubiquity of this theme in the novel relates closely to the fact that there *can be* no significant action for the father's story.

Instead of going through a linear action, Chiron displays himself in a series of confrontations which reveal his personality and the quality of his will even though he has worked himself into a network of tensions that confine him entirely and make any change but death impossible. This tension uses an enormous amount of energy, and in this respect it is dynamic; it vibrates with its contained force and so gives a powerful sense of life.

There are some striking similarities in the unusual actions of *The Centaur* and *The Catcher in the Rye*. In both cases the hero has come to a point where he does not seem to be able to do anything to change his condition; he is in a state of tormented arrest — not easy rest but the immobility of tension or frustration. Both characters could be seen as acting out of this tense immobilization. Holden sets about getting pneumonia and ends in a sanitarium. George Caldwell moves in tightening vibrations from confrontation to confrontation, harried by debt, fear, cold, and his spavined automobile (to list only a few of his agonies), until the physical machine gives way and he dies. Neither character changes, learns anything much, or faces a realized decision. George cannot, Holden will not see any way out of his situation. Holden indeed cannot either; for different reasons both heroes have failed to manage their lives in ways that would give them the large varieties of choices that society offers to others. Of course, the future is before Holden; he may pass through a crisis, which various critics have seen as entering into a general compassion, giving up his dream of being a catcher in the rye by some crazy cliff ("purged of the fantasies that tortured him"), going off to live apart where he can be separate from the phony world, achieving the communication that everybody refuses him during the story, overcoming his own phoniness, or even (since he is in California) making use of his talents as an actor. Warren French in his judicious book proposes as title "A Portrait of the Artist as a Very Nervous Young Man," to indicate what is going to become of Holden.

Thus whether Holden will grow and change is hotly debated, but one can say that George Caldwell is finally bounded by his obligations; he cannot stop whirling and bouncing among his tasks, his fears, and his concerns; each confrontation defines him anew by showing *how* he reacts to a situation, but the confrontations do not offer him choices that will take him to new choices; he moves freely, but only in and out among the same complexities, which contain him entirely. He is the centaur, endowed by the gods with immortality in recognition of the divine part of his nature, and yet suffering incredible agonies from his wound that will not heal, his wound that would kill a mortal creature, as indeed it kills George Caldwell, though his humanity may be deathless and godlike. Holden's paralysis is less pathetic, much less lovable, and not the consequence of the sort of social involvement that has closed in upon George, yet it has the same quality of holding him in a tension where he cannot act himself out of his predicament. (When Holden acts, it is often from tenderness, which he confuses with whim and defiance, his other motives.) So he too whirls in desperate gyrations of un-choice. The myth of the centaur expresses with the beautiful Greek lucidity what twentieth-century man is reduced to bandaging in sanitary psychological abstractions: unconsciously, both heroes "want out."

These novels have a new sort of "action" — where the hero is free in a way that enables him to reveal himself as a character because he *relates* to many issues and people, but where his actions do not permit him to get out of the network of forces that contain him. George's are social, Holden's personal, but their part in the action of each book is the same. From Aristotle's stately conception of an action "of a certain magnitude" that brought about significant changes in the lives of its actors we have come all the way to the action that has slowed down until it is not a movement but a tense balance of forces in which the actors make no linear progress but only vibrate at constant tormented wave lengths. The naturalistic novel, which presumed to show man dominated completely by forces of heredity and environment, nevertheless contrived actions that moved its characters from one state to another. What we have here is a step beyond — the action as a field of force, as a closed circuit of energy in which the character can only react in a repetitious pattern, although unlike the naturalistic novel the emphasis is on character rather than economic or social movements, or the presumed demonstration of any scientific explanation of human affairs.

Updike's earlier novel, *Rabbit, Run* (1960), shows the same kind of character-action relation although with many differences. The hero has been a "great" high-school basketball player; at twenty-six he finds himself trapped with a dull job, a querulous wife, a squalling baby, and a headful of nostalgia carrying back through his basketball days to his childhood when the grass was green and the woods were bright with freedom and promise. His nostalgia resembles Holden Caulfield's, though it does not lead him to quite such violent rejections. His life with his stupid wife is utterly dreary, and although he loves his child he doesn't feel that he can do anything for it. The interesting point is that Rabbit is sensitive and generous; he has on the whole the sympathy of the reader, for the people around him all seem to be inferior in quality of mind and heart. So he gets deeply in trouble with established proprieties by leaving his wife and home and going to live with a semi-professional streetwalker whose heart he has won, on a casual encounter one night, by his tenderness and need. He is made a project of by a somewhat disorganized young minister, goes in circles of humor, frenzy, and despair — and comes out actually running down the street toward nothing. The action is purposefully inconclusive, as the title of the book indicates. Rabbit is questing for order and achievement in a setting that offers no satisfactory way for him. He is clever, sensitive, vital, and good; and there is great subtlety in Updike's usual richly textured prose as he shows Rabbit liked, admired, often effective in human relations, and more clever than most of his associates, including the young minister. Yet he is not strong: he is rich and complex and full of potential but *weak*. He just does not know what to do with himself. Again character is achieved by the series of confrontations in which the form of his wit and spirit is revealed although no linear action appears in which Rabbit could make decisions that would carry him into significant changes, developments, discoveries. The basketball player, running in tight patterns over the bounded court, running afterwards in desperation, symbolizes the relation of character and action. The centaur in the later novel adds the dimension of myth to the same centripetally diminished man. Holden Caulfield, Rabbit, and George Caldwell are three of a kind.

An interesting consequence of this sort of action is the fact that many readers will not acknowledge that it produces the meaning of the story. We have seen how a generation of young people have ignored the action and glorified Holden Caulfield's protest. The same reading of Updike will not surprise us. A recent article contends that Rabbit and Chiron are saints who sacrifice themselves in the service of a "high-er" ideal for mankind. It concludes with the following sentences: "So long as he has strength, [Chiron] continues the struggle; there is no more compelling requirement for any of Updike's characters than that of existing — no matter how essentially absurd the struggle for life may be. The individual is the sole hope in the dislocated modern environ-ment. The demonstration of Rabbit's and Caldwell's pursuit of their particular saintly visions is an optimistic assertion of man's ability to overcome his environment and to project his compassion and concern to the degree of intensity at the heart of the religious experience."*

Here the critic simply ignores the fact that the hero's life and prob-lems are made of "the dislocated modern environment," which is what makes Rabbit run or Chiron limp. Their problems rise from the pres-sures to act exerted upon them by that society, plus the limited oppor-tunities it offers them. The perspective that sees them as saints must ignore the action in which they are enmeshed and treat them as es-sences who really live somewhere else. If I am not mistaken, it is this notion that lies somewhere behind the sneer of a typical Marlon Bran-do role or the yowl of a beatnik.

Wright Morris has searched in many nooks and crannies of this prob-lem in a series of oblique but engaging novels. In his latest (*One Day*, 1965), he puts his finger precisely upon the American freedom-aliena-tion syndrome, in a passage I should like to quote at much greater length than space permits:

In representing nothing bigger than himself, Lee Oswald represented more than enough. He did in Texas. He did in all of America. A free man, he testified to the horrible burden of freedom: how connect with some*thing*? How relate to some*one*? It was no accident that he singled out the man who represented the maximum of human connections, and displaced this man, this symbol of connections . . .

So this senseless crime not only made history: it made American sense. In each American ear the word from Dallas would acquire its own troubled burden of meaning, and its own intolerable burden of meaninglessness. What word was it? How well Cowie knew it. *Im-potence* . . .

Hooded like a falcon, seen but unseeing, impotence persuaded Oswald not to strike out blindly but with cunning at the heart of the

* David D. Galloway, "The Absurd Man as Saint: The Novels of John Updike," *Modern Fiction Studies*, Summer 1964, pp. 111–27.

matter: a man who could act. The one man with the power to act as he could not. In its extremity such impotence made a man murderously potent. If he could not act he could *protest* . . . On this day without end impotence and protest would lie down in darkness, like lovers, and issue from that union would turn up in Dallas, in Escondido, and in towns yet to be heard from . . . In one voice they would cry for Havoc, in another for Help. [Pages 365–67.]

Morris here seems to me to define the real meaning of Holden's and Rabbit's stories. I believe it is the meaning that Salinger intended when he wrote. If so, this is far from being the first time that the public has imposed its own meaning on a work. *Hedda Gabler* is regularly performed in Oslo as high tragedy. Bernard Shaw confessed in a letter that the public would stone him if they knew what he thought (and what he thought he had unequivocally expressed) about Candida.

Ihab Hassan in *Radical Innocence: Studies in the Contemporary American Novel** gives the fullest and most uncompromising exposition of the approach that is diametrically opposite to mine. The rebel-victim, the anti-hero — "the fool, the clown, the hipster, the criminal, the poor sod, the freak, the outsider, the scapegoat, the scrubby opportunist, the rebel without a cause, the 'hero' in the ashcan and 'hero' on the leash" (page 21) — "is not a product of the eccentric vision, the enervated sensibility, or the alienated condition of the 'writer in America,'" he says, but "it is rather the image of man — modern and strictly contemporary too — which the lackeys of our culture cannot bring themselves to recognize" (page 9). This rebel-victim, whose "capacity for pain seems very nearly saintly, and his passion for heresy almost criminal . . . finally appears as an expression of man's quenchless desire to affirm, despite the voids and vicissitudes of our age, the human sense of *life!*" It is this quality of his passion that Hassan calls "radical innocence." It is, he says, "a property of the mythic American Self, perhaps of every anarchic Self. It is the innocence of a Self that refuses to accept the immitigable rule of reality, including death, an aboriginal Self the radical imperatives of whose freedom cannot be stifled." (Page 6.)

Hassan cites persuasive sources in philosophy, history, psychology, and social and political science that have drawn the picture of alienated man. He proceeds to describe the condition by which this anti-hero

*Princeton, N.J.: Princeton University Press, 1961.

dictates the form of the novel: "The dialectic forces of history and society (the World) affect our idea of the self (the Hero). A new type of hero emerges, and from the two critical moments in his encounter with experience, the moments of initiation or defeat, the form of fiction takes its shape." (Page 8.) This is clearly a condition in which the situation of the hero is a plight, a spiritual tension, rather than a place in an action. In short, "The disparity between the innocence of the hero and the destructive character of his experience defines his concrete, or existential, situation." (Page 7.) In this plight, what the world does around him is a counterpoint to what he spiritually *is*, and what he does is in counterpoint both to what he is and to what the world around him does.

With the background of assumptions provided by Hassan, it is not difficult to endow Holden Caulfield or Rabbit with insights to make them archetypes of the modern self. "Between nihilism and sainthood, the modern self wavers, seeking still the meaning of life. In its concrete encounter with absurdity, with dread and the obscene corporeality of death, with mystical anarchy and organized nothingness, with abstract truth and experienced reality, the modern self discovers ways of affirmation that heroes of yore did not envision." (Pages 19–20.) Among this complex of abstractions, if that is where he indeed is, a boy of sixteen like Holden Caulfield would scarcely be aware of setting foot on the pavements he treads, or of being represented by any of his physical actions, or of being involved with immediate concrete choices having to do with his place in the world.

Without being unduly critical of Hassan's position, which is earnestly expounded, I should just like to suggest how heavily it rests upon the separation of character from action. His conclusion to a chapter entitled "The Modern Self in Recoil" is particularly instructive in the very abstractness of statement to which he is driven in expressing the attempt to separate being from doing: "The problem of the anti-hero is essentially one of identity. His search is for existential fulfillment, that is, for freedom and self-definition. What he hopes to find is a position he can take within himself. [Note here, with the word *position*, the jump from slippery abstractions to metaphor, which is traditionally and essentially concrete but which cannot bring more than the illusion of substance to insubstantial referents; as he proceeds, the metaphors proliferate into their own confusions.] Society may modulate his aware-

ness of his situation, but only existence determines his stand. The recoil of the modern self is its way of taking a stand. The retreat weakens
its involvement in the living world." (Page 31.) The metaphors of
position, stand, recoil, involvement, fulfillment, modulation, and retreat all apply to actions in social or physical situations, yet they are
here all enlisted to make appear concrete and substantial a condition
of being apart from doing, of existence apart from involvement and
decision, of character apart from action.

The new hero is identified as an outraged intellectual, a moral
visionary, or a crippled saint whose "primary function is to liberate
those values whose absence from our common experience is the cause
of his predicament." (Page 95.) A bit further along he becomes still
more of an actual person, existing apart from any mere novel and
indeed using the novel as a weapon. He seems to move among
ideas, self, society, and the novel — and again as the focusing concept
of the *action* is pushed aside, the critic falls more deeply into abstraction and climbs out on metaphor and simile. A linguistic phenomenon
of some interest is the fact that abstractions of this sort drive their
author to metaphor. The genius of language is concreteness. Metaphor
is the only possible concreteness where the discourse has been composed of abstractions without discoverable referents. But of course its
concreteness is illusory too, being only verbal. Here is a sparkling
example, where the writer's instinct for the concreteness of language
struggles with the slipperiness of his abstractions. I quote it not just to
illustrate my comments on language but to show how Hassan has to
make action *out of language itself* in order to give apparent substance
to the theoretical hero he has conceived. Through metaphor, the hero
is seen in action, a diver exploring down under a frozen sea. There he
is before our eyes, although he does not exist in any real or fictive sea:
"The central fact about fiction in a mass society may be this: that
as the modes of behavior congeal into a hard, uniform crust, the hero
attempts to discover alternate modes of life on levels beneath the
frozen surface. The new hero is a diver, a subterranean, and this
accounts for the aesthetic distance which the formal resources of the
novel put between him and the standardized realm of social behavior.
A diver, however, moves where light is seldom sharp, and the shadowy
contours of things melt into the strange imaginings of the eye. Forced
beneath the surface, the hero in a mass society lacks some measure of

definition, lacks the basis to distinguish between illusion and reality which the traditional novel afforded." (Page 107.)

Hassan acknowledges that art is in the vanguard of society, shaping the forms in which man recognizes himself. He realizes that the alienated anti-hero is partly an invention of philosophers and cultural historians. He seems to be only a step from seeing that the novelists have been impelled to participate in the creation of this mask by their own imposed or willful renunciation of significant actions.

The immediate source — or perhaps it would be better to say the nearest landmark on the road leading to Hassan's book — is R. W. B. Lewis' *The Picaresque Saint.** Lewis is more concrete in presentation and therefore much more reserved in his pronouncements. He has also an advantage in dealing with a small group of Western novelists — Proust, Joyce, Mann, Moravia, Silone, Camus, Faulkner, Greene, Malraux — who make better exhibits for the case. Lewis has the further advantage of dealing with an intellectual trend. Only occasionally does he lapse into the dogma of asserting that his pattern must be the pattern of "great" modern fiction.

A PATTERN OF UN-PATTERN

Anthony Powell's trilogy, *A Dance to the Music of Time* (*A Question of Upbringing*, 1951; *A Buyer's Market*, 1952; *The Acceptance World*, 1955), owes a great deal to its brilliant title, which suggests mysteries and subtleties of structure for what might otherwise seem to be a reverie in mandarin prose over the sort of pattern that we find in a Persian carpet — a baroque exposition of an intricate but essentially formless arabesque. Color and tone produce unity of a sort, but not structure that leads into meaning. It is a book of tableaux and vignettes, of university, manor-house, and ballroom scenes, and of little bizarre incidents generally involving coincidental connections between various of the narrator's acquaintance. There are a considerable number of characters in the trilogy, whose relations through friendship, business, and love (including marriage) constitute the Persian arabesque I have mentioned. Just as the little dramatic incidents are odd rather than significant (let alone crucial), so the developing network of relations among the characters is interesting rather than in any clas-

*Philadelphia: Lippincott, 1959.

sical sense an action. What stands out about the incidents is just this fact that they don't tell us anything final about the characters who enact them. They are marked by the unexpected convergences of people from different areas of the narrator's life, not by problem and choice. In fact, one or two of the characters are singled out as having strong *wills* by which they force their ways in the world — in contrast to the great majority who exist in the eddies of life without striking out in any direction. One of the closest approaches to significant event comes when the narrator mentions a university acquaintance of his host and himself. He is one of the fellows with will — a pushy upstart who has bulled his way into some authority as a literary pundit — and at a strange party years before he had met the rather vulgar model who is now the wife of the wellborn host. The narrator is weekending with this oddly matched couple, and the wife insists that he telephone the critic and invite him straight out to lunch. The host had always been a great success with the ladies; but now he is under his wife's thumb, and, to make matters worse, she is attracted by the clumsy critic, who used to be painfully shy with women. The situation is fantastic; somewhat later we learn indirectly that the critic and the ex-model have eloped and are living together. It makes a little corner of the arabesque that is not connected with anything else.

Anthony Powell is obviously aware of these qualities in his work, for they constitute its statement: people in modern England move back and forth in a floating dance to the music of time; time passes and carries them from one situation to another, irreversibly; in time everybody touches almost everybody else. The pattern is composed to demonstrate the uncontrolled and elusive meandering of experience, to suggest how modern life happens to people. One is reminded of Emerson's wry comment in "Days" on the discovery that he has enjoyed the spectacle of life and so forgotten to seize its opportunities:

> I, in my pleached garden, watched the pomp,
> Forgot my morning wishes, hastily
> Took a few herbs and apples, and the Day
> Turned and departed silent. I, too late,
> Under her solemn fillet saw the scorn.

Powell, in a new climate, draws upon the image of life as a business transaction, a "deal" in which one may fail or flourish, but in which there is an imperfect relation between outlay and intake. With the

same effort, some drudge, some starve, some get rich. The unexpected
dominates. T. S. Eliot touched the same thought in "Gerontion," to
portray confusion, if not despair:

> Think now
> History . . . gives when our attention is distracted
> And what she gives, gives with such supple confusions
> That the giving famishes the craving. Gives too late
> What's not believed in, or if still believed,
> In memory only, reconsidered passion. Gives too soon
> Into weak hands, what's thought can be dispensed with
> Till the refusal propagates a fear.

Ernest Hemingway took up the idea with the image of a business transaction in a key passage of *The Sun Also Rises*, where the moral cast of
the image is broken by the last sentence: "You paid some way for everything that was any good. . . . Either you paid by learning about them,
or by experience, or by taking chances, or by money. Enjoying living
was learning to get your money's worth and knowing when you had it.
You could get your money's worth. . . . It seemed like a fine philosophy. In five years, I thought, it will seem just as silly as all the other
fine philosophies I've had." (Chapter 14.) Getting your money's worth,
for Hemingway, is not any conventional idea of success but rather the
achieving of inward control, outward indifference, and a mask of
worldliness. The inward control comes hard and at the high price of
abandoning the common social values and niceties and reducing your
life to basic, often violent, essentials.

A generation later the business image appears, modified, in Powell's
explanation of the title of the third volume of his trilogy, *The Acceptance World*. It is taken from a credit transaction having to do with
the financing of overseas sales. The narrator explains, "The Acceptance World was the world in which the essential element — happiness,
for example — is drawn, as it were, from an engagement to meet a bill.
Sometimes the goods are delivered, even a small profit made; sometimes the goods are not delivered, and disaster follows; sometimes the
goods are delivered, but the value of the currency is changed. Besides,
in another sense, the whole world is the Acceptance World as one approaches thirty; at least some illusions discarded. The mere fact of still
existing as a human being proved that." (Page 170.)

Because Powell has conscientiously eliminated the last traces of plot,
his characters are obscured by veils of mandarin prose, secondhand re-

portage and commentary, and the fact that they appear only occasionally and briefly as bits of color in the large tapestry. Their deeper problems and aspirations simply do not exist. Even the narrator himself never tells us what sort of novels he wrote, though he does mention having written some; he watches the dance very much as he engages in it, which is the way an accomplished ballroom dancer performs — relaxed, formal, and elegantly going through minor variations of an exterior and superficial set of postures. The characters are revealed in the clever little dramatic episodes, but these too are studiously chosen for their oddness, when unacquainted people meet in bizarre and unexpected situations; floating on time as they do, they are not given occasions for serious involvement in crucial problems, and the author does not permit us to know them or to take them seriously.

CODA: BECKETT, OR MAN AS NOTHING

When Lear mutters, "Pray you, undo this button," a door opens momentarily into the twilight of a mind close to death. Polonius in a few lines concentrates the ultimate bore:

> My liege, and madam, to expostulate
> What majesty should be, what duty is,
> Why day is day, night night, and time is time,
> Were nothing but to waste night, day, and time.
> Therefore, since brevity is the soul of wit
> And tediousness the limbs and outward flourishes,
> I will be brief. Your noble son is mad.
> [II, ii, 86–92]

T. S. Eliot expresses a sterile dying thought:

> I sat upon the shore
> Fishing, with the arid plain behind me
> Shall I at least set my lands in order?
> London Bridge is falling down falling down falling down . . .
> These fragments I have shored against my ruins . . .
> [The Waste Land]

Samuel Beckett in Malone Dies (1956) works these two elements — the twilit, wandering mind, groping, spinning free, lingering, repeating, striving feebly for order — up into 120 full pages. He has, as one critic said, emptied the "novel of its usual recognizable objects — plot, situation, characters," yes, but whether he has also kept "the reader interested and moved" is a question. I have interviewed a number of avowed "readers" of *Malone Dies* but have been able to find only one person who insists that he has indeed read every page of it. More typical performances range from eight to twenty-five pages by readers who kept steadily on in the belief that some order or action *must* presently emerge. Somewhere about page 20 they found themselves nodding, and thereafter they merely let their eyeballs roll down every fifth or sixth page looking for a sign of action or focus — which they did not find.

Believing he is near death, Malone undertakes to set his house in order. His program is to define his present state, tell (or invent) three stories, and make an inventory of his possessions. He is in a room, he knows not where, outfitted with a few receptacles, and he assumes that his hat, stick, pencil, writing pad, and perhaps a few shabby items of clothing are strewn about. He struggles with his inventory from time to time as he wanders about in his stories, but he can't decide whether the bed or the chamber pot is really "his," and so he founders over the semantics of the possessive case. He slips in and out of dreams and deliriums (apparently); and without further ado I shall quote a typical passage, although I must admit that it is tantalizing to try to find *the* ultimate epitomizing passage. Perhaps this will do — it is long, but you must have the beauty of it hot, as T. S. Eliot says:

I fear I must have fallen asleep again. In vain I grope, I cannot find my exercise-book. But I still have the pencil in my hand. I shall have to wait for day to break. God knows what I am going to do till then.

I have just written, I fear I must have fallen, etc. I hope this is not too great a distortion of the truth. I now add these few lines, before departing from myself again. I do not depart from myself now with the same avidity as a week ago for example. For this must be going on now for over a week, it must be over a week since I said, I shall soon be quite dead at last, etc. Wrong again. That is not what I said, I could swear to it, that is what I wrote. This last phrase seems familiar, suddenly I seem to have written it somewhere before, or spoken it, word for word. Yes, I shall soon be, etc., that is what I wrote when I realized I did not know what I had said, at the beginning of my say, and subsequently, and that consequently the plan I had formed, to live, and cause to live, at last, to play at last and die alive, was going the way of all my other plans. I think the dawn was not so slow in coming as I had feared, I really do. But I feared nothing, I fear nothing any more. High summer is truly at hand. Turned towards the window I saw the pane shiver at last, before the ghastly sunrise. It is no ordinary pane, it brings me sunset and it brings me sunrise. The exercise-book had fallen to the ground. I took a long time to find it. It was under the bed. How are such things possible? I took a long time to recover it. [Pages 33–34.]

Or this bit of a paragraph some 4500 words long about one Macmann who is lying in the rain. Keep in mind that this is just a snip of the whole paragraph, which has a uniform texture:

But to pass on now to considerations of another order, it is perhaps not inappropriate to wish Macmann, since wishing costs nothing, sooner or later a general paralysis sparing at a pinch the arms if that is conceivable, in a place impermeable as far as possible to wind, rain, sound, cold, great heat (as in the seventh century) and daylight, with one or two eiderdowns just in case and a charitable soul say once a week bearing eating-apples and sardines in oil for the purpose of postponing as long as possible the fatal hour, it would be wonderful. [Page 73.]

If we are to believe the title, Malone dies at the end. Anyway, he stops speaking. Or is it writing? The "novel" projects a certain quality of mind, but I cannot tell whether it is that of a courageous spirit maundering *in extremis*, or of Irish blarney verbalizing its merely verbal defiance. Since there is no action, one cannot be more precise about this diminished self than to say that he is indeed diminished to a wavering, disoriented voice.

Beckett seems to be the ultimate triumph of negation (though who knows what the future will bring?), the assertion of power by the act of rejection and destruction. He performs the symbolic action of saying that nothing counts, the world is either phony, or crazy, or ridiculous. Salinger and his kind are performing parts of the same act with quite different tones — the act of destroying the world in order to give themselves superiority over it. Thus they defeat what has defeated them. Their power, ironically, derives from society's continued responsibility toward them. Society cares about them, feels that they are a part of its life and being, wants to cherish, perhaps to control, certainly to be loved by them.

Society, as we have seen, provides the manners, activities, and values to make the substance of character. Without these man has only consciousness. Consciousness achieves the form of character only when it can act in and with these substantial elements provided by society. The union of consciousness and these elements in making character is thus a product of the centuries of human civilization — given form and meaning by the literary tradition; for as we have seen in novel after novel it is the literary treatment that shapes the character, literally creating the parts (the roles) that people thereafter understand and enact. In the literary tradition — especially in drama and story — these elements are organized and selected and concentrated into significant actions, which consist of fusions of the elements of society in and with language. Character as we know it, then, is made of consciousness, the social elements, and language, the three so interfused that they are conceptually separated only by another miraculous power of language, namely abstraction.

The heart of man lives in this amazing human achievement of literature, and even the unliterary recognize and respect the power of language and its instrument of story in this making of man. First the minstrel or storyteller, now the printed page enjoy a special status. If it's in print typical people accept it as fact, for print embodies the tradition that springs from the original bard. When the form that has in such a literal sense *made* man is used as the weapon against itself for the rejection and negation of human values, it is generally heeded because of our veneration for literature. Thus the positive values of our tradition are intimately involved in the undertaking of a Beckett to reject or destroy them. Society's devotion to its people is combined with the magical instrument of language speaking through the golden medium of story in this destructive enterprise!

In *Malone Dies* a special power is drawn upon by the use of the great literary tradition of Western civilization to express a sequence of trivial nothings — and not even a sequence, but a pattern of trivial associations showing the human mind at its most superficial. Here it makes a virtue of disorder and triviality. The sentences are little more than automatic writing — a continued dribble of words excreted by verbal twitches; a noun, then any verb, then an object — or something and then its opposite — or a frowzy statement repeated with variations and modifications. We are bamboozled by a modern tradition of patience and humility before artistic experimentation. (After all, Beethoven, Brahms, Cézanne, Renoir, Degas were scathingly denounced by the best critics: let *us* be cautious!)

The mere action of the pen here creates an un-character, to be sure, and then it goes on to demand and receive respect for this un-character because he exists and is human. Then the character becomes a role and his attitudes become established and therefore respectable, and it is no time until we may find ourselves saying that it may be good to be this way, or at least that since such a person exists and speaks he must be acknowledged and heard in deference to the literary artist who has put these words down one at a time. In the art world — shades of Cézanne and Renoir — almost anything now goes. People throw or dribble paint on a canvas; Franz Kline makes two or three black smears on a huge white area with a twelve-inch brush and a critic raves about the "profound treatment of space": "he is probably the one who has been accepted the most readily by the French. He is in fact a remarkably approachable painter. There is nothing secret or ambiguous in his dynamic carving-up of space, his unorthodox but infectious rhythms, his straightforward architectonics. . . . In addition, Kline offers a romantic view of space which is typically American and has always proved attractive to the French, from the poetry of Whitman down to our present-day Westerns. The space in a Kline . . . is a kind of storehouse of possibilities, both plastic and spiritual, and its vastness is casually alluded to rather than defined."* Here the critic outdistances mere tolerance and throws himself avidly into the enterprise of inventing profundities.

Of course the great artist must be a perpetual innovator. Of course he must create and educate the taste that appreciates him. But just as the great artist works with and from the established tradition, so he must cope with a firm and established taste in the public. One shudders at the venomous ferocity of the critical attack on the French impressionists, but the critics' resistance was essential for the artists. It was infinitely more helpful than the supine acceptance that drools in flabby rapture over anything new and eagerly abases itself to discover profound meanings in nonsense. If this latter is all the taste, all the judgment that the great artistic innovator has to work against, he might as well give up before he starts. How can he educate a taste in a public that refuses to discriminate or to judge, but instead improvises deep meanings in its abject haste to appear open-minded? The critics who attacked Cézanne had beliefs and took a stand. They let the artist see what he had to work, not against, but *with*. They were a resource and a challenge.

The critics who go into raptures over anything rob the artist of a responsible current audience. They give him happy pills and toss him

* John Ashbery in the Paris edition of the *New York Herald Tribune*, July 7, 1964.

into a void of stupid beatitude where anything is equal to nothing. This is chaos. Its signs today are the total eclecticism of our painting — every traditional style shown beside color splashes that are at best decorative, and at worst dribbles or splotches or thrown paint that is not even decorative, let alone meaningful. Recently the critics in Sweden were hoaxed by a series of canvases painted by a chimpanzee. They wrote rave reviews. But actually they were not particularly hoaxed, for what the chimp painted was no less conventional than what hundreds of abstract expressionists or "action" painters are doing every day. With no formulated standards, how could the un-judging critic possibly judge?

My tirade is not directed against innovation in the novel, which will continue as long as there is life in our society regardless of my screeches. I most certainly do not want to join the ranks of the stiff-necked who have always denounced art that turns from the pretty and looks at the sordid and ugly. I am rather concerned lest we too readily allow ourselves to be influenced by a spirit of flabby, passive, destructive negation that takes its un-form in novels that lead through a maze into a social chaos. The exploration of "letting go" can become a way of life; merely because it happens it need not be celebrated as either good or inevitable. We may let it speak without jumping to the conclusion that it is the only voice and making a cult of it in our lives.

Truman Capote caused a sensation in 1965 with what he describes as a new kind of book, "a nonfiction novel." He is reported in the press as saying that he "had been playing since 1954 with the idea of a book that would synthesize fictional techniques with journalism" so that he could "live more in the world that other people live in." He spent two years training himself to record conversations from memory, practiced, worked at length on various experimental projects, and then found his subject in the wanton murder of a family in Kansas, and the apprehension, trial, and execution of the two young killers. Their neurotic motives were much too complex for us to be able to dismiss them with a phrase like "thrill-killers." Indeed, their motives were different. What they had in common was a social alienation that made them heedless of personal ties or human obligations; yet at the point of execution, one of them did admit (but almost as an aside) that what he had done was wrong.

The horror of the crime, the lives of the killers before and after it, the complexities of American justice, and perhaps the unspoken reflections on the question of capital punishment make the book more interesting than most contemporary novels. But this considerable interest cannot repress certain questions. Has Capote got all the facts? Obviously not; it would be impossible to have them all, and the gaps are obvious in the story at times. Has he arranged the facts he has? Obviously, too, for the story has to be told, and is told very well. Has he selected among the facts that he did have? and if so upon what principle of selection? These important questions seem unanswerable. It is certain that Capote has selected and emphasized, but the only principle I could assign would be that he meant to leave a final impression of the irreducible mystery of actuality. The killers don't understand themselves, and they don't communicate well or freely enough to reveal what they do know of themselves. We see a society that by its failure of manners and discipline, along with its abundance of money and emphasis on material things, makes these horrors possible; yet one could not say that Capote writes with a tone of indignation. His tone is *interested*, certainly tender where he treats the good and charming people who were killed, but it's an interested objectivity with respect to the killers. Theoretically, I should say, a perfectly accurate account of the crime could not have any explicit or implied interpretation by the author, whose art might be devoted to making it vivid and interesting. If this describes *In Cold Blood*, it suggests an extraordinary shift in the intent of the artist, from bringing form and meaning to chaos, to accepting the disorder of actuality as more interesting (or more manageable?) than the significant form of art. Yet even this statement is an oversimplification: the act of writing implies the use of a writer's powers of expression. Even the form of a sentence makes an order. Capote has written artistically but let actuality provide his *action* — and hence avoided interpretation. That is, no matter how effectively he renders the events, he does not set up the conflicts or control his characters' responses to them.

Obviously this marks a change in the nature of the transaction between the author and his reader — a change that might be considered the next step after Beckett. Instead of making characters in an action of some magnitude, who discovered themselves as they made their significant decisions, the author became increasingly prominent as he used his "story" to explore and bare his own troubled heart — or to dabble provocatively among Chaos and Nothing. When such tortuous pursuits moved further and further into labyrinths, nuances, evasions, negations, a new direction seemed indicated. Capote has taken this further step that leaves the author with his impenetrable esoterica of spirit and allows him to commit his powers of expression to a new sort of action, an action that calls for rendering and *some* understanding, but not for ethical judgment, not for a structured comment on the condition of man. Aristotle's famous rule is reversed: the possible supersedes the probable.

SIGNS OF NEW TRENDS

The diminished man is unsatisfactory to be, and he is a dead end for the novelist. Something will replace this grotesque mask, and there are signs of new openings and new directions today, which will lead to new sorts of characters. New characters, possibly, but what of the living models of these fictional characters? I believe it is the other way round — that the prevalence of the diminished man in the recent novel is the result of a literary circumstance rather than a copying of "real life" (although, as I said at the beginning of this book, real life always follows very close on the heels of art and soon offers itself as an example of what art has "copied"). The character of the diminished man, that is, has evolved from a trend of literary theory rather than entirely from the impact of life itself on the writer. The literary theory is the doctrine of objectivity; this has produced the aimless hero. As the relation becomes increasingly clear — and there are many signs that it is already doing so — its consequences will generate new values and new ways of expressing them in fiction.

How can literary theory or method be a creator of diminished men? The answer is to be found in the connection between ambiguity as a praiseworthy quality in literature and the celebration of aimlessness in character. What links them is the notion, which rests very heavily on the example of James Joyce, that the author should stand apart from his work, detached, "paring his nails," as Joyce said, letting his language alone render reality with brilliance and clarity. Stephen Dedalus explains this aesthetic in the last part of *A Portrait of the Artist as a Young Man* (1916). Up to this section Stephen has gone through various stages of growth and discovery, beginning with his earliest childhood, and while the story is told through his mind and eyes one cannot be sure that what he thinks at any point represents the opinions of Joyce as he is writing. The extent of the author's distance from his narrator is not made clear, nor is it even constant. At any point in the book we will have Stephen's brilliant vision of his world along with what may be his enlightened or his fatuous views on it. Whether these views are ignorant, childish, romantic, or pompous must be inferred from the language of the narrator; and how difficult it is to determine Joyce's opinion may be discovered by a review of the extensive scholarship on the subject. The best critics have stood at opposite extremes on point after point. Looking at the explanations in "Stephen Hero," the earlier and much fuller version of *A Portrait*, in which many of Joyce's interpretations are presented in detail, furthermore, one of the best critics of the novel concludes that *no* reader could be expected to infer Joyce's opinions reliably.* He demonstrates, in fact, that the distance between the author and his narrator is continually changing, without signals to the reader. The intention of brilliant objectivity and clarity has come out as ambiguity.

Now, classically the literary artist has acknowledged by a variety of conventional signals not only that he was selecting and organizing his materials but also that he was thereby making a statement about them. His attitude toward his hero and the moral standards by which his hero's conduct should be judged would be made quite clear enough for the typical interested reader. Not always, of course. Defoe's *Shortest Way with the Dissenters* (1702) landed him in the pillory. Swift's "Voyage to Laputa" (*Gulliver's Travels*, 1726) is still found somewhat ambiguous. Rogue heroes like Richard III, Moll Flanders, and Barry Lyndon draw the reader to identify with their immoral attitudes and conduct. But on the whole these exceptions merely underline the fact that the author's attitude toward his narrator or his characters was made clear by traditional signals; they underline it because they have always been noticed as exceptions to what the typical reader would expect. To take a giant step, Agatha Christie's *The Murder of Roger Ackroyd* (1926) was a sensation because the narrator himself was the

---

* Wayne C. Booth in *The Rhetoric of Fiction* (Chicago: University of Chicago Press, 1961) has a dazzling exposition of both the criticism and the ambiguities of *A Portrait of the Artist*. Analyzing fictional method (which he calls the rhetoric), Mr. Booth has come by a different route to many of the conclusions that I have set forth in perspectives of character and action. "Distance" is Booth's useful term.

murderer; the book has been considered to violate all the proprieties of detective fiction.

Joyce's objectivity is ambiguous, then, not because he has no opinions about his subject but because he conceals them behind his pose of not getting between the reader and the story. Seen against the old naive methods of writing fiction, where the author explained at every step how the reader should be judging and feeling, the objectivity of writing so well that the facts speak for themselves appears to be a tremendous advance in technique; but the achievement of its most illustrious practitioner has been taken on faith by two generations of dedicated critics: they have assumed that all Joyce's work was virtually perfect and that it was up to them to dig out the facts and refine their insights until they saw exactly what Joyce had carved into his cameo-perfect pages. Now Wayne Booth has shown not only that the texture is too thick to be seen clearly through by anyone, and that the judgments are too subtle to be inferred from the language, but also that Joyce has repeated unsignaled shifts of attitude that make it impossible to evaluate his hero with any confidence that one will reach general agreement with other careful readers. Interesting corollaries to these discoveries are to be found in a volume by Robert M. Adams, who demonstrates that an extraordinary proportion of the names and other references in *Ulysses* when pursued to the very roots turn out to have no significance whatsoever.* Digging deep for gold he found what seems in the most ironic sense to be fool's gold.

To carry this analysis a step further, I should say that objectivity is a purely aesthetic literary value; specifically it is the ideal of reducing auctorial commentary and explanation to zero and at the same time writing so vividly that the concrete facts presented tell everything. When this end is not achieved and ambiguity results rather than supreme clarity, the aesthetic term "objectivity" is modulated into the moral term "detachment." The latter suggests the artist's independence, his removal from what he describes. He is no longer "responsible" for it. Aesthetically Joyce would seem to be rendering Dublin with minutest accuracy in *Ulysses*, letting the facts speak. But as commentators found it impossible to define his attitude toward the city, it became fashionable (indeed it became essential if they were to main-

---

* Robert M. Adams, *Surface and Symbol: The Consistency of James Joyce's Ulysses* (New York: Oxford University Press, 1962).

tain the greatness of *Ulysses*) to speak of the writer as morally objective, that is, detached from his subject, presenting it in a spectrum of good and bad, beautiful and ugly, without moral comment because without any attitude toward it — as aloof and godlike as a scientist.*

This notion must be false; it is impossible for a writer to assemble and organize materials and describe them in words that he chooses (every one of them!) without having and showing attitudes toward these materials. What it means, then, is that his attitudes are either inconsistent, or unclear, or both. The pose of detachment (for that is what it is) grows out of the failure to be crystal clear. Then it becomes a cult.

If we cannot judge the hero, it must be because we do not have clear standards set up to evaluate the choices he meets and makes. Without

* The theory was supported for the novelist by somewhat earlier trends in the aesthetic of painting and poetry that gathered support after the turn of the twentieth century. With painting it was easier to say that the subject did not matter because the patterns that can be made with line and color do not require human problems, actions, or morals as subject. Ortega y Gasset published in 1925 his famous essay on "The Dehumanization of Art," in which he noticed the "progressive elimination of the human, all too human, elements predominant in romantic and naturalistic production." As Thomas Parkinson explains in his fine *W. B. Yeats: The Later Poetry* (Berkeley: University of California Press, 1964), "When the artist has no allegiance to visible nature outside the art work, he can ultimately divorce the art work even from his own feelings, so that his only responsibility is to the 'scrupulous realization of the artifact.' . . . For if one accepts the point of view ascribed to modern artists by Ortega, art should be considered completely apart from subject matter." (P. 9.) And, closer to our problem, "The artist was technician, practical joker, or agent who with detachment shaped artifacts pertinent to his experience of his medium. In literary art, an analogous coolness, Ortega thought, led to the sense of poetry as 'the higher algebra of metaphor.'" (P. 11.) Whereas T. S. Eliot said that literary art should not depend upon the experience of the artist, yet charged his own verse with religious commitment, Ezra Pound went on to insist that it should be dedicated to no creed or philosophy. These trends of theory all reveal a genuine concern for technical mastery, for the discovery of form and expression through the dedicated exploration of the medium. The novelist has echoed the same beliefs, but he has never even approached the scrupulous textures of a Pound or an Eliot.

As fast as one writes, the writers keep a step or so ahead. Just off the press, in June 1965, right in the middle of a novel, comes an author's description of his craft that makes my own somewhat harsh words seem like understatement. Halfway through his novel the author says that when he began it, "I secretly decided that though I would exercise a strict selection of the facts to write down, be they 'fictional' facts or 'true' facts taken from newspapers or directly observed events from my own life, once I had written something down I would neither edit nor censor it [myself] . . . Novels, in theory anyway, are supposed to be slices of life, slices of plum cake. So once the cook has created and stirred up the mixture *he has no moral right or obligation to censor, or select* [italics mine]: all the cook-writer can do is taste and smell and say 'Yum-yum' or 'This stinks!'" *The Catacombs* by William Demby, (New York: Pantheon, 1965).

plain moral signposts, without clear issues, without defined problems, neither he nor the reader can evaluate (perhaps not even discover) his problems; both are in the same soup (classically a *satira laux*, today a minestrone). There comes, then, a connection between the author's hidden, ambiguous, inconsistent judgments and the hero's moving along without clearly defined choices. They are in fact two inseparable sides of the same coin. One guarantees the other. So what appears to begin as a program of supreme objective lucidity in rendering the thing in its diamond dazzling essence easily slips into a mode by which it is impossible to locate the author's attitude toward his characters *or* the moral values involved in the choices they face. From here it is a short step to the undigested chaos of novels where raw unsorted experience is poured out to splash in every direction. *Malone Dies*, which makes a virtue of negation (nothing means, nothing matters), is the ironic but predictable upshot of Joyce's "detachment." If critics, having exhausted themselves these many years trying just to establish the tone of *Ulysses* without success, still agree on its greatness, the way to a Malone is paved and the gates are wide open. Indeed, any budding author is pushed toward ambiguity, which he of course sees as a commendable detachment. And in this direction the aimless hero must emerge as the inevitable product of the objective, which is to say the ambiguous, which is to say the detached author — who rapidly becomes the irresponsible author. In the process, the action will be reduced on the same scale, for without firm choices the substance of a traditional action, of some magnitude, cannot exist.

Philip Roth, in *Letting Go* (1962), seems to have been aware of the plight of the aimless hero even while he was committed to the sort of narrative mode that produced him. His people in this book are desperately aimless, so aimless that they practically consume each other with their violent and meaningless dialogue. Paul and Libby Herz wrangle each other to exhaustion, and their discussions are almost without subject, passionately illogical, devoutly incoherent. Whether Paul agrees or disagrees with Libby, she will respond with a new flight from reason. Roth has an ear comparable to Salinger's for catching the diction and speech rhythms of his intelligent maniacs, and he brings his reader right into the heart of these disputes, where identification most certainly takes place: they and their reader are engaged, totally engaged, in the meticulous exploration of every minutest detail. Indeed, it is this intense and frantic absorption in the homemade chaos of their lives that gives the book energy and makes the characters live.

Daniel Aaron says that the "literary sixties can scarcely be described as a time of apathy. Rather, it is a time of positive nonbelief in the stability or even the reality of contemporary life. . . . The very subject matter of recent fiction has become blurred and unreal: subjective views of a protean world, explorations into private voids, depersonalization of fictive characters into archetypes. Much of it suggests the contemporary writer's inability to identify himself with concrete issues in a world which he apparently can't even see, much less understand."* Yes, this is the created literary world I have been describing; but Paul and Libby throw themselves with incredible energy into their tangle of hope, need, and despair; and somewhere deep in that tangle there gleams, for both of them, the notion of a decent, ordered life. But Libby is too neurotic ever to make sense, and Paul has to disengage himself somewhat from her and face up to a private crisis. This happens with a kind of mystical experience, a burst of vision, that somehow unites him with his family, at the burial of his father, in an ecstasy of confusion: "For his truth was revealed to him, his final premise melted away. What he had taken for order was chaos. Justice was illusion. Abraham and Isaac were one. His eyes opened, and in the midst of those faces — the faces of his dream, the faces of the bums, all the faces that had forever encircled him — he felt no humiliation and no shame. Their eyes no longer overpowered him. He felt himself under a wider beam." (Page 451.)

The issue not having been defined, I cannot determine just what happens to Paul here. The next thing we know he is back with Libby,

*New York Times Book Review, February 14, 1965.

The ubiquity of the diminished man today has inspired almost endless commentary. Substantial volumes published in two recent years include Charles I. Glicksberg's The Self in Modern Literature (University Park: Pennsylvania State University Press, 1963); Maurice Friedman's Problematic Rebel: An Image of Modern Man (New York: Random House, 1963); Julian N. Hartt's The Lost Image of Man (Baton Rouge: Louisiana State University Press, 1963); Davis D. McElroy's Existentialism and Modern Literature (New York: Citadel, 1963); Ralph Freedman's The Lyrical Novel: Studies in Hermann Hesse, André Gide, and Virginia Woolf (Princeton, N.J.: Princeton University Press, 1963); John Edward Hardy's Man in the Modern Novel (Seattle: University of Washington Press, 1964); Frederick J. Hoffman's The Mortal No: Death and the Modern Imagination (Princeton, N.J.: Princeton University Press, 1964); Arthur Mizener's The Sense of Life in the Modern Novel (Boston: Houghton Mifflin, 1964); and Marcus Klein's After Alienation: American Novels in Mid-Century (Cleveland, Ohio: World, 1964).

but he absolutely vanishes as a character from this point on because we never again see into his mind and it is not possible to find in his speech or conduct the consequences of whatever decision or choice was made in the burst of vision at the cemetery. Roth is engaged, committed, but his materials, as he develops them, will not fit into an action that gives them order and meaning.

Aaron continues, "These seekers . . . are not cast in the heroic mold. They are marginal people, misfits, children, picaros, hipsters and underdogs operating on the fringes of society — all reflections of their creators' want of interest in 'issues' as subjects." But these modern writers, he notes, are not irrevocably alienated. Their works, whether "determinedly antirealistic [or] dealing with the daymares of goofs, may turn out to be much closer to the marrow of reality when we have had them around longer." If they do, then either their formless actions are an end point, a culmination, or else new actions will be devised through which such people can manifest themselves more coherently. But it appears to me that these new actions have already been tried and found wanting. Roth is not looking for actions that will bring substance to the daymares of goofs; he has turned back toward some old virtues of family, work, and decency. His problem is to break loose from the zany sort of activities in which novelistic heroes commonly engage today and find actions that move through less frantic extremes. But how to do so and still be "new"?

Well, there's Saul Bellow's Herzog — forty and frantic, a new kind of transparent eyeball, who knows everything and is nothing, who is one with all the world's ills and yet paralyzed, squeezed dry like a used lemon, witless before the demands of bread, butter, bed, board, and bitches. Like Updike's centaur he is caught in a network of responsibilities; like Huxley's hero of *Eyeless in Gaza* he lives with a head full of ideas that have come from many books, conversations, and events. But whereas the centaur is confined in his maze, Herzog travels frantically around the eastern seaboard and west to Chicago. He rushes wildly off for a rest on Martha's Vineyard by train and boat, staggers in to greet his hosts, and then sneaks off and 300 miles back to New York while they suppose he is emptying his suitcase. Meanwhile and all the while he is fighting a dozen old battles, composing unsent (and often unwritten, and nearly always unfinished) letters to Eisenhower, Stevenson, anybody who has a finger on one of the world's problems —

as well as to the people who have exasperated him and a host of authors who have churned up the muddy waters of philosophy, sociology, anthropology, political science, and history in which Herzog finds himself thrashing and drowning.

Herzog careens back and forth among ideas and places for over 300 pages just gathering together — no, let us say trying to bring into momentary focus the jiggling kaleidoscope of his past, so that he can see to take one firm step. All the way through this engaging book we live with Herzog in the present moment of his discontent. We watch him go through ridiculous acrobatics of intrigue in order to obtain an antique revolver with which to kill his ex-wife and her lover, get himself arrested and humiliated for carrying it (after he had abandoned the idea of using it), and finally return to the great empty house in the Berkshires into which he has poured all his money while he was letting Madeleine destroy him before she divorced him. At the end he has come to rest, but one could not say that he had drawn the exploded pieces of his life together into order. He appears rather to have stopped whirling for a breather.

The character Herzog hides behind a series of masks of the author's devising. He is an intellectual, with a wide-ranging knowledge of philosophy, history, and literature, to say nothing of a good deal of science. He is socially inept because he cannot give himself to most human relations. He is almost insanely self-destructive, having got himself into a tangle of human relations that threatens to destroy him. Chief example is Gersbach, his friend, whom he has brought to live with them so that he can destroy Herzog's marriage. He is sentimental and tragic, wallowing in pity and despair. But his wailing wall is, may I say, whitewashed and decorated by the author with masks of comic and grotesque evasion. Another way of saying this is that, behind all the mad traveling and near-hysteria, old Herzog is *aware* of everything that is going on, like a destructive delinquent brandishing a huge knife to see what sort of reaction he will get. It is true that such masks become the man, that the delinquent may slash someone fatally with his big knife; but Herzog is never lost in his gestures; he is always thinking furiously behind them, giving himself time to compose three or four letters before he takes the fatal step that he does not then take. He tells his story, persuading us from time to time that he is on the very edge of cracking up; but all the while he is carrying on his dialogues with his other selves and with the sick world around him. He is a juggler, keeping the balls of his frenzy aloft while he grimaces below them; the deftness of his prestidigitation diverts us from the fact that it is controlled by the mind below.

If Roth's and Salinger's characters hide behind incoherence, Herzog camouflages himself with clowning. He can interrupt a tremulous sob with a deft penetration of his own pose, piercing it with a shaft of lightning wit. What on one level is the heroic struggle of a shattered man to hold onto his sanity is on another a feverish dance of self-parody, a Bacchanalia of zesty abandon, a masque of mockery.

It goes without saying that the action of *Herzog* (1964) is incidental. There is no moment of significant choice that marks a turning point, unless it is the moment when the hero looks through the bathroom window and sees Gersbach giving his child a bath. He has the gun in his pocket, to kill both Gersbach and Madeleine; but there was no suspense over this issue; the reader could not have feared that he would shoot them. Herzog knew he wouldn't because his family were not killers but sufferers. The slight detail of the loaded gun is drowned in the spate of language that pours from Herzog as he conducts imaginary conversations and composes his unfinished, unwritten, unposted letters. Demonstrating the tendency of culture to make idealists of us, Emerson tells in *Nature* how the poet "unfixes the land and the sea, makes them revolve around the axis of his primary thought, and disposes them anew. Possessed himself by a heroic passion, he uses matter as symbols of it." Ironically — and I mention the irony to stress how the old symbols and techniques are bent to new misuses in the modern world — Herzog uses language to disorient society and make it revolve around the axis of his chaos. Where for Emerson the idea dominates the mere physical world, for Herzog it is confusion that makes the social and intellectual world a glittering bauble to be tossed and whirled until he and we and it are dizzy.

But after all this, I must conclude that *Herzog* evinces a powerful drive toward order and morality. The hero is trying to wrestle himself back into shape (if he indeed ever had a shape), and the form of the enterprise embodies his constant awareness that whatever self he can mold must be an expression of the manners and values of his society. Finding the world absurd, but not liking it so, he constantly reaches for *family* ties. Stretched, then, between the search for order and the unstable intelligence of its hero whirling through chaos, *Herzog* is a pretty pickle. It can't be made back into a good old cucumber, but perhaps it may stimulate the appetite for newer and more substantial dishes.

We cannot deny, after all, that mankind is now in a pretty pickle — or that science, technology, commerce, in short all the activities of human reason that exasperate Herzog, are what have led us into that pickle. This being so, it might appear that only the aggressively nonrational forms of the various modern arts could combat the dreadful products of rationality. But just as the extreme left and the extreme right of social opinion are found holding hands in the philosophical anarchist and the ultra-reactionary, so the blind follies of modern reason and the passionate nihilism of artistic un-form seem to join forces in assailing human measure and dignity. A true science of man can be imagined that would be both rational and humane. And art can protest in forms that do not lead to detachment, irresponsibility, and despair. Reason and beauty, form and passion, lucidity and humanity are married in the best science and the best art.

Index

THE names of fictional characters are followed, in parentheses, by "ch." and the title of the work in which they appear.